The Nitpicker's
CLASSIC
TREKKERS

STAR TREK NOVELS

STAR TREK GIANT NOVELS

OTHER STAR TREK PUBLICATIONS

STAR TREK ADVENTURES

The Nitpicker's Guide for
CLASSIC TREKKERS

PHIL FARRAND

TITAN BOOKS

THE NITPICKER'S GUIDE FOR CLASSIC TREKKERS
ISBN 1 85286 587 3

Published by
Titan Books Ltd
42-44 Dolben Street
London SE1 0UP

First Titan edition November 1994
10 9 8 7 6 5 4 3 2 1

The trademark Dell ® is registered in the U.S. Patent and
Trademark Office.

Developed and produced by Ettlinger Editorial Projects, New York.

Cover illustration © 1994 Bob Larkin.

Star Trek and *Star Trek: The Next Generation* are trademarks of
Paramount Pictures. This book is not sponsored, approved, or
authorised by Paramount Pictures.

British Library Cataloguing-in-Publication Data. A catalogue record for
this book is available from the British Library.

Printed and bound in Great Britain by Cox and Wyman Ltd, Reading,
Berkshire.

Dedicated to Jeanne Cavelos,
trekkie/nitpicker/editor extraordinaire,
without whom there would be no Guides

TABLE OF CONTENTS

THIRD SEASON

ACKNOWLEDGMENTS

A great host of individuals contribute to make any book a reality. The acknowledgments for this particular book must begin with Gene Roddenberry. He and his talented group of producers, directors, writers, actors, and production specialists created a rare commodity in the television industry—a show that has endured for almost three decades. Without your excellent work, ladies and gentlemen, there would be no fans, there would be no nitpicking, and there would be no *Nitpicker's Guide.* Please understand, I really do love your creation.

Steve Ettlinger not only acted as agent, but served as the book producer as well. He coordinated William Drennan's copy editing, Sharon Guskin, Daniel Pinchbeck and Sean Sullivan's editorial assistance and manuscript preparation, Geoff Notkin and Jacqueline Ho's page buildup, Miriam Sarzin and Gene Aretsky's proofreading, and Jane Farnol's indexing, all done on a crash basis. Thanks again, Steve. My gratitude to each member of your team.

Jeanne Cavelos once again applied her considerable talents as editor for this installment of the *Nitpicker's Guide.* As always, Jeanne, it was a joy to work with you and the rest of the able individuals at Dell Publishing, especially Mary Carlomagno, Evan Boorstyn, and Danielle Clemens.

My wife, Lynette, and daughter, Elizabeth, lent me a great deal of support and strength during this project, especially when the deadlines grew short and the hours long. As I've said before, I am privileged to have you stand with me, ladies.

A special thanks also needs to go to David Pogue. He's the one who originally introduced me to Steve. Sorry I forgot to mention you in the Acknowledgments of the *NextGen Guide,* David.

Of course, many members of the Nitpicker's Guild made significant contributions to this *Guide.* Otto "Hack-Man" Heuer—who's been collecting *Star Trek* nits far longer than I—shot me his list over Internet. Stuart Davis and Joshua M. Truax spent hours compiling information on the *Star Trek* movies. Joe Ryan loaned me vital reference materials and even suggested a topic for a sidebar. Cliff Cerce loaned me his tapes.

In addition, all of the following individuals contributed at least one nit to this tome. I do thank you for taking the time to write. Steve Ballard, Erick Banks, Bret Barrett, Kurt C. Bellhorn, Lisa Boyes, Jonathan Bridge, Chris Browne, Graham Buckingham, Laurie Calvert, Pete Carter, Phyllis "Tiny" Carter, Cliff Cerce, Michelle Cerce,

Robert Chisnall, Jeremy Dabbs, Danny Da Silva, Matthew Davis, John S. DiGianno, Lisa Ferrington, Adam Fuller, Alex Frazer-Harrison, Sara Green, Richard Hahn, Jessica Hall, John "KRIS" Halvorson, Steve Hannah, Myles S. Hildebrand, Scott Heise, Adam Hincks, Darrin Hull, Edward Huspeka, David Jackson, Gary G. Kerr, Josh M. Kielty, Mikal Krueger, Andrew LaMance, B. Keith Lawson, Eric G. Lemmon, Paul R. Lilly, Brian Lombard, Rachel Lunneborg, Wells P. Martin, Craig Mason, Stephen Mendenhall, Jeff Millward, Becky Monsess, Douglas Murray, Chad Nielson, Simon Nonington, Quimby Olmstead, Mark S. Painter, Sr., Annie Percik, Patricia Pozywak, Anne Price, Phillip Ramati, James K. Rone, Leland Sanders, Celia Shires, Mark A. Shore, Maryann Smialkowski, David K. Smith, Lance Smith, Robert C. Smith, Christopher Steeves, Matthew Strommer, Ruth and Ian Stuart-Hamilton, Julie Watson, Lee Whiteside, Geoffrey H. Wood, and Edward Yee. I wanted to list each of you by your entry, but time and space precluded that approach.

And finally, as always, I am forever grateful to you, Jesus Christ, for your kindness, your generosity, and your love.

INTRODUCTION

reetings, fellow nitpickers! So now we turn our attention to classic *Trek*. In case you do not know, this guide is a follow-up to the earlier book, *The Nitpicker's Guide for Next Generation Trekkers*. In my travels, I've come across an interesting attitude toward the original *Star Trek* series. I've found that many fans of *Star Trek: The Next Generation* view the original series like the crazy old uncle that no one wants to talk about at the family reunion. That's unfortunate, because you can't really understand *NextGen* unless you go back to its beginnings. And go back to the beginnings I have.

It has been my delight to spend four months revisiting the seventy-nine episodes of the most popular science fiction television series of all time, along with the first six *Star Trek* movies. There really is good work here. There really is a reason this series has survived for almost three decades. Once you get past the less polished sets and cheap-looking effects, you find great stories performed by talented actors. Stories worth discussing. Stories worth nitpicking. Stories that have spawned everything that we call *Star Trek* today—the movies, *NextGen, Deep Space Nine*, and *Voyager*. So much has already been written about classic *Trek*, I feel very honored to add my little

rock-throwing to the fray. As always, I've tried to be fair. After all, the series was produced almost three decades ago.

If you are unfamiliar with a *Nitpicker's Guide*, let me offer a quick tour. In this book you'll find reviews for all seventy-nine episodes of *Star Trek;* the first pilot, titled "The Cage"; and the first six movies. For each I will list the title, star date, and a brief summary. I'll add a few ruminations along the way and offer my picks for great moments. Knowing how much Trekkers love trivia, I'll even toss two questions your way. As readers of the *NextGen Guide* know, I like *real* trivia. Then it's on to the good stuff! I've taken the nits for each review and placed them in one of four major categories: Plot Oversights, Changed Premises, Equipment Oddities, and Continuity and Production Problems.

Plot Oversights is a catchall. Anything that concerns the plot, or won't fit anywhere else, goes here. Under Changed Premises you'll discover that sometimes information given in one show directly contradicts information in another. In Equipment Oddities I'll point out any technical problems I can find with the machinery of the *Trek* universe. Lastly, the section Continuity and Production Problems will expose errors in the actual creation of any of the installments of *Star*

Trek that feature the classic cast.

The episodes of the television series contain two additional categories: Syndication Cuts and Closing Stills. As you probably already know, *Star Trek* originally aired on network television. The program content of each episode ran fifty-one minutes, including opening credits, the teaser for the next week, and the closing credits. For syndication, the creators cut the program content to forty-six minutes, thirty seconds—deleting the teaser and approximately four minutes of each episode. Often these cuts are simply establishing and reaction shots. However, some edits actually change the meaning of the dialogue and even remove nits. Most surprising, there are twenty episodes that contain no edits. They are the same as the ones aired on network television (see "The Unsyndicated" for more information). I will list each episode's cuts under Syndication Cuts.

Under Closing Stills, I will identify the shots that serve as background for the closing credits. Since these change every week, I thought it would be fun to identify the episode from which the stills are taken. Interestingly enough, when the creators originally broadcast the episodes over network television, some of the stills in the closing credits came from episodes not yet aired. For instance, the first episode to air on network television, "The Man Trap," has the garden scene from "Where No Man Has Gone Before" as a closing still. When this happened, the closing stills functioned as a sneak preview for later episodes. You will notice that there are a few stills I couldn't identify. If you can identify them, write me at the address at the back of this *Guide* and become a member of the Nitpicker's Guild (if you aren't already).

A word about the resources I used while constructing this guide. I purchased a complete set of video rental tapes from Paramount through my local Blockbusters. These tapes included-the network versions of the seventy-nine episodes and "The Cage." I also purchased the six-pack of *Star Trek* movies from a local wholesale club. Some of these tapes contain additional footage not seen in the theaters. The copies of the syndicated episodes were taped here in Springfield, Missouri from regular television over the past several years. (It airs only once a week.) It is possible that the episodes are syndicated differently around the world. However, I have it on good authority that the masters used by my local television station came from Paramount. In addition, Jeanne Cavelos, my editor, loaned me a few of her tapes—recorded ten years ago in Syracuse, New York—and a spot check revealed that they had edits identical to the ones recorded locally.

Diehard fans of classic *Trek* will immediately realize that I do not discuss the television episodes in production order. Instead, I have listed them in their original air date order. (Believe me, I can hear the howls ascending even as I write this! Wink, wink.) I realize that *all* the other reference materials list the episodes in production order. (Then again, I've never been one to follow the crowd quietly.) Certainly, Jeanne and I had more than one discussion on this topic. As a purist, I felt it was important to view the episodes as the creators originally offered them to the fans. I understand that for the past twenty years television stations have played them in production order. Television stations also play *Star Trek: The Next Generation* in production order. This method results in "Skin of Evil" playing before "Symbiosis" because it was produced before "Symbiosis." So Yar gets killed in "Skin of Evil" and then magically resurrects in "Symbiosis." (In addition, "Unification II" was actually produced before "Unification I," but the television stations play that particular combination in air date order, not production order.) Because of these types of problems, I listed the episodes in air date order in the *NextGen Guide*. For consistency, I did the same in the classic *Guide*. Having said all that, let me add that someone at Paramount seems to agree with my air date approach. After the twelfth episode in the original television series—"The Conscience of the King"—all the teasers on the prerecorded tapes for the "next voyage" of the *Enterprise* are in air date order

(except when they're just plain wrong). Of course, this raises an interesting point for dyed-in-the-wool nitpickers. For instance, the tape I purchased from Paramount unequivocally states that "Who Mourns for Adonais?" follows "Amok Time." Yet the reference materials from Pocket Books say that "The Doomsday Machine" follows "Amok Time." What are we to believe? The printed word? Or that which we see with our own eyes on a copy of the original version of the episode that aired on network television? (Oh, the grand tribulations of being a nitpicker.)

In any order, if you happen to have the episodes on videotape, pull them out and grab the remote as you work your way through the *Guide.* If you find something I missed, disagree with a nit I picked, or even find an error in the classic *Guide* itself, drop me a line at the address at the back of this book. That entry will make you a member of the Nitpickers' Guild.

As always, the Nitpicker's Prime Directive remains in full force. However, it has been significantly modified. The main rule of nitpicking now reads, "All nits picked shall derive from sources the creators consider canonical." In other words, anything that Paramount claims is authoritative can be nitpicked. Before I tell you what Paramount claims as authoritative, a brief word of explanation for this change. The Nitpicker's Prime Directive—as stated in *The Nitpicker's Guide for Next*

Generation Trekkers—originally read, "The information in this book comes solely from the television series." At the time, there were 152 hours of *Star Trek: The Next Generation* available. I felt that everything the creators needed to tell us about *NextGen* could be told somewhere in those 152 episodes. On the other hand, there are only 79 episodes in the original series. The creators really didn't have time to tell us everything they might have intended to tell us about the *Star Trek* universe. Reference books can fill in these gaps as long as the contents are approved by Paramount. In addition, any television show would soon get bogged down in minutiae if the creators took the time to explain every little piece of equipment. Reference books can help here as well, as long as the explanations match what is shown on the screen (and the creators use the devices in a consistent fashion).

So, what does Paramount consider authoritative? I've heard the same list from several different sources. Any of the television episodes in any incarnation of *Star Trek* are canonical. So are the movies and the reference materials available from Pocket Books. In addition, I consider the blueprints of the original *Enterprise*—drawn

by Franz Joseph Designs and approved by Gene Roddenberry himself—authoritative. Not only do they bear the mark of the Great Bird of the Galaxy himself, they are actually displayed on the bridge science station in *Star Trek: The Motion Picture.*

On the other hand, the creators do not consider the *Star Trek* novels authoritative. Those stories have never actually happened. Trying to prove a nit by citing a passage from a novel violates the Nitpicker's Prime Directive. And, as you know, nitpickers *never* violate the Nitpicker's Prime Directive. Please believe me when I say that I, as the chief nitpicker, am as dedicated to the Nitpicker's Prime Directive as the captains of the *Enterprise* are to Starfleet's Prime Directive. After all, violating the Nitpicker's Prime Directive could get me kicked out of the Guild!

One final note: At times in this Guide, I have picked nits in *Star Trek: The Next Generation* by using information in the original series and vice versa. This "interseries" nitpicking is certainly not exhaustive. There were just a few things that jumped out at me or that fellow nitpickers submitted. I thought you might find them interesting if you are also a fan of *NextGen*.

Happy nitpicking!

FIRST
SEASON

Star Dates: 1513.1-1513.8

The *Enterprise* arrives at planet M-113 to provide annual physicals for a pair of isolated researchers, Robert and Nancy Crater. Only one fact keeps the inspection from being completely routine: McCoy and Nancy Crater were once romantically involved. Unexpectedly, the medical assignment turns deadly. Crewmen begin dying of complete salt deprivation. On the surface of the planet, Kirk and Spock force some answers from Robert Crater. In fact, Nancy has been dead for a year. A creature indigenous to M-113— the last of its kind—killed her. It lives on salt, draining it from its victims, and can assume any shape. When the first two landing parties arrived, it posed as Nancy Crater. Now it has gained access to the ship by assuming the appearance of a crew member.

Putting the ship on security alert, Kirk returns to the *Enterprise* with Spock and Robert Crater. Eventually the creature ends up in McCoy's quarters. It resumes its impersonation of Nancy Crater and pleads for the doctor's protection. When Kirk enters with a phaser, McCoy confronts his captain in disbelief. The creature seizes the opportunity to attack Kirk and almost kills him before the doctor can bring himself to fire on the image of the woman he loved so many years ago.

Trivia Questions

1. What is the name of the crewman Uhura asks to fix her door?

2. What are the designations on McCoy's doorplate?

RUMINATIONS

Shatner really does scream well. As the creature begins to drain the salt from his body, he lets loose and contorts his face very convincingly. Allan Asherman, in his book The Star Trek Compendium, *notes that a reviewer of William Shatner's science fiction, fantasy, and horror acting dubbed him the "male Fay Wray" because of this ability. I like that title.*

Also, this episode features an interesting female costume. One hallway shot shows a woman wearing pants! Are the microminiskirts reserved as a perk for female officers? (I realize that all the women wear pants in "Where No Man Has Gone Before," but we'll get to that episode later.)

PLOT OVERSIGHTS

• Shortly after beaming down the first time, Kirk asks Crewman Darnell to step outside. Moments earlier, Darnell had made a few untoward comments about Nancy Crater. Nancy then strolls out of the building and presents herself to Darnell as the image of a girl he met on Rigley's Pleasure Planet. She tosses a scarf toward him and slinks away. Immediately, Darnell goes panting after her. What kind of discipline is this? Setting aside the fact that the woman is married, does Darnell really think that Kirk brought him down just so he could have a romp in the sand? For that matter, why *did* Kirk bring this guy down? (So he could die maybe?)

• Someone should teach Kirk a few infantry techniques. I realize that the man's training covers starship operations and command, but he should at least have a passing knowledge of what makes a good barricade against enemy fire. Shortly after Kirk and Spock beam down to get some answers, Crater shoots at them. The phaser blast hits a stone structure near the pair. Specifically, it hits the center column of an object that has only three uprights supporting a long, heavy-looking stone. Kirk responds by falling to the ground while jumping forward *under* the structure. Bear in mind that Crater has already taken out the middle support. One more shot and the whole thing would come down on the captain. Moments later, Kirk repeats his mistake! He dives under a pile of stone slabs. The entire weight of this structure also rests on two uprights. Thankfully, Crater is just trying to scare them and doesn't take the opportunity to bury Kirk under a pile of rubble.

• As noted under *Ruminations,* Kirk screams heartily as the creature drains the salt from his body. This begs the question: Why didn't the other crewmen scream? On the planet, both Kirk and McCoy heard Nancy scream after she killed the first crewman. If Darnell had screamed, wouldn't they have heard him as well?

CHANGED PREMISES

• In this episode, Spock states that Vulcan has no moon. However, the planetscape in *Star Trek: The Motion Picture,* during the scene when Spock seeks the Vulcan state of *Kolinahr,* shows something that certainly looks like a moon. Then again, there is another planet in the distance. Maybe the moon orbits that planet?

EQUIPMENT ODDITIES

• This equipment oddity occurs so often throughout the series that listing all the instances would add several pages to this book! In the opening shot of the episode, the *Enterprise* orbits M-113. As it flies away from the camera, you can clearly see spherical projections on the back of the engine nacelles. A moment later, during the opening credits, the *Enterprise* flies away from the camera and there are vents on the backs of the engine nacelles. Evidently the creators changed the engine nacelles between the creation of the second pilot, "Where No Man Has Gone Before," and the first episode of the series, "The Corbomite Maneuver." Every time the creators reuse a ship shot from "Where No Man Has Gone Before," the backs of the engine nacelles revert to vents. Unfortunately, the creators never redid the opening credits, so this problem shows up in many, many episodes. (Only the fact that some episodes do not contain the "spherical" footage keeps the nit from appearing in every show!)

• Evidently the crew is still getting used to the communicators. For instance, Kirk has trouble getting his communicator open. It happens twice—the first time, just after Darnell dies, and the second, after Spock finds Green. Also, when Kirk decides to call the ship at the start of the second landing party mission, he pulls out his communicator, pauses for a split second like he's thinking about flipping it open, and then reaches over with his free hand to do it manually! (With the day he's having, I can understand Shatner wanting to play it safe.) The sound editors are also figuring out the communicators. Several of the opening chirps are missing.

• Along the same line, the crew is still learning about the companels, those little speakers with the lights that shine when they're on. Kirk correctly uses the one on his chair by pushing it to talk and pushing it again to end the conversation.

Spock, on the other hand, pushes it only once when responding to the call that the first landing party has returned. Uhura makes the same mistake just after the creature tries to attack her in the hall. She runs up to a companel, presses the button, the light comes on, she talks, and then she hurries onto a turbolift. The light indicates that the companel is still on. She probably just wants to get away from the creature and intends to order some hapless crewman to go turn it off later! Finally—and I mention this *solely* for the sake of completeness—the light on the companel mounted to the top of the transporter station stays on constantly, even though Kirk correctly flips a switch on and then off.

• At this point in the series, the crew obviously didn't know about all the features of a tricorder, either. Toward the end of the second landing party mission, McCoy wants to run off to look for Nancy, but Kirk restrains him. The captain wants to return to the ship and use its infrared sensors to locate both researchers. Of course, McCoy is holding a tricorder, but he probably hasn't read the operator's manual and doesn't know that it can scan for life signs.

• Additionally, the infrared sensors of the ship beg a question. There are two freshly murdered crewmen nearby. Since it takes time for a body to lose its heat, shouldn't Spock's infrared sensors detect the corpses?

CONTINUITY AND PRODUCTION PROBLEMS

• At the beginning of the first landing party mission, Kirk carries a tricorder for McCoy. As they approach the Craters' main building, Kirk has the tricorder slung over his left shoulder. Making a joke, he leans down to pick some weeds for McCoy to present to Nancy. When he does, the tricorder suddenly disappears. Subsequent shots show that the tricorder has jumped to Kirk's right hand.

• After the creature changes into a crewman and gains access to the ship, it starts following Yeoman Rand. She has a tray of food that includes a salt shaker, a plate of celery, and a bowl of colored food cubes. The creature follows Rand to Sulu's work area. In the scene that follows, we see Sulu happily munching on the cubes in the bowl. A close-up of the tray shows that the cubes are suddenly on a plate! Afterward, they are back in their bowl again. True, there is enough time for Sulu to grab a plate, dump the cubes out, let the camera take a close-up, grab the bowl, and shovel the cubes back into it, but . . . why would he?

TRIVIA ANSWERS

1. Bobby.
2. 3F 127.

CLOSING STILLS

• Smoking bridge, "Where No Man Has Gone Before"
• Talosian, "The Cage"
• Fortress on Rigel VII, "The Cage"
• Laser cannon, "The Cage"
• Garden scene, "Where No Man Has Gone Before"
• Vina as the green Orion slave girl, "The Cage"

CHARLIE X

Star Dates: 1533.6-1535.8

The *Enterprise* has a rendezvous with the cargo vessel *Antares* to pick up a young man named Charlie Evans. The *Enterprise* will transport him to Earth Colony Alpha Five, where he has relatives. Fourteen years ago, the crash of a transport ship left Charlie stranded on the planet Thasia. Somehow, he managed to survive. McCoy certifies Charlie as a normal seventeen-year-old, but his activities soon hint at extraordinary powers. In Recreation Room 3, he performs card tricks, magically transforming three of them into pictures of Yeoman Rand. When Rand realizes that Charlie has a deep crush on her, she asks Kirk to speak with him. In the process, Kirk decides to teach Charlie how to fight as a way of spending time together. However, when a crewman in the gym laughs, Charlie makes the man fade into nothing.

Kirk knows he cannot take Charlie to Colony Alpha Five. The undisciplined young man with his abilities would wreak havoc on the planet. Unfortunately, Charlie commandeers the ship and forces it to fly according to his will. Just in time, a Thasian ship arrives. Their spokesman explains that they gave Charlie the power to transmutate matter so he could survive on their planet. Once they realized he had departed, they quickly came to retrieve him, knowing the damage he would cause by his immaturity.

Trivia Questions

1. What card does Charlie materialize inside Yeoman Rand's dress?

2. For Spock, where is the tiger burning bright?

GREAT LINES

"He had a mean look. I had to freeze him. I like happy looks."— Charlie, explaining his actions to Kirk.

GREAT MOMENTS

This episode is filled with moments well played by the actor who portrays Charlie Evans. He does an excellent job of depicting a young man torn by his rites of passage into adulthood with gifts that far outweigh his temperament.

SYNDICATION CUTS

• Several moments from Charlie's beam-in.

• Two scenes from Charlie's first tour of the ship: a man lowering a pipe into the floor, and two men working in a Jefferies tube. The latter cut causes a small problem. After setting up his first rendezvous with Yeoman Rand, Charlie says, "You've got a deal, friend," and slaps her on the posterior. The two men in the Jefferies tube actually provide the motivation for his behavior. The pair speak of getting together in the rec room. Then one says the same line that Charlie repeats later and slaps the other before leaving. Once the exchange disappears, it makes one wonder where Charlie learned to slap others on the posterior. Did he practice on himself during all those years on Thasia?

• Uhura distracting Spock as he tunes up his lyre just before she launches into an ad-libbed song. Spock smiles!

• Two women in leotards turning handsprings, and a sequence in which Kirk teaches Charlie to break his falls.

• In the gym, several more seconds of Charlie resisting Kirk's order to go to his quarters.

• Little pieces of both the briefing room discussion and Kirk's questioning of Charlie.

• Charlie leaving the bridge, traveling rapidly in a turbolift, freezing a female crew member, and shoving his way through three men.

• More pleading by Charlie not to return to Thasia, lending credence to Kirk's decision to argue for Charlie staying.

PLOT OVERSIGHTS

• Kirk identifies the ship that brings Charlie Evans as the cargo vessel *Antares*. Then the ship explodes and Kirk notifies his superiors of the mysterious loss of the "science probe vessel *Antares*." (Yes, these two statement can be reconciled. It just seems like an awfully wide swing in assignments.)

• Following Charlie's card tricks in the rec room, Kirk speaks with someone in food service. He tells the man that it is Thanksgiving on Earth and that he wants the meat to *look* like turkey at least. The captain finishes the conversation, turns, and starts toward a turbolift. Charlie rounds the corner and begins a conversation with Kirk. Moments later, on the bridge, the food service guy calls to inform Kirk that there are real turkeys in the ovens. Charlie snickers. Obviously, the creators wish us to believe that Charlie caused the transformation. However, it doesn't appear that Charlie could have overheard Kirk's prior conversation, and nothing in the episode indicates that Charlie can read minds. He can only alter matter. Does Charlie also know that it is Thanksgiving? Was Kirk's hall conversation merely coincidental?

• At one point in the show, Charlie plays chess with Spock. Of course, the Vulcan soundly tromps him in only two moves. After Charlie becomes argumentative, Spock leaves. At this point, the young man rolls his eyes up into his head and melts all the white pieces. The interesting thing here is that Charlie melts his own pieces! At first glance, I thought he melted Spock's pieces. I suppose he could be angry that his own pieces made him look bad.

EQUIPMENT ODDITIES

• The doors on the *Enterprise* behave oddly in several places during this episode. The first time occurs during a chess game between Kirk and Spock. The scene begins with the pair seated at a table and a crew member standing in the open doorway behind Kirk. In the close-up that follows, the door is no longer open, and no sound accompanied its closing. Also, when Charlie walks in, the door reopens with a very odd gurgling. (Actually, it sounds like the editor didn't have the tape cued quite right and the machine wasn't up to speed when he or she began recording the effect.) Another instance occurs when Charlie leaves Rand's quarters. The door opens, but not all the way. It sticks out a good six inches trom the jamb.

• After taking over the ship, Charlie pays Rand a visit. As he enters, she is seated—clothed in her loungewear—writing on a noteboard. Rand stands up and backs into her viewscreen. Stealthily, she reaches around and flips the switch. A close-up of her hand shows the red indicator light going *off*. In other words, up to this point, the viewscreen was *on*. Yet Rand wasn't talking with anyone. Was she providing a little viewing enter-

tainment for the rest of the crew? ("And so, as this day draws to a close, we invite you to join us tomorrow for another installment of . . . *The Captain's Yeoman*.") Thankfully—even though Rand turns the viewscreen off —Kirk and Spock still manage to hear her discourse with Charlie.

• It's true that Charlie disposed of the phasers, but couldn't McCoy put him under with a sedative?

• Trying to regain some control over the situation, Kirk and Spock manage to trap Charlie in a room equipped with a force field. What's the point of this? Charlie's powers are mental in nature. In the *Star Trek: The Next Generation* episode "Night Terrors," Lieutenant Commander Data states that there is no known technology for blocking telepathic transmissions. Presumably, telepathic transmissions operate in the same domain as transmutational powers. If there is no known blocking technology in the twenty-fourth century, there is no known technology in the twenty-third century, and Spock should know this. Sure enough, Charlie simply dissolves away the whole wall and walks out!

CONTINUITY AND PRODUCTION PROBLEMS

• Shortly after arriving on the *Enterprise,* Charlie gets a physical from McCoy. In one scene, Charlie lies on his back and pushes some blocks with his feet. Periodically, McCoy glances up at a medical panel that is beside the blocks, to check Charlie's readings. Every close-up clearly shows Charlie's face. The only explanation is that Charlie must be jumping on and off the exercise table.

• Following his card tricks in the rec room, Charlie meets up with Kirk in a hallway. The captain wears his gold shirt with the black collar. During their conversation, Uhura pages him from the bridge. A message is coming from Captain Ramart of the *Antares*. Kirk boards a turbolift with Charlie. The camera cuts to the bridge, the turbolift doors pop open, and Kirk walks into the scene wearing his green V-neck captain's shirt.

• Escaping from the force field-enhanced room, Charlie leans toward his would-be captors and freezes them in their tracks. Well . . . almost. Spock still manages a blink. It must be that incredible Vulcan physique.

TRIVIA ANSWERS
1. The ace of clubs.
2. In the forest of the night.

CLOSING STILLS
• Flying Kirk on bridge, "The Naked Time"
• Laser cannon, "The Cage"
• Sulu with foil, "The Naked Time"
• Salt creature, "The Man Trap"
• Rock explosion after Robert Crater fires, "The Man Trap"
• Lithium cracking station on Delta Vega, "Where No Man Has Gone Before"

WHERE NO MAN HAS GONE BEFORE

Star Dates: 1312.4-1313.8

Approaching the edge of the galaxy, the crew of the *Enterprise* encounters the ship recorder of the USS *Valiant*. According to the two-hundred-year-old record, the *Valiant* encountered an energy barrier at the edge of the galaxy. Six crewmen died. A seventh finally recovered. Then the crew became very interested in ESP. Although uncertain, Spock thinks the last item on the tape is the captain ordering the ship's destruction. Kirk decides to press on with the mission and continues to the edge of the galaxy. Soon the *Enterprise* hits the energy barrier as well. Control panels short-circuit, the ship tosses about, and two officers collapse on the bridge before Kirk retreats. The two officers, Lieutenant Commander Gary Mitchell and Dr. Elizabeth Dehner, seem to recover quickly.

Mitchell soon develops new abilities—among them, the ability to read minds and move objects by thought command alone. When Kirk tries to strand him at the lithi- um cracking station on Delta Vega, Mitchell escapes with Dehner. She has begun to develop supernatural abilities as well. Desperate to stop Mitchell, Kirk grabs a phaser rifle and pursues them. He manages to convince Dehner of the dangers of ultimate power. Aided by the sacrifice of her own life, Kirk kills Mitchell before the newly formed "god" can destroy them all.

Trivia Questions

1. What was the name of Elizabeth Dehner's father?

2. What animal threw poison darts at Kirk on Dimorus?

RUMINATIONS

For those of you who don't know, this episode is actually the second pilot. I try to go easy on pilots, since a significant amount of time usually elapses between the production of the pilot and the production of the actual series. If you try to compare this episode with the others of the first season, differences abound. A complete list would become tedious very quickly, but here's a sampling:

• There's a big screen in the rec room.

• The uniforms are the style featured in "The Cage," including women in pants (poorly fitted

pants, I might add).
• *Spock's eyebrows sweep up at a more severe angle.*
• *Kirk has only two bands on his sleeve; Spock, only one.*
• *Kirk's chair has a nameplate, and a gooseneck that terminates in a communication hood.*

The episode does have a nice matte painting for the lithium cracking station on Delta Vega, and the integration of live action with the still works quite well.

PLOT OVERSIGHTS

• I'm puzzled about the title of this episode. *Who* is going where no man has gone before? Does the title refer to Gary Mitchell? Didn't the person who recovered on the *Valiant* go through the same process? Does the title then refer to *that* person, and, if so, why title the episode concerning events that happened two hundred years ago?
• All the graphics of the energy barrier show it as a relatively thin band. So why doesn't Kirk just fly over it? Isn't the object of this exercise to see what's *beyond* the galaxy? They already know that something bad happened to the *Valiant*. Doesn't this seem motivation enough to avoid contacting the barrier? Of course, if they did fly around it, the show would end very quickly!
• After Mitchell begins to change, Kirk and Spock worry over his progress. In one scene they watch how quickly he zips through the text on his library screen. What's the big deal? If you look closely

you can see that Mitchell reads the same pages over and over!
• Evidently Mitchell isn't as godlike as everybody thinks. He can't even get the captain's name right! The tombstone he creates for Kirk reads "James R. Kirk." Many other episodes refer to the distinguished captain as "James T. Kirk."
• During the last scene of the episode, the communications officer looks like he's asleep at his post! Did he have too much stress over the past few days? Is he distraught that he never acted on his feelings and asked Dehner for a date?

EQUIPMENT ODDITIES

• An overhead view of a turbolift doorway offers an interesting oddity. There's no break between the hall floor and the turbolift floor! Are we to believe that twenty-third-century floor technology looks seamless?
• Computer records indicate that Elizabeth Dehner is five feet, two inches, and Gary Mitchell is five feet, nine inches. Yet when Mitchell escorts Dehner into the detention cell, she is very close to his height. And—in case any of you are wondering—the scene does show the heels on her boots. They are the same height as Mitchell's.
• Computer records also indicate that Elizabeth Dehner is twenty-one—born on star date 1089.5—and Gary Mitchell is twenty-three—born on star date 1087.7. So, in other words, the digit preceding the decimal point approximates

years? That can't be right, because this episode lasts from star date 1312.4 to star date 1313.8—over a year by that standard.

CONTINUITY AND PRODUCTION PROBLEMS

• Who *are* these guys fighting at the end of this episode? The altercation begins between Kirk and Mitchell, and then the scene changes and these two strangers start duking it out. Honestly, it's tough to tell who's supposed to be who. (I realize that this is the pilot and it was done on a budget, but the stunt stand-in business had flourished for many years in Hollywood before this episode was created. Couldn't they find *anyone* who had the same color hair as Shatner?)

• During the fight, Kirk gets several cuts on his face. Yet, on the bridge afterward, only his hand is bandaged. His countenance is unmarred.

TRIVIA ANSWERS

1. Gerald.
2. A "rodent thing." (I chose this as a trivia question mainly because it sounded so similar to Worf's description of the attackers on Q's planet during the *Star Trek: The Next Generation* episode "Hide and Q." Worf called them "animal things.")

CLOSING STILLS

• *Enterprise* and energy barrier, "Where No Man Has Gone Before"
• Fortress on Rigel VII, "The Cage"
• Mitchell and Dehner, "Where No Man Has Gone Before"
• Laser cannon, "The Cage"
• Scientific Research Center on Psi 2000, "The Naked Time"
• Vina as the green Orion slave girl, "The Cage"

THE NAKED TIME

Star Dates: 1704.2-1704.4

The *Enterprise* arrives at planet Psi 2000 to pick up a scientific team. Beaming down in isolation suits, Spock and Lieutenant Joe Tormolen find all six scientists dead. Absentmindedly, Tormolen pulls off a glove to scratch his nose. Then he places his hand on the side of a desk, and small drops of red liquid trickle onto the hand. Moments later, Spock and Tormolen beam back to the ship. In the briefing that follows, Kirk reviews the current mission. Earth Science needs the closest possible observation of this ancient world as it collapses. Accordingly, the *Enterprise* will spiral inward as the diameter of the planet shrinks.

Meanwhile, Tormolen begins acting strangely. After stopping Tormolen's suicide attempt, Sulu and Lieutenant Kevin Riley begin acting strangely as well. Sulu charges the halls with a foil, while Riley commandeers the ship from Engineering. Kirk finally regains control as McCoy discovers that the water from the planet acts like

Trivia Questions

1. Where does Riley want to hold the formal dance?

2. What message is painted on the inner turbolift doors?

alcohol, and he devises an antidote. By this time the *Enterprise* is in danger of burning up in the planet's atmosphere. The crew performs a never-before-attempted implosion in the ship's engines. The tactic works but throws the *Enterprise* backward in time three days—a side effect that Kirk muses might be useful someday.

RUMINATIONS

The creators recycled the plot of this show into the Star Trek: The Next Generation *episode "The Naked Now." Personally, I think that the classic* Trek *episode has a more believable reason for the ship's peril. In "The Naked Now," Picard simply could turn on the tractor beam and tow the* Tsiolkovsky *out of the danger zone long before things turn nasty. But, of course, he doesn't.*

GREAT LINES

"Sorry, neither."—Uhura, commenting on Sulu addressing her as a "fair maiden."

SYNDICATION CUTS

• An establishing shot of the rec

room and a man and woman playing three-dimensional checkers before Tormolen gets his food and sits down.
• After Kirk's log entry, comments from the bridge crew on the breakup of the planet.
• Kirk checking communication status with Uhura before Riley begins rubbing his hand on his pants.
• Part of Tormolen's operation.
• Riley departing a turbolift, leering at a woman, and blowing on the sick bay doors.
• Sulu poking his thumb with the foil. (This is a very cute moment.)
• Part of Scott's work in the Jefferies tube.
• An establishing shot of the med-panel before it pulls back to reveal Sulu. Also, McCoy sitting down to page the biopsy lab.
• Spock entering sick bay and asking Chapel the location of McCoy.
• Kirk approaching Engineering as Scott finishes cutting through the bulkhead.
• Spock walking down a hall and then ducking into the briefing room. This edit deletes a really good nit. When Spock enters Briefing Room 2, the room description plate is stuck on the wall to the left of the doors. Several minutes later, when Kirk exits the room, the plate is stuck on the wall to the *right* of the doors. Obviously some crew member had a secret desire to rearrange doorplates and—once freed from his or her inhibitions by the alcoholic water—acted.

PLOT OVERSIGHTS

• Lieutenant Joe Tormolen beams into a situation where all the researchers have died very strangely. He transports down dressed in an isolation suit. Obviously, *someone* thought it might be wise to *isolate* the landing party from *something* at the research center. So what does Tormolen do? He takes his glove off and presses his hand against the side of a desk. (Need I say more?)
• One other item concerning Joe Tormolen and his gloveless hand: Apparently, on this planet not only does water act like alcohol, it also can run uphill! His hand is clearly above the red splotch on the side of the desk, yet the drips still find him.
• After a commercial break, Kirk makes an additional log entry containing these statements: " . . . our orbit tightening, our need for efficiency critical. But unknown to us, a totally new and unusual disease has been brought aboard." How can Kirk know that a "totally new and unusual disease has been brought aboard" if that fact is "unknown" to him?
• After Riley seals himself in Engineering, Scott uses several precious minutes cutting a hole in the wall to open the doors. Wouldn't it be easier to cut open the door or maybe even beam into Engineering, as Kirk did in "Day of the Dove"? (I remind you that Kirk accomplished that beam-in while the *Enterprise* hurtled through space at warp nine.)

• Just a tidbit of information, not really a nit. At one point, Spock bumps into a graffiti artist with an insane laugh. Spock orders him to the "lab." (An interesting destination; I would have picked sick bay.) Much later, after isolating the cause of the madness, McCoy pages the lab. Guess what? The graffiti artist followed Spock's orders! The same maniacal cackling floats over the intercom.

• Once Kirk gets infected with the alcoholic water, he launches into a soliloquy on the demands of the captaincy. This scene answers one of the burning questions of *Classic Trek:* Why does Kirk go after every alien female he meets, including androids? Answer: Because he's not allowed to fraternize with any of the women on his ship!

CHANGED PREMISES

• At this point in the series, the creators obviously didn't know about Spock's incredibly sensitive hearing. Near the end of "Operation—Annihilate!," McCoy whispers to Kirk not to mention that he said Spock was the best first officer in the fleet. At this point, Spock turns at his station and thanks the doctor for the compliment. In "The Naked Time," Sulu has a conversation about leaving the bridge, does so, and Spock just keeps looking into his scanner.

EQUIPMENT ODDITIES

• Just after the opening credits, an establishing shot shows the *Enterprise* orbiting Psi 2000. The planet rotates right to left with respect to the ship. However, the scene then cuts to the bridge, and the main viewer shows the planet rotating left to right.

• The aforementioned isolation suit seems to be lacking an important quality: *isolation.* The hood on the suits is a loose-fitting affair with plenty of gaps for airborne particles to slip through.

• The automatic doors display an amazing degree of sensitivity in this episode. When Spock becomes infected he flees to Briefing Room 2 for a place to cry. He barely gets inside the doors when they close. Then he leans back against the doors and they stay closed! How did they know to do this? Did they sense that he was in emotional turmoil and needed their support?

• After cutting through the bulkhead to force open the doors to Engineering, Scott pulls off the panel with his bare hands. Just how fast does this bulkhead metal cool down? In essence, Scott has just burned through it with a welding torch.

• At the end of the show, the *Enterprise* travels backward in time until Kirk can reverse engines and slow them down. A close-up of the ship's chronometer shows it moving backward, stopping, and then moving forward. The chronometer uses cylinders inscribed with numbers. Unfortunately, the gearing mechanism for the cylinders is off. This problem causes the chronometer, as it moves forward, to read, "7:59," "7:00," and then "8:01." Wouldn't that be a bit confusing?

CONTINUITY AND PRODUCTION PROBLEMS

• When the ship's engines implode, Kirk, McCoy, Uhura, and Rand grimace in pain. Their behavior is contrasted by the two officers at Conn and Navigation and the one at Scott's position. These guys seem fine. Is the pain a localized phenomenon?

TRIVIA ANSWERS

1. The bowling alley.
2. SINNER REPENT.

CLOSING STILLS

• *Enterprise* heading into the energy barrier, "Where No Man Has Gone Before"
• Engineering, "The Enemy Within" (this is the establishing shot just before the good Kirk and Spock walk into the scene)
• Talosian, "The Cage"
• Scott in Jefferies tube, "The Naked Time"
• Sulu with foil, "The Naked Time"
• Vina, poster child for *The Male Dominated Society,* a magazine dedicated to satirizing the masculine need to assert supposed superiority, and published by Intelligent Orion Women Anonymous (IOWA), "The Cage"

★ THE ENEMY WITHIN

Star Dates: 1672.1-1673.1

During a specimen-gathering mission on planet Alpha 177, Scott beams Kirk back to the ship. When the captain stumbles off the platform, a worried Scott escorts him to his quarters. As soon as they leave, the transporter reengages and beams up yet another Kirk. Unknown to the crew, a transporter malfunction has split Kirk into his two halves—good and evil. While the good Kirk relaxes in his quarters, the evil Kirk attacks Rand. At the same time, Scotty attempts to beam an animal up from the surface and sees the transporter split it into two halves. After examining the results, Spock and the good Kirk realize that an evil Kirk exists somewhere on the ship. A stranded landing party—including Sulu—further complicates matters. Nightfall is coming, and the temperature on the surface usually reaches minus 120 degrees.

As Scotty races to repair the transporter, the good Kirk and Spock locate the evil Kirk. With repairs completed, the good Kirk

Trivia Questions

1. What are the designations on Rand's doorplate?

2. What does McCoy call Technician Fisher as he leads him back to bed?

takes the evil Kirk into the machine. The transporter successfully puts the two halves of Kirk back together, and the landing party is beamed to safety.

RUMINATIONS

One scene in this episode affords a quick view of Scott's right hand. In case you aren't aware, James Doohan—the actor who plays Scott—is missing the middle finger on that hand. It's amazing the lengths the creators went to cover up this fact throughout the entire television series. Watch the hand in any scene and you'll see that Doohan keeps it curled or hidden.

I bring this up for one reason: Why did the creators worry about this in the first place? He's missing a finger. So what? He's an engineer. Doesn't it seem likely that he would have a few accidents during his career? By the time Star Trek V: The Final Frontier rolls around, the creators have done away with this foolishness. In that movie, there's a scene with Scott and Uhura eating rations that clearly shows Doohan's hand. (A less clear view

18

also exists in Star Trek IV: The Voyage Home.*)*

SYNDICATION CUTS
• Several moments before Scott beams Kirk back to the ship.
• After the evil Kirk demands brandy from McCoy, Spock goes to the captain's quarters to check on him. The uncut version has several seconds of dialogue before the good Kirk says he recognizes the look on Spock's face and asks what is wrong. These disappear in the syndication version, making Kirk look amazingly perceptive.
• The evil Kirk playing peekaboo in Rand's quarters a few moments longer.
• Two sections of the good Kirk's discussion with Rand and Technician Fisher in sick bay.
• Moments of the dialogue between Kirk and Spock in the transporter room.
• The entrance of the good Kirk and Spock into main engineering to look for the evil Kirk.
• Sulu's last two reports from the planet's surface. One of the deleted sections contains a very odd editing sequence. Kirk gets the call, Sulu starts talking, and suddenly there's a shot of the *Enterprise* orbiting the planet. Then the action returns to the conversation.

PLOT OVERSIGHTS
• The transporter malfunctions after Scott beams Technician Fisher back to the ship. Yellow ore dust covering Fisher's clothing

causes the problem. The chief engineer expresses concern about the equipment and—after perusing the instruments—he tells Technician Wilson to fetch a "synchronic meter" so they can double-check the device. Yet, before Wilson returns, Scott beams the captain aboard. So he didn't need the synchronic meter after all?
• Shortly after arriving on the ship, the evil Kirk attacks Yeoman Rand. She seems deeply disturbed by his actions when relating them in sick bay. In addition, when the evil Kirk tries to make amends and asks to visit her later, Rand grimaces. These reactions would be perfectly normal. The man did try to rape her. However, at the end of the show, Rand suddenly acts like everything is fine. Her recovery is a bit too quick. Then Spock comments to her that the evil Kirk possessed some "interesting qualities." What's that supposed to mean? Is Spock wondering if Rand secretly enjoyed the evil Kirk's "forthrightness" (to use a very bad euphemism)? (My wife also noted that Spock leers quite intently at Rand following these comments. Doesn't seem very Vulcan-like, does it?)
• In one scene, Spock tells the good Kirk that they must not inform the crew of the transporter malfunction. He says that the captain cannot afford to be "anything less than perfect." Spock claims that any imperfection will cause Kirk to lose the crew's respect, and the captain will lose his ability to com-

mand. Evidently this necessary image of perfection extends to the physical as well. When the evil Kirk wants to hide the scratches on his face, he walks over to the dressing area of his quarters and opens a jar of *makeup*. Kirk probably keeps it around to hide those unsightly skin blemishes and age lines. (Thankfully—by the time the movies roll around—the crews of the *Enterprise* have matured, and the senior staff is allowed to show the progress of the years.)

• While attempting to convince the good Kirk to get back into the transporter, Spock makes an odd statement. He says, "I have a human half you see as well as an alien half, submerged, constantly at war with each other." Did he just call his Vulcan half "alien"? I thought Spock prided himself on his Vulcan heritage. Wouldn't he be more likely to identify his human half as alien?

• Having made a decision to reenter the transporter, the good Kirk unstraps the evil Kirk from his bed in sick bay. A fight ensues, and the evil Kirk wins. He quickly proceeds to the bridge, where Lieutenant John Farrell gives him an update on the landing party. Specifically, Farrell says, "No word from Mr. Solo, sir." Who's Mr. Solo? Did the person in *The Man from U.N.C.L.E.* get stranded on the planet, too? (Or, perhaps the Millennium Falcon from *Star Wars* crashed there.)

EQUIPMENT ODDITIES

• Of course, the great oddity of this episode is: Why doesn't the crew send down a shuttle to pick up Sulu and the others? (The unofficial answer is the production crew hadn't *built* a shuttle for the *Enterprise* yet. This answer must be unofficial because, as a nitpicker, I don't deal in reality!)

• Sulu seems to have some sort of rotating head on his phaser. In one scene, he uses it to heat up several rocks. He holds it perfectly still but the beam sweeps back and forth.

• Just before the fight between the Kirks in sick bay, the medpanel above the evil Kirk's bed thumps away in rhythm with his heart. During the fight, the pace of the rhythm increases as the evil Kirk exerts himself. There's only one problem. The evil Kirk isn't on the bed anymore. He's on the other side of the room! Why is the medpanel still thumping when no one is in the bed?

CONTINUITY AND PRODUCTION PROBLEMS

• For some reason, the creators spliced the film in backward for the opening scene on the planet. Note the parts in Kirk's and Sulu's hair. Also note that no one on the planet has an emblem on his or her shirt. After Technician Fisher falls, Kirk and Sulu run over and everything reverts to normal. However, the emblem doesn't reappear on Kirk's shirt until after he leaves the transporter room. (Personally I think the creators did this to make their planet set look bigger. Flipping the set makes the area appear completely different. If that's true, they purposefully left off the insignias. Of course, if the creators really wanted to be clever, they could have put the insignias backward on the wrong side.)

• Knowing the evil Kirk will try to hide in Engineering, the good Kirk and Spock go there to capture him. At one point, the evil Kirk points a phaser at the good Kirk and backs away. In the long shots, it looks like the evil Kirk holds the smaller Type I phaser. In the close-up, the evil Kirk holds the larger Type II phaser.

• During the final confrontation between the good and the evil Kirks on the bridge, the scratches on the evil Kirk's face switch sides! For most of the show, they are on the left side of his face. In a few close-ups here they jump to the right side. Either that or someone scratched him on the right side as well.

• There's a small continuity problem after Kirk is reunited. McCoy asks him how he feels, Kirk turns to answer, and then, in the close-up, turns to answer again. (Of course, it may not be a mistake. Kirk's head may rotate 360 degrees!)

TRIVIA ANSWERS
1. 3C 46.
2. Bucko.

CLOSING STILLS
• *Enterprise* orbiting Alpha 177, "The Enemy Within"
• Talosian, "The Cage"
• Garden scene, "Where No Man Has Gone Before"
• Laser cannon, "The Cage"
• Balok puppet, "The Corbomite Maneuver"
• Vina as the low-mileage Orion pit woofie, "The Cage" (Please note: I didn't come up with this term. The creators of *Star Trek: The Next Generation* did in "The Neutral Zone.")

MUDD'S WOMEN

Star Dates: 1329.8-1330.1

The *Enterprise* pursues an unidentified cargo vessel. When the craft goes into an asteroid field, Kirk extends the *Enterprise*'s deflector shields to protect it. At the same time, Spock and Scott beam its inhabitants aboard: a man—Harcourt Fenton "Harry" Mudd—and three strikingly beautiful women. Unfortunately, the entire operation burns up all but one of the *Enterprise*'s lithium crystals. Kirk sets course for Rigel XII—site of the nearest lithium mining operation—and charges Mudd with unlawful operation of a space vessel. When Mudd learns of the ship's difficulties, he quickly dispatches his women to gather a communicator and information on Rigel XII.

As Kirk attempts to negotiate with Ben Childress, the head miner on Rigel XII, he finds that Mudd has already done so. Childress refuses to sell Kirk any crystals. Instead, he wants to trade the crystals for Mudd's women. In addition, Childress demands that Mudd be allowed to go free. After the women beam down, however, Childress is too "busy" to get the crystals. Only when Kirk discovers the truth about the women does Childress uphold his part of the bargain. In fact, Mudd used the "Venus drug" to make them more attractive than they are. In spite of this, Childress asks one of the women to remain behind to discuss their future together.

Trivia Questions

1. What type of vessel does Harry Mudd pilot at the beginning of this episode?

2. How much did Harry Mudd weigh the last time his records were updated?

SYNDICATION CUTS

• Shortly after rescuing Mudd and his women, Kirk orders Spock to bring them to his quarters. The entire sequence of Spock, Mudd, and his women going from the transporter room to Kirk's quarters disappears. This cut features a close-up of the women's backsides as they saunter down the halls.

• Two different sections from Mudd's hearing.

• A few extra moments of dialogue on the state of the ship as it arrives at Rigel XII.

• Brief moments during Harry's search for the Venus drug.

• Parts of the party scene on

Rigel XII.

• A significant portion of footage after Eve McHuron runs out of the party. It shows her struggling against the wind with both Kirk and Childress desperately searching for her.

• It takes considerably longer in the uncut version for Eve to transform herself into the seductive temptress at the end of the episode after swallowing the gelatin pill.

PLOT OVERSIGHTS

• After finding out that the *Enterprise* needs new lithium crystals, Harry Mudd gets an inspiration. He tells the women that they will soon wed rich miners and that he will be ordering Kirk around. He tells the women this in the conference room where Kirk held Mudd's hearing. In the background two guards listen to the entire exchange. Are these guys completely mesmerized by the women? Do they think Mudd is just a blowhard? Why don't they report this exchange to the captain?

• Just after beaming aboard, Childress meets with Kirk. Halfway through the meeting, Mudd comes barging in with his women. Wait a minute: Kirk confined Mudd to his quarters and posted a guard. Is that guard zoned out just like the ones in the briefing room?

• As fellow nitpicker Sara Green wrote, "According to this episode, the best way to give yourself a nice makeover is wishful thinking."

• At the end of the episode, Kirk calls Spock from Childress's quarters on the surface of Rigel XII. He tells his first officer that he and Mudd are beaming up with the lithium crystals. Then Kirk offers to be a character witness at Mudd's trial and walks out without the crystals! (He probably came back when we weren't looking.)

EQUIPMENT ODDITIES

• Mudd keeps the drug that he gives to his women in a little oval box with a hinged lid. Yet, when he approaches Eve to give her a pill, the box loses its lid. Then the shot changes and suddenly the lid is back.

• This Venus drug is hot stuff. It smooths out wrinkles. It fixes your hair. It can even give you a complete makeup job, including false eyelashes.

• Why didn't Uhura pick up Mudd's transmission to the miners? In "Elaan of Troyius" she picked up the transmission from a Klingon communicator.

CONTINUITY AND PRODUCTION PROBLEMS

• McCoy seems to have some trouble deciding which shirt to wear in the transporter room at the beginning of the episode. When the women first beam aboard, he's wearing his long-sleeved velour shirt. Then, as the camera takes another look at the women, he changes into his short-sleeved medical shirt. Evidently he thought he looked better in the long sleeves, because the next time the camera finds him, he's changed back! (Actually, the creators wanted a close-up reaction shot of McCoy and didn't have one, so they edited in a close-up from sick bay. You can even see a medical scanner in the background.)

• When one of Mudd's women visits McCoy in sick bay, she passes in front of a medical panel and it starts blinking. The long shots show her head clearly within the boundaries of the readout area, but the close-ups do not.

• I suppose it shouldn't have surprised me, but I never thought the *Enterprise* would have bugs. Those little pesky critters would be awfully hard to get rid of once they came on board. There certainly would be plenty of places to hide. As Mudd tries to give Eve a Venus

pill in his quarters and she contemplates accepting, a moth flies by!

TRIVIA ANSWERS

1. A small Class J cargo ship.
2. Two hundred forty pounds.

CLOSING STILLS

• *Enterprise* orbiting Rigel XII, "Mudd's Women"

• Kirk, Spock, and Mudd on Rigel XII, "Mudd's Women"

• Mudd's women, "Mudd's Women"

• Lithium cracking station on Delta Vega, "Where No Man Has Gone Before"

• Flying Kirk on bridge, "The Naked Time"

• Vina, beginning to wonder how long it will take Pike to tire of this adolescent fantasy, "The Cage"

CAPTAINCY APTITUDE TEST

(FROM AN IDEA SUGGESTED BY JOE RYAN)

Because the opportunities for commanding a starship are extremely rare, The Powers That Be have developed this test to classify potential commanders according to their abilities. Bear in mind that the results of this test will forever categorize you into one of three possible command tracks (CT). Your CT rating—once determined—will dictate all the possible opportunities that you will be offered in the course of your career. The test will be administered by the interactive workstation in front of you. This workstation will display five hypothetical scenarios concerning a fictitious starship, the USS *Hopeful*. Three possible options will follow each scenario. You must respond in fifteen seconds by typing "A," "B," or "C."

The following addendum was added to this software after the passage of the "Reaffirmation of Personal Rights During Testing" bill on star date 5370.8: Under the laws guaranteeing freedom of expression, this workstation has been modified to allow you to input your own answers. If you wish to supply your own response, you may exercise your option to do so—under Governmental Regulation 80982, Paragraph 12, Subparagraph AA—by typing "D," followed by the statement you wish to make. Answers created by the user will be displayed in an italicized font.

Testing will commence in five seconds. Have a nice day.

1. Suddenly disappearing from the bridge of the *Hopeful,* you awake on planet EADF-82, a world dominated by three bodyless brains called "The Masters." These multicolored brains control the waiflike inhabitants of the planet, forcing them to compete in three-dimensional chess tournaments, and wagering on the results. The Masters explain that their games have grown routine. They need new blood to spice up the competition. They indicate that they intend to destroy your ship and crew, stranding you here for the rest of your life. Do you:

A. Wager your life and the lives of your crew that you can beat three of the best players on EADF-82 not only at three-dimensional chess but in arm wrestling as well?

B. Argue forcefully for the definition of sentience as the standard by which a society guarantees personal rights and eventually convince The Masters to let you go? They are certain that your insipid pontifications would hopelessly bog down any possible excitment you might bring to the games.

C. Assure The Masters that they've made a huge mistake because you don't play three-dimensional chess, but offer to test the inhabitants' skill at one-dimensional checkers?

D. *This isn't the commander's test for the merchant marine, is it? I thought the room number was 225, not 255. Now what am I supposed to do? Well . . . as long as I'm here, I suppose I could answer a few questions. Let's see . . . Personally? I'd see if I could get The Masters to sign me as their agent. I know this guy who does brain juggling on Sidesholotis IV. He's got a machine that temporarily gives him the knowledge to remove the brains of three members of the audience. Then he does this acrobatic program and returns the brains before his surgical knowledge fades. It's a great show, but multicolored brains would be a much bigger draw than those dull gray ones.*

2. The *Hopeful* receives a transmission from a freighter in the Neutral Zone. Its engines have failed, and sensors show the approach of four decloaked Romulan warbirds. Like you, it will take them four hours to reach the freighter. The lives of two hundred humanoids on board the freighter are at stake as well as the supposed inviolable nature of the Neutral Zone. If you attempt to rescue the freighter, the *Hopeful* probably will be destroyed, and you will start an intragalactic war. Do you:

A. Career in with phasers blasting, hoping for that one-in-a-million chance that you will survive?

B. Put out an urgent call to any cloaked Klingon vessels for assistance, and then head into the Neutral Zone at maximum warp with phasers at the ready?

C. Send your regrets to the commander of the freighter?

D. *Take up a position outside the Neutral Zone and ask the commander of the freighter for salvage rights if there's anything left when the Romulans get through.*

3. The *Hopeful* falls into a time-space anomaly and arrives in a completely unknown region of the galaxy. All navigational sensors are useless, but a quick visual check reveals a planet nearby. On arrival, you discover an energy being who lives in a box. The being claims he could return you to Federation space if you transported him aboard. Unfortunately, his assistant, a humanoid of the opposite sex, is violently jealous and will not allow it. Do you:

A. Use your considerable charm to distract the assistant while your science officer spirits the box back to the ship?

B. Spend the next several hours reasoning with the assistant in a respectful manner?

C. Avoid a confrontation by returning to the *Hopeful* and spending the rest of your life wandering around in space looking for home?

D. *Call United Planetary Service! Those guys can get anything from any-where to anywhere. They'd come in, slap a label on that pupster, and you'd have that box on the* Hopeful *in no time.*

4. Your science officer has just informed you that a creature that can assume any appearance has beamed aboard the *Hopeful* from the planet below. It is the last of its kind, but it has already seriously debilitated four crewmen by draining all the male hormones from their bodies and forever damaging their ability to create more. Do you:

A. Run around the ship alone until the creature attacks you—all the while hoping that your senior officers will have the presence of mind to follow you and kill the thing?

B. Conduct a careful deck by deck search with large teams of security officers with tranquilizer equipment and orders to capture the creature and return it to the planet?

C. Make sure that absolutely no lives are at risk by beaming the entire crew down to the planet and waiting for reinforcements?

D. *Capture the creature, sell it to the clinics on Tranvestis V, and tell ship's store to issue the four crewmen some of those miniskirt outfits that the women wear.*

5. A plague that plasticizes humanoid epidermal tissue has struck the inhabitants of the fourth planet in the Delta Omicron Alpha system. In four days, all humanoid life will cease. The only known cure is an exotic compound called DLF-37. The only known source for the compound is the outer asteroid belt of the Strathmed system. Unfortunately, the miners on the outer asteroid belt have recently stopped delivery to the chief distribution center on Strathmed III. They are ashamed of their current compensation package and are demanding lower wages and fewer benefits before returning to work. The government of Strathmed III refuses to pay the miners any less, believing that the current arrangement constitutes the only equitable option. Do you:

A. Have your science officer locate the highest-ranking miner of the opposite gender and attempt to seduce that person into giving you the DLF-37?

B. Convince the government to lower the miners' wages and compensation packages and use the extra profits from the sale of DLF-37 to fund better educational facilities for the children of the miners in the outer asteroid belt?

C. Send a message to Delta Omicron Alpha on the status of the negotiations, informing them that you will bring the DLF-37 as soon as it is available?

D. *Visit Rigley's Pleasure Planet for a week and then set up a mannequin supply operation from a satellite orbiting Delta Omicron Alpha IV.*

SCORING

For every "A" answer, give yourself 100 points; for every "B," 10 points; for every "C," one point; and for every "D," no points. (The Powers That Be are required to allow you to supply your own answers, but they are not obligated to reward you for them.) After adding up your score, please refer to the following grading:

IF YOUR SCORE IS GREATER THAN 250:

Congratulations on qualifying for Command Track 1! A wonderful career awaits you commanding the most exciting starships in the galaxy. *Note:* If you are a woman, you must drop to Command Track 2.

IF YOUR SCORE IS GREATER THAN 25 AND LESS THAN 250:

Congratulations on qualifying for Command Track 2. Your sensitive and insightful answers certainly demonstrate your capability to command a starship. Unfortunately, your viewpoints will not prevail for another eighty years or so. For instance, if you responded "B" to the second question, you simply forgot that the Klingons are *still* our enemies! Hopefully you will live long enough to see your sensitivities come to fruition.

IF YOUR SCORE IS GREATER THAN 2 AND LESS THAN 25:

You qualify for Command Track 3. There are many old rusting space stations—some of them quite deep in space—that will benefit from your abilities. Of course, you can always hope that a stable wormhole will open up near your assignment and add some prestige to your job.

IF YOUR SCORE IS 2 OR LESS:

The Ferengi are always looking for individuals of your caliber. You can contact their "DaiMons in Training Program" through the Ferengi embassy.

WHAT ARE LITTLE GIRLS MADE OF?

Star Date: 2712.4

The *Enterprise* approaches planet Exo III in search of Nurse Chapel's former fiancé, Dr. Roger Korby. Moments after the ship drops into orbit, Korby calls and states that he has made a tremendous discovery. He asks Kirk and Chapel to beam down alone. In caves below the surface, the pair find Korby, a young woman named Andrea, and a being named Ruk. Korby then explains that Andrea and Ruk are androids. To demonstrate the ancient technology of this world, Korby creates an android replica of Kirk and dispatches it to the ship. When it returns, Andrea destroys it, thinking the real Kirk has escaped.

At the same time, Kirk turns Ruk against Korby. Ruk was constructed by the "old ones." At one point millennia ago, the old ones became afraid of their machines and started turning them off. The androids rebelled and killed their creators. Kirk reawakens the memories in Ruk, forcing Korby to dis-

Trivia Questions

1. Dr. Korby revolutionized immunization techniques after translating medical records from the ruins on what planet?

2. Numbering the 5 buttons from left to right, what are the last 6 numbers in the combination to Kirk's safe?

tegrate the huge android. The captain then attacks Korby. The struggle reveals that the scientist is also an android. Korby claims it makes no difference. Chapel responds that it does. The compassionate man she once knew no longer exists. Suddenly Korby realizes that what she says is true. Demoralized, he commits suicide, killing Andrea in the process.

RUMINATIONS

This episode is filled with wonderful elements. The creators did a fabulous job on Ruk. They made him look huge, and the way he tosses Kirk around gives the impression of great strength. Kirk shines as well. Filling his mind with prejudice against Spock is a brilliant tactic, and the logic he uses to reawaken Ruk's memories proceeds beautifully. Finally, Dr. Roger Korby's confusion over his humanity easily evokes pathos.

GREAT LINES

"*Existence . . . survival must cancel out programming.*"— Ruk, upon realizing the logical path that would allow him to attack Korby.

GREAT MOMENTS

There's a lovely exchange between the real Kirk and the android Kirk at a dinner table. The creators did an excellent job blending the two shots together.

PLOT OVERSIGHTS

• Just after Chapel meets the lovely Andrea with the breathy voice, Korby tries to allay his fiancée's fears by assuring her that androids can't love. Well . . . isn't he an android? Doesn't he think that *he* can love?

• Apparently Kirk and company don't think much of the technology discovered by Korby. To my knowledge, there is no indication in the television series or the movies that the Federation ever made it back to Exo III to do more research.

CHANGED PREMISES

• Nurse Chapel seems very much in love with Korby during this episode. Yet just a few shows ago—when alcoholic water loosened her up a bit in "The Naked Time"—Chapel seemed very much in love with Spock. (I suppose this really isn't a changed premise. It is possible. I just thought I would note it.)

• Near the beginning of the episode, Spock asks Chapel if she is certain that the voice she hears belongs to Korby. Chapel responds by asking if Spock has ever been engaged. Spock gives her a noncommittal look, as if she had just

zinged him. In fact, the answer to her question is "yes." "Amok Time" reveals that Spock and T'Pring are betrothed. (It is possible that Spock doesn't answer because—up until the third season—he's a little shy about the whole *Pon farr* thing. Of course, then he starts gushing about it with a woman he has just met. See "The Cloudminders.")

EQUIPMENT ODDITIES

• The little oval light next to Uhura's speaker must be burned out. It stays off the entire show, though both Korby and Ruk communicate through it.

• Just after the second security guard dies, Kirk pulls out his communicator to contact the ship. He has to flip the communicator twice before he finally gets it open.

• To duplicate Kirk, Ruk locks him down on one side of a giant turntable and then slips a generic humanoid form into the other. As the turntable spins, the generic humanoid form resolves into a copy of Kirk. If you watch the form during the overhead shots, it looks a little stubby in the leg department. Obviously, the legs stretch because the final product is the same height as Kirk.

• For an android, Ruk isn't very observant. In one scene, Kirk unties the binding on a chair leg and uses it to attack Korby. While the captain's left hand does the work, Ruk stands just to the left and behind but never picks up on this activity.

• The next oddity occurs just after

the incident above. Kirk successfully attacks Korby by wrapping the binding around his throat and threatening to choke the doctor if Ruk charges. Then Kirk shoves Korby at Ruk and exits through a door. Korby coughs, sputters, and sends Ruk after Kirk. Isn't Korby an android? According to the show, these androids don't have to eat. Do they have to breathe? Why would a cord around his neck cause Korby so much difficulty?

CONTINUITY AND PRODUCTION PROBLEMS

• Evidently, on Exo III your personal status determines how much clothing you get to wear. Korby wears a full jumpsuit. His assistant, Brown, wears a dark shirt and pants that have integrated suspenders. On the other hand, poor Andrea must wear only pants and suspenders.

• Early on, the episode contains a shot of the *Enterprise* orbiting Exo III. It looks like there are smudges of some sort on the film of the ship, because they move in perfect sync with the ship. This happens again later in the show.

• When Ruk and Andrea duplicate Kirk, Korby first shows Chapel the real Kirk and then rotates the turntable to reveal the android Kirk. The creators had to shoot two pieces of film—one with Kirk on the near side and the other with Kirk on the far side of the turntable. They then put the film together to make one continuous shot. It works very well except for

one minor flaw: Watch the real Kirk as he rotates out of view. Just as the android Kirk appears, the opposite side of the turntable goes completely flat—suddenly missing the depression in which the real Kirk rested.

• At times during any television production, some problem forces the creators to bring the actor back into the studio to fix a line or two of dialogue. Most often this involves "dubbing" over the existing film. They keep the pictures and fix the sound. You can find these places by listening carefully to the dialogue. Whenever you hear an instant change in the tone of a person's voice, it's an indication that the line might have been dubbed. I usually don't comment on this type of nit. Often, overdubbing is hard to detect. This episode has an overdubbed line that isn't. It occurs as Chapel talks with the android Kirk over a meal. She thinks it's the real Kirk and says, "Please, go ahead and eat." Listen to the volume and tone of her voice. It's different from the dialogue before and after this line.

• Arriving on the ship, the android Kirk heads for the captain's quarters and grabs the "command pack"—an official list of their itinerary. He then heads out of his quarters and into a turbolift. This stroll down the hall actually comes from "The Man Trap." In that episode, Kirk didn't have anything in his hands. Kirk is supposed to be returning to Exo III with the command pack.

TRIVIA ANSWERS

1. Orion.
2. 554334.

CLOSING STILLS

• *Enterprise* orbiting Rigel XII, "Mudd's Women"

• Scientific research center on Psi 2000, "The Naked Time"

• Ruk tossing Kirk, "What Are Little Girls Made Of?"

• Smoking bridge, "Where No Man Has Gone Before"

• Korby making the android Kirk, "What Are Little Girls Made Of?"

• Andrea, Ruk, "What Are Little Girls Made Of?"

• Rock-filled terrain with city in background, "The Conscience of the King" (I'm guessing on this one. It looks similar to the view out Dr. Leighton's window. The city is also identified as Mojave in "The Cage.")

MIRI

In the "distant reaches" of the galaxy, the *Enterprise* discovers a planet that looks exactly like Earth. Kirk, Spock, McCoy, Rand, and two security guards beam down to a decaying and apparently deserted city. As McCoy inspects a broken tricycle, a humanoidlike beast attacks, claiming the tricycle is his. Then the beast dies. Next they find an older girl named Miri. Miri can only talk of evil "grups" that do hurtful things, get sick, and die. Rand makes the connection that "grups" means "grown-ups," and soon they discover that the only inhabitants of the city are children. They also make another disturbing discovery: The disease that killed off all the adults, causing deformation and madness, has now attacked them. They learn that three hundred years ago, the planet's scientists attempted to slow the rate of aging. It worked, but only for the children, and only until they reached puberty.

In a laboratory on the surface, Spock and McCoy begin their research and finally formulate a cure. Unfortunately, the suspicious children take their communicators, and the pair cannot determine the correct dosage without the ship's computer. Knowing he will die anyway, McCoy takes the first shot. Moments later, he recovers, and the crisis passes.

Trivia Questions

1. According to McCoy, what are the early symptoms of the disease (aside from the splotches, of course)?

2. What "chart" hangs on the wall of the lab?

RUMINATIONS

This is the first of many episodes featuring a planet that developed "just like Earth." Of course, these episodes accomplished one very important thing for Roddenberry: They made the accountants happy. Sets and costumes already existed for many different eras of American history as well as a few for European history. Reusing them saved money. As I consider this whole parallel Earth business, I find myself agreeing with Captain Kirk, who said, "It seems impossible, but there it is."

SYNDICATION CUTS

• Several brief moments just after the landing party beams down.

• McCoy comments that buildings in the city are the most horrible conglomeration of antique architec-

33

ture he has ever seen.

• When the creature attacks McCoy, Kirk actually hits the creature three times before he stays down.

• Just after the creature dies, the landing party hears a noise. The syndicated version shows them running up to a doorway. This is their second destination. First, they run to the end of the street and look at some buildings. One bears the label "Bartlett Stables." This whole episode stresses the similarities between this planet and Earth, yet this planet has a place in the city—among all the brick buildings and automobiles—to rent horses?

• Spock and the guards dispersing after Miri's first appearance.

• Spock and the guards searching for a while and then arriving at an alley.

• A reaction shot of Miri after the landing party discovers the information on the life-prolongation experiment.

• A section including Spock announcing the availability of his calculations, and Kirk dispatching the guards to carry out another search.

• Rand reacting to Spock's assertion that the children age one month for every one hundred years.

• A child singing "Oli oli umpum free" (however it's spelled) when Jahn talks about taking the communicators.

• Miri sharpening pencils for Kirk shortly after Louise dies.

• Miri witnessing Kirk grabbing Rand by the shoulders after McCoy announces his discovery of the disease.

• A single child's attack on Kirk before the rest of the children swarm him.

(You may notice that some of the cuts deal with the security guards. In fact, the syndicated version shows so little of the guards that I almost wrote it down as a nit. They arrive, search with Spock for a few moments, and then disappear until the very end of the show.)

PLOT OVERSIGHTS

• Two days after the children steal the communicators, Kirk and the others still can't contact the ship. I realize that Kirk ordered the rest of the crew to stay on board. Doesn't it seem odd, however, that no one on the *Enterprise* wonders if they're having communicator problems and sends down a few usable communicators for good measure? They know Kirk and the landing party are still alive. They can track them on infrared sensors. (I know. It would be a short show if they could talk to the ship.)

• Along the same lines, what happens to the security guards' communicators? The guards are out on patrol when the children sneak off with the rest of the landing party's communicators. Wouldn't the guards carry their communicators in case they needed to contact Kirk?

• Just after McCoy gives himself a shot of the drug and passes out, Spock comments that he will never understand the medical mind. I think that Spock understands McCoy all too well. The Vulcan knew they needed a guinea pig to test the drug. He loads the syringe and then makes some excuse about needing to check on Kirk's progress with the children. Spock's departure conveniently leaves the hypo in plain view and McCoy all by himself. Right on cue, the doctor picks it up and injects himself.

• At the end of the episode, Kirk tells Spock, "Full ahead, warp one." Why isn't Kirk telling this to the navigator, who sits a few feet in front of him? Are they not on speaking terms?

EQUIPMENT ODDITIES

• At one point, Spock comments to McCoy that their concoction could be a "beaker full of death." According to my sources, Spock looks at a flask, not a beaker, and—being a scientist—the Vulcan should know that.

CONTINUITY AND PRODUCTION PROBLEMS

• Twice in this episode, the sound technicians forgot to dub in the chirping of the communicator as it opened—once with Kirk and once with Spock.

• Toward the end of the show, the children kidnap Yeoman Rand and tie her to a chair. In all the long shots the rope wraps around her waist and below her elbows. In the close-up, the rope wraps *above* her elbows.

TRIVIA ANSWERS

1. Intense fever, pain in the extremities, and fuzzy vision.
2. The Chart of Mutations.

CLOSING STILLS

• *Enterprise* approaching a small, blue planet. (Up to this point in the series, I cannot find this shot. There are other shots of the *Enterprise* and a planet in the distance, but none of the planets are blue.)
• Laser cannon, "The Cage"
• Kirk and Louise, "Miri"
• Kirk and Onlies, "Miri"
• Penal Colony, Tantalus V, "Dagger of the Mind"
• Sulu with foil, "The Naked Time"
• Vina as the green Orion slave girl, "The Cage"

DAGGER OF THE MIND

Star Dates: 2715.1-2715.2

After resupplying the penal institution on Tantalus V, the crew of the *Enterprise* beams aboard a box of records bound for Earth. Unknown to them, the box really contains an escapee. The highly agitated and distraught man eventually charges the bridge, demanding asylum. He claims that he is Dr. Simon Van Gelder, an associate of Dr. Tristan Adams, the head of the institution. Adams confirms the man's statements, stating that Van Gelder is the victim of an experimental new therapy gone wrong. Under McCoy's urging, Kirk decides to investigate. The captain beams down to the institution with Dr. Helen Noel. Adams graciously gives them a tour of his facilities, including the neural neutralizer—the machine that injured Van Gelder. At the same time, Spock learns from Van Gelder that Adams is using the neutralizer as a torture chamber to reshape individuals' minds.

That night, Kirk and Noel return to investigate the neutralizer. Moments later, Adams breaks in and uses the neutralizer on Kirk, giving him an agonizing demonstration. Once they are returned to their quarters, the captain sends Noel into the air-handling ductwork to shut off the institute's force field. She succeeds long enough for Spock to beam down. The first officer finishes the job and calls for security teams to take control of the situation.

SYNDICATION CUTS

• Kirk's second log entry is dropped. It occurs after a commercial break and recaps the action up to this point. It also includes the statement, "As for my last entry, it seems I shall get to meet Dr. Adams at last." However, Kirk's last log entry didn't say anything about wanting to meet Dr. Adams. Kirk made that comment to McCoy after the captain completed the log.

• Spock's log entry is also dropped. If occurs after a commercial break and speaks of how he must use an ancient Vulcan technique—a highly personal thing to his people—on Van Gelder. He then tells McCoy that the joining of two minds is part of Vulcans' private lives.

Trivia Questions

1. What is the destination of the records the *Enterprise* crew beams aboard?

2. How long had Van Gelder worked with Adams?

36

• Finally, the syndicated version does not contain Kirk's recovery from his initial session with the neural neutralizer. During that session, Adams suggested that Kirk was deeply in love with Noel. Back in her quarters, Kirk awakens and reiterates his love for her. Noel quickly reminds him of Adams' actions, and Kirk snaps out of it.

PLOT OVERSIGHTS

• This penal colony really needs better security. Van Gelder, in a crazed state, manages to escape in the *only* box beamed up to the ship. In addition, the living quarters of the institution have air conditioning ducts big enough to crawl through. Of course, without this laxness, there would be no show because Van Gelder couldn't make it to the ship and Noel couldn't shut off the force field to save the day.

• Once Kirk is under the influence of the neural neutralizer, Adams orders Kirk to take out his phaser and drop it on the floor. Kirk brings the weapon out slowly, points it at the beam emitter in the ceiling, and then drops it. Next, Adam asks Kirk to do the same with his communicator. Kirk slowly pulls it out, opens it up, and tries to hail the *Enterprise*. Adams turns up the power. Even still, Kirk hails the *Enterprise* a second time. If Kirk had enough strength to call the *Enterprise* not once but twice, why didn't he have the strength to fire the phaser and destroy the infernal machine?

• When Kirk discovers the effectiveness of the neural neutralizer, Adams decides to use it on the captain to its fullest extent. He wants to convince Kirk that everything is fine at the penal colony. There's only one problem with the scenario. Everyone who has been treated with the neural neutralizer ends up acting like a zombie or a maniac. Wouldn't the crew notice the difference when the captain returned? And if Kirk didn't return, wouldn't they send down more investigators? (I just don't understand what Adams is trying to accomplish by torturing Kirk.)

• Kirk still isn't on speaking terms with his navigator. The person sits a few feet in front of the captain's chair, and Kirk tells Spock to take them out of orbit. Spock just grins and does nothing. In the background, you can hear the officers at navigator and conn pressing their switches to carry out Kirk's order.

CHANGED PREMISES

• It is interesting that Spock refers to the Vulcan mind meld as a "highly personal" thing and a part of Vulcans' "private lives." But evidently it is not *too* personal, given that Spock uses it over and over again during the television series.

EQUIPMENT ODDITIES

• Obviously McCoy doesn't care whether Adams hears him accuse the penologist of lying. During a ship-to-planet conversation between Kirk and Adams, McCoy walks up and says that Adams's statements don't quite ring true. Kirk then tells Adams to stand by and turns off the speaker. Clearly, Adams should be able to hear McCoy's statement.

• In "The Naked Time," McCoy ripped Kirk's shirt to give him a hypo. Evidently the uniform stewards on the *Enterprise* chewed him out, because in this and many other episodes, McCoy gives shots right through clothing.

• The control panel on the neural neutralizer has an interesting feature, a large, centrally located indicator to tell the operator when the machine is *off*. Note that the machine does not have an indicator to tell the operator when it is on.

• When Kirk tells Spock that he will spend the night at the penal colony, Van Gelder overhears the conversation from his sick bay bed and yells, "No!" Appropriately, the thumping sound indicating his heart rate picks up speed. Yet the pulse light on the medpanel above him remains constant.

• For some reason, the neural neutralizer room has a regular twentieth-century hinged door. All the other doors in the complex are the automatic opening pocket doors seen on the *Enterprise*.

CONTINUITY AND PRODUCTION PROBLEMS

• Dr. Helen Noel's uniform seems a bit short in back and a tad too low in front. There are several scenes where other items of clothing—not normally seen on a regular basis during *Star Trek*—make an appearance. Good taste precludes a detailed description.

• The Tantalus penal colony matte painting is actually a remake of the lithium cracking station on Delta Vega ("Where No Man Has Gone Before"). Also, Tantalus V bears a striking resemblance to Alpha 177 ("The Enemy Within").

TRIVIA ANSWERS

1. The Central Bureau of Penology in Stockholm.
2. Six months.

CLOSING STILLS

• *Enterprise* approaching energy barrier, "Where No Man Has Gone Before"

• Engineering, "The Enemy Within" (This is the establishing shot just before the good Kirk and Spock walk into the scene.)

• McCoy and security guard, "Dagger of the Mind"

• Helen Noel, "Dagger of the Mind"

• Scientific research center on Psi 2000, "The Naked Time"

• Fortress on Rigel VII, "The Cage"

• Rock explosion after Robert Crater fires, "The Man Trap"

THE CORBOMITE MANEUVER

Star Dates: 1512.2-1514.1

Three days into a star mapping mission, the *Enterprise* encounters a cube that blocks the ship's path. Kirk tries to fly around it, but the cube begins emitting radiation and approaches the ship. After destroying the object with phasers, Kirk presses forward. A short time later, a massive, spherical vessel approaches. Commander Balok announces that the crew has violated the territory of the First Federation. At the end of ten minutes, he vows to obliterate them.

Faced with no other alternative, Kirk bluffs Balok. He claims the *Enterprise* contains a special substance known as "corbomite." When an enemy attacks, it reflects the attacker's energy and destroys their ship. After the ten minutes, Balok grants them a stay. He says he will tow their vessel to an internment planet. A small cruiser appears as the rest of the giant ship speeds away. Knowing that Balok's tractor beam must be consuming much of the cruiser's power, Kirk attempts to break free

and succeeds. This action apparently damages Balok's cruiser, so Kirk returns with the *Enterprise* to offer assistance. Beaming over, the captain discovers that their enemy is, in fact, a diminutive, pleasant being who has tested the compassion of the crew of the *Enterprise* and desires to know them better.

GREAT LINES

"*Oh, he's starting a countdown.*"—Bailey, after Sulu corrects him that they have only seven minutes, forty-five seconds left, not eight minutes.

GREAT MOMENTS

*W*hen Balok's ship approaches, the creators did a superb job of presenting its immensity in contrast with the Enterprise. *It flies up and keeps getting bigger and bigger and bigger.*

In addition, Spock has two excellent moments in this episode. Minutes before Balok's deadline expires, the first officer comments on the game of chess, stating that once checkmate exists, the game is ended. Kirk comes back with irritation, and the human side of

Trivia Questions

1. How many degrees of overlap does Spock allow during the star field photography?

2. How often does McCoy give Kirk a physical?

Spock almost says, "I'm sorry" before his Vulcan side kicks in to provide a more emotionless response. Then, just as the ten minutes come to a close, Spock glances around the bridge and makes a comment about Balok's similarity to his father. It appears that he does so merely to invoke a snide response from the crew. He knows that he can counter the response with a zinger and break the tension in the air.

SYNDICATION CUTS

• Much of the first encounter with the cube, including evasive maneuvers.

• As the cube first approaches, McCoy gives Kirk a physical. The captain eventually sees the alert light and calls the bridge from sick bay. After Spock displays a picture of the cube, Kirk heads out. In the uncut version, Kirk hops a turbolift and then calls the bridge again. He finds out there is no immediate danger and decides to stop off to get changed. In the syndicated version, Spock apprises Kirk of the crisis, and the captain wanders off to his quarters!

• A shot tracking Kirk's backside as he heads from his quarters to the bridge.

• Several establishing shots before Kirk arrives on the bridge.

• Kirk trying to elude the cube before Bailey shouts that it is coming toward them.

• Reaction shots from Sulu and Bailey on the approach of Balok's big ship.

• Reaction shots after Kirk relieves Bailey of duty.

• Just after Scott comments on Sulu's affinity for timepieces, Kirk pacing into the scene and then back to Spock.

• After Sulu announces one minute until destruction, the syndicated version cuts straight to Bailey's arrival on the bridge. This deletion actually does away with a nit. In the uncut version, Sulu gives the time, pauses, and makes the cryptic comment, "I knew he would." According to Allan Asherman in *The Star Trek Compendium,* the sound editors forgot to dub in the voice of Balok saying, "One minute." Up to this point, Balok counts down the minutes for the crew of the *Enterprise.* The dialogue was constructed for Sulu to predict that Balok would announce the one-minute mark as well.

• Portions of the towing sequence.

PLOT OVERSIGHTS

• Kirk must be an incredibly charismatic speaker. When he encourages the crew, a second cutaway, to a hallway scene, shows a man frozen in midstride. Kirk has spoken for several seconds, and the guy hasn't even put both feet flat on the ground yet!

• At one point, Spock describes the warning buoy as "flypaper." Do they still use flypaper in the twenty-third century? (My neighbor's son, James Strathdee, didn't know what it was, and this is only the 1990s.)

• After Balok produces a drink

40

from his home world, Kirk hesitates to partake. Obviously, Kirk wonders if the impish alien has drugged the potion. To assure them that he has not, Balok picks up the ladle in the punch bowl and pours himself a glass. Then he drinks it. At this, Kirk and the rest imbibe as well. If Kirk is suspicious of Balok's motives, why would these actions allay his fears? The drinks that Balok handed to them didn't come from the punch bowl. They arrived already prepared on the tray. Balok easily could have doctored them and still enjoyed the untouched liquid in the bowl. In addition, McCoy doesn't even take a reading on the liquid. How do they know that the alien substance isn't poisonous to humans?

CHANGED PREMISES

• During the final minutes of Balok's countdown, Spock reminisces about his father and mother. Interestingly enough, he continually refers to them in the past tense. "Journey to Babel" shows that they are both alive and mostly well.

EQUIPMENT ODDITIES

• Great confusion surrounds the hailing whistle used for communications. Sometimes a page follows it, sometimes not. Yet Kirk always seems to know when the page is for him. For instance, after the encounter with the cube, Kirk and McCoy discuss the day's events in Kirk's quarters. The whistle sounds, and Kirk immediately leans over and responds. Some

time afterward, the whistle sounds again, and Kirk just sits there. True, Lieutenant Bailey announces—moments later—that the message is for the crew, not Kirk, but the captain doesn't make even the slightest movement toward the viewscreen. How did he know that the message wouldn't be for him before he heard the page? (I know . . . he read the script!)

• In "The Naked Time," I discussed the fact that the gearing mechanism for the ship's chronometers is off. This problem causes the minutes to read incorrectly whenever the seconds read "00." Even Sulu gets confused by it. When he announces that there is one minute left, the actual sequence on the clock is "2:01," "1:00," and then "1:59." Knowing the clock's faulty design, doesn't that mean that the crew has just less than *two* minutes left?

CONTINUITY AND PRODUCTION PROBLEMS

• As the crew repairs the minor damage caused by destroying the cube, Kirk and Spock discuss the next move. In one shot, Spock has an earpiece inserted in his right ear. The camera angle changes, and the earpiece instantly disappears.

TRIVIA ANSWERS

1. One.
2. Quarterly.

CLOSING STILLS

• *Enterprise* in the energy barrier,

"Where No Man Has Gone Before"
- Balok puppet, "The Corbomite Maneuver"
- Balok, Kirk, and McCoy, "The Corbomite Maneuver"
- Crew thrown about, "The Corbomite Maneuver"
- Scott in Jefferies tube, "The Naked Time"
- Vina showing off her Lee press-on nails, "The Cage"

THE MENAGERIE, PART I

Star Dates: 3012.4-3012.6

The *Enterprise* receives a message to divert to Starbase 11. When they beam down, Commodore Mendez claims the starbase sent no such message. While Kirk and Mendez try to figure out who sent the false message, Spock visits an old friend. Christopher Pike—captain of the *Enterprise* prior to Kirk—is interned at this starbase. A reactor accident has crippled and scarred all but his mind.

After sending false orders to the *Enterprise,* Spock commandeers the ship, taking Pike with him. The ship's computer then sets course for Talos IV, a destination forbidden by General Order 7—the only remaining Starfleet order that carries a death sentence. Kirk and Mendez give chase in a shuttle, forcing Spock to return for them. The first officer places himself under arrest but refuses to release computer control of the vessel. In the court-martial that follows, Spock presents a visual record of the events in "The Cage" (the original pilot for the television series). Moments after watching the replay of Pike's capture, Mendez receives a communiqué from Starfleet. Subspace monitors show that the *Enterprise* is receiving transmissions from Talos IV. Mendez is ordered to relieve Kirk of command for violating General Order 7.

Trivia Questions

1. Which tape does Spock order the computer to execute just prior to Kirk's arrival on the *Enterprise*?

2. What is the name of Pike's chief medical officer?

RUMINATIONS

If I didn't know that all the footage of the encounter between Pike's Enterprise *and Talos IV came from the first pilot for* Star Trek, *I would be very, very impressed with this episode. On the surface, it looks like the creators built a completely new set for the* Enterprise *just for two episodes! Even still, the creators did a very clever job of crafting a story to make use of the old footage—and a good story at that.*

GREAT MOMENTS

At the end of the episode—after ardently defending his first officer to McCoy and then finding that the doctor was right in suspecting the actions of the Vulcan—Kirk suddenly faces the prospect of a court-martial because of Spock's actions. It is a chilling moment.

SYNDICATION CUTS

• Kirk and Mendez sitting at the controls as the craft runs out of fuel, and Kirk shutting down the sidewall computers.

• Kirk's comments about storing the shuttle just prior to beaming aboard.

• When the computer refuses to release control, Kirk reiterating that this is a voice command and giving the order to disengage more slowly. (This episode was obviously filmed in the States. It is so typical of Americans, I almost burst out laughing. Having grown up in the Philippines, I cannot count the number of times I've seen tourists raising their voices and talking slower to Filipinos who didn't understand English. It does no good to talk slower and louder if the person doesn't speak your language. Neither does it do any good to give orders more slowly to a computer that's been programmed not to obey!)

• Scott turning on the viewscreen for the court-martial.

• Before the crew of Pike's *Enterprise* receives the distress call, an entire sequence of uncertainty about the radio signal.

• Pike walking to his quarters after deciding to ignore the call for help.

• Spock reinforcing that the events they see on the viewscreen are the actual events after Pike indicates the same.

• Pike's landing party preparing to beam the crash survivors back to the ship.

• Reaction shots just before the end of the episode.

• In the uncut version—at the very end of the show—Kirk walks around the table, pauses, walks to another table, and then out of the scene. The titling reads "To Be Concluded Next Week." In the syndicated version, Kirk is frozen for some time and the screen reads, "To Be Continued."

• Finally, when Spock introduces the preview of the next episode on the uncut version he says, "You will learn next why returning Captain Pike . . . " If you listen closely you can hear an audio edit on the word "next." Leonard Nimoy never finishes the "t," and there's a "k" sound in its place. That's because he originally said "next week." The pause between "next" and "why" is just long enough for the word "week."

PLOT OVERSIGHTS

• In one scene, Mendez pulls out the top secret file on Talos IV. Kirk hesitates reading it, but Mendez say he will vouch that he allowed Kirk to read it. Yet in the background, Miss Piper listens as Kirk and Mendez go over the file. If this file is so secret, what is she doing in the room?

• I hope this doesn't ruin the story for anyone, but "The Menagerie, Part II" reveals that Mendez is an illusion created by the Talosians. Bear in mind that this is the same

Mendez who boarded the shuttle at Starbase 11. Starbase 11 is six days from Talos IV at maximum warp. That's a long way. Can the Talosians really transmit illusions from that far away, or did Spock sneak a Talosian on board the shuttle? And if they can transmit illusions over this distance, shouldn't the entire area be forbidden?

• Spock must pluck his eyebrows. In the scenes from "The Cage" they are really bushy, but in most other *Star Trek* episodes they make a nice thin line.

EQUIPMENT ODDITIES

• Pike's room in the infirmary on Starbase 11 has a hinged door. Is the medical staff trying to keep him from driving off?

• Evidently Starbase 11 bought the dismantled control panel for the neural neutralizer from the Tantalus V penal colony. At the end of "Dagger of the Mind," Dr. Van Gelder claimed they had dismantled the machine and, sure enough, the control panel is in the computer room of Starbase 11. Those crafty technicians even rewired it and made it into a communications panel. They also fixed the problem with the "off" light (see "Dagger of the Mind"). Now it illuminates when Spock opens a channel (instead of illuminating when the machine was turned off, as it did in "Dagger of the Mind").

• Again, I trust I won't ruin the plot for anyone, but Pike ends up on Talos IV. I sure hope Eveready or Duracell has a local outlet on that planet, because Mendez claims Pike has a battery-driven heart.

• The viewscreens on the *Enterprise* are nothing short of amazing. Just as Kirk and Mendez beam aboard, Spock watches them from the viewscreen in his quarters. Then—when Kirk finds out he can't regain control of the *Enterprise*—the viewscreen automatically zooms back to include a reaction shot from Mendez. Hats off to those designers.

CONTINUITY AND PRODUCTION PROBLEMS

• When Kirk, Spock, and McCoy beam down to Starbase 11, the matte painting shows that it is day. In the next scene, the windows of Mendez's office show that it is night. Then an establishing shot shows that it is day once again. Then the windows show that it is night.

• Just after Pike disappears from Starbase 11, Mendez pauses and suddenly goes for a switch on his viewscreen. He says, "Mendez here. What is it?" He sounds exactly like he's answering a hail except . . . there is no hail. I think the sound editors forgot to put in the whistle.

• "Number One" from Pike's *Enterprise* and Nurse Chapel from Kirk's *Enterprise* bear a striking resemblance to each other. (Hmmmm; I wonder why?)

• Evidently the creators hadn't yet fashioned a dress uniform for Scott. In the hearing, everyone wears one except him.

TRIVIA ANSWERS

1. Alpha 7 Baker.
2. Phil. (I'm kind of partial to that name.)

CLOSING STILLS

• *Enterprise* in orbit around Psi 2000, "The Naked Time"
• Laser cannon, "The Cage"
• Pike and Vina having a picnic, "The Cage"
• Spock and the blond guy, "The Cage"
• Spock's court-martial, "The Menagerie, Part I"
• Talosians gas Pike, "The Cage"
• Survivors' encampment, "The Cage"
• Vina as the green Orion slave girl, "The Cage"

THE MENAGERIE, PART II

Star Dates: 3013.1-3013.2

Spock's trial proceeds in closed session as the court-martial board continues watching the Talos IV transmissions. They depict the expedition Pike led there many years ago. According to the visuals, Pike soon realized the Talosians possessed an awesome power. They could make him live in any illusion they desired. One constant remained: a woman named Vina. When pressed about this fact, Vina eventually answered Pike's questions. She was the only survivor of a cargo vessel crash eighteen years ago. The Talosians desired to use humans to repopulate their planet and, thus, needed an "Adam" for their "Eve." In time, the Talosians realized that humans could not be domesticated, and they let the *Enterprise* depart. Vina stayed behind. The Talosians did well when they pieced her back together after the crash, but they didn't know what a human looked like. In reality, Vina is misshapen.

The viewscreen dims, and then the head Talosian appears on it.

She offers to let Pike live out the rest of his days with Vina. With their power of illusion the Talosians can restore his image of strength. At this point, Commodore Mendez fades. He was never in the shuttle or on the ship. The Talosians created this illusion to distract Kirk from regaining control of the *Enterprise*. As the episode ends, a renewed Christopher Pike walks underground with Vina.

Trivia Questions

1. What does Vina ask Pike to fetch from the horse during their picnic illusion?

2. What is Commodore Mendez's middle initial?

GREAT LINES

"You want me to test my theory out on your head?"—Pike to the head Talosian after he guesses that the laser weapons really are working.

GREAT MOMENTS

The creators did a great job on the opener for the conclusion to this tale. They actually shot new footage of Kirk, Spock, and Mendez against a black backdrop. It works well.

SYNDICATION CUTS

• During the fortress illusion from Rigel VII, a shot of the doorway before the giant walks back out and a reaction shot from Pike and Vina.

• A reaction shot of Spock just before the view of Pike sleeping in his wheelchair.

• The first discussion between Pike and Vina in Pike's cage.

• The crew of Pike's *Enterprise* setting up the laser cannon on the surface of Talos IV.

• Pike exploring his cell before the liquid nutrient appears.

• Three different sections of Vina's dance as the green Orion slave girl.

• Vina assessing the qualifications of the two women the Talosians beam down from the ship.

• Pike spouts off not once but twice about his primitive thoughts.

• A portion of Pike's rest period before the head Talosian tries to abscond with the lasers.

• Several sections of reaction shots after the Talosians suspend transmission to Kirk's *Enterprise*.

• The ascent to the surface by the head Talosian and the humans.

• A brief section during Pike's return to the bridge.

• A reaction shot of Pike after Commodore Mendez calls from Starbase 11.

PLOT OVERSIGHTS

• At the end of "The Menagerie, Part I," Kirk learns that the images on the viewscreen come from Talos IV. He also receives word that Starfleet has relieved him of command because of this fact. Yet, at the beginning of Part II, the court-martial board marches back into the room and starts watching the picture show again. The creators explain this by having Kirk say that the crew has tried everything to stop the transmission of the images and has failed. Just because someone is transmitting images, does that mean you have to watch them? True, Mendez, Kirk, and Pike need to continue Spock's court-martial, but couldn't they move to another room or at least hang a sheet over the viewscreen?

• Toward the end of the show, the navigator pages Mendez by saying, "Bridge to commander." Isn't Mendez a commodore? (I realize that "commander" may be correct from a generic standpoint but during "The Doomsday Machine," Decker is constantly referred to as "commodore.")

• At the end of the show, it sounds like Kirk calls his first officer "Miss Spock." This is not a good sign and may indicate that Kirk intends to exact his own personal retribution on Spock for the events of the past few hours. (Actually, Kirk almost always sounds like he's saying "Miss Spock.")

EQUIPMENT ODDITIES

• Doesn't the computer act as court reporter? As the officers filled the room for the court-martial in Part I, a female ensign turned on the computer. During recess, she turned it off. Yet once the board begins meeting in closed session, no one bothers with the computer anymore.

• Oddly enough, after all these years the Talosians still have not fixed the top of their elevator to the surface. Many years ago, Pike's crew blasted off the top of the elevator shaft in an attempt to rescue their captain. The final scene of this episode shows Pike boarding the elevator with Vina, and the top of the knoll is still sheared. I guess Vina wasn't kidding when she said the Talosians had forgotten how to fix their machines. The open shaft must be really inconvenient when it rains.

CONTINUITY AND PRODUCTION PROBLEMS

• At one point Pike and Vina discuss the Talosians in Pike's cage. The Talosians decide to punish Vina and she disappears, screaming. The scene then transitions back to the court-martial room as the images flicker on the viewscreen. At this point there are some really weird sound effects that don't seem to correspond to any action on the screen.

TRIVIA ANSWERS

1. A thermos of coffee.
2. I.

CLOSING STILLS

• *Enterprise* in the energy barrier, "Where No Man Has Gone Before"
• Vina and Pike, "The Cage"
• Talosian beast illusion, "The Cage"
• Talosian, "The Cage"
• Fortress on Rigel VII, "The Cage"
• Pike in hell, "The Cage"
• Vina growing restless with Pike's predilection for this particular fantasy, "The Cage"

TRIATHLON TRIVIA ON ALIEN RACES

MATCH THE RACE TO THE DESCRIPTION TO THE EPISODE:

RACE	DESCRIPTION	EPISODE
1. Argelians	A. Fought humans on the *Enterprise*	a. "The Apple"
2. Capellans	B. Didn't know they rode in a spaceship	b. "Balance of Terror"
3. Ekosians	C. Played games with Thralls	c. "Is There in Truth No Beauty?"
4. Elasians	D. Rock creatures who staged pageants	d. "A Taste of Armageddon"
5. Eminians	E. Telepaths who wanted to be left alone	e. "Charlie X"
6. Excalbians	F. Master tunnelers	f. "The Mark of Gideon"
7. Eymorg	G. Enslaved by females	g. "Friday's Child"
8. Fabrini	H. Construct tractor beam webs	h. "By Any Other Name"
9. Feeders of Vaal	I. Hideous to behold	i. "Amok Time"
10. Gideons	J. Parallel Communists	j. "Spock's Brain"
11. Gorn	K. Peaceful protectors of dilithium	k. "Spectre of the Gun"
12. Halkans	L. Live one month for every hundred years	l. "A Piece of the Action"
13. Horta	M. They wore dilithium crystals for luck	m. "Errand of Mercy"
14. Iotians	N. Sadistic telekinetics	n. "The Cage"
15. Kalandans	O. Gave fruit to a machine	o. "Wolf in the Fold"
16. Kelvans	P. Built an asteroid deflector	p. "Day of the Dove"
17. Klingons	Q. Peaceful lovers of pleasure	q. "The Devil in the Dark"
18. Kohms	R. Moved in a flash	r. "The Gamesters of Triskelion"
19. Medusans	S. Developed a cloaking device	s. "For the World Is Hollow and I Have Touched the Sky"
20. Melkotians	T. Lived with their heads in the clouds	t. "Arena"
21. Morg	U. Lived on the fantasies of others	u. "What Are Little Girls Made Of?"
22. Onlies	V. For them, combat is better than love	v. "The Tholian Web"
23. Organians	W. Wanted to reduce the surplus population	w. "The Savage Curtain"
24. Platonians	X. Gave Charlie Evans his powers	x. "The Empath"
25. Preservers	Y. Got stupid sniffing zenite	y. "The Lights of Zetar"
26. Providers	Z. Constructed asteroid outposts	z. "The Omega Glory"
27. Romulans	AA. Fought wars with computers	aa. "Mirror, Mirror"
28. Scalosians	BB. Their king married Elaan	bb. "Patterns of Force"

50

29.	Stratos dwellers	CC.	Normally have a hundred arms	cc.	"The Cloudminders"
30.	Talosians	DD.	Givers of pain and pleasure	dd.	"Miri"
31.	Thasians	EE.	Their males experience *Pon farr*	ee.	"The Paradise Syndrome"
32.	The Old Ones	FF.	Forced a peace treaty	ff.	"Plato's Stepchildren"
33.	Tholians	GG.	Became like Nazis	gg.	"That Which Survives"
34.	Troglytes	HH.	Slang for Yankees	hh.	"Wink of an Eye"
35.	Troyians	II.	Adopted a mob culture	ii.	"Elaan of Troyius"
36.	Vians	JJ.	Tried to help the Ekosians		
37.	Vulcans	KK.	Reptile warriors		
38.	Yangs	LL.	Wanted to live in Mira Romaine		
39.	Zeons	MM.	Tortured Kirk to prove Gem's worth		
40.	Zetarans	NN.	Built Ruk		

SCORING
(BASED ON NUMBER OF CORRECT ANSWERS)

0-10	Normal
10-25	Exceptional
26 and up	Put away *The Star Trek Encyclopedia* and try it again.

RACES ANSWER KEY: 1. Q o 2. V g 3. GG bb 4. M ii 5. AA d 6. D w 7. DD j 8. B s 9. O a 10. W f 11. KK t 12. K aa 13. F q 14. II l 15. Z gg 16. CC h 17. A p 18. J z 19. I c 20. E k 21. G j 22. L dd 23. FF m 24. N ff 25. P ee 26. C r 27. S b 28. R hh 29. T cc 30. U n 31. X e 32. NN u 33. H v 34. Y cc 35. BB ii 36. MM x 37. EE i 38. HH z 39. JJ bb 40. LL y

THE CONSCIENCE OF THE KING

Star Dates: 2817.6-2825.3

When a good friend is murdered, Kirk wonders if the man's suspicions are true. He believed that Anton Karidian—the head of an acting troop—is actually Kodos the executioner. When a plague wiped out the food supplies on Tarsus IV twenty years ago, Governor Kodos executed more than four thousand colonists to stretch the remaining provisions. Although the authorities found a burned body, they never absolutely determined it was that of Kodos. Of the nine who could identify him, only two eyewitnesses remain: Captain Kirk and Lieutenant Kevin Riley.

Kirk arranges to transport the troop to their next engagement. En route, he searches the library computer for links between Kodos and Karidian. Then a phaser set on overload almost destroys his quarters, and Kirk adopts a more direct approach. He forces a meeting with Karidian and demands that the man read the death sentence spoken by Kodos many years ago. The computer matches the two voiceprints, but not exactly. Later, during the troop's complimentary performance for the crew, Kirk overhears Karidian confess to being Kodos. He also hears Karidian's daughter, Lenore, tell her father that she is the one who's been silencing the voices against him. Lenore tries to escape by fighting her way out with a phaser but accidentally kills her father. She then promptly goes insane.

Trivia Questions

1. What is the name of the captain of the *Astral Queen*?

2. What was the poison used on Lieutenant Riley?

RUMINATIONS

The first time I watched this episode, I thought Karidian criticized Kirk by referring to him as "the perfect symbol of our technical society, mechanized, electrolicized . . . " I thought finally understood why Kirk doesn't have any hair on his chest. He's been electrolicized! Unfortunately—for the sake of humor—Karidian actually says, "electronicized."

GREAT MOMENTS

The actress who plays Lenore gives a very convincing portrayal of insanity after her character kills Karidian. As she hovers *over the dead body, you can almost see Kirk remembering that he was romantically involved with the woman and getting the heebie-jeebies.*

PLOT OVERSIGHTS

• This whole business of only nine witnesses to the massacre of four thousand colonists deserves scrutiny. There were four thousand other colonists who lived. None of them saw Kodos? He must have been an extreme recluse. In essence, he was the mayor of a small town, population eight thousand. Normally, everybody knows the mayor in a town that size.

• Along the same lines, if the computer records have a picture and a voiceprint, why does the prosecution need eyewitnesses? Surely there is some absolutely identifiable piece of datum stored somewhere. (I realize that DNA matching wasn't in vogue at the time the creators filmed this episode, but what about simple fingerprints?)

• The audience for the complimentary performance for the crew must wonder what is going on backstage. Kirk sneaks around in view of the attendees and talks in a normal tone of voice to Riley, who then argues back.

• The actress who plays Lenore deserves an award for service above and beyond the call of duty. After she confesses to the murders, Karidian draws her to himself and grieves that he has lost the only precious thing in his life. In the process he shouts, "You've left me

nothing!" right in the actress's ear. That had to hurt.

CHANGED PREMISES

• Growing concerned about Kirk's behavior, Spock visits McCoy in sick bay. During the discussion, McCoy imbibes and offers Spock a drink. Spock declines, claiming that his ancestors were spared the effects of alcohol. McCoy concludes that this must be the reason "they" were conquered. "They" who? Vulcans? In "The Immunity Syndrome," Spock emphatically says that Vulcans have never been conquered. Granted, McCoy's remark in this episode is offhand, but—throughout the entire series—Spock consistently responds to this type of statement from the good doctor.

EQUIPMENT ODDITIES

• After giving Kirk general information about Kodos, the computer moves on to the details. It starts out by saying, "Star date 2794.7, Kodos . . . " and then Kirk interrupts it. The computer has already stated that the last record it has of Kodos dates back twenty years. There are many episodes that precede star date 2794.7, and those episodes show Kirk in charge of the *Enterprise*. Kirk hasn't been in command of the *Enterprise* for twenty years. How can the star date on the Kodos file be correct?

• The computer continues with the bad day it's having. Kirk asks the machine about eyewitnesses to the massacre, and it responds that there are nine who can testify against Kodos. Later, Spock—using the same computer—determines that of the nine, only two still live. How can the other seven people testify if they are dead?

• The computer finally redeems itself by giving Spock the right answer even though he asks the wrong question. The first officer gives the computer a list of names and then orders the computer to correlate any past episode that they *all* have in common. Those named in the list are: James Kirk, Thomas Leighton, Kevin Riley, and Anton Karidian. A few scenes later, Spock tells McCoy about the massacre on Tarsus IV. The dialogue leads us to believe that the computer kicked this event out as the common incident. It shouldn't have, because Anton Karidian didn't exist during the massacre on Tarsus IV. Only Kodos did.

• It probably would be tacky to mention the *squirt bottle* that Lenore uses to fill Riley's glass with poison.

• One of the medpanels in sick bay needs adjusting. Just after collapsing in Engineering, Riley is brought to sick bay. When the camera pans up from his body to the medpanel, the pulse light and thumping sound aren't synchronized.

CONTINUITY AND PRODUCTION PROBLEMS

• The city seen through the window of Dr. Thomas Leighton's home evidently had the same architect as the city on the home world of Captain Christopher Pike. "The Menagerie, Part II" features a picnic scene between Pike and Vina. In the distance you can see the city. ("The Cage" identifies this city as Mojave and the planet as Earth.)

• Leighton's home world bears a striking resemblance to Alpha 177 ("The Enemy Within").

• In air date order, this is the first time numbers have appeared on the pipes behind the big screen mesh in Engineering.

• With this episode, the previews of upcoming shows on my uncut, prerecorded tapes switch from production order to air date order.

TRIVIA ANSWERS

1. Jon Daily.
2. Tetralubisol.

CLOSING STILLS

• *Enterprise* firing phasers, "The Corbomite Maneuver"
• Salt creature, "The Man Trap"
• Karidian as Macbeth, "The Conscience of the King"
• Lenore with phaser, "The Conscience of the King"
• Sulu with foil, "The Naked Time"
• Rock explosion after Robert Crater fires, "The Man Trap"
• Lithium cracking station, "Where No Man Has Gone Before"
• Vina auditioning for the part of Jolly Green Giantess, "The Cage"

BALANCE OF TERROR

Star Dates: 1709.2-1709.6

Patrolling near the Neutral Zone, the *Enterprise* loses contact with Earth Outposts 2 and 3. Established by subspace treaty a century ago, the zone defines a no-man's-land between the Federation and the Romulan Empire. Earth set up the outposts to monitor the area for violations. Suddenly a vessel appears near Earth Outpost 4 and fires a glowing plasma ball that destroys it. Afterward, the craft simply fades from view. When motion sensors show the craft heading back to the Neutral Zone, Kirk decides it must be a Romulan with a cloaking device. Spock captures a picture of the Romulan bridge and recommends immediate attack. Evidently the Romulans are a Vulcan offshoot and still warlike. All they will understand is strength. After an intricate battle of move and countermove, Kirk comes out victorious and offers to beam the Romulans from their crippled vessel. The commander simply replies that it isn't their way and pulls a lever that destroys his ship.

Trivia Questions

1. What Earth outpost section is displayed on the viewscreen at the beginning of the episode?

2. What is the name of the Romulan who gets demoted two steps in rank?

RUMINATIONS

This episode starts out with a wedding. Kirk takes his place behind a podium and begins speaking of the happy privilege that ships' captains enjoy. The monologue is later reused as part of Miles and Keiko O'Brien's wedding in the Star Trek: The Next Generation episode "Data's Day."

GREAT LINES

"He's a sorcerer, that one."—The Romulan commander, commenting to a subordinate about Kirk's abilities to guess the Romulan ship's next move.

SYNDICATION CUTS

• After Spock puts up the star map for the outposts, a shot of the viewscreen and some reaction shots from Kirk.

• Several of the reaction shots after the destruction of Outpost 4.

• Uhura's comment about the Romulan message sounding like it's in code.

• Spock working to lock in on the transmission to get a picture of the Romulan bridge.

• Reaction shots from both Uhura

and Sulu.

• After the commercial break, an establishing shot of the ship and the bridge before going to Spock at his console.

• Spock listening to the tape Uhura creates.

• After reporting something at extreme range, Sulu stating that the Romulan ship is changing course, and Kirk encouraging him to stay with the other vessel.

• While the *Enterprise* is still an hour away from the Neutral Zone, a shot of the viewscreen.

• In the briefing, Kirk asking for comments, and a reaction shot showing Sulu, Scott, and Stiles before Spock speaks of the Romulans' superior weapons.

• After the commercial break, an establishing shot of the comet, Kirk and the navigators, and the viewscreen.

• Part of the *Enterprise*'s journey through the tail of the comet.

• The impact of the first phaser shot, and Tomlinson firing phaser two.

• The *Enterprise* resuming its shadowing of the Romulan vessel after outrunning its plasma weapon.

• An establishing shot of the ship, Spock wandering down to Stiles's position, Stiles giving Spock a dirty look, and Spock wandering off.

• The commander of the Romulan ship ordering evasive procedures. The sound effects used as the Romulan twists the control are the same as the ones used during the creation of the

android Kirk in "What Are Little Girls Made Of?"

• After Kirk states that the *Enterprise* has been motionless for nine hours, forty-seven minutes, the uncut version segues to Kirk's quarters. He lies on his bed, thinking. Rand enters and asks if he'd like some coffee. McCoy enters as Rand leaves. Kirk talks about longing to be on a voyage and then starts questioning why he has to be the one to make this decision. The editing sequence is abrupt in the syndicated version. The last shot has Kirk on the bridge. Then the log entry occurs, and suddenly Kirk is in his quarters, with McCoy torn over the decision he faces.

• A reaction shot of Kirk after Spock finishes his work, closes the vent, and picks up the tricorder.

• After Spock fires the phasers, a shot of the viewscreen showing the Romulan vessel drifting in space, Kirk telling Sulu to bring them closer, Uhura opening hailing frequencies, and the image on the viewscreen fading to a shot of the Romulan bridge.

• The Romulan commander actually says, "No . . . no, it's not our way."

PLOT OVERSIGHTS

• One of the interesting things about the Milky Way Galaxy is that it's always moving. Not only does it rotate internally, it also rotates with respect to other galaxies. I started wondering how the Federation could establish outposts on asteroids in a fairly straight line along the Neutral Zone. Do these asteroids orbit stars? You can't just drag an asteroid into space and stick it where you want, because it will drift. Or do the asteroids have some sort of propulsion mechanism that is constantly adjusting their position?

• While giving his report on the Romulans, Spock calls their home worlds "Romulus" and "Remus." Aside from the fact that these names come from Earth mythology, why does the viewscreen say "Romulus" and "Romii"?

• On pages 324 through 326 of *The Making of Star Trek,* Stephen E. Whitfield quotes from the writer's guide for *Star Trek.* The excerpt contains a test of the writer's understanding of *Star Trek* science fiction. The test makes it very clear that the captain of a starship would never hug a female yeoman during a crisis—specifically, a crisis that represented the imminent destruction of the *Enterprise.* The writer's guide states that this would be completely unbelievable. Of course, in "Balance of Terror," guess what Kirk does just before the Romulan plasma weapon hits the ship? He hugs Rand!

• Tomlinson really seems to enjoy his work in the phaser room. The word comes down from the bridge to fire the phasers, and he pauses for a dramatic second before hollering, "Fire!" Wouldn't it be better just to hit the button?

• When the two ships play dead in space, the crews whisper.

Sound doesn't travel in a vacuum. Why are they whispering? (I know. It's the old silent running thing from the submarine days.)

• Did Kirk really chase the Romulans around for three weeks? Didn't the dialogue at the beginning of the show indicate it would take three weeks to get word from Starfleet command? At the end of the show, Rand trots in and informs Kirk that Starfleet has responded.

EQUIPMENT ODDITIES

• After the complete destruction of Outpost 4, the *Enterprise* still manages to receive video from it for several seconds.

• Upon learning that the Romulan vessel heads for a comet, Kirk hands Spock a book. A book? What happened to the library computer banks?

• Kirk consistently orders the crew to fire phasers, but in each case the exterior shot of the ship shows it firing photon torpedoes. Even the explosions look like those from photon torpedoes.

• After the first engagement with the Romulan vessel—an engagement in which the *Enterprise* suffered no hits—the phaser transfer coil suddenly burns out. Are the weapons systems on this ship really this bad? No one on the bridge seemed to think that Kirk was overtaxing them, and yet they just quit working!

• According to Scott, the Romulan vessel has only impulse power. That means it travels slower than the speed of light. Yet their weapon overtakes the *Enterprise* when the ship is traveling at emergency warp speed. Emergency warp speed must be much, much faster than the speed of light. How could the Romulans understand enough about subspace to build a weapon that, in essence, has a warp drive and still have only impulse engines on their ships?

• When the *Enterprise* is retreating from the plasma weapon, why doesn't Kirk tell Sulu to go sideways and get out of the line of fire? Is this plasma cloud smart enough to follow them? If so, how? The cloud looks transparent (no circuitry that I can see).

• Some of the bulbs in the red alert panels seem to be burned out. When Spock hurries back to fire the phasers, neither of the red alert panels flashes in the corridor.

CONTINUITY AND PRODUCTION PROBLEMS

• After capturing the first ever view of the Romulans, Spock's eyebrows rise in amazement. No wonder. His father commands the Romulan vessel! (Just joking. They are played by the same actor.)

• The creators cleverly dressed most of the Romulans in ear-covering helmets for this episode. It saved them some money on pointed ear appliances.

TRIVIA ANSWERS

1. Z-6.
2. Decius.

CLOSING STILLS

• *Enterprise* in energy barrier, "Where No Man Has Gone Before"

• Romulan commander, "Balance of Terror"

• Crew thrown about, "The Corbomite Maneuver"

• Romulan ship, "Balance of Terror"

• Balok puppet, "The Corbomite Maneuver"

• Scott in Jefferies tube, "The Naked Time"

• Vina starting to worry that she might spend the rest of her life in this idiotic costume and green body paint, "The Cage"

★
SHORE LEAVE

Star Dates: 3025.3-3025.8

The *Enterprise* orbits a planet in the Omicron Delta region, looking for a place to take shore leave. Sensors have reported only plant life on the planet, and a landing party is making the final inspection. Then McCoy sees something very unusual. A large white rabbit approaches, pulls out a gold pocket watch, exclaims that he is late, and runs away. Of course, McCoy realizes the scene comes straight from *Alice in Wonderland* but can find no explanation for it. He reports to Kirk, who immediately beams down. Other oddities soon appear. Sulu finds an old-style police special. Yeoman Barrows is attacked by Don Juan.

Then tragedy strikes when a knight on horseback thrusts a lance through McCoy's heart.

Having joined the landing party, Spock formulates a theory. Apparently, thinking about an object or a person causes it to come into existence on this planet. Soon the "Caretaker" appears. He explains that the entire planet is an amusement park, built as a playground for

another race. Until moments ago, he was unaware that they didn't understand this fact. After presenting a fully repaired and recuperated Dr. McCoy, the Caretaker invites them to stay and enjoy themselves.

SYNDICATION CUTS

• Kirk's initial embrace of Ruth lasts a bit longer before the commercial break.

• The captain's log star date 3025.8 disappears from the syndicated version after a commercial break.

• After another commercial break, the captain's log supplemental also disappears.

PLOT OVERSIGHTS

• Ensign Angela Martine has certainly recovered quickly. In the previous episode, "Balance of Terror," she lost her fiancé. In this episode she's cozy with a man named Rodriguez. (Actually, in production order there are seven episodes between these two, giving Martine a chance to recover from her loss. When they were aired, the creators put them back to back.)

• I want to know who's been thinking about bugs. Supposedly

Trivia Questions

1. In what order will the shore parties depart the ship?

2. Where has McCoy previously seen the tribble-equipped pleasure girls who hang from his arms at the end of the show?

this planet has only plant life. In addition—according to the plot line—the objects appear because someone thinks of them. Since there are three different scenes that feature insects, someone must be thinking about bugs. The first scene occurs when Kirk encounters Ruth. Just after Kirk orders his people to rendezvous in the glade, the reaction shot of Ruth has a bug flying by. Next, after McCoy encourages Barrow to put on the princess dress, a white butterfly makes its way across the screen. Finally, after Sulu retreats from a samurai warrior, Kirk asks his helmsman if he has seen anyone else from the landing party. Watch very closely. An insect flits up, and Kirk actually moves to avoid it. (I know they shot these scenes outside and the insects were unavoidable, but I thought it was interesting to note.)

• It's grungy nitpicking time. When Spock begins to materialize, Sulu says, "Someone beaming down from the bridge." Crew members beam down from the ship. They also beam down from the transporter room. They don't beam down from the bridge.

• Of course—after Spock barely manages to beam down to the planet—no one bothers to mention the possibility of a shuttle coming down to get the "stranded" group.

• Kirk and Spock seem genuinely frightened when a tiger appears in their vicinity. What are they worried about? Look closely and you'll see that the poor animal is chained up.

• Doesn't Sulu know how to operate a tricorder? After Kirk shoots the knight who skewered McCoy, Sulu notices that the rider looks like a mannequin. He also tells Kirk that the tricorder still functions. At this, Kirk shouts to Spock. The first officer walks all the way across the glade, gets the tricorder from Sulu, and takes the reading. Did Kirk not trust his helmsman—who is ofttimes noted as head of life sciences—to do this?

• The Caretaker seems a tad prejudiced against Spock. He calls everyone else by their rank and last name, yet refers to the Vulcan as "Mr. Spock."

• What happened to Martine? Rodriguez apparently runs her into a tree and knocks her unconscious as they flee from the strafing airplane, but she never shows up in the rest of the episode. Did the bullets from the plane kill her? At the end of the episode, the Caretaker says everything's been fixed, and McCoy certainly looks recovered (if the silly grin evoked by the pleasure girls is any indication). But if Martine survived, shouldn't she show up at the end of the episode as well?

EQUIPMENT ODDITIES

• Sulu finds an interesting "police special" revolver. It fires seven bullets! He fires four during target practice, and Kirk fires three more at the knight.

CONTINUITY AND PRODUCTION PROBLEMS

• The footprints made by the rabbit are distinct impressions set side by side. However, the actual footage of the large rabbit shows it shuffling along. (I live in the woods with a fair sprinkling of wild animals around. Those prints were definitely not made by that rabbit.)

• When Kirk first encounters his old flame Ruth, the creators use background music that features a melody on flute. The instrumentation flows along and lends its support nicely—all except the cello part, that is. First, the cello is out of tune. Second, the notes it plays sound like they come from a different piece of music! It is really bad. Every time I hear it I burst out laughing. Also, when Kirk says "Ruth" the first time, listen for the cello. It sounds like the musician plays a note for no particular reason.

• The teaser for this episode contains a shot never used in the episode. It is a close-up of Barrow's left side as she leans against a tree. She is already dressed in the princess outfit. A hand reaches around the tree to grasp her wrist.

• All the dialogue speaks of a singular airplane, and most of the shots show only one. However, for several brief seconds the sky suddenly contains two.

• After McCoy's body disappears, Kirk and Spock walk back to that location. As they do, the ground makes an odd clunking sound, as if they are walking across sheets of plywood.

• These Starfleet uniforms have some odd characteristics. In one scene, Kirk has a fistfight with an old Starfleet Academy nemesis named Finnegan. Kirk's shirt holds up well until Finnegan kicks him in the groin and flips him over onto his back. At this point Kirk's shirt is still in one piece, but when the scene cuts to a close-up, it's torn completely off his right shoulder. Also, when Don Juan roughs up Yeoman Barrows, her tunic is torn from her right shoulder. Yet at the end of the episode, when she dons the miniskirt again, the right shoulder seems completely repaired.

• Just as the Caretaker appears, watch the tree trunk near the center of the screen. You'll see the shadow of a boom mike pass across it.

TRIVIA ANSWERS

1. Alphabetical. (Listen to the background voices in the conversation between Kirk and Spock in the captain's quarters at the beginning of the episode.)
2. A cabaret on Rigel II.

CLOSING STILLS

• *Enterprise* orbiting amusement planet, "Shore Leave"
• Sulu with foil, "The Naked Time"
• Finnegan, "Shore Leave"
• Lake scene, "Shore Leave"
• Kirk running, "Shore Leave"
• Knight on horseback, "Shore Leave"
• Vina as the Orion slave girl, "The Cage"

THE GALILEO SEVEN

Star Dates: 2821.5-2823.8

ncountering a quasarlike formation on the way to planet Makus III, Kirk dispatches the shuttle *Galileo* to investigate. Unfortunately, the formation grabs hold of the shuttle and sucks it inside. The formation has ionized all the surrounding area of space, making the ship's sensors useless. On top of this, the *Enterprise* carries medical supplies that must be delivered to Makus III on schedule, limiting the crew's search time.

On the *Galileo*, Spock and Scott assess the damage caused by their crash landing on an unknown planet, while two other officers scout out the land. A giant spear kills one of them almost immediately. Evidently the planet is home to a race of savage giants. Needing fuel, Scott suggests draining the energy from the hand phasers even though they are the only source of protection for the shuttle crew. When the shuttle starts lifting off, the giants grab on to it and hold it down. Seeing no alternative, Spock engages the thrusters. The

Trivia Questions

1. What is the length of the *Galileo*?

2. The giants are similar to life forms discovered on which planet?

action burns a great amount of fuel, but it allows them to break free. The shuttle achieves orbit, but the *Enterprise* has already left for Makus III. In one last desperate attempt, Spock jettisons the remaining fuel and ignites it. The giant flare draws Sulu's attention, and Kirk instantly turns the ship around to rescue them.

SYNDICATION CUTS

• The *Galileo* rotating to face the hangar doors, Spock doing a preflight check, and Kirk ordering the shuttle to launch. The last deletion causes a minor problem. If a nitpicker watches the syndicated version, he or she might note that Kirk never gives the *Galileo* the order to launch, even though he does so for the *Columbus* later in the show.

• After Spock comments that they may be on the planet for a very long time, an establishing shot of the *Enterprise* and Kirk checking with communications, sensors, and the transporter room before contacting the *Columbus*.

• A portion of interchange

between Spock and Boma concerning the Vulcan's callous attitude toward Latimer's death.

• The discussion about bringing Latimer's body back to the shuttle.

• The commissioner reminding Kirk of the deadline, a reaction shot from Kirk, an establishing shot of the shuttle, and Spock making a suggestion that Scott discounts before the doors to the shuttle's rear compartment open.

• Gaetano reacting to Spock's assertion that they should fire to frighten, not to kill. The trio heads outs and goes through one passageway before reaching the location where a giant throws a spear.

• McCoy hesitating before giving Spock his phaser to power the shuttle.

• Part of the discussion between McCoy and Boma after Spock wanders off to find Gaetano. Also, Spock searching through another section of the set before locating the dead man.

• Returning with the body of Gaetano, Spock sits beside Scott, who is working near an access panel on the floor. In the uncut version Boma walks up, stops, and then wanders up to the front before McCoy comes forward and starts speaking with Spock. The syndicated version has Boma walking up and stopping. The scene then cuts straight to Spock's conversation with McCoy. Since Boma's head cannot be seen, it looks like McCoy has become an African American and reduced in rank to lieutenant.

• A portion of the giant bashing the shuttle with a rock.

• A few reaction shots after Scotty realizes that Spock was trying to send a distress signal when he jettisoned the fuel.

PLOT OVERSIGHTS

• Supposedly the *Galileo* is taking flight to study a quasar phenomenon. Yet McCoy and Scott accompany the scientists. True, they are needed in the end but their assignment in the first place seems a bit dubious.

• Trying to frighten the giants away, Spock, Boma, and Gaetano travel into the rocks and fire in their general direction. First of all, why not stun the big guys? I realize that Spock doesn't want to kill them, but isn't that the whole point of the stun setting? Then Spock leaves Gaetano behind. How is this a logical choice? Latimer was killed when traveling as part of a team. Doesn't it seem likely that a lone guard will be murdered as well?

• At the end of the episode, Uhura reports that they have recovered five survivors from the shuttle. Kirk smiles and sets course for Makus III. Wait a minute: How does he know the other two aren't still on the planet? For that matter, why isn't he concerned with *which* of the five beamed aboard? Does he automatically conclude that all the senior officers survived? (Come to think of it, this may be proof that there is some unwritten law in Starfleet. If you are a junior officer, it's your duty to get killed off first! That law would explain *a lot* of things.)

• After searching for the *Galileo* until the deadline to leave, piddling along to Makus III, and then going back for the shuttle crew, Kirk sets course again for Makus III, warp one. Warp one? Shouldn't they be going faster than warp one? Didn't Kirk wait until the last possible moment to leave?

EQUIPMENT ODDITIES

• When leaving the shuttle to attend Latimer's funeral, Boma uses his hand to close the lower portion of the shuttle exit. The rest of the time, the exit opens and closes automatically.

• The shields that the giants use look like simple wood and leather. However, they seem to employ a very sophisticated enlargement technology. When a giant tosses his shield to the ground, it grows to monstrous proportions almost instantly.

• I really am impressed with the speed of the window shutters on the *Galileo*. When the giants assault the craft, the scene from inside of the shuttle shows that the windows are open. An instant later, an outside shot shows them closed. Evidently these things can seal up tight in the blink of an eye. That's a great feature to have in case of attack.

• Those clever creators tried to pull a fast one on us with the placement of the switch labeled "Fuel Jettison." If you watch Spock's hand movements you might think that the switch is on the center panel between the two chairs in front. Not so. Study the console that houses the "Fuel Jettison" switch carefully and you will see that it is actually one of the boxes that hangs on the side of the shuttle!

CONTINUITY AND PRODUCTION PROBLEMS

• Arguing about whether to conduct burial services, McCoy snaps that Spock should allow them to die as men, not machines. As the doctor says these words, there is a weird effect on his voice, almost like an echo.

• As Spock carries Gaetano's body back to the shuttle, two spears fly his way. The second one hits a rock, and chips of Styrofoam fly everywhere! No wonder it's so easy for a giant to lift up this huge boulder and pound it into the top of the shuttle. Of course, this also explains why the shuttle can take such horrendous punishment.

• Speaking of giants, I do think that the creators could have done a more consistent job with the size of the giants. One team reports that they are ten to twelve feet tall. Yet when one kills Gaetano, the fur-covered beast tops out at about eight feet. When another attacks the shuttle, he towers over it from the waist up. Finally, one of the giant's footprints looks to be about three feet long. I'm just over six feet tall and my feet are approximately one foot long (no pun intended). I have no problem with stability. On the other hand, these giants are supposedly twice as tall as I am, and their feet are *three* times as long! I bet they don't have any problem standing upright in a brisk wind.

• Back on the subject of rocks, Spock makes a brave but ultimately futile attempt to convince us at the end of the episode that a ponderously heavy boulder has pinned his leg against the rock face.

TRIVIA ANSWERS

1. Twenty-four feet.

2. Hansen's Planet.

CLOSING STILLS

• *Enterprise* orbiting Psi 2000, "The Naked Time"

• Spock, Gaetano, Boma, "The *Galileo* Seven"

• Giant, "The *Galileo* Seven"

• Kirk in court, "The Squire of Gothos"

• *Galileo* in shuttle hangar, "The *Galileo* Seven"

• Gorn, "Arena"

• Vina celebrating St. Patrick's Day, "The Cage"

THE SQUIRE OF GOTHOS

Star Dates: 2124.5-2126.3

While warping across a "desert" in space, the *Enterprise* encounters a previously unknown planet. In the next moment, first Sulu and then Kirk disappear. A landing party finds Kirk and Sulu frozen like wax figures in a castle on the surface. Suddenly a being appears, unfreezes the pair, and introduces himself as Trelane, the squire of Gothos. Apparently he can change matter into energy and back at will. After careful observation, Kirk and Spock surmise that Trelane's abilities come from a machine. Since the squire never ventures far from a large mirror, Spock hypothesizes that the machine lies beyond it. Moments later, Kirk challenges Trelane to a duel. Then he uses a pistol to shoot out the mirror. As Trelane throws a fit, everyone beams back to the *Enterprise*. Kirk orders maximum warp, but no matter which way the ship turns, the planet blocks its path. Incensed, Kirk heads back to the surface. An angry Trelane stages a mock trial

and convicts the captain of treason. Just as he is about to run Kirk through with a sword, Trelane's parents—energy beings of great sophistication—apologize for their child's behavior and make him come home.

Trivia Questions

1. What is the magnitude of the planet Gothos?

2. According to Trelane, what is Spock's one redeeming virtue?

RUMINATIONS

Trelane seems to be the precursor of Q in Star Trek: The Next Generation. *He's impudent and possessed of great power. He even puts Kirk on trial, just as Q does later with the crew of the* Enterprise 1701-D.

GREAT LINES

"I object to you. I object to intellect without discipline. I object to power without constructive purpose."— Spock to Trelane.

SYNDICATION CUTS

• Kirk getting an update from McCoy after Trelane releases the captain from suspended animation.

• After a commercial break, Spock's first log. Also, Spock advising Scott to narrow the focus of the sensor beams and ordering him to beam up, indiscriminately, every life form found on the planet.

Finally, a portion with Trelane showing off his battle flags. This edit does away with a plot oversight. Spock tells Scott to beam up any life form they find on the planet but does not post any security in the transporter room. Since the sensors are barely working, isn't there a possibility that Scott could beam up something dangerous?

• A discourse between Spock and McCoy over Spock's use of the word "fascinating." Spock states that he uses the word "fascinating" whenever something unexpected occurs.

• An extra pair of reaction shots of Trelane and Yeoman Ross dancing and Kirk and Spock watching.

• More reaction shots—including Uhura playing the harpsichord—just before Kirk mentions that Trelane never strays far from his mirror.

• In the syndicated version Kirk comes to the conclusion that the mirror is Trelane's source of power. In the uncut version, Spock prompts Kirk to this conclusion by carefully guiding the discussion.

• Following a commercial break, Kirk making a "delayed report" before the actual duel.

• A pair of reaction shots from Kirk and Trelane directly after the captain appears in the squire's courtroom.

• Spock's short entry in the captain's log following a commercial break.

• Several moments of Kirk running through the forest before heading up the castle steps.

• Pieces of the final discussion between Kirk and Trelane about winning and losing.

PLOT OVERSIGHTS

• The dialogue seems to indicate that Trelane did his research on Earth using methods that would allow him to view the light coming from that planet. Since Gothos sits nine hundred light-years from Earth, Trelane's information is supposedly nine hundred years old. However, Trelane also comments about how much he admires Napoleon and talks of Alexander Hamilton's death. Napoleon rose to power in about A.D. 1800, and Hamilton died in 1804. That would make the time frame for "The Squire of Gothos" about A.D. 2700—four centuries too late.

• At one point, Lieutenant DeSalle tries to get the drop on Trelane by sneaking up behind him with a phaser. Of course, Trelane sees DeSalle's reflection in the mirror and freezes the officer. I have a hard time believing that DeSalle can't figure out that Trelane could see him. Didn't he even stop to consider that there is a huge mirror directly in front of him?

• After Spock beams up the first landing party, Kirk orders the *Enterprise* to warp out of orbit immediately. Obviously he's in a hurry. Well . . . sort of. Knowing the *Enterprise* must escape Trelane's sphere of influence as quickly as possible, Kirk takes a few moments to chitchat with Spock in the transporter room before giving the actual orders to warp away.

EQUIPMENT ODDITIES

• At the beginning of the episode, Spock scans the space ahead of the *Enterprise* and announces that it is barren. Kirk sets course across the void as the first officer wanders down to the navigator's station. Then Spock announces that a large disturbance has suddenly appeared. He does this while looking at the navigator's station. Kirk asks DeSalle—who happens to be sitting in the navigator's chair—to confirm this, but at first the officer cannot. Is there some configuration on the instrument readouts that only Vulcan eyes can see? They are both staring at the same panel!

• While deciding to destroy Trelane's mirror, Kirk asks if the machine would be the same one that is maintaining the friendly atmosphere. Spock replies that the machine maintaining the atmosphere would have to be much larger. Who says? When does size automatically denote capability? Earlier in this episode, the creators show us a breathing apparatus that featured a small mask and a book-size belt pack. Presumably the creators wanted us to believe that this was the twenty-third century equivalent of an air tank and a face mask. As equipment becomes more sophisticated, doesn't it also have a tendency to shrink in size? If Trelane is so advanced, doesn't it seem fallacious to assume that his machinery must be of a certain size?

CONTINUITY AND PRODUCTION PROBLEMS

• After the first group beams down to the planet, DeSalle flips open his communicator and hails the *Enterprise.* Receiving no answer, he snaps the communicator shut. Then a wide shot shows him snapping it shut again.

• In the syndicated version, the multiple edits in the scene where Trelane dances with Yeoman Ross create a very strange piece of music. It proceeds in fits and spurts, making very little musical sense. Of course, Uhura *is* playing the harpsichord at this point, and she *did* tell Trelane that she couldn't play the thing. Maybe that explains it.

• The planet of Gothos seems transparent at times.

TRIVIA ANSWERS

1. 1E.
2. Spock is ill-mannered.

CLOSING STILLS

• *Enterprise* approaching energy barrier, "Where No Man Has Gone Before"

• Kirk and Trelane in duel, "The Squire of Gothos"

• Lazarus's vessel, "The Alternative Factor"

• Lawgivers leaving Hall of Audience, "The Return of the Archons" (This scene is never shown in the episode.)

• Kirk in corridor, "The Alternative Factor" (I'm guessing on this one. The scenes in the corridor are all shown as negatives.)

• Starbase 11, "Court-Martial"
• Vina, hoping the author of this book has finally exhausted all his idiotic labels for her present persona, "The Cage"

ARENA

Star Dates: 3045.6-3046.2

After an unknown vessel savagely attacks Cestus III, Kirk gives chase. Just as the *Enterprise* begins to overtake the enemy, a powerful force from a nearby star system reaches out and halts both ships. The Metrons announce that the two ships have entered their space on a mission of violence. They refuse to allow this. Instead, they have determined that the ships' captains will fight alone on a barren planet. The winner and his ship will go free. The loser and his ship will be destroyed. The Metrons indicate that the planet is rich in weapon-making materials. Moments later, Kirk finds himself face to face with a lizardlike biped called a Gorn. He soon discovers that the Gorn is much stronger, though less agile. After pushing a huge boulder from a high ledge and dropping it directly on top of the Gorn, Kirk discovers another disturbing fact: The Gorn can withstand a tremendous amount of physical punishment. Running from that engagement, Kirk stumbles into a Gorn trap and injures his leg. Thankfully, Kirk realizes that he has the chemicals on hand to make gunpowder. Fashioning a crude cannon, he knocks the Gorn unconscious with a load of raw diamonds. He refuses to finish the job and kill his enemy, however—an act the Metrons commend as showing promise.

Trivia Questions

1. What did Kirk put in his bamboo cannon?

2. How far across the galaxy did the Metrons toss the *Enterprise* after they returned Kirk to the ship?

RUMINATIONS

I am amazed at how many stunts the actors actually performed in this series. After the landing party beams down to Cestus III at the beginning of the episode, the Gorn attack. Both Kirk and Spock run through an exploding debris field.

GREAT MOMENTS

There's a fun moment in this show when Kirk struggles to pick up a basketball-size rock and toss it at the Gorn. The rock hits the biped lizard in the chest and bounces off without even slowing him down. Then the Gorn hoists this gigantic boulder and lobs it up at Kirk's position. If I were Kirk, this interchange would not inspire confidence in my ability to defeat this guy.

SYNDICATION CUTS

• After Sulu decides to take the *Enterprise* out of orbit, the uncut version shows the ship warping away, Kirk running into the armory, and Spock checking on the injured man before taking a new reading on the Gorn.

• In sick bay, a portion of the wounded man's ranting that there must be a reason why the Gorn attacked.

• Coming back from a commercial break, the captain's log, star date 3046.2, and Kirk's discussion with the navigator and Spock.

• After going to warp eight, Kirk ordering all phasers to battle ready and Scott giving the bridge a worried look.

• Following a commercial break, Kirk's thoughts on the Gorn as it rips a large branch from a tree.

• Spock conferring with Uhura about sensor readings after talking with Scott about bypassing the transformers and feeding the impulse engine directly.

• Part of the conversation between Spock and McCoy when the doctor initially asks the Vulcan what he is going to do to help the captain. Also, reaction shots after Spock answers that there is nothing they can do.

• Kirk initially finding the bamboo patch, beating a stick on the ground, and finally running up the hill.

• Toward the end of the show, Kirk breaking a stick to make a tamper, the Gorn wandering down a road (more on that later), and

Kirk packing the gunpowder into the bamboo tube.

PLOT OVERSIGHTS

• When Kirk disappears from the bridge of the *Enterprise,* Uhura screams. Why? Kirk disappeared from the bridge in the last show and Uhura didn't scream.

• In the first encounter with the Gorn, Kirk allows the big lizard to grab his legs and then get him in a bear hug (lizard hug?). I don't understand why this Gorn doesn't just bite Kirk. The Gorn looks as if he has some pretty nasty teeth. Maybe he had a few of the colonists on Cestus III for lunch and discovered that he doesn't like how humans taste. (See, now that was a very Terracentric remark, and you should be ashamed of yourself if you smiled when you read it. Just because an alien is big and green and has rows of razor-sharp teeth doesn't mean his eating habits are any less civilized than ours. For all we know, the Gorn may enjoy crumpets and tea every afternoon . . . yeah, right.)

• This Gorn captain needs to improve his aim or get himself a pair of glasses. Trying to make a hand weapon, the big lizard uses a rock to chip away at a chunk of crystal. Watch closely the first time the scene appears and you'll see him completely missing the crystal!

• The first things Kirk gathers to make his cannon are a bamboo tube and a length of rope. At least it looks like a piece of bamboo. (I grew up in the Philippines, and some of my friends would use bamboo of the same diameter to fashion gasoline cannons.) If it is bamboo, Kirk must have knocked out the segments when we weren't looking. Notice the outside of the tube. Every horizontal line represents the start of a segment. The bamboo is only hollow between these segment boundaries.

• And speaking of the rope Kirk finds, remember that he only wants it to wrap around the bamboo for strength. Yet, for some reason, Kirk thinks the rope he finds is too long and so consumes several precious seconds making it shorter by cutting it with a rock. Oddly enough, the piece he discards is only a few feet in length. Why not just wrap it around the tube a couple more times?

• Looking for Kirk, the Gorn captain walks out onto a dirt road. A road? Who built a road on this barren planet?

• Collecting the chemicals he needs for gunpowder, Kirk shovels each element into his bamboo tube. Then he dumps the contents out onto a rock. By this time the powders have thoroughly mixed. This is to be expected. After grinding the coal into carbon, however, the sulfur and potassium nitrate have magically separated themselves back into neat piles so Kirk can mix them in the right ratios.

• I must admit that these Metrons really are quite civilized. When they return Kirk to his ship, they wash his face, clean his clothes, and apparently heal his leg.

CHANGED PREMISES

• Evidently the Federation developed the technology to create precious gems between the time of this episode and "Catspaw." In this episode, Kirk finds a stash of uncut diamonds and proclaims that they are an "incredible fortune." Yet in "Catspaw," Kirk claims they can manufacture the baubles at will.

EQUIPMENT ODDITIES

• Beaming down to Cestus III, Kirk and the others find it completely destroyed. Soon after, the Gorn attack. Looking for better weapons, the captain heads for the armory and locates a photon grenade launcher. He and Spock set it up in a large depression on the bank closest to the enemy. Then they drop a grenade into the launcher and dive for the opposite bank. I'm confused. Wouldn't the far bank expose them to more of the blast? If they are worried about being too close to the launcher when it fires, why not duck into the armory? It's right beside them.

• So that the opponents can record a log of their engagement, the Metrons provide Kirk and the Gorn captain with hand-held devices. It turns out that these devices also instantaneously translate English to Gorn and back. And they act like walkie-talkies. Even more impressive is the fact that the Metrons conveniently placed some sort of flintlike device on the top of the recorder so Kirk could get a spark to light his cannon. (The translator must be like a Swiss

Army knife. I wonder if the Metrons make a model with a couple of blades, a screwdriver, and a pair of those tiny scissors. I might buy one if they did. It might come in very handy.)

CONTINUITY AND PRODUCTION PROBLEMS

• During the Gorn attack on Cestus III, Kirk finds a photon grenade launcher. He comes out of the armory and sets down a metal box. Then the shot changes and Kirk has the box in his hand again.

• When it appears that Kirk will lose, the Metrons let the crew of the *Enterprise* watch. Shortly afterward, a wide shot of the mountainous region shows a tiny Kirk hobbling forward. If you watch closely, you'll see that Kirk actually pops into the scene moments after it begins.

TRIVIA ANSWERS

1. Diamonds, potassium nitrate, sulfur, and coal.
2. Five hundred parsecs.

CLOSING STILLS

• *Enterprise* leaving Earthlike planet, "Miri"
• Kirk as lawgiver, "The Return of the Archons"
• Metron, "Arena"
• Kirk in decompression chamber, "Space Seed"
• Gorn, "Arena"
• SS *Botany Bay*, sleeper ship, "Space Seed"
• Vina as the green Orion leaf lady, "The Cage"

PERSONAL FAVORITES

Don't ask me why these are my favorites of all the nits in Classic Trek and the first six movies, because I'm not sure. As I said in *The Nitpicker's Guide for Next Generation Trekkers,* many of my favorites don't show up until the third or fourth viewing of a particular episode. In a way, they are like gold. I watch and think and dissect and ruminate, and in the process of all that expenditure of mental energy I suddenly catch a glint of something I haven't seen before. I flash the remote at the VCR, back up the tape, and watch the scene again. A smile spreads across my face, and I can't believe I didn't see the nit before. Then there are the ones I don't find. A fellow nitpicker writes, "Did you notice when. . ." I scamper for my tapes, fast-forward to the right spot and there it is, another entry for *The Nitpicker's Guide.* (I know, I need a life!) As before, I've listed the nits by episode. Each episode review contains the nit, as well.

1. "Charlie X." At one point, Charlie Evans accompanies Kirk to the bridge. Kirk steps on the turbolift wearing a gold shirt and steps off wearing a green V-neck.

2. "The Enemy Within." The opening scene on the planet is spliced in backward. The hair on both Kirk and Sulu parts on the wrong side. Interestingly enough, the insignias are missing from their shirts. Evidently the creators planned to reverse this scene because Kirk's insignia suddenly reappears after he returns to the *Enterprise.*

3. "The Return of the Archons." As Kirk and the landing party run from a mob scene just after beaming down, a rock the size of a cantaloupe arches down and whacks a crew member on the top of his head. It bounces off, and the guy keeps running.

4. "The Devil in the Dark." While searching through tunnels for a silicon-based creature, Kirk and Spock come to a fork in the path. Kirk points to the *right* and says to Spock, "You go left." Then he gestures back to the *left* and says, "I'll go right."

5. "The City on the Edge of Forever." At one point, Kirk and Edith Keeler meet on the stairs leading to her apartment. She stumbles, and Kirk immediately catches her. The wide shot shows that she still wears both shoes. Then close-ups show her thanking Kirk for saving her life. The scene cuts back to a wide shot, and Keeler continues up the stairs, wearing only one shoe.

6. "A Private Little War." This episode features an angry, snarling beast known as a mugato. It has dinosaur ridges down its back and lethal, venom-filled fangs. However, when the creators needed a close-up of mugato prints they simply went back and grabbed the footage of the foot prints made by the large white rabbit in "Shore Leave." So—according to the scene in "A Private Little War"—this ferocious beast called a mugato leaves bunny prints!

7. "The Savage Curtain." In this episode, Kirk splits his pants. At one point, the captain ends up on his back and uses his legs to shove away an attacker. As Kirk draws his knees to his chest, a white line appears on his posterior.

8. *Star Trek: The Motion Picture.* At the end of the movie, Spock and McCoy chat with Kirk on the bridge. Spock wears a coat with an orange armband. McCoy wears one with a green armband. Then the shot changes, and instantly Spock wears the coat with the green armband and McCoy wears the one with the orange armband.

9. *Star Trek II: The Wrath of Khan.* At the beginning of the movie, Saavik participates in the *Kobayashi Maru.* The shots of her in the captain's chair contain the starboard turbolift doors in the background. A piece of paper hangs on the door, looking very much like a stencil that was used to create the door's decorative markings. Moments later, a similar shot shows that the paper has disappeared and only the markings remain.

10. *Star Trek III: The Search for Spock.* After the *Enterprise* enters space dock, sensors detect a break-in at Spock's quarters. When Kirk leaves the bridge to investigate, a close-up shows a layout of the *Enterprise* and a square to indicate the location of the intruder. The graphics come from the blueprints of the original *Enterprise,* and on those plans the section is labeled "Brig."

11. *Star Trek V: The Final Frontier.* Those clever creators pulled a fast one in the scene at the beginning of the movie where Spock catches Kirk just before he hits the ground. Instead of attaching a suspension wire to Shatner's foot and hanging him upside down, they attached the wire to his side and suspended him horizontally. Then they built a set with trees running horizontally to make it look like he is hung upside down, and tipped the camera on its side. However, as the camera rotates and pulls back to show the full view of Kirk, you can see the wire sticking out of his side.

12. *Star Trek VI: The Undiscovered Country.* Uhura's name is spelled "Uhuru" in the closing credits.

TOMORROW IS YESTERDAY

Star Dates: 3113.2-3114.1

After breaking away from the gravitational pull of a black hole, the *Enterprise* hurtles backward through time—eventually arriving at Earth in the late 1960s. As the ship drifts over Nebraska, the Air Force sends up an intercept plane. Learning from Spock that the airplane may carry missiles tipped with nuclear warheads, Kirk locks a tractor beam on the craft. Unfortunately, it can't take the strain and begins breaking up. With no other choice, Kirk beams the pilot aboard. Captain John Christopher soon learns enough about the future from touring the *Enterprise* that he could change it. At first Kirk solves this by deciding not to allow the man to return to Earth. Later investigation proves that Christopher must return. His son, as yet unborn, will make a significant contribution to the Earth's expansion into space.

After retrieving all the physical evidence recorded by Christopher's plane, Kirk sets course for the sun. Spock has calculated that accelerating toward and then breaking away from the sun will first throw the *Enterprise* back in time and then far forward. At the exact moment Christopher first saw the *Enterprise,* the crew transports him into the pilot's seat of his plane and then continues on to their own century.

Trivia Questions

1. En route to what starbase did the *Enterprise* encounter the black hole?

2. Where did the computer receive its feminine disposition?

SYNDICATION CUTS

• Assessing the damage caused by the slingshot effect, Kirk asks about auxiliaries, Spock wonders about Scott, and Kirk helps Uhura up from the floor.

• Kirk and Christopher exiting the transporter room, and Christopher ogling a female crew member before walking onto the turbolift.

• In sick bay a large section of dialogue is deleted while Kirk and McCoy wait for Christopher to return to consciousness. The missing dialogue puts an entirely different spin on a question Kirk asks as the uncut and syndicated versions sync back together. The question has Kirk asking McCoy if Christopher could be retrained to forget his family. In the syndicated version, Kirk precedes this question by saying that he cannot send

Christopher back with what the pilot knows. This makes the question sound like Kirk is asking McCoy if the doctor could make it easier on Christopher by *helping* him forget his family. The uncut version presents the question in a completely different light. After Kirk says he can't send Christopher back, McCoy asks about the crew. The doctor points out that they are trapped as well. If they try to beam down to Earth, it is inevitable that one of the 430 individuals would change the future. Kirk changes the subject and says that even if the *Enterprise* does make it back to the future, Christopher won't fit in. McCoy counters that the pilot could be retrained. Then Kirk makes a point by asking the question, "Could he be trained to forget his family?" In other words, in the uncut version, Kirk presents the question as an impossibility, while in the syndicated version he presents it as an option.

• Kirk asking Christopher if he is all right as the pilot awakens in sick bay.

• Kirk and Sulu walking over to the computer in the records area of the base and making comments about seeing them in museums. Then the episode transitions to an establishing shot of the *Enterprise* in orbit before cutting to a worried McCoy in the transporter room.

• Following a commercial break, the captain's log by Spock, star date 3113.9, recapping events.

• Spock commending Sulu for returning to the ship, and talking with Scott about starting up the engines before commenting on the poor photography of the Air Force.

• The first part of Kirk's interrogation by the Air Force.

• The *Enterprise* moving away from Earth, and several reaction shots before Christopher comments about making it into space. The edit removes a serious production problem. Something is very wrong with the ship as it leaves orbit. The starboard engine nacelle has an entire section eaten out of it!

PLOT OVERSIGHTS

• When first checking on relevant contributions by Christopher, Spock forgets to check his descendants. This is useful for the plot but completely inconsistent with the normally outstanding precision of Spock's work. Later in this show, he calculates more than a hundred variables on the time warp equation while standing in the transporter room. Oddly enough, no one says, "Are you sure you didn't forget a variable like you forgot to check on Christopher's descendants?"

• Great confusion surrounds star dates. Are they really a date of some kind? The *Enterprise* is orbiting Earth in the 1960s and the top two officers of the *Enterprise* make log entries with star dates in the range 3113.2-3114.1. How can this be correct? They have no guarantee that they can even return to the future, and even if they do, they have no guarantee that their arrival time will be anywhere close to their departure time.

• Kirk refers to the process of flying toward a high-gravity object, jamming the engines into reverse, and snapping free as a "rubber-band effect." They must have a different definition of "rubber band" in the future. The creators illustrate the effect at the end of the episode. The *Enterprise* accelerates toward the sun, stops dead, slowly turns, and starts accelerating again.

• Temporal logic—the application of logic to the weirdness of time travel and its associated anachronisms—is a mind-bending exercise fraught with loopholes, but let's explore one small problem with the return of Christopher. After traveling backward in time, the *Enterprise* shoots forward, depositing Christopher into his plane at the moment he originally sighted the *Enterprise*. Note that the *Enterprise* immediately disappears from the skies over Nebraska. The *Enterprise* that disappears is the one that dropped into Earth's atmosphere at the beginning of this episode. I draw the following conclusion from that fact. The creators' model of time travel states that only one physical manifestation of an entity can exist in any time frame. (Actually, this model neatly handles one of the standard time travel problems. Suppose you work all your life to figure out how to make a time travel machine. When you do, you decide that it was a waste of time to spend all those years working on it. So you travel back in time to tell your younger self how it works. This, of course, changes the future, because you won't need to spend your life working on it and, therefore, when you get old you'll have no reason to travel back to tell yourself how to make it work. Because you don't travel back to tell your younger self how it works, you spend your life trying to figure out how to build a time travel machine. It gets very convoluted.) Since only one manifestation can exist of the *Enterprise* in any given time frame, as soon as the *Enterprise* reaches the time frame when it originally appeared, the prior *Enterprise* blinks out of existence.

There is a problem with this scenario. If only one entity can exist in a given time frame, Christopher should have disappeared from Earth as the *Enterprise* moved backward in time past his original sighting of the *Enterprise*. At that moment, he existed at two different physical locations in the same time frame. Therefore, he could not have flown the airplane up to meet the *Enterprise* in the first place. (I could go on with this, but it would give everyone, including me, a headache.)

CHANGED PREMISES

• Spock states that it is logical for the *Enterprise* to move backward in time as it accelerates toward the sun. Why didn't this occur during *Star Trek IV: The Voyage Home?*

• In "Patterns of Force," Kirk orders a full Gestapo uniform for McCoy from the ship's clothier, yet in this show, Kirk and Sulu sneak around the base in their Starfleet uniforms. Couldn't the clothier make Kirk an outfit from the 1960s? (Of course, I guess it wouldn't do Kirk much good to show up in ratty jeans and a tie-dyed shirt.)

EQUIPMENT ODDITIES

• This transporter is a wonderful device. It can grab a seated pilot from the cockpit of his plane and rematerialize him in a standing position.

• When the air police sergeant disarms Kirk and Sulu, the shot clearly shows that both communicators have flipped open. Moments later, the sergeant himself opens one again. The communicators never chirp. Has the crew finally figured out how to rig these things for silent running? It makes sense that they shouldn't chirp during a

covert mission, but the creators never give us any dialogue to support that feature.

TRIVIA ANSWERS

1. Starbase 9.
2. Signet XIV.

CLOSING STILLS

• *Enterprise* firing phasers, "The Corbomite Maneuver"

• Air police sergeant, "Tomorrow Is Yesterday"

• Talosian beast illusion, "The Cage"

• Balok puppet, "The Corbomite Maneuver"

• Laser cannon, "The Cage"

• Spock, dusted by the plants of Omicron Ceti III, "The Side of Paradise"

• Vina, thinking about filing a sexual harassment lawsuit against the Talosians, "The Cage"

COURT-MARTIAL

Star Dates: 2947.3-2950.1

When the computer's visual log contradicts Kirk's version of the events during an ion storm, Commodore Stone of Starbase 11 launches an investigation. During the storm, Kirk dispatched Lieutenant Commander Benjamin Finney into a pod to take measurements. As per regulations, Kirk states that he initiated red alert before jettisoning the pod to give Finney a chance to get to safety. However, the computer records show Kirk jettisoning the pod *before* initiating red alert. If that's true, Kirk killed Finney. Privately, Stone advises Kirk to accept a ground assignment and Starfleet will dispense with the matter. Kirk refuses, forcing Stone to convene a general court-martial.

At the trial, all the evidence works against Kirk. When all seems lost, Spock discovers that he can beat the computer at chess. Since he programmed the game in the first place, that shouldn't be possible. Obviously someone has tampered with the computer and its records.

The trial reconvenes on the *Enterprise*, and—using the ship's sensors—Kirk discovers that Finney is still alive. Evidently Finney hoped to destroy Kirk as payback for an incident that put Finney at the bottom of the promotion list years ago. Accordingly, Stone drops all charges.

Trivia Questions

1. What are the names of the members of the court-martial board?

2. According to this episode, what are some of the awards of valor that Kirk has received?

GREAT MOMENTS

As the time approaches for the court to offer a verdict in Kirk's trial, McCoy discovers Spock playing chess in a briefing room. The doctor accuses the Vulcan of being the most cold-blooded person he's ever met. At this, Spock politely replies, "Why, thank you, Doctor." Then he lets McCoy turn back toward the door before quietly announcing that he has beaten the computer four times already. It's a great scene with a lovely twist at the end.

SYNDICATION CUTS

• The initial chitchat between Kirk and Lieutenant Areel Shaw, the prosecuting attorney.

• Spock's statements during the court-martial are shortened. During

80

the deleted section, Spock refers to himself as part "Vulcanian."

• Captain's log, star date 2949.9.

• Just after Spock informs McCoy that the computer has been tampered with, their exits from the briefing room, as well as the reconvening of the court-martial.

• Two sections of Samuel T. Cogley's speech about human rights.

• After Cogley announces—in the briefing room—that Finney is still alive, the uncut version has a Batman-style transition, with the whole screen appearing to rotate as the scene changes to show the court's new location on the bridge.

• Reaction shots on the discovery of Finney's heartbeat.

• In the uncut version, when Kirk leaves the bridge, the camera zooms in on Stone. His face fades into a shot of Kirk walking down the hallway on B deck, outside Engineering. The syndicated version has a commercial slot in this transition. To cover the fade, an establishing shot of the *Enterprise* was added.

• Reaction shot of bridge and Kirk walking into Engineering.

• Kirk walking around Engineering.

• The entire sequence of the *Enterprise* reestablishing a stable orbit after Kirk restores power disappears from the syndicated version. This actually covers up a rather bad production error. As the sequence starts, Spock assigns Uhura to the navigator's position. She remains there until the

Enterprise is out of danger. Yet all her close-ups show her seated at the communications station!

PLOT OVERSIGHTS

• At the court-martial, the personnel officer of the *Enterprise* testifies that *Ensign* Kirk discovered Finney's mistake. On the other hand, Gary Mitchell—in "Where No Man Has Gone Before"—refers to the fact that *Lieutenant* Kirk taught at the Academy. Did Kirk actually go out into space and then return to teach at the Academy for a while?

• When the court-martial moves to the *Enterprise,* Kirk, Spock, and McCoy change out of their dress uniforms into their regular ones. Shouldn't Kirk at least remain in his dress uniform out of respect for the court? Spock's court-martial was held aboard ship, and he wore a dress uniform the entire time.

• Just before performing the experiment to determine if Finney still lives, Kirk speaks of the capability of the auditory sensor and mentions that they can install a booster to increase its effectiveness "on the order of one to the fourth power." One to the fourth power is . . . one!

• When Kirk finds Finney, the deranged lieutenant commander tells Kirk that he has shut down the engines and the *Enterprise* will burn up as its orbit decays. A few moments later, Kirk attacks Finney, and the two wrestle around in Engineering for some time. I realize Kirk told everyone to stay on the bridge, but that was before he knew of the danger to the ship. Wouldn't it make more sense for Spock to head to Engineering and assist the captain in restoring the engine? Or, at the very least, to beam Scott back on board?

CHANGED PREMISES

• Starbase 11 seems to have changed. The establishing shots of it in this episode and "The Menagerie, Part I" are different. Also, this episode has Commodore Stone at the starbase, while "The Menagerie, Part I" has Commodore Mendez. (I realize that both of these points can be explained, but the creators make no effort in dialogue to do so and could have saved themselves the trouble simply by calling one of the locations "Starbase 10.")

• Why didn't Spock have a prosecuting attorney at his court-martial during "The Menagerie, Part I" and "The Menagerie, Part II"? The Star Trek: The Next Generation episode "The Measure of a Man" establishes that Starfleet has regulations for all types of legal situations.

• The dialogue in the episode "Wolf in the Fold" seems to indicate that the computer's ability to tell when a person is lying is admissible in court as evidence, yet this episode never addresses the issue.·

• The playback of the computer's visual log looks pretty good in this episode. It even offers the ability to zoom in tight on Kirk's right hand and present the picture from a reverse angle. However, when Spock begins replaying the logs of the Enterprise's mission to Talos IV during "The Menagerie, Part I"— logs that look similar to the ones in this episode—Kirk says that no vessel makes record tapes that perfect and detailed.

• During the experiment to find Finney, McCoy masks each person's heartbeat with white noise. Aside from the fact that the instrument he uses looks suspiciously like a microphone, the doctor holds the object over the center of Spock's chest. According to "Mudd's Women," Spock's heart is on the left side of his chest.

EQUIPMENT ODDITIES

• This entire episode hinges on the fact that Kirk might have pushed the jettison pod button on the right arm of his chair before he pushed the red alert button. Kirk has only five buttons on the right arm of his chair. Are we supposed to believe—given all the complicated operations that a captain must perform as part of his duties—that jettisoning a pod is so high up on the list that the designers of the Enterprise actually dedicated a button on the captain's chair to this function? And when have we ever seen Kirk use the buttons on his chair to signal a red or a yellow alert? Doesn't he always simply give the order? Oddly enough, the button that the captain uses over and over on the right arm of his chair doesn't have a label—namely, the communications button.

• The court reporting computer seems to have a little trouble with names. It announces Spock and Kirk but forgets to announce the personnel officer and McCoy.

• I'm intrigued by the large wrench Finney swings at Kirk during the final fight scene. Does the *Enterprise* really have nuts that big?

CONTINUITY AND PRODUCTION PROBLEMS

• As Kirk and Finney duke it out, the creators—once again—artfully rip Kirk's shirt to show his manly chest. Unfortunately, they forgot to rip the stunt double's shirt in the same manner.

TRIVIA ANSWERS

1. Commodore Stone, Space Command Representative Lind-strom, and Captains Krasnowsky and Chandra.
2. Medal of Honor, Silver Palm with Cluster, Starfleet Citation for Conspicuous Gallantry, Kragite Order of Heroism.

CLOSING STILLS

• *Enterprise* orbiting Psi 2000, "The Naked Time"

• Starbase 11, "Court-Martial"

• Flying Kirk on bridge, "The Naked Time"

• Scientific research station, Psi 2000, "The Naked Time"

• Engineering, "The Enemy Within" (This is the establishing shot just before the good Kirk and Spock walk into the scene.)

• Vina as the nimble Orion nymph, "The Cage"

THE RETURN OF THE ARCHONS

Star Dates: 3156.2-3158.7

The *Enterprise* arrives at Beta III to investigate the disappearance of the *Archon,* a ship lost one hundred years ago. Kirk, Spock, McCoy, and three security guards beam down to find a simple city where all the inhabitants seem heavily tranquilized. Then, at six o'clock in the evening, almost everyone goes crazy—burning, looting, and assaulting each other. The crew members escape into a house and ask for a place to stay the night. Kirk questions the citizens' behavior, but their host replies that it is the will of Landru, their leader.

Eventually Kirk and Spock come face to face with Landru, a highly sophisticated computer that controls the lives of millions on Beta III. Millennia ago, in the midst of raging war, the real Landru showed the people a better way—the way of peace and tranquillity. Before dying, he programmed a computer with his knowledge and gave it the power to control the lives of his subjects. A century ago, the survivors of the crash of the *Archon* either submitted or were killed. To spare the *Enterprise* the same fate, Kirk argues that the highest good requires that individuals must have freedom to express their creativity. He convinces the computer that it is restricting creativity and therefore is harmful to the body. In response, Landru short-circuits.

Trivia Questions

1. Who stays behind to help the inhabitants of Beta III cope with their freedom?

2. Where is Beta III located?

RUMINATIONS

In this episode, Spock wonders if their interference is a violation of the Prime Directive. Kirk indicates that the Prime Directive applies only to developing worlds. This one is stagnant. If that's true, why was Picard hesitant to help the Ornarans in the Star Trek: The Next Generation *episode, "Symbiosis"? In that show, an entire planet was addicted to a drug called felicium. Crusher wanted to help them, but Picard refused. Is an entire culture dedicated to working solely to support their collective habit not stagnant enough?*

SYNDICATION CUTS

• O'Neil convincing Sulu that the lawgivers are everywhere, just

84

before Sulu calls for beam-up.
- Sulu repeating "paradise" on returning to the ship.
- Kirk waking up the others after sleeping through festival.
- Reger objecting to bringing O'Neil along after they find him in the street.
- Reger arguing for a second time to keep O'Neil sedated.
- After a commercial break, captain's log, star date 3157.4. Also, Kirk waking up in the dungeon.
- When the lawgivers take Kirk away, Spock asking McCoy what will happen to him.
- Reger and Marplon's entrance into the dungeon.
- Marplon, Kirk, and Spock walking down the long corridor to the Hall of Audience.
- Reaction shots when Landru appears in the Hall of Audience.
- Just after blowing a hole in the wall, comments by Kirk and Spock that it had to be a machine—reiterated moments later.

PLOT OVERSIGHTS

- During his recitations about the benefits of his society, Landru claims that it is without conflict or disease. Two point of interest here. During festival, men carry women like sacks of produce, rocks smash through windows, and shops are plundered. Doesn't this qualify as conflict? Also, after festival, McCoy takes Reger's daughter into another room, and Kirk tells him not to worry because McCoy will give her a shot. If there's no disease, why does Reger act like he knows the

definition of "shot"?
- For some reason, Spock clubs a lawgiver with his fist instead of neck-pinching the guy. Even Kirk comments on this unusual behavior. Did Spock think the neck pinch wouldn't work because of Landru's mind control?

CHANGED PREMISES

- Supposedly the Prime Directive is still a consideration at the beginning of the show, yet Kirk and the landing party beam down to a main thoroughfare with people walking around. In "Bread and Circuses," the landing party beamed down out in the country so their technology wouldn't be seen.

EQUIPMENT ODDITIES

- At the beginning of the episode, Sulu joins the body when a lawgiver zaps him with a rod. Then Kirk beams down and the lawgivers have to take him and the others to an absorption chamber to accomplish the same thing. Why don't the lawgivers just zap them?
- After escorting the crew members to a place of safety, Reger unwraps a light panel, a device created before the time of Landru. At first the light panel seems to radiate light in all directions, but when Reger sets it on a mantel, it casts a shadow on the wall. If both the front and the back of the panel produced light, there would be no shadow.
- When Landru trains heat beams on the Enterprise, Scott makes an intriguing statement. He tells Kirk

that the shields are consuming all the power of the *Enterprise*. Scott says they can't use the warp drive or even the impulse engines. So, Scott knows how to use the warp drive to supplement the shields? That's very interesting, because when Barclay did the same thing in the *Star Trek: The Next Generation* episode "The Nth Degree," La Forge seemed to think that was a really big deal.

• The door to the absorption chamber bears a striking resemblance to the doors in the underground civilization on Exo III (see "What Are Little Girls Made Of?").

• After blowing a hole in the wall of the Hall of Audience, Kirk and Spock train their phasers on Landru. The computer then neutralizes the phasers. If Landru could neutralize the phasers, why didn't it do so before Kirk and Spock ripped an opening in the wall?

CONTINUITY AND PRODUCTION PROBLEMS

• Just after festival begins, Kirk and the others scamper for cover. In one shot, a rock about the size of a cantaloupe arches down and whacks a crew member on the top of his head. Surprisingly, the man seems unaffected, and the rock simply bounces off. Now, that's the kind of guy you want to take on landing party missions!

• Kirk and the others find shelter from festival in the home of Reger. He takes them upstairs to a bunk room with an interesting set of windows. In every wide shot, the windows are completely black. Yet in the close-ups with Kirk they are suddenly transparent, offering a clear view of the street and the happenings below.

• As Kirk and the landing party follow Reger to a hiding place, Landru summons the body to attack them. Kirk orders phasers on stun, wide field. Then he shouts, "Fire!" Everyone acts like they are firing, but nothing comes out of McCoy's phaser.

• Landru seems to use the same technology as McCoy's medical wand. At least they use the same sound effect.

• When Landru first appears in the dungeon, watch the guards in the back by the door. One of them puts his hands up to his ears while the rest of the landing party acts very comfortable with the level of sound. Then Landru turns on his hypersonic pulse, and everybody puts their hands to their ears. (I'm wondering if the actor mistook his cue and put his hands to his ears too early.)

• Shortly after McCoy returns to the dungeon, a close-up shows Kirk, and his hair is parted on the wrong side!

• After Kirk exposes Landru's true nature, a reverse shot from the computer's perspective shows the captain and Spock standing in the Hall of Audience. In the background you can see through the big doors to a blue wall. There was no blue wall outside the Hall of Audience when Kirk and Spock approached. The view through the doors should show a long hall.

• When Landru short-circuits, a line of gunpowder burns just below the lower yellow panel on the left, leaving a large black discoloration. As soon as Kirk and Spock enter the computer room, the black smudge disappears.

TRIVIA ANSWERS

1. Sociologist Lindstrom.
2. In the star system C-111.

CLOSING STILLS

• *Enterprise* in energy barrier, "Where No Man Has Gone Before"
• Kirk on trial, "The Squire of Gothos"
• Lawgivers leaving Hall of Audience, "The Return of the Archons" (This scene is never shown in the episode.)
• Lake scene, "Shore Leave"
• Engineering, "The Enemy Within" (This is the establishing shot just before the good Kirk and Spock walk into the scene.)
• Sulu with foil, "The Naked Time"
• Vina as the promiscuous Orion plaything, "The Cage"

SPACE SEED

Star Dates: 3141.9-3143.3

F inding the SS *Botany Bay* drifting in space, Kirk and a landing party beam over to the ancient craft. According to their calculations, the ship is at least two hundred years old. Once aboard, they discover more than seventy humans in suspended animation. The presence of the landing party triggers an alarm, and a man begins awakening. In sick bay, McCoy stabilizes him. Later Kirk tries to question the man, but he will say only that his name is Khan. A library search by Spock reveals Khan's identity. He is Khan Noonien Singh, one of a select breed of genetically enhanced humans who tried to conquer the world in the 1990s. According to Spock's count, eighty or ninety of these supermen were never accounted for. Obviously they fled Earth in the *Botany Bay*.

With his powerful charisma, Khan seduces the ship's historian, Lieutenant Marla McGivers. She helps Khan awaken his companions, and they take over the *Enterprise*. When Khan tries to kill

Trivia Questions

1. Where is Starbase 12?

2. Where and when did Khan rule?

Kirk, McGivers switches sides and helps the captain recapture the ship. Knowing that Khan and his group would never be happy without a world to conquer, Kirk maroons them on Ceti Alpha V. He knows that life there will be difficult, but he also understands that Khan would rather "reign in hell than serve in heaven."

RUMINATIONS

S cience fiction always runs a risk whenever it sets specific dates for events in the future. I'm sure the decade of the 1990s sounded very distant in 1967, when this episode originally aired. I wonder if Gene Roddenberry—in his wildest dreams —ever imagined that we would still watch his creation so many years later.

Khan Noonien Singh has a familiar ring to it, doesn't it? Evidently the creators liked the rhythm of the name so much that they took off "Khan," changed "Singh" to "Soong," and used it for the name of Data's creator, Dr. Noonien Soong.

GREAT LINES

"It would be most effective if you would cut the carotid artery just

under the left ear."—McCoy to Khan, refusing to answer the superman's questions even with a knife at his throat.

GREAT MOMENTS

*R*icardo Montalban gives a powerful performance as Khan. His seduction of McGivers in his quarters is gripping (no pun intended).

SYNDICATION CUTS

• After an establishing shot of the *Enterprise* during the opener, an interchange among Kirk, Spock, and Uhura over the vessel's approach.

• Kirk ordering full security alert and everyone scurrying around on the bridge.

• An establishing sequence of McGivers in her quarters before beaming over to the *Botany Bay*.

• McCoy's second report on Khan's vital signs as he awakes in the sleeper compartment.

• After a commercial break, the words "captain's log, supplemental."

• An establishing shot of McCoy dismissing a nurse before Kirk arrives to check on Khan.

• Kirk leaving sick bay and returning to the bridge, claiming that he is letting Khan look through the technical manuals as a courtesy. This is a very weak explanation of Kirk's reckless behavior concerning Khan and the technical manuals.

• Just after McCoy tells Kirk that Khan could overpower McGivers because of her preoccupation with the past, the syndicated version

jumps to Khan in McGivers' quarters, looking at her paintings. The uncut version has Khan entering and complimenting McGivers on her hair. The problem with the syndicated version is that the establishing shot of McGivers' quarters earlier in the show is also deleted. So the viewer who has never seen the uncut version is suddenly thrust into a scene with Khan standing in the middle of several pictures and no idea how he got there or even where he is!

• A pair of reaction shots before Khan, during the dinner, compliments Kirk on being an excellent tactician.

• Moments later, Khan actually says, "excellent" twice, accompanied by another pair of reaction shots.

• After Khan tells McGivers to go or stay but do it because it is what she wants to do, McGivers hesitantly says she'll stay. Then Khan sarcastically asks her how many minutes she "graciously" offers. He says that her presence grows tiresome and now she must ask to stay. This sequence illustrates Khan expertly manipulating McGivers' emotions and provides more motivation for her betrayal of Kirk and the crew.

• Khan's realization that they used the computer to identity him after Kirk speaks his full name.

• An establishing shot of the *Enterprise* and the *Botany Bay* and then the helmsman reporting that they are maintaining warp two, following the scene with Khan and his newly awakened traveling companions.

• Spock double-checking Kirk's assertion that life support has been cut off.

• Khan's statement to the captors that he sees that he made one serious error. (He allowed them to suffocate together on the bridge, thereby creating a sense of camaraderie.)

PLOT OVERSIGHTS

• Supposedly Khan is the product of genetic engineering. Yet he looks about 35. At the very latest, he disappeared from Earth in the year 1999. That means he was born sometime before 1965. Were scientists really able to engineer a human genetically in 1965? Or did the creators imagine that Khan was the result of some type of high-speed cloning and aging?

• Just after Khan wakes up, Kirk gives him access to all the technical manuals of the entire ship. Does this seem like a reasonable thing to do? His ship is named the *Botany Bay*. Kirk knows that *Botany Bay* was the site of a penal institution. Wouldn't it be more reasonable to wait until you have just a tad more information on this guy before giving him this kind of information?

• This episode purports that in 1993, a group of genetically engineered humans took over forty nations. I must have been watching *Star Trek* that day because I completely missed it.

• I don't know. I realize that Kirk claims the men of the 1990s were more adventurous than those of the twenty-third century, but I just can't imagine anyone I know using the pickup line that Khan shoots at McGivers. The first time she visits him in sick bay, he thanks her for helping to revive him and then says, "Please sit and entertain me."

• This crew is really into celery. It must be a delicacy. In "The Man Trap," Rand brings a tray of food to Sulu. It has colored cubes and several stalks of celery. In this episode, McCoy walks into the preparations for the dinner for Khan, raises his eyebrows, and comments on the spread. Each person has a bowl of colored cubes, and, smack dab in the middle of the table there is . . . a tray of celery! (Is Dr. Who paying a visit?)

• When Khan takes over the ship he shuts down all life support to the bridge. While suffocating, Kirk makes a log entry and recommends commendations for five of the crew members on the bridge. The scene clearly shows seven crew members on the bridge, not counting Kirk. Why didn't the last two get commendations?

CHANGED PREMISES

• The dialogue indicates that the wars begun by this group of genetically engineered humans at the end of the twentieth century were worldwide. However, the *Star Trek: The Next Generation* episode "Encounter at Farpoint" indicates that World War III occurred in the mid-twenty-first century. If the eugenic wars were worldwide and occured in the twentieth century, shouldn't the war in the twenty-first century be called World War IV?

EQUIPMENT ODDITIES

• After watching "Shore Leave," I thought the Velcro belts that hold phasers a far better invention than the holsters used in the supposedly more advanced *Star Trek: The Next Generation* series. (You may recall that *NextGen* phasers have a nasty habit of popping out of their holsters whenever the crew runs too fast.) In "Shore Leave," Kirk goes through an entire knock-down, drag-out fight, and the phaser stays securely fastened. Alas, my confidence in these belts suffered a fatal blow with this episode. When Kirk breaks the glass on Khan's sleeper compartment, his arm brushes against the phaser and it unceremoniously plops to the floor.

• Attempting to convince the crew to follow him, Khan places Kirk in a decompression chamber and evacuates the air. A gauge near the door of the chamber clearly shows the current pressure. A close-up puts the level at 10 HG and dropping. Yet moments later, a brief glimpse of the gauge before the camera pans to Kirk shows the level at 20 HG.

CONTINUITY AND PRODUCTION PROBLEMS

• Kirk, McCoy, Scott, and

McGivers are beaming over to the *Botany Bay*. In the transporter room, Scott's assistant is at the controls and wears a blue jumpsuit. When the transport starts, the close-up shows a red uniform with two strips of braid and hands that look suspiciously like those belonging to Scott.

• The creators chose to place blinking lights all over the *Botany Bay*. Watch them very closely when the landing party rematerializes. Every light stutters just a bit. The creators came very close to executing this very difficult scene flawlessly.

• The head with helmet sculpture shown in McGivers' quarters is a popular knickknack. Dr. Adams had one just like it in "Dagger of the Mind."

TRIVIA ANSWERS

1. On a planet in the Gamma 400 star system.

2. Khan ruled Asia and the Middle East from 1992 to 1996.

CLOSING STILLS

• *Enterprise* leaving Earthlike planet, "Miri"

• Sleeper ship, "Space Seed"

• Pergium production station, Janus VI, "The Devil in the Dark"

• Kirk and Spock fighting, "This Side of Paradise"

• Kirk and the silicon creature, "The Devil in the Dark"

• Kirk sprayed by plant, "This Side of Paradise"

• Vina as a titillating Orion tease, "The Cage"

A TASTE OF ARMAGEDDON

Star Dates: 3192.1-3193.0

The *Enterprise* arrives at planet Eminiar VII to open diplomatic relations. Although the Eminians warn the *Enterprise* not to approach, Kirk has orders to do so anyway. After beaming down with a landing party, Kirk and Spock are cordially escorted to the council chambers. Anan 7, leader of the High Council, expresses his concern over their arrival. After all, Eminiar VII has been at war for five hundred years. His statements confuse Kirk. The planet shows no signs of the usual destruction of war.

Suddenly an alarm sounds and large doors open to reveal a bank of computer systems. The Eminians speak of the fierce attack they have just sustained, of the half a million people who've just died. A tricorder sweep reveals nothing. Anan 7 then reveals that the war is fought with computers. The machines calculate who has died, and those individuals report to disintegration chambers. Unfortunately, the computers say that the *Enterprise* has been destroyed. Anan 7 expects the crew to beam down so that the Eminians can kill them. To ensure this, he holds the landing party as hostages. After escaping, Kirk and Spock return to the war room and destroy the computers. This action forces the Eminians to face the prospect of real war. Given its devastation, they opt to talk with their enemies about peace.

Trivia Questions

1. In what star cluster is Eminiar VII located?

2. Where does the Enterprise set course for at the end of the episode?

SYNDICATION CUTS

• Spock's identification of the ship that contacted Eminiar VII fifty years ago as the USS *Valiant*. This edit ruined a perfectly good trivia question!

• The introductions when Kirk meets Anan 7 for the first time.

• Spock's comments that there is a certain scientific logic to the Eminians' computerized warfare.

• Mea 3 leaving the room that imprisons the Starfleet officers.

• Part of the discussion between Scott and McCoy just before Uhura informs Scott that there is a message from the planet.

• Part of the discussion between Scott and McCoy just after the Eminians open fire on the *Enterprise*.

• Just after Kirk asks Mea 3 how to get to the war room, his assurances that he is trying to help her planet. This edit caused a continuity problem. Kirk's arms are at his side when he asks about the war room. In the syndicated version, Mea 3 then asks, "What are you going to do?" If you look closely in the area of Mea's right shoulder you'll see the top of Kirk's thumb. In other words, his hand jumped instantly from his side to her shoulder.

• Anan 7 pouring himself a drink in his quarters before Kirk arrives.

• Spock giving instructions to Yeoman Tamura and then leaving the room that previously imprisoned the Starfleet officers.

• Spock and security skulking down the hall toward the High Council chambers.

PLOT OVERSIGHTS

• As the *Enterprise* approaches Eminiar VII, the High Council of that planet sends a message for the ship to stay away. Specifically, Uhura says that they are sending "*Starfleet* code 7-10." Later Spock says the last contact with Eminiar VII occurred fifty years earlier, when the USS *Valiant* visited the planet. Starfleet codes must not have changed much in the past fifty years, since the *Valiant* is the only way the High Council could have learned about Starfleet code 7-10.

• Kirk and the landing party are not included in the casualties of the attack, yet a woman named "Mea 3" is declared dead. Mea was standing right next to Kirk when the

assault occurred. In the computer simulation, the enemy supposedly materialized fusion bombs over their targets and detonated them. Fusion bombs don't discriminate. If the attack that Kirk witnessed killed Mea, it killed the captain as well. Was there a prior attack that the dialogue neglects to mention?

EQUIPMENT ODDITIES

• Evidently Starbase 11 has upgraded its computer system, because the Eminians have purchased the ones featured in "The Menagerie, Part I." This includes the communication panel that the starbase originally purchased from the Tantalus penal colony (see "The Menagerie, Part I"). Actually, this makes sense. When Commodore Stone replaced Commodore Mendez at Starbase 11, he probably had some discretionary funds to upgrade the facilities. What is really interesting in this episode is that the Eminians also managed to buy the scrapped computer system from Beta III, the one that used to call itself Landru. Just before Kirk destroys all the computers, look in the background and you'll see a computer that looks just like the one seen at the end of "The Return of the Archons." True, it has a few panels that are different, but that's because it short-circuited and needed a few new parts.

• The depiction of the explosion that marks the *Enterprise* as destroyed has a wiggle in it. On the planetary map in the war room, it grows as a white oval and then bobs up and down as it fades from view.

• The doors on Eminiar VII look suspiciously like the ones on the entrance to the absorption chamber in "The Return of the Archons" and those in the underground civilization on Exo III (see "What Are Little Girls Made Of?").

• After realizing that Scott will not beam the crew down to the surface for annihilation, Anan orders an attack on the ship by planetary disrupters. The helmsman of the *Enterprise* refers to the beams as "extremely powerful sonic vibrations" and gives their power rating in decibels. If I recall correctly, "sonic" and "decibels" are terms used to refer to sound waves. But if that's true, how are these disrupters hitting the *Enterprise?* All the graphics show the ship well above the atmosphere, in the vacuum of space. Sound waves don't travel in a vacuum!

• When the first attack on the *Enterprise* fails, Anan talks with Federation ambassador Fox—still aboard the ship—and convinces him that it was a mistake. At the same time, Anan orders the planetary disrupters to wait for the *Enterprise*'s defensive screens to drop and then fire again. On the *Enterprise,* Fox orders Scott to lower the screens, but the chief engineer refuses. Even so, Fox accepts Anan's invitation to come to the surface for further discussion and promptly beams down. Doesn't the *Enterprise* need to lower its screens to operate the

transporter? When the Gorn attack the *Enterprise* near the beginning of "Arena," the dialogue between Sulu and Kirk seems to indicate this. If the screens dropped while Fox transported to the surface, why didn't the Eminians attack?

CONTINUITY AND PRODUCTION PROBLEMS

• The shot just before Spock destroys a disintegration chamber clearly shows the chamber's door open. When the scene changes to a side view of the chamber, its door is suddenly closed.

TRIVIA ANSWERS

1. NGC-321.
2. Argama II.

CLOSING STILLS

• *Enterprise* and *Botany Bay,* "Space Seed"

• Council chambers and war room, "A Taste of Armageddon"

• Exploding disintegration chamber, "A Taste of Armageddon"

• Knight on horseback, "Shore Leave"

• Scientific research station, Psi 2000, "The Naked Time"

• City, Eminiar VII, "A Taste of Armageddon"

• Vina, just after sending an appeal to the members of Intelligent Orion Women Anonymous pleading with them to start a letter-writing campaign urging the author of this book to refrain from any more derogatory aliases, "The Cage"

THIS SIDE OF PARADISE

Star Dates: 3417.3-3417.7

On Omicron Ceti III, Kirk and a landing party find a pleasant surprise. Unknown to the colonists who came here three years ago, their new home was bathed in Berthold radiation. Spock had predicted that all would be dead. Instead, they find a flourishing colony. Looking for answers, Spock questions Leila Kalomi, an old friend. Promising to show him the reason why the colonists have survived the lethal radiation, they approach a cluster of plants. Suddenly a plant sprays the Vulcan with a fine dust. Moments later, Spock smiles. The dust contained spores that thrive on Berthold radiation. When the spores inhabit a humanoid body, they bring perfect health and joy.

Soon McCoy begins beaming up the plants to the *Enterprise,* infecting the entire crew. En masse, they depart for the surface. Then Kirk succumbs to the spores. Just before beaming down, however, a surge of anger pulses through him at the thought of leaving his ship. The strong emotion kills the spores. Having made this discovery, Kirk beams Spock back to the ship and goads him into a fight. The spores quickly vacate the first officer as well. Using sound waves transmitted through the communicators, the pair cause fights to break out all over the colony. Freed from the spores, the crew members contritely return to their posts.

SYNDICATION CUTS

• Establishing pan of the colony before the landing party beams down.

• Sandoval and landing party walking to Sandoval's house.

• *Enterprise* officers walking up to the barn door before opening it.

• After McCoy's examination of the African-American man, he speaks longer with Kirk before Sandoval arrives.

• The front portion of the establishing shot showing Spock scanning for insects.

• Leila telling Spock she missed him, and the Vulcan countering that they should all be dead.

• Sections of the discussion between Kirk and Sandoval about

Trivia Questions

1. Where did Spock see a dragon?

2. Numbering the buttons—left to right—from 1 to 5, what is the combination of Kirk's safe?

leaving the colony.

• After Spock asserts that the colonists aren't leaving, Kirk ordering him to report back immediately.

• Kirk calling again for Spock and tapping his communicator several times after the Vulcan lets his fall to the ground.

• Kirk, Sulu, and a third officer approaching Spock, who is hanging from a tree limb.

• A section of dialogue with Kirk asking for McCoy's help precedes McCoy saying, "Who wants to counteract paradise, Jim boy?"

• After talking with Spock and Sandoval on the planet, Kirk returns to the bridge and walks around for a while before making the log entry. The syndicated version actually contains an additional establishing shot of the *Enterprise* in orbit to smooth the transition.

• Kirk packing his uniforms in his quarters.

• Kirk and Spock exiting the transporter room after the captain frees his first officer of the spores.

• A portion of the planet retreating on the viewscreen.

PLOT OVERSIGHTS

• Despite the spore infection, these colonists have accomplished amazing things. With very few mechanical devices, they have managed—in just three years—to construct some very nice buildings, including a home with asphalt shingles! I realize that they may have brought some supplies with them, but I would have expected the buildings to look much more modu-

lar. Of course, they may have wanted the "back to nature" look. In that case they should have used wood shakes on the roof.

• Even after McCoy certifies that the colonists are healthy, Kirk receives orders to evacuate them. Why? What's wrong with leaving these people on this planet? They are happy and healthy. If Kirk wants to go through life scratching and clawing and struggling and fighting and marching, fine. But why can't Starfleet leave these people alone?

• And speaking of Kirk, he really is a party pooper in this episode, isn't he?

• When taking Spock to see the spores, Leila comments, "It's not much further." Having been beaten about the head severely on the difference between, "further" and "farther," I believe I can say with some trembling confidence that she should say, "It's not much farther." "Further" means "to a greater extent or degree" whereas "farther" means "to a greater distance." (I know this is really picky, but hey, that's my business.)

• Supposedly the microbes die when exposed to intense emotion, yet when Spock is infected, he goes through some pretty intense emotions. Shouldn't the microbes die even as they are trying to infect him?

• McCoy loses his deep southern accent for a moment after telling Kirk, "Who wants to counteract paradise, Jim boy?" DeForest Kelley delivers his next line,

"McCoy out," in his usual accent.

• Just before Kirk gets sprayed, a side shot of the navigator's position clearly shows an empty floor. Then Kirk sits down at the helmsman's position, and one of the plants slowly raises up and sprays him. In the first place, how does this plant move? In the second place, where did it come from?

• Hot stock tip for the week: Buy Samsonite! It's still in business in the twenty-third century. When Kirk gets ready to leave the ship, he packs his belongings in a suitcase that's vintage 1960s. Maybe it's an heirloom.

• Someone really should keep the address of this planet. At the end of the episode, McCoy reports that all the colonists have retained their good health. That means that any time Starfleet has people with a really-bad disease, they can just fly them here, let the spores infect them, beam them back to the ship, get them mad, and return them to duty! Even if the patient has to stay on the surface for a few years, perfect health seems a big enough incentive. And think of the tourist trade . . .

• This episode qualifies Kirk for the award for "The Most Clichés Strung Together in One Speech by a Starship Captain." He uses no fewer than five in a row during his last soliloquy about the destiny of mankind. They are: "fight our way through," "claw our way up," "scratch for every inch of the way," "stroll to the music of the lute," and "march to the sound of the drums."

EQUIPMENT ODDITIES

• The communicators seem to be infected by the spores as well. Several times they fail to chirp.

• Someone has been repainting the doors on the *Enterprise*. In this episode, the doors down the hall from the transporter room are red. In "Tomorrow Is Yesterday," the doors are blue. (In case you're wondering, *this Enterprise* has only one transporter room. In "Tomorrow Is Yesterday," Kirk knows Captain Christopher will try to beam off the ship and tells Scott that he's heading for *the* transporter room.)

CONTINUITY AND PRODUCTION PROBLEMS

• The infamous romantic music described first in "Shore Leave" is back in force with this episode. The creators use it many times during the episode's touching moments. Unfortunately, this music ruins every one of them for me.

TRIVIA ANSWERS
1. Berengaria VII.
2. 5231.

CLOSING STILLS
• *Enterprise* firing phasers, "Balance of Terror" (Actually, they look like photon torpedoes.)

• Kirk and Spock fighting, "This Side of Paradise"

• Kirk sprayed by plant, "This Side of Paradise"

• Kirk and Spock escaping from jail, "Errand of Mercy" (This shot isn't shown in the actual episode.)

• Kirk and Spock eyeing tools, "The Guardian on the Edge of Forever"

• Balok puppet, "Where No Man Has Gone Before"

• Vina, "The Cage" (Pending a review of policy, the author hereby suspends all descriptions with respect to Vina and her various Talosian incarnations.)

ROMANCE TOTE BOARD

1. Number of past loves for Kirk: eight
2. Number of women who swoon over Spock: five
3. Number of marriages for McCoy: one
4. Number of episodes or movies in which Scott worries over the *Enterprise*'s engines: twenty-three
5. Number of times Sulu gapes at an alien female: two
6. Number of love interests for Uhura: one
7. Number of women who find Chekov attractive: three
8. Number of euphemisms Kirk uses for "pressing of the lips": two
9. Number of times the life-force of a male Starfleet officer has resided in a feminine body: two (as far as we know)
10. Number of times Spock mesmerizes females so they will do his bidding: one (as far as we know)
11. Number of times a woman gives Spock the shove-off: one
12. Number of times that the creators strongly hint that "something" happened when we weren't looking: two
13. Number of times members of the crew have been engaged and simultaneously in love with someone else: two
14. Number of times Kirk refuses the attentions of a female: one

REFERENCES

1. The blond lab technician Mitchell refers to in "Where No Man Has Gone Before." Lieutenant Helen Johanson described Kirk to Miss Piper prior to the events in "The Menagerie, Part I." (From Kirk's reaction, it appears the relationship was more than casual.) Ruth—reincarnated by the Caretaker—in "Shore Leave." Lieutenant Areel Shaw in "Court-Martial." Edith Keeler in "The City on the Edge of Forever." (Since the romance occurred in the 1930s, it qualifies as a "past love.") Dr. Janet Wallace in "The Deadly Years." Dr. Janice Lester in "Turnabout Intruder." Dr. Carol Marcus in *StarTrek II: The Wrath of Khan.*

2. Nurse Chapel in "The Naked Time." Leila Kalomi in "This Side of Paradise." The Romulan commander in "The *Enterprise* Incident." Droxine in "The Cloudminders." Zarabeth in "All Our Yesterdays."

3. To Natira in "For the World Is Hollow and I Have Touched the Sky."

4. Actually, I could probably just list every episode in which he appears, but here's the short list: "Where No Man Has Gone Before," "The Naked

Time," "Mudd's Women," "The Corbomite Maneuver," "Arena," "Tomorrow Is Yesterday," "The Return of the Archons," "The Changeling," "Obsession," "The Gamesters of Triskelion," "The Immunity Syndrome," "The Ultimate Computer," "The *Enterprise* Incident," "And The Children Shall Lead," "Is There in Truth No Beauty?," "Day of the Dove," "The Tholian Web," "Elaan of Troyius," "That Which Survives," *Star Trek: The Motion Picture, StarTrek II: The Wrath of Khan, Star Trek V: The Final Frontier*, and *Star Trek VI: The Undiscovered Country.*

5. Ilia in *Star Trek: The Motion Picture* and Vixis in *Star Trek V: The Final Frontier.*

6. Scott in *Star Trek V: The Final Frontier.* (Also possibly the salt creature in "The Man Trap.")

7. Yeoman Martha Landon in "The Apple." Sylvia in "Spectre of the Gun." Irina Galliulin in "The Way to Eden."

8. Kirk "helps" Shahna in "The Gamesters of Triskelion" and "apologizes" to Kelinda in "By Any Other Name."

9. Spock inhabited Chapel's body in "Return to Tomorrow." (They "share conciousnesses." Ooooooh.) Kirk inhabited Lester's body in "Turnabout Intruder."

10. Spock ordered Cloud William's woman to open a communicator at the end of "The Omega Glory." (Yes, Henoch—in Spock's body—did make Chapel forget that the metabolic formulas were different in "Return to Tomorrow," but Spock was tooling around inside Henoch's globe at the time.)

11. Kelinda outside the cave in "By Any Other Name."

12. After Kirk puts on his boots in "Wink of an Eye." As Kirk and Odana walk out of his quarters in "The Mark of Gideon."

13. Chapel expressed her love for Spock in "The Naked Time" while still engaged to Dr. Roger Korby, as we discover later in "What Are Little Girls Made Of?" Spock falls for Leila Kalomi in "This Side of Paradise," but "Amok Time" reveals that he is betrothed to T'Pring.

14. Losira in "That Which Survives." (Of course, the fact that any contact would prove deadly for our beloved captain is cause enough for his hesitation.)

THE DEVIL IN THE DARK

Star Date: 3196.1

When dozens of men die in the tunnels beneath the mining colony on Janus VI, the *Enterprise* comes to assist. An eyewitness claims that the deaths are caused by a large creature. A perfectly round sphere of silicon in the colony director's office triggers a theory in Spock. The killing began shortly after the miners opened a new tunnel and discovered thousands of the spheres. Because of this, Spock wonders if the creature might be a life form based on silicon rather than carbon. A foot search confirms Spock's suspicions. When he and Kirk first encounter the creature, it apparently is made of rock. A combined phaser blast stops the creature's attack but the next meeting produces an uneasy standoff. The creature is hesitant to evoke another phaser blast. Likewise, Kirk and Spock hesitate to fire unless forced to do so. Through a mind meld, Spock discovers that the creature is called a Horta. It is intelligent and the mother of its race. Every fifty thousand years, all but one Horta die, leaving thousands of eggs behind. The last remaining Horta becomes a maternal guardian. When the miners broke into her nursery, the Horta attacked to protect her young. As the episode ends, Spock negotiates an agreement that benefits both the Horta and the miners.

Trivia Questions

1. Who does Schmitter relieve from guard duty at the beginning of the episode?

2. What are the odds that Kirk and Spock will both be killed during the search for the Horta?

SYNDICATION CUTS

• A small section of the exchange between Vanderberg and Schmitter.

• Kirk ordering the first search teams to start on the twenty-third level and then instructing Vanderberg and his people to stay on the top level.

• Several small pieces of the first search.

• Spock informing Kirk that the search team is gathering in the main tunnel, and Kirk's pep talk before Spock gives the men the last known location of the creature. During the pep talk, Kirk tells the men that the creature is wounded and dangerous. In the uncut version, this makes the third time he says this.

• Bits and pieces of the second search, and Kirk's discovery of the Horta.

• Kirk's summons of McCoy to heal the Horta. This deletion causes a small problem in the syndicated version. After Kirk and Spock discuss a full Vulcan mind meld with the Horta, McCoy comes running in without Kirk ever requesting his presence. It makes the doctor look psychic.

• Mere seconds of the miners coming down the hall and upon the Horta.

PLOT OVERSIGHTS

• One of the tension points of this plot comes from the capture of a recirculating reactor pump by the Horta. Supposedly the miners have no spare parts for their reactor. (This in itself is a bit unbelievable, but moving right along . . .) Without the pump, their only power source will go supercritical in just a few hours. Spock comments that the Horta knew exactly which part to steal. How? The Horta's environment shows no evidence that it has ever built any type of mechanical device. In addition, at this point in the episode, the Horta is interested only in ridding the planet of this carbon-based infestation. It has killed fifty men to accomplish its mission. Why would it bother to save the pump? Why not just destroy it and force the miners to leave?

• While examining the silicon nodule on Vanderberg's desk, Spock quotes the director as saying there were "thousands of them." Actually, Vanderberg com-

mented that there were "a million" of them. Of course, a million is a thousand thousands, but wouldn't Spock be a little more accurate than this—even if he did consider Vanderberg's statement an exaggeration?

• Why are the Horta's tunnels nicely circular when the cross section of its body is elliptical?

• At the beginning of the second search, Kirk suggests that Spock assist Scott with the makeshift circulating pump. The captain doesn't want both him and his first officer killed by the creature. Spock counters that the odds of both of them dying are very high, and Kirk acquiesces. Then Kirk and Spock go looking for the creature together! Doesn't this significantly increase the odds of both of them being killed simultaneously?

• Starfleet must concentrate almost exclusively on the directional terms "port "and "starboard" to the exclusion of all else. I had great fun in The Nitpicker's Guide for Next Generation Trekkers describing an error by Riker in "Encounter at Farpoint." The computer tells him to go right, and he goes left. It turns out he's in good company. When Kirk and Spock look for the creature and come to a fork in their path, Kirk points to the right and says to Spock, "You go left." Then he gestures back to the left and says, "I'll go right." Spock—ever the loyal first officer—ignores what Kirk says and does what the good captain meant.

EQUIPMENT ODDITIES

• Vanderberg has a button on the underside of his desk to open the door of his office. It's either really big or it moves, because the first time he uses it, he grabs the desk near the end. The next time, he grabs the desk almost a foot from the end.

• Several times in this episode, Kirk's communicator forgets to chirp when it's opened.

• McCoy heals the Horta by using a hundred pounds (note: pounds, not kilos) of thermal concrete. He identifies the substance as the kind they use to build "emergency shelters." Sure would have been nice to load some of this stuff into a shuttle and fly it down to Sulu and company on the frozen surface of Alpha 177 during "The Enemy Within."

CONTINUITY AND PRODUCTION PROBLEMS

• Speaking of Alpha 177, Janus VI is yet another world that bears an amazing similarity to the planet seen in "The Enemy Within."

TRIVIA ANSWERS

1. Sam.
2. 2,228.7 to 1.

CLOSING STILLS

• *Enterprise* firing phasers, "The Corbomite Maneuver"

• Kirk, Spock, and the Guardian of Forever, "The City on the Edge of Forever"

• Kirk and Spock wounding the Horta, "The Devil in the Dark"

• Kirk and Spock looking for period clothing, "The City on the Edge of Forever"

• Pergium production station, Janus VI, "The Devil in the Dark"

• Vina, "The Cage"

ERRAND OF MERCY

Star Dates: 3198.4-3201.7

The *Enterprise* travels to Organia. Hostilities between the Federation and the Klingon Empire have erupted, and Starfleet wants the cooperation of the strategically important planet. Beaming down, Kirk and Spock find a completely passive people. The captain warns them that the Klingons are coming, but their council leader, Ayelborne, simply tells him everything will be all right. Unfortunately, the arrival of Klingon starships traps the pair on the surface. As the *Enterprise* leaves to bring help, the Organians provide disguises for Kirk and Spock. Soon a Klingon commander named Kor arrives, declaring himself military governor of Organia.

That night, the pair try to give the Organians a lesson in resistance by blowing up a Klingon weapons pile. The Organians find such violence appalling. Knowing Kor will torture Kirk to discover his identity, Ayelborne freely discloses the information. Then, several hours later, Ayelborne appears at the detention cell and leads Kirk and Spock to safety. When Kor begins killing Organians for their return, the pair attacks the Klingon headquarters. Suddenly everyone's weapons grow very hot. The same is true for the ships massing for battle above the planet. Ayelborne quietly announces that the Organians will not allow such a violent war to occur. If the Federation and the Klingons do not reach a peace agreement, their weaponry will be useless. Begrudgingly, Kirk and Kor acquiesce.

Trivia Questions

1. What unit reported a Klingon fleet in their sector?

2. How many guards were on duty outside Kirk and Spock's cell?

RUMINATIONS
The Klingon commander wears an interesting sash. It is the same one that Worf wore during the first season *of* Star Trek: The Next Generation.

GREAT LINES
"You are stopping us? You?"— Kirk responding to the Organian claim that they are stopping the war.

GREAT MOMENTS
*K*irk's demand that the Federation has the right to make war is a wonderfully crafted moment. The

captain becomes more and more agitated at the Organian interference until he exclaims, "We have the right—" At this instant, Ayelborne interrupts and asks if he is really demanding the right to kill millions of innocent people. A reaction shot of Spock shows that the Vulcan is immediately both impressed with the Organians and amused at the hot seat on which they have placed his captain (no pun intended).

SYNDICATION CUTS

• Several moments from Kirk's initial discussion with the council.

• The Organians confiscating Kirk and Spock's phasers and assigning them false identities. This deletion ruined a perfectly good trivia question: What is Spock's fake occupation? He poses as a dealer in kevas and trillium.

• Kor's description of Organians, "smile and smile."

• A moment from the first discussion between Kirk and Kor.

• A large portion of Kirk's speech about staging a resistance after he and Spock blow up the Klingon munitions dump. This edit does away with a plot oversight. The tone of Kirk's talk obviously comes from an outsider's perspective, and Spock tells the Organians that the "fleet" will arrive soon. Yet when Kor arrives, Ayelborne still has to tell him that Kirk and Spock are members of Starfleet, even though the Klingon commander overhears the entire conversation.

• A few side comments when Kor

comes to pick up Kirk and Spock from the Organian council chambers.

• Two snide remarks by Kor, directed at the Organians after the commercial break.

• The transition from the council chambers to Kor offering Kirk a drink.

• Kor questioning Kirk about the munitions dump explosion. Just after Kor says, "I must confess to a certain admiration . . ." watch his jaw during the syndicated version. Kor talks, but the jaw movements don't match up with his words. The syndication editor grabbed this piece of footage from another spot in this scene.

• Kirk's journey from Kor's office to the dungeon.

• A mistrustful discussion among Kirk, Spock, and Ayelborne before the pair decide to leave with the Organian leader.

• The transition between the Organians preparing themselves and the Klingon lieutenant walking up to Kor in the hallway.

• Just after Ayelborne announces that he is going to put a stop to the war, Kor says, "You're what?"

PLOT OVERSIGHTS

• Ayelborne claims that the Organians will comply with all Klingon rules, but when Kor reads some of them to Kirk, he states that not more than three Organians can meet in a public assemblage. Surprisingly, the Organian council continues to meet, even though they have five members. Even more surprising, Kor says nothing about this flagrant disregard of Klingon rule.

• After using a mind scanner to determine that Spock is a trader, Kor tells the Vulcan that since he is an alien, the Klingon troop will keep him under scrutiny at all times. Spock must have given them the slip, because that night he and Kirk blow up the munitions dump.

• Of course, this next nit may explain why Spock had no trouble losing the Klingon "scrutineers." Shortly after leaving Kor's office, a Klingon bumps into Kirk and shoves the captain aside. Spock quickly steps in front of Kirk to prevent him from striking the Klingon. The Vulcan then apologizes, and the Klingon departs. Then Spock calls Kirk "Captain," and they discuss strategy in a moderately loud tone of voice. The entire time another Klingon stands a few feet away, listening. Has this guy been drinking too much Klingon warnog? Shouldn't he do something about what he's hearing?

• At the end of the episode, Kirk comments that they—referring to humans—think of themselves as the most powerful beings in the universe. He says it is disturbing to find out that they are not. Kirk must have been disturbed a lot during the episodes so far. In one way or another, all of the following races or individuals have shown their superiority to date: Thasians, "Charlie X"; Talosians, "The Menagerie, Part I"; Balok, "The

Corbomite Maneuver"; the builders of the amusement planet, "Shore Leave"; Trelane, "The Squire of Gothos"; and the Metrons, "Arena."

CHANGED PREMISES

• After the Organians rat on Kirk and tell Kor his real name, the Klingon commander takes the captain back to his office and offers him a drink. Evidently Kor doesn't know about the Klingon code, "Drink not with thine enemy." (Worf demonstrated this code in the *Star Trek: The Next Generation* episode "Hide and Q.")

• Spock tells Kirk that he finds the Organians' behavior most peculiar. Presumably the first officer refers to their refusal to do anything to resist the Klingons. Isn't pacifism one of the highest virtues of Vulcan society? Didn't Surak—the father of all that Vulcans hold dear—eloquently demonstrate this belief in "The Savage Curtain?"

EQUIPMENT ODDITIES

• The fact that Kirk, Spock, and the Klingons all fail to notice the anachronistic doors on the council chamber boggles my mind. At the beginning of the episode, Spock says that the Organians are a "D-" on the Richter scale of culture. After discovering that Organian society has not changed in thousands of years, the Vulcan says that the Organian society is not a primitive one making progress toward mechanization, as the Federation previously thought. In other words, the Organians may have figured out how the wheel works, but very little beyond that. So why isn't anyone intrigued that the doors on the council chamber open and close by themselves with no apparent mechanism?

• Either the Klingons buy their weapons from the Eminians (see "A Taste of Armageddon"), or vice versa. They are too similar to be coincidental.

• I do not understand Kirk's choice of cover when Spock drops the sonic grenade into the munitions pile. The shots leading up to this event clearly show a nearby passageway that goes around a corner. Instead of availing himself of this quick and potentially safer exit, Kirk runs across a flat courtyard area and stands up against a wall that is completely exposed to the force of the blast. Of course, the other small problem with the munitions dump is that all the guards seem to be missing!

CONTINUITY AND PRODUCTION PROBLEMS

• Organia sure does look like Alpha 177, doesn't it?

• Near the end of the episode,

Kirk and Spock creep into the Klingon fortress and apprehend Kor. Spock takes his disrupter. Then Kor's forces burst in, and the Organians turn up the heat. All drop their weapons. Kor rushes back to his communications box and suddenly he is wearing his disrupter. Afterward, he walks back around his desk and it's gone again.

TRIVIA ANSWERS

1. XY75A47.
2. Ten.

CLOSING STILLS

• *Enterprise* approaching energy barrier, "Where No Man Has Gone Before"

• Kirk introducing Spock to Ayelborne, "Errand of Mercy"

• Kor and Kirk, "Errand of Mercy"

• Fortress on Rigel VII, "The Cage"

• Spock's circuitry shorting out, "The City on the Edge of Forever"

• Buildings, Deneva, "Operation—Annihilate!"

• Vina as the often misunderstood Orion slave person, "The Cage"

THE ALTERNATIVE FACTOR

Star Date: 3087.6-3088.7

While surveying a barren planet, the *Enterprise* encounters a series of violent energy disturbances. At the same instant, a lifeform appears on the surface. Beaming down, Kirk finds a craft and a highly agitated individual named Lazarus. Back on the ship, Lazarus claims that he chases a perverse enemy, an evil destroyer who must be killed. He pleads for a pair of dilithium crystals to end the battle once and for all. When Kirk refuses, Lazarus steals them and beams down to the planet. Kirk follows close behind. Accidentally, Lazarus's craft pushes him into a magnetic corridor, a link between the universe of matter and the universe of antimatter. On the other side, he finds a parallel Lazarus. With great calm, this one claims that his people first discovered the way to open the corridor. When the first Lazarus discovered the existence of a twin, he went insane and vowed to kill his double even if it meant his destruction. Unfortunately, if the two ever meet

Trivia Questions

1. What is Lazarus's body temperature when Spock first detects him on the surface?

2. What is McCoy's terminology for the security guard Kirk brings to sick bay?

outside the corridor, not only will they destroy each other, but both universes as well. Under the second Lazarus's urgings, Kirk returns to his universe and shoves the first Lazarus into the corridor, where his twin awaits. Then the captain quickly beams back to the *Enterprise* and destroys Lazarus's craft, trapping the warring pair inside.

GREAT LINES

"*Aches.*"—Lazarus answering McCoy's inquiry about his head. (Lazarus has a gift for understatement. The guy just fell off a cliff!)

SYNDICATION CUTS

• Kirk, Spock, and the security team approaching Lazarus's ship.

• After returning from the planet, Kirk calling battle stations, McCoy giving his first report on Lazarus, and Uhura informing Kirk that the message from Starfleet is ready.

• Before the commodore begins speaking, Kirk acknowledging the message, and reaction shots from Spock and Uhura.

• The second half of the captain's log, star date 3088.3. Also, Kirk returning to the bridge, and the first part of his discussion with Spock.

• Just after Lazarus enters Engineering for the first time, an establishing shot of the crystals and Lieutenant Masters.

• When the first set of crystals disappear, Kirk takes Lazarus and a landing party back to the surface of the planet. The uncut version contains a longer terrain search before Lazarus has his next experience in the corridor. During this search, he wanders off in one direction while everyone else takes another. At this point, Kirk has some suspicions about Lazarus, but the landing party seems oblivious to the fact that Lazarus has just left them!

• A long explanation by Lazarus before he tells Kirk the truth in sick bay.

• Four different pieces are edited from Kirk's approach to Lazarus's ship, his travel through the corridor, and his meeting with the antimatter Lazarus.

PLOT OVERSIGHTS

• Kirk gets in a little old-fashioned bootlicking when conferring with a Starfleet commodore at the beginning of this episode. Prior to the conversation, Uhura informs the captain that she has received a Starfleet command code factor 1, invasion status. A few moments later, the commodore asks Kirk his opinion on the energy disturbances. With very little information at his disposal, Kirk opts for the safe answer. He agrees with the

top brass and says he thinks it might be a prelude to invasion! The commodore seems gratified with this response and says Starfleet command thinks so as well. Of course it's what Starfleet command thinks. They transmitted a command code that ordered everyone to invasion status!

• At one point, McCoy comments that Lazarus has the recuperative powers of a dinosaur. Evidently by the twenty-third century, the recuperative powers of dinosaurs will be known.

• Lazarus's easy access to vital areas of the ship during this episode boggles the mind. Kirk has already said that he thinks the energy distortions are a prelude to invasion and Lazarus appeared at the precise moment of an energy distortion. The man is visibly agitated and possibly mentally deranged, yet he manages to stroll down to Engineering. Once there, he creates a diversion and steals two dilithium crystals.

CHANGED PREMISES

• The Starfleet commodore at the beginning of this episode states that the energy distortions were felt in every quadrant of the galaxy and far beyond. This would indicate that Starfleet has a way to quickly communicate with every quadrant of the galaxy and far beyond. (Does this mean Starfleet can speak with other galaxies? With a minimal time delay?) In fact, many shows in the original series reference the galaxy as if Starfleet has already traversed its length. On the other hand, *Star Trek: The Next Generation* seems to indicate that Starfleet has covered only a limited part of the galaxy. For instance, Kirk and crew travel to the center of the galaxy in *Star Trek V: The Final Frontier* and give no indication that this is an unusually long journey. On the other hand, when Picard and crew travel to the center of the galaxy in "The Nth Degree," everyone seems amazed at the distance they have covered.

EQUIPMENT ODDITIES

• Asserting that Lazarus's forehead wound has completely healed, McCoy takes Kirk to find him. When they do, Kirk escorts Lazarus back to the bridge. One final shot shows McCoy standing near a hallway intersection. In the background you can see two red alert light panels. Only one is flashing. Evidently the bulb is burned out in the other one.

• The medpanels above the bed in sick bay can apparently function even if the patient is standing across the room. The medpanel thumps away in rhythm with Lazarus's heart as he convalesces. Then he gets up and stumbles across the room and the medpanel just keeps on thumping.

• Someone at Starfleet really likes the layout of the control panel used on the neural neutralizer in "Dagger of the Mind." Avid readers of this guide will note that it has made several appearances already. In this episode it shows up

in Engineering.

CONTINUITY AND PRODUCTION PROBLEMS

• For this episode, a female lieutenant named Masters functions as chief engineer. Kirk consistently addresses her as "Lieutenant," but her uniform has no stripe on its sleeves. Several episodes establish that the creators designate the rank of lieutenant by a single gold braid on each sleeve.

• Lazarus's planet sure does look like Alpha 177, doesn't it? (This footage has appeared in many episodes to date, including, "The Enemy Within," "Dagger of the Mind," "Conscience of the King," "The Devil in the Dark," and "Errand of Mercy.")

• Lazarus's beard goes through a host of amazing transformations during the show, from thick to thin and back.

• One of the final shots of the viewscreen during this episode shows the planet without a star field.

TRIVIA ANSWERS

1. 98.5 degrees Fahrenheit.
2. Muscleman.

CLOSING STILLS

• *Enterprise* leaving Earthlike planet, "Miri"
• Antimatter Lazarus's ship, "The Alternative Factor"
• Crew thrown about, "The Corbomite Maneuver"
• Kirk's court-martial, "Court-Martial"
• Scott in Jefferies tube, "The

Naked Time"
• Garden scene, "Where No Man Has Gone Before"

• Vina as the mature, insightful Orion slave woman, "The Cage"

THE CITY ON THE EDGE OF FOREVER

Star Date: 3134.0

When time disturbances from an uncharted planet buffet the ship, McCoy injects himself with cordrazine by accident. The heavy dosage induces extreme paranoia, and McCoy flees to the surface. Kirk and Spock follow him down with a security team but soon make an astonishing discovery: A living machine is the source of the temporal ripples. It is the "Guardian of Forever" and can serve as a gateway to any time or place. To demonstrate, the Guardian begins projecting Earth's history. At this point, the drug-crazed McCoy leaps through the portal. Suddenly all communication with the *Enterprise* ceases. Evidently McCoy has changed the past and radically altered history.

The Guardian replays Earth history again, and Kirk and Spock follow McCoy, arriving in the year 1930. A turn of events leads them to the Twenty-first Street Mission, run by Edith Keeler, a true visionary. By accessing Spock's tricorder recordings, the pair learns that her peace movement will eventually stall the United States' entry into World War II, allowing the Nazis to win. They also determine that McCoy kept Keeler from dying in an auto accident. When the moment comes, Kirk restrains McCoy and himself. The captain has fallen in love with Keeler. As she dies, the Guardian returns them to their own time, stating, "All is as it was."

Trivia Questions

1. Why does Spock need a block of platinum?

2. What is the number of Edith Keeler's apartment?

RUMINATIONS

This was a great episode, and the creators did a very nice job on the shape and look of the Guardian of Forever.

GREAT LINES

"I am endeavoring, ma'am, to construct a mnemonic memory circuit using stone knives and bearskins."—Spock to Keeler after she asks about his invention.

GREAT MOMENTS

The end of this episode is gripping—the sudden happy reunion of Kirk and McCoy immediately overpowered by Kirk's necessity to restrain his friend from saving Keeler, then McCoy's accusatory questioning, and finally Kirk's angry retreat from the Guardian of Forever.

SYNDICATION CUTS

• Just after encountering the Guardian of Forever, Kirk asks Spock what it is. When Spock replies "Unbelievable," Kirk responds, "That's funny." The editors made a good choice in cutting out these two lines. I suppose it was meant to be humorous, but it doesn't work.

• When Spock comments that they have no past or future, a reaction shot from Kirk and an admission by Uhura that she is frightened.

• Reaction shots of Scott and Uhura when Kirk and Spock prepare to jump into the portal.

• The front section of the scene where Spock almost gets hit by a car.

• After escaping from the policemen, Kirk and Spock run down a street before turning and running across the front of the Twenty-first Street Mission.

• A few comments between Kirk and Spock after meeting Keeler and the pair receiving their meal and finding a seat.

• After Keeler's speech, Kirk and Spock handing in their plates.

• An establishing shot of the building that houses Kirk and Spock's "flop."

• Kirk and Spock sweeping, and a reaction shot of the two men working at the table before Spock points out the fine tools one of the men uses.

• Following a commercial break, an establishing sequence with a milk delivery cart and an old man stealing a bottle of milk from the doorstep just as McCoy arrives. This edit destroyed a perfectly good trivia question: What was the name of the company that delivered the milk? Windin Dairy Farm.

• Kirk and Keeler walking up her stairs and discussing the future.

• Establishing shot of McCoy walking past Walt's Restaurant before going into the Twenty-first Street Mission. (Another perfectly good trivia question down the drain.)

• After a commercial break, an establishing shot of the Twenty-first Street Mission before the scene changes inside to Keeler looking through a file cabinet drawer as McCoy awakes.

• The first time I watched the uncut version, I made a note to talk about the awful music the creators used under two key scenes—Kirk's catch of Keeler as she starts to fall down the stairs, and Kirk's restraint of McCoy after the truck kills Keeler. The music on the uncut version sounds like something from a 1930s radio program. It is true to the period but very distracting because it sounds so dated. It turns out that somebody had the same viewpoint as I did! The syndicated version has different music at these two spots.

PLOT OVERSIGHTS

• After McCoy injects himself with the cordrazine, Kirk and Spock stand and watch, apparently dumbfounded. Even when McCoy begins screaming, they still stand and watch. Why doesn't Spock pinch him? I would expect this type of emotional behavior from Kirk but not from Spock. And—as long as we're on the topic of McCoy on the bridge pumped full of drugs—does anyone else find it amazing that McCoy can throw off Spock's grip and run away so easily?

• To access the tricorder recordings of Earth's history, Spock builds the twentieth-century equivalent of a mnemonic memory circuit. He manages to play back Keeler's obituary from 1930 as well as a meeting that Keeler has with President Roosevelt in 1936. From this he deduces that Keeler is the focal point in time that has drawn all three Starfleet officers. One question: How could Spock see Keeler's obituary? The Vulcan begins recording the Guardian's playback of history. As the playback nears the time frame of the Great Depression, McCoy jumps through and saves Keeler from dying. The *Enterprise* instantly disappears because McCoy has changed history. Wouldn't the Guardian's playback change instantly as well? (Remember that Spock's tricorder also records the meeting between Keeler and Roosevelt in 1936.) If the Guardian's playback instantly changes, then there would be no

obituary, since McCoy saved Keeler's life. (I suppose the Guardian could have helped Spock out a little and included the obituary anyway to give the Vulcan some clue as to what they were supposed to do.)

• And speaking of the recording of the obituary, why does Spock tell Kirk that he doesn't know exactly when Keeler will die? Don't obituaries usually have this information in fairly precise detail?

EQUIPMENT ODDITIES

• While leaving the bridge, McCoy doesn't wear a utility belt—the kind the crew uses to hold their phasers and communicators. Neither does he wear one when manipulating the controls in the transporter room, although he does grab a phaser from the transporter chief. Yet when he is captured on the surface of the planet, McCoy suddenly wears a belt. An additional oddity exists with the transporter chief. He wears a belt when McCoy first approaches but doesn't when the security guards find him. The only solution to both these oddities is that McCoy headed for the transporter pads, changed his mind, came back, got the belt, put it on, and then manipulated the controls a second time to beam himself down to the surface. Of course, this entire sequence occurred while we weren't looking.

• Somehow McCoy makes it to twentieth-century Earth with a hand phaser. Look at the sequence of events. McCoy goes crazy. He attacks the transporter chief and takes his phaser. He transports himself to the surface of the planet. Kirk, Spock, Scott, Uhura, and a security detail follow. The security people grab the doctor. Spock pinches him. Everyone looks at the Guardian replaying Earth's history. McCoy wakes up, runs for the portal, and jumps in. He has no time to grab a phaser from anyone. The only phaser he possibly could have is the one he stole from the transporter chief. In other words, the security team didn't bother to disarm McCoy after Spock pinched him?

• Why doesn't Uhura use her tricorder to locate McCoy on the planet's surface?

• It's cheap-shot time! The Guardian's playback of Earth's history occurs twice. During the first run-through, McCoy jumps through the portal. During the second, Kirk and Spock do the same. Since Kirk and Spock arrive at the Twenty-first Street Mission before McCoy, they must have entered the time stream prior to the doctor. The Guardian of Forever claims that its review of history can proceed at only one rate. With this statement, the creators give hard-nosed nitpickers an absolute standard by which to judge if the scene is executed correctly. Since the playback of Earth's history proceeds at a fixed rate, the timing of both sessions must be identical. A persnickety nitpicker can choose a scene that occurs in both ses-

sions—for instance, a cannon blast followed by infantry charging up a hill—and time from this spot, first, to the entry of McCoy and second, to the entry of Kirk and Spock. *The time for Kirk and Spock must be less than that for McCoy.* Of course . . . it isn't! About twenty-five seconds elapse from the infantry charge to McCoy's entrance of the Guardian. Compare that to fifty-six seconds from the infantry charge to the entrance of the Guardian by Kirk and Spock. (Now, I don't know why anyone would bother to time this in the first place. No one could possibly expect the creators to look after these types of details, could they?)

• Spock's tricorder has a little playback screen, but the screen can play back only what the tricorder recorded if the tricorder is hooked up to a computer. Does this seem right?

CONTINUITY AND PRODUCTION PROBLEMS

• During Edith Keeler's speech at the Twenty-first Street Mission, Kirk looks at Spock and freezes for a moment. If you watch carefully, you'll see that this footage actually comes from a close-up of Kirk several seconds later. In that close-up he looks at Spock and begins talking. Evidently the creators needed an extra reaction shot and grabbed it from the close-up.

• At one point Keeler stumbles down the stairs leading to her apartment, and Kirk catches her. After the stumble, she wears both shoes. Then she thanks Kirk for saving her and continues up to her apartment. Suddenly she's wearing only one shoe; the other is nowhere to be seen.

TRIVIA ANSWERS

1. To construct a duodynetic field core.
2. Thirty-three.

CLOSING STILLS

• *Enterprise* leaving Earthlike planet, "Miri"

• *Galileo* preparing for departure, "The *Galileo* Seven"

• Kirk and Keeler, "The City on the Edge of Forever"

• Spock's circuitry shorting out, "The City on the Edge of Forever"

• Kirk, Spock, and the Guardian of Forever, "The City on the Edge of Forever"

• Gorn, "Arena"

• Buildings, Deneva, "Operation—Annihilate!"

• Vina, skilled exotic dance artist by night, baker of cookies by day, collector of aluminum cans by morning, assistant of little old ladies who wish to cross the street by afternoon, and all-around nice person by evening, "The Cage"

OPERATION—ANNIHILATE!

Star Dates: 3287.2-3289.8

Just before arriving at the planet Deneva, Kirk witnesses a Denevan pilot exclaiming that he is finally free. Then he plunges his vessel into the planet's sun. The situation on Deneva is no less peculiar. A mob tries to attack while they shout that they do not wish to cause any harm. Soon Kirk and Spock find a nest of odd-looking creatures, one of which attaches itself to Spock's back. The stinger of the creature rapidly entwines itself throughout the Vulcan's nervous system and attempts to control him with intense pain. With his Vulcan training, Spock thwarts the attempt and explains the creatures to Kirk. Each is like a giant brain cell. Though not physically connected, they function as a unit.

From the Denevan pilot's transmission, the crew determines that the creatures are sensitive to light. Knowing the need for a test subject, Spock volunteers, and McCoy subjects him to the full spectrum of intense light. It blinds Spock, removing the creature in the process. Unfortunately, later test results show that the creature is sensitive to ultraviolet light only. Spock didn't need to be blinded. Saddened by the loss of their first officer, the crew place special satellites in orbit. As the ultraviolet light from the satellites destroys the creatures, a forgotten "inner eyelid" opens, and Spock regains his sight.

Trivia Questions

1. What are the call letters and frequency of Sam Kirk's personal subspace transmitter?

2. What is Sam Kirk's occupation?

SYNDICATION CUTS

• The opening scene with the Denevan pilot flying into the planet's sun has four different edits: a reaction shot from Sulu and an establishing shot of the viewscreen; Kirk asking Scott about using the tractor beam; more reaction shots of the bridge crew; and Spock's report of the hull temperature.

• Spock's report in the transporter room just before the first landing party beams down. This edit gives the syndicated version a small nit. Spock is nowhere to be seen in the transporter room and then suddenly appears with the landing party during the beam-down.

• Kirk and the others running up

to a building and then entering after they hear a scream. This edit helps deflate a nit. In the uncut version, Kirk is clearly some distance from the building and must go through two closed doors to get to his brother's wife, Aurelan. The episode seems to indicate that Aurelan is the one Kirk hears screaming. She must have a great set of lungs. She's inside a closed room inside a building, and Kirk still hears her clearly from at least fifty feet away!

• Kirk saying with a sigh, "Oh . . . Sam," when identifying his brother's dead body.

• Kirk demanding answers from Spock before beaming back to the ship, conferring with McCoy, and then speaking with Aurelan. During the conference with Kirk, McCoy says he won't know anything until he gets the "plates" back from the lab. It sounds like McCoy still uses X rays. Remember that this episode originally aired well before the arrival of CAT scanners and MRI machines.

• Kirk asking about his nephew as McCoy gives him a report on the bridge.

• After subduing Spock on the bridge, Kirk ordering McCoy to take him back to sick bay and put him in restraints.

• In sick bay, Spock grimaces and says, "I am a Vulcan" prior to repeating the statement and breaking free.

• Two edits come from the transporter room scene before Spock beams back to the planet: Scott gives Kirk a report, and McCoy objects to Spock leaving sick bay.

• After Kirk says he wants the analysis in an hour, there are several reaction shots between Spock and McCoy.

• McCoy closing the door of the test chamber on Spock.

PLOT OVERSIGHTS

• The end of the episode makes note of Spock's supersensitive hearing. McCoy whispers to Kirk at the captain's chair, and Spock overhears them. Near the beginning of the show, however, Kirk seems to have *better* hearing than the Vulcan. As they check out a buzzing noise, one of the creatures chirps, giving away its location. Although Kirk and Spock stand side by side, it is the captain who follows the sound to its source.

• After discovering the creatures, Kirk wonders if their situation might be a trap and orders a strategic withdrawal. Oddly enough, everyone stands and walks out with their backs to the creatures! If it might be a trap, I don't think you want to turn your back on your enemy. Right on cue, one of the creatures swoops down and hits Spock in the back (or the posterior, if you happen to be watching the blooper reel).

• The pain Spock endures in this episode must be incredible. His logic seems sporadic. He gives a perfectly reasonable discourse on why he must be the one to fetch a creature for study. His arguments are so compelling that Kirk agrees to let him go. Instead of trying this approach to begin with, Spock goes to the transporter, attempts to disobey a direct order to stay on the ship, and beats up two fellow officers in the process.

• After performing the first test with light and discovering that it kills the creature, Kirk demands that they push forward and test the blinding light on a humanoid subject. He says they need to know now! Why? What's the rush? The *Enterprise* can ensure that no ships leave Deneva. Surprisingly, Spock comes back and agrees that they must proceed quickly. Isn't it more logical to wait for the test results? They come back in less than ten minutes. The only reason for this breakneck speed is to get Spock into the chamber so they can blind him so he can recover. (This is classic plot trickery.)

• I can still remember seeing this episode for the first time and the emotion I felt as I realized that Spock was blind. I can still remember how cheated I felt when the creator suddenly invoked the plot trapdoor, "Oh, by the way, Vulcans have an inner eyelid and everything is okeydokey fine." (A deep and prolonged groan escaped me when I saw the same thing happen with Worf in the *Star Trek: The Next Generation* episode "Ethics.")

CHANGED PREMISES

• Kirk and the landing party follow Aurelan's screaming to Sam Kirk's office. Inside they find Sam dead, Aurelan screaming, and Peter unconscious. Peter is Sam and Aurelan's son. Everyone acts like this is the entire family. Where are the other two boys? According to to "What Are Little Girls Made Of?," Sam has three sons.

EQUIPMENT ODDITIES

• After thwarting Spock's attempt to leave the ship without permission, Scott keeps a phaser trained on the Vulcan while he, Scott, walks around to the transporter station. At one point the phaser crosses in front of the hood that sits in the middle of the transporter panel. If Spock had chosen that moment to attack, how could Scott have fired with the hood in the way? ·

CONTINUITY AND PRODUCTION PROBLEMS

• Discovering that ultraviolet light kills the creature, Kirk orders the crew to place satellites in orbit. Sulu, as helmsman, indicates that they are in place. Note that Sulu wears a gold shirt with one armband. Kirk says "Energize," and the scene cuts to a shot of the navigator and helmsman stations. The helmsman now wears a red shirt with no bands on his sleeves. What happened to Sulu?

TRIVIA ANSWERS

1. GSK 783, subspace frequency 3.
2. Research biologist.

CLOSING STILLS

• *Enterprise* approaching small blue planet. (I have no idea.)

• Knight on horseback, "Shore Leave"

• Spock in lawgiver's robe, "The Return of the Archons"

• Penal colony Tantalus V, "Dagger of the Mind"

• Sulu with foil, "The Naked Time"

• Scott in Jefferies tube, "The Naked Time"

• Vina as the green Orion slave girl, thankful that Pike's fantasy has finally come to an end, "The Cage"

IS STARFLEET MILITARY?

f anyone had asked me this question while I was writing *The Nitpicker's Guide for Next Generation Trekkers,* my immediate response would have been, "Obviously!" Aside from the discipline of the crew, everything I saw smacked of the military: the uniforms, the armament, the ships, the ranks, the command structure. I just assumed that Starfleet was the equivalent of our current-day military forces, and I took every opportunity to criticize the lack of military disciple on Picard's *Enterprise.* Then the letters began pouring in claiming that Picard had specifically said that Starfleet *wasn't* military. In addition, there's a story going around Trekdom that the Great Bird of the Galaxy himself, Gene Roddenberry, unequivocally asserted that Starfleet is not military. As to exactly what it is, I heard it mostly likened to a fleet of ships run by people like Jacques Cousteau. What follows is a small collection of statements and situations dealing with this matter. I leave it for you to decide.

1. Who ya gonna call? Whenever there's a threat of invasion by the military of another group, Starfleet answers the challenge ("Balance of Terror," "Errand of Mercy," "The Immunity Syndrome"). If someone threatened the United States with invasion, we wouldn't call Jacques, we would call . . . the military.

2. "Tomorrow Is Yesterday." In this episode, Kirk tells Christopher that Starfleet is a combined service when asked if the Navy built the *Enterprise.*

3. "Errand of Mercy." Kirk tells the Organians that he's a soldier, not a diplomat.

4. "A Private Little War." In this episode, Starfleet supplies weapons for their allies. Doesn't supplying weapons for an ally usually fall within the purview of the military?

5. "Whom Gods Destroy." Garth comments that Kirk is the finest military commander in the galaxy—except for himself, of course. To this, Kirk replies that he is primarily an explorer now. (Just trying to be fair.)

6. *Star Trek II: The Wrath of Khan.* In reference to Starfleet, David Marcus states that scientists have always been pawns of the military. His mother replies that Starfleet has kept the peace for a hundred years.

7. *Star Trek V: The Final Frontier.* Starfleet Command sends Kirk to rescue

the kidnapped ambassadors on Nimbus III. Isn't rescuing hostages usually a military operation?

8. *Star Trek VI: The Undiscovered Country.* In the initial briefing, a female captain asks if they are talking about mothballing Starfleet. The man in charge of the meeting replies that the exploration and scientific programs would be unaffected. What would be affected then? Wouldn't it be . . . the military? In the same meeting, another person comments that if they dismantled the fleet, they would be defenseless against an aggressor. I believe that defending against aggressors is one of the roles of the military. (By the way, while we are on this topic, Klingons aren't the only enemies of the Federation. Why are they even considering "mothballing Starfleet" if they have a possible agreement with only *one* of their foes?) Later, during the dinner between the crew of the *Enterprise* and the Klingons, Chang asks Kirk if he would be willing to give up Starfleet. Spock jumps into the conversation by diplomatically suggesting that Kirk feels that Starfleet's mission has always been one of peace. When Kirk begins to dispute this statement, Chang interrupts, saying that there is no need to mince words. He says that in space "All warriors are cold warriors."

SECOND
SEASON

AMOK TIME

Star Date: 3372.7

When Spock's behavior becomes erratic, Kirk orders him to sick bay for a complete physical. McCoy's disturbing report reveals a growing chemical imbalance in Spock's system. In the first officer's quarters, Kirk demands clarification. Hesitantly, Spock reveals that Vulcan males experience *Pon farr*, a time of mating when primitive emotions overwhelm logic. He must return to his family's ritual grounds or die in the attempt. When the ship arrives at Vulcan, Spock asks Kirk and McCoy to join him for the *Koon-ut-kal-if-fee*, the "marriage or challenge" ceremony.

All goes well until T'Pring—Spock's chosen mate—refuses the marriage. According to Vulcan traditions, she opts for challenge, and she chooses a champion. Unfortunately, she chooses Kirk. Not understanding the implications of the challenge and wanting to keep Spock from fighting anyone else in his weakened condition, Kirk accepts. Only then does he learn that he must kill Spock to survive.

Trivia Questions

1. McCoy claims that Spock is as tight-lipped about his condition as what animal?

2. The great eel-birds of what planet must return every eleven years to their hatching grounds?

In the middle of the fight, McCoy injects Kirk with a drug. The doctor claims it will help the captain function in the hot, thin atmosphere. In reality, the drug is a neural paralyzer and simulates Kirk's death, thereby halting the contest. Of course, Spock is greatly relieved once he beams back to the ship and finds that his friend is still alive.

RUMINATIONS

With the start of the second season, DeForest Kelley moves into the front credits, and the titles of the episodes are now in the same font as the title of the series.

GREAT LINES

"I shall be honored, sir."—McCoy responding to Spock's invitation to accompany him to the *Koon-ut-kal-if-fee*. (For all their bickering, this line and Spock's invitation demonstrate that the first officer and doctor are, in fact, good friends.)

GREAT MOMENTS

This episode has many, many great moments, but I think my favorite comes when Spock tries to dissuade T'Pau from allowing Kirk

125

to accept the challenge. She drills to the heart of his objections by questioning whether he is Vulcan or human.

SYNDICATION CUTS

• A reaction shot just before Spock asks to take his leave on Vulcan.

• Kirk's words, "Spock . . . I'm asking you" just before he says, "What's wrong?"

• Kirk resting in his quarters before he calls the bridge.

• Kirk leaving his quarters after learning that the ship is on course for Vulcan.

• Kirk giving a destination of deck 5 before he talks with Spock in the turbolift.

• Spock wandering down the hall to sick bay, arguing with McCoy over the examination, and finally submitting.

• After walking into Spock's quarters, Kirk reiterates McCoy's report and demands to know why. This edit did away with a continuity problem. At one point Spock forces his hand to his desk, dropping a stylus. Kirk grabs Spock's hand, the shot changes, and Spock suddenly holds the stylus again.

• Spock refusing to explain his situation to Kirk even in light of a direct order.

• After Spock finishes discussing the *Pon farr*, Kirk walks around the desk, assures the Vulcan of his silence, tells Spock he will get him to Vulcan somehow, and leaves. This edit also does away with a nit—this time a production prob-

lem. Spock has a large sculpture in his bedroom. It has a light in its belly that constantly changes color. In this scene, smoke starts pouring from the belly. I don't think it's incense. The stream of smoke is too thick and rapid, and it never shows up in any of the other shots. Something caught on fire!

• Reaction shots from McCoy and Kirk after the captain decides to disobey orders and take Spock to Vulcan. Also, Chapel's approach to Spock's bed.

• After telling Spock that the ship heads for Vulcan, Chapel indicates that they will arrive in just a few days. This edit does away with an equipment oddity! (Who ever edited this one for syndication sure knew where the problems were.) Just prior to this scene, Kirk gives orders to head for Vulcan at warp eight. Now Chapel says they will be traveling for a few days. In "Arena," Kirk orders the *Enterprise* to warp seven, and everyone immediately reacts with worried looks. Spock comments that a sustained warp seven will be dangerous. Yet in the uncut version of this episode, the *Enterprise* evidently maintains a sustained speed of warp eight for several *days*.

• Several reaction shots as the marriage party approaches.

• The close-ups of the marriage party as everyone settles into position.

• Reaction shots as Spock introduces Kirk and McCoy.

• T'Pau asking Spock who will pledge Kirk and McCoy's behavior,

Spock answering that he will, and a few reaction shots.

• McCoy smirking to himself after Kirk and Spock leave for the bridge at the very end of the episode.

PLOT OVERSIGHTS

• After Spock "kills" Kirk, McCoy comments that it may seem strange, but the first officer now commands the *Enterprise*. Does this seem right? Wouldn't Starfleet have some sort of regulation prohibiting the acquisition of command by assassination?

CONTINUITY AND PRODUCTION PROBLEMS

• In the early part of the episode, a shot shows the *Enterprise* flying toward the viewer, with a star field in the background. This footage has a terrible production problem. Watch carefully and you see that something has eaten away most of the starboard engine nacelle.

• Just before calling for the challenge, a wide shot shows T'Pring walking toward the gong over the fire pit. Then a close-up shows her standing beside Stonn once again. Moments later, she moves toward the gong.

• For being "deep in the *Plak-tow*," Spock sure seems relaxed during this *Koon-ut-kal-if-fee*. At times he has his hands behind his back as he leans against a wall.

TRIVIA ANSWERS

1. An Aldebaran shellmouth.
2. Regulus V.

CLOSING STILLS

• *Enterprise* orbiting what looks like North America, "Miri"
• T'Pau, "Amok Time"
• T'Pring and Stonn, "Amok Time"
• Hand gripping *Enterprise*, "Who Mourns for Adonais?"
• Rocky terrain.
• Balok puppet, overjoyed at his agent's report that he's been tapped to fill the final slot in the closing credits for the entire second season in syndication, "The Corbomite Maneuver"

WHO MOURNS FOR ADONAIS?

Star Date: 3468.1

After a large hand composed only of energy grasps the ship, a face appears in space. Using the mannerisms of a Greek god, the face invites Kirk and fellow officers to the surface. The captain brings along Lieutenant Carolyn Palamas, an expert in ancient civilizations. Beaming down, they find a being who claims to be Apollo. With a point of his finger, he melts phasers, and with a wave of his hand changes Palamas's tunic to a flowing Greek gown. Apollo demands that the entire crew evacuate the ship, live on the planet, and worship him.

Meanwhile, Spock and the crew of the *Enterprise* manage to punch holes in the energy field, restoring communications. He then informs Kirk that they have located a power source on the planet. At the same time, Kirk orders Palamas to spurn Apollo, since he obviously cares for her. The tactic works, and he becomes very angry, expending much of his energy in the process. Keeping up the pressure, Kirk orders Spock to fire the phasers. With the power source destroyed, Apollo mourns its loss and—realizing that humanity has outgrown the need for gods—spreads himself thinner and thinner on the wind until nothing is left.

Trivia Questions

1. Where is Pollux IV located?

2. What is the animal on Antos IV that Chekov identifies as able to generate and control energy with no harm to itself?

RUMINATIONS

Stephen Whitfield in his book The Making of Star Trek *has some interesting comments about Lieutenant Palamas' s Grecian gown in this episode. Apparently the top had only one anchor point. It fastened to the hip-hugging waistline of her skirt. Whitfield claims that only the weight of her cape—tossed over her shoulder—held the rest of it in place. Theiss, the designer of the outfits for* Star Trek, *certainly has a talent for engineering. It does cause one to wonder how carefully the actress had to move during storm scenes, when the wind whips the costume around. There is a moment during the sequence that is startling in terms of the amount of female anatomy revealed, especially for 1967. At one point Palamas falls to the ground and her skirt peels back, leaving her side exposed from waist to ankle.*

I also had another thought on the matter of Scott's missing finger. In the Ruminations *for "The Enemy Within," I commented that the creators should have written an engineering accident into a script to account for James Doohan's missing finger. They also missed a perfect opportunity to explain it in this episode. At one point Apollo shoots an electric charge at Scott and melts the phaser he holds in his right hand. If it did that much damage to the phaser, wouldn't it be believable to have the charge do collateral damage to his hand?*

GREAT LINES

"Well, I'm sure that's very flattering, but I must get on with my work."—Palamas to Apollo after he reminds her that he has "chosen" her.

GREAT MOMENTS

C hief Engineer Montgomery Scott takes quite the hit in this episode. He makes the mistake of charging Apollo, and the Greek god fires a lightning bolt at him. The charge lifts Scott off his feet, slings him backward, and even after he hits the ground, he keeps sliding for several more feet. The stunt is very well executed.

SYNDICATION CUTS

• Chekov asking if he is seeing things just after the hand appears.
• After a commercial break, a

large section containing Spock and the crew's efforts to establish communications and perform sensor sweeps. This edit removed a bit of very grungy nitpicking. In a close-up, Uhura's hand operates one of the center panels on her work station. In the wide shot that immediately follows, her hand rests near the left-most panel on her workstation.
• Kirk saying "Apollo" and a reaction shot of Apollo before the captain continues to explain that they do not bow to every entity with a bag of tricks.
• After a commercial break, Kirk asking McCoy about Scott's condition.
• The second scene showing Spock's continued efforts.
• A portion of the discussion between Kirk and Apollo just before the captain and the others try to evoke Apollo's anger.
• After the incident just mentioned, Apollo retires with Palamas to a garden. In the syndicated version, the scene starts with Apollo saying, "Fools!" and then turning and speaking to Palamas about her future as a mother of gods. The transition is rough because a significant portion of monologue was deleted. In the uncut version, Apollo rants about man forgetting that there is an order of things in the universe and how he has come to restore it. Then he calms himself and speaks with Palamas.
• After a commercial break, Kirk attempts to contact the *Enterprise* before Palamas strolls into the

scene.
• Several moments from Apollo's generation of the storm.

PLOT OVERSIGHTS

• Apollo doesn't identify himself until after Kirk and company beam down. Since Spock stays on the ship, he has no way of knowing who the being claims to be. Yet near the end of the episode, when Kirk speaks with Spock and addresses Apollo by name, the Vulcan acts as if he knows precisely what his captain is talking about.

CHANGED PREMISES

• To convince Palamas to shun Apollo, Kirk gives a rousing speech about the bond of humanity, how we're all the same and share the same history. As he holds her hand, he says that man or woman, it makes no difference. He states that they are all human. All well and good, but if we're all the same, why isn't there a female captain of a starship? "Turnabout Intruder" states that a human woman has *never* served as captain of a starship. (I wonder what happened to Number One? She was the second-in-command on Christopher Pike's *Enterprise*—see "The Cage"—and certainly seemed like command material.)

EQUIPMENT ODDITIES

• In this episode, Sulu adjusts the tractor beam to repel. This capability of the tractor beam was lost somewhere in the years that follow, because everyone is shocked

when Wesley does it in the *Star Trek: The Next Generation* episode "The Naked Now."
• As the storm increases, Kirk decides to order Spock to fire on Apollo's temple. He pulls out his communicator and flicks his wrist. The communicator doesn't open, so he flicks his wrist again. Oddly enough, the communicator chirps both times. In other words, it chirps even though it doesn't open! (It's probably making up for the times in the past when it didn't chirp at all.)

CONTINUITY AND PRODUCTION PROBLEMS

• Throughout the entire show a hand grips the *Enterprise*. Then, when Spock fires the phasers, it suddenly disappears. If the crew of the *Enterprise* succeeded only in punching holes in Apollo's force field, shouldn't the graphics show a hand with holes in it?
• At the very end of the episode, Apollo mourns for the loss of his temple and man's inability to believe. Close-ups show a tree in the background. Then he grows tall again and the close-ups still show a tree in the background. The wide shots, however, prove that Apollo now towers over every tree in sight.
• On the uncut video, the preview of the next voyage of the *Enterprise* concerns the episode "Space Seed"—an episode from the first season!

TRIVIA ANSWERS
1. In the Beta Geminorum system.

2. The giant dryworm.

CLOSING STILLS
• *Enterprise* orbiting what looks like North America, "Miri"
• Fortress, Rigel VII, "The Cage"
• *Enterprise* charm over candle, "Catspaw"
• Salt creature, "The Man Trap"
• *Galileo* on Gamma Canaris N, "Metamorphosis"
• Balok puppet, "The Corbomite Maneuver"

Star Date: 3541.9

Just after all humanoid life disappears from the Malurian system, energy bolts from a tiny vessel rock the *Enterprise*. When Kirk hails the vessel, the attack abruptly stops and the vessel introduces itself as *Nomad*. Given its size, the crew beam it aboard. *Nomad* then states that its purpose is to eliminate all nonperfect life. Accordingly, it sterilized the imperfect biological life in the Malurian system. Spock's research fills in the rest of the details. *Nomad* was built by Earth scientist Jackson Roykirk to search for alien life. Damaged sometime after its launch in 2020, *Nomad* drifted until it contacted Tan-Ru—a probe from another civilization, designed to collect soil samples and sterilize them. Somehow the two merged to become the current *Nomad*. Evidently *Nomad* confused the name "Jackson Roykirk" for "Captain James Kirk." Thinking its creator was on the *Enterprise*, *Nomad* ceased its attack.

In time, *Nomad* discovers that Kirk is a biological life form and starts to cleanse the *Enterprise* of biological infestation. The captain then reminds the machine of its programming. It must destroy all nonperfect life. He reveals that he is not the creator. *Nomad* has made an error. Therefore *Nomad* is not perfect. Just after the crew beam the powerful machine into space, it destroys itself.

Trivia Questions

1. What chart does Kirk display to *Nomad* to show the *Enterprise's* point of origin?

2. What other episode contains the song Uhura sings while holding for Lieutenant Singh? (Believe me, even I wouldn't try a pun that bad. It was definitely not intended.)

RUMINATIONS

The creators revisit this plot idea in Star Trek: The Motion Picture. *Both this episode and the movie concern an Earth probe that meets and is modified by alien machinery. Both story lines use the threat of their respective probes destroying all life on Earth and reference humans as biological units.*

By the way, Scott takes another hit in this episode (see Great Moments, "Who Mourns for Adonais?"). This time he flips over the railing on the bridge and slams into a wall.

GREAT LINES

"*No, sir.*"—Spock admitting to

Kirk that he didn't think the captain capable of the flawless logic used to convince *Nomad* to destroy itself.

GREAT MOMENTS

T here is a very cute moment when Nomad *tells Kirk that the unit "Spock" is different and well ordered. The Vulcan looks at his captain with a smug expression that almost borders on pride.*

SYNDICATION CUTS

• After Kirk tells Uhura to put *Nomad*'s initial transmission on audio, a large section is deleted. It includes Uhura assigning the message to the ship's analysis sector; Spock identifying it as a rapid, multilayered binary; the message slowing down and collapsing to a single binary stream; Uhura identifying the one symbol it contains as "repeat"; Kirk repeating his message and requesting the attacker's identity; and Uhura identifying a second message.

• After Kirk lets the attacker take it at its own speed, Spock's computer shorts out.

• During *Nomad*'s message, Kirk comments that the attackers apparently got what they needed to communicate before the computer overloaded.

• After *Nomad* agrees to come aboard, Kirk asks if it needs any special conditions, Scott objects to bringing it aboard the *Enterprise* and the captain orders a repair crew for the computer. There's a line by Spock later in the show that

suffers with the removal of the three preceding edits. By eliminating all references to Spock's computer short-circuiting, the syndicated version removes the motivation for Spock's request that *Nomad* draw the medical information on Scott only as fast as his computer can supply it.

• In the transporter room, a discussion between Spock and *Nomad* on the meaning of "opinion."

• Lieutenant Singh attempts to speak with *Nomad* before Uhura hails him.

• *Nomad*'s approach to Uhura on the bridge.

• Kirk's exclamation, "Bones!" after *Nomad* knocks Scott over the railing.

• *Nomad* asks if Kirk will effect repairs on Scott, and Kirk tries to explain that Scott is dead. *Nomad*'s offer to repair Scott follows this section.

• In sick bay, a few light moments after Kirk tells Scott that McCoy will explain what *Nomad* did to him.

• Uhura reads about the dog running before she reads that the dog has a ball.

• Spock punches buttons before telling Kirk that his examination of *Nomad* is insufficient.

PLOT OVERSIGHTS

• When worrying about how to deal with *Nomad*, Kirk misses the simple solution. Why not order it back into the transporter, begin beaming it out, and then have a transporter accident? The *Enter-*

prise has enough of those by chance. Surely it wouldn't be that difficult to make it happen on purpose.

- At one point, *Nomad* scans Uhura's mind and erases her memory. Since there's no brain damage, McCoy and Chapel set about to retrain her. It generates some cute moments but a plot oversight as well. If the teaching facilities aboard the *Enterprise* are so advanced that they can take a person and completely reeducate him or her to function on a starship in just *one week,* why does Starfleet need an Academy? Startlingly enough, the *Enterprise*'s facilities are actually better than any found on Vulcan. It takes the testing stations on Vulcan *three months* to retrain Spock after his death and resurrection in the movies.

- To learn more about *Nomad,* Spock uses his Vulcan mind meld technique. My wife brought up a good point about this scene. In all other instances of the Vulcan mind meld, the participants shared each other's thoughts completely. Then why doesn't *Nomad* learn the truth about Kirk from this incident?

EQUIPMENT ODDITIES

- In *Equipment Oddities* for "The Return of the Archons," I mentioned that a statement by Scott seemed to indicate that he was using the warp engines to supplement the shields. I noted that when Lieutenant Barclay did this in "The Nth Degree," everyone was amazed. This episode absolutely establishes that Scott can use the warp engines to supplement the shields. As the second energy bolt approaches the ship, Sulu reports a loss of navigational power, and Scott immediately pipes up that he has rerouted the energy from the warp engines into the shields.

- In retaliation for the attack, Kirk fires a photon torpedo at *Nomad.* It has no effect, and Kirk wonders out loud about what kind of entity could absorb that much energy. Wait a minute: Spock said that each of *Nomad*'s energy bolts had the power of ninety photon torpedoes. The shields of the *Enterprise* have absorbed three such attacks. That's equivalent to the power of 270 photon torpedoes, and Kirk is amazed that *Nomad* can absorb the power of one photon torpedo?

- The transporter room gains a sensor scanning station with this episode.

- Where did *Nomad*'s planet-killing capabilities come from? True, Spock says that it met an immensely powerful probe, but that probe's mission was simply to collect soil samples. Did the alien designers really equip a soil-collecting probe with the ability to obliterate entire worlds? (Just a bit of overkill, don't you think?)

- Engineering now has two large round cannisters on the floor in the center of the room. (It's probably where they keep the coffee.)

CONTINUITY AND PRODUCTION PROBLEMS

- When *Nomad*'s first energy bolt

hits the *Enterprise,* the bridge crew goes flying back and forth across the set. At one point Spock trots down to the navigator's station before the violent rocking throws him back in the direction from which he came. Just as Spock changes direction, the shot shows the navigator hanging on to the console. Then the shot changes and Kirk is suddenly behind the navigator's chair, holding on to it with a firm grip. Uhura also magically appears between these two cuts behind the captain's chair.

• After finding out that Kirk is also a biological unit, *Nomad* goes to sick bay to look at the captain's records. Kirk meets the probe as it leaves the infirmary. The shot showing *Nomad* coming toward the camera actually comes from earlier in the episode, when *Nomad* departs from a turbolift.

TRIVIA ANSWERS
1. 14A.
2. Uhura sings it for Lieutenant Riley in "The Conscience of the King."

CLOSING STILLS
• *Enterprise* orbiting what looks like North America, "Miri"
• Kirk and the imperial Spock, "Mirror, Mirror"
• *Enterprise* and doomsday machine, "The Doomsday Machine"
• Sylvia as a cat, "Catspaw"
• Vaal, "The Apple"
• Balok puppet, just after investing in a large-screen TV, four-head VCR, all eighty original series tapes, and the six movies so he can bone up on all the plots just in case he's asked to do a convention appearance, "The Corbomite Maneuver"

MIRROR, MIRROR

Star Date: unknown

As the episode begins, Kirk confers with the leader of the Halkan council for mining rights to their dilithium crystals. The leader politely declines, fearing that the crystals would be used for other than peaceful purposes. Kirk asks them to reconsider and then beams up to the ship with McCoy, Scott, and Uhura. An ion storm disrupts the process, and when they arrive back on the ship, the *Enterprise* and its crew have changed. Officers step up in rank by assassinating their superiors. "Agonizers" are used to discipline crew members, and, worst of all, the Federation is now an empire that rules by terror. Apparently the transporter switched the landing party with their counterparts in this parallel universe. Using the ship's computers, the landing party computes the power and configuration needed to return home.

Meanwhile, Spock becomes suspicious of Kirk's suddenly benevolent behavior after the captain refuses to obey Starfleet orders to obliterate the noncooperating Halkans. The first officer launches an investigation and uncovers the truth. In the end, he helps Kirk and the others return to their own universe. He wants his ruthless captain back. Their relationship has proven most profitable. Just before he departs, however, Kirk challenges Spock to consider the logic of serving an empire that must eventually fail. Intrigued, Spock says he will.

Trivia Questions

1. How many colonists did imperial Kirk slaughter on Vega IX?

2. According to imperial Spock, approximately how long before the Empire falls?

GREAT LINES

"Captain Kirk, I shall consider it."— Imperial Spock to Kirk after the captain challenges him to change the Empire. (This is also a great moment. It definitely gives the impression that the imperial Spock will make a difference in the Empire.)

SYNDICATION CUTS

• Sulu and Chekov locking phasers on Halkan targets before Uhura arrives.

• Scott checking out main phaser control, being stopped by a security guard, and reporting "no damage" to Kirk before Spock arrives on the bridge. This edit removes a very minor production problem. When Scott calls the bridge, Kirk reaches over and hits his communications button with his thumb. Hit thumb immediately slides off, and he has to hit the button a second time. (Yes, this type of thing would happen in real life. It just looks funny to see such a mundane problem bother our impeccable captain.)

• After the thwarted assassination attempt, Kirk agrees to the agony booth for Chekov and then speaks with McCoy and Scott in the captain's quarters. Two points of interest in this edit. First, during this exchange, McCoy relates his shock that sick bay resembles a chamber of horrors. These statements seem consistent with an imperial empire. However, imperial Spock later comments that McCoy is sentimental and soft. If the imperial McCoy is so sentimental and soft, why does our McCoy find sick bay so appalling? Is it a matter of degree? Second, the edit puts a different twist on Scott's statement as the two versions sync back together. In the syndicated version, Kirk clouts the man looking for a promotion as a reward for saving the captain's life. The scene instantly changes to Kirk's quarters and Scott says, "Everything's exactly where it should be, except us." "Everything" in this context seems to refer the general layout and capabilities of the *Enterprise*. In the uncut version, Kirk clouts the guy,

goes to his quarters, and starts the discussion with McCoy and Scott. At the end of the edit, Kirk asks about star readings and Scott replies, "Everything's exactly where it should be, except us." In other words, all the *stars* are where they should be.

• Kirk walks down the hall, meets Spock, and speaks to him before coming upon Chekov in the agony booth.

• In the captain's quarters, Kirk and Marlena discuss Chekov's assassination attempt.

• After a commercial break, the captain's log recaps events thus far in the episode.

• Spock discovers that Kirk and Scott are conducting secret computer research.

• Kirk hears a door open and spins to see Marlena in her loungewear. This edit does away with a line I could not believe actually made it past the censors. Just after Kirk turns, Marlena unfolds her arms, and places her outstretched hands high on the doorway. After giving Kirk the full view, she explains her behavior by saying, "Oiling my traps, darling."

• Uhura backs away from Sulu and exits the bridge after seducing him away from his security panel. Also, a shot of Scott working in a Jefferies tube, and Uhura in the turbolift after she leaves the bridge.

PLOT OVERSIGHTS

• At the beginning of the episode, Kirk tries to persuade the

Halkan council that the mission of Starfleet is peaceful. Bear in mind that the Halkans are extreme pacifists. Their leader even worries that, in the future, Starfleet might change and one life might be lost through the use of Halkan dilithium crystals. One question: How is Kirk going to explain Starfleet General Order 24 to these peace-loving people? That's the order to obliterate an entire planet (see "A Taste of Armageddon"). For the Halkans, there could never be a reason to carry out such an order. Wouldn't the very existence of such codified destruction be enough to cause the Halkan council to refuse?

• This is one of those unavoidable plot oversights. In reality, this scenario could not occur. You could not have two radically different universes in sync with each other for long. It just isn't reasonable that both *Enterprise*s would be orbiting the same planet at precisely the same time, conducting the same negotiations. (Of course, it made for a great episode, and Kirk's speech at the end, driving Spock to consider the irrationality of the Empire, is absolutely wonderful. Having said all that, we now return to our regularly scheduled nitpicking.) The sequence of events in such radically different universes would quickly diverge. Even within this one episode, Marlena kills several crew members with a device called the Tantalus field. Did those men somehow die on our *Enterprise* as

well? And what about all the episodes that have preceded this one? For instance, would Imperial Starfleet Command put Kirk on trial for "murdering" Finney, as our Starfleet Command did in "Court-Martial"? Wouldn't Imperial Starfleet Command just chalk those events up as another assassination? And what would the imperial Kirk be doing during the time of the court-martial? Wouldn't he be traveling to his next assignment? As another example, would imperial Kirk fiddle around with Kodos in "The Conscience of the King," or would he simply kill the guy? The sequence of events in episode after episode depends on Kirk behaving in a certain way. Imperial Kirk behaves in a diametrically opposite way and therefore creates a very different sequence. Each difference compounds the next, pushing the two universes farther and farther apart. The chances of both Kirks speaking with the Halkans at precisely the same time are slim indeed. In addition, it's highly unlikely that the senior staff would be the same. Yes, Spock seems content to remain second-in-command, but Sulu and Chekov both jump at the opportunity to try to kill Kirk. Doesn't it seem likely that they would have tried to do so in the past? If so, at what point does imperial Kirk just wipe them out with the Tantalus field?

• During the captain's logs, Kirk continually says, "stardate . . . unknown." Why is it unknown?

Does the Empire use another standard for keeping time?

• At one point, Sulu makes his move to kill Kirk and Spock at the same time. Coming to the captain's rescue, Lieutenant Marlena Moreau—the imperial Kirk's consort—uses the Tantalus field to eliminate Sulu's guards. Strangely enough, she stops short of killing Sulu. (I suppose she wants to allow Kirk to do the manly thing and pay back Sulu with a punch.)

• At the end of the episode, Spock greets Kirk and the others as they finally make it home. Three security guards stand in the background. Evidently, Spock had just beamed the imperial group back to its own *Enterprise*. It boggles the mind to think that these two beamings occurred simultaneously. The imperial landing party was in the brig. Our beloved landing party waited for the last second to transport only because Kirk wanted to preach at imperial Spock on the illogic of supporting the Empire. What stopped our Spock from getting the computer to solve the problem just as Kirk did and then immediately beaming the imperial landing party home?

EQUIPMENT ODDITIES

• After calling for beam-up, Kirk closes his communicator and drops his arm. Yet when the captain initially appears on the transporter pad before fading into the parallel universe, his arm is raised, as if speaking into a communicator.

• The interior of the imperial *Enterprise* is richly adorned with the symbols of the Empire. Why, then, is the exterior the same as the *Enterprise* we've grown to love?

• When Kirk and the others finally make it home, Uhura reappears with her tricorder. During the initial beam-up, they switched clothes and equipment with their imperial counterparts. Presumably the tricorder Uhura carried arrived in her imperial cousin's hands. Since imperial Uhura didn't have it when Spock threw them in the brig, someone on board our *Enterprise* must have taken it from her. How then does it get back in her hands at the end of the episode?

CONTINUITY AND PRODUCTION PROBLEMS

• When imperial Spock confronts Kirk and the others in sick bay, a fight breaks out. Evidently the creators couldn't find a stunt double for Spock with straight hair, because every time Spock performs some difficult move he suddenly has curls.

TRIVIA ANSWERS
1. Five thousand.
2. Two hundred forty years.

CLOSING STILLS
• *Enterprise* orbiting what looks like North America, "Miri"
• Vaal, "The Apple"
• *Enterprise* and doomsday machine, "The Doomsday Machine"

• Romulan warbird, "Balance of Terror"

• Shuttle *Columbus* returning, "The *Galileo* Seven"

• Balok puppet after hearing Lieutenant Marlena Moreau say, "Oiling my traps, darling," "The Corbomite Maneuver"

THE APPLE

Star Dates: 3715.0–3715.6

Kirk beams down with a landing party to Gamma Trianguli VI. Too quickly, three crewmen die in the beautiful paradise, and Scotty reports that the *Enterprise* has lost power. In just a few hours, a tractor beam from the surface will pull the ship into the atmosphere. The local inhabitants offer no explanation. They are called the Feeders of Vaal. Led by a man named Akuta, they live a very simple life. Kirk asks to see Vaal. Readings show that the god of this world is actually a powerful and intelligent machine. It protects the inhabitants in exchange for food.

Unfortunately, Vaal has recognized that the *Enterprise* and its crew constitute a threat to the order of the planet. Having already attacked the ship, Vaal orders Akuta to kill the strangers. Of course, the landing party quickly overpowers the unskilled Feeders, and the next time Vaal rings its dinner bell, Kirk concocts a plan. He forces the inhabitants to stay away and orders the *Enterprise* to fire on Vaal's feeding point. Vaal tries to fend off the attack, but it overloads and quits functioning. With the *Enterprise* saved, Kirk and the others return to the ship after congratulating the people on their newfound freedom.

Trivia Questions

1. What is Kaplan's nickname after the lightning bolt hits him?

2. How did Mallory's father assist Kirk's career?

SYNDICATION CUTS

• The first time Kirk wanders off to look for the person who spies on them, Chekov approaches Spock and asks what is happening. Spock answers, and Chekov returns to his place beside Yeoman Martha Landon. Because of this cut, the syndicated version has Chekov doing a little dance. He starts moving away from her, the scene cuts, and he moves toward her.

• Part of the walk through the jungle before Spock finds the rock.

• Spock puts the unexploded half of the rock back on the ground, the landing party wanders off, and leaves rustle.

• After a commercial break, a captain's log recaps the events so far.

• Part of the communication between Mallory and Kirk.

• After a commercial break, a captain's log, star date 3715.6, recapping the events so far.

• After meeting Vaal, the journey by Kirk and the others to the village, and a reaction shot of Vaal.

• A few more comments by McCoy after he says the Feeders aren't growing old, including his assertion that he cannot tell if they have been this way for twenty or twenty thousand years.

• Feeders departing village, and a fade to Vaal.

• A section of the argument between Spock and McCoy in the bushes, including an assertion by McCoy that the Feeders have remained unchanged for ten thousand years. As you can see, this edit and the one above did away with a plot oversight.

• After a commercial break, Landon angry over the possibility of the *Enterprise* burning up in the atmosphere.

• Three different sections of the discussion concerning who would teach the Feeders to reproduce if one of them died in an accident. The sections consist mainly of reaction shots.

• A section during the attack on Vaal by the ship's phasers.

• Akuta discussing the other benefits of serving Vaal, including the fact that Vaal put the fruit on the trees.

• A wisely deleted statement from Kirk's speech. "There's no trick to putting fruit on the trees." (Yeah? Maybe you'd like to try to build a tree and make it sprout some fruit, Kirk!)

PLOT OVERSIGHTS

• While wandering in the moonlight with Chekov, Landon comments that if it weren't for Vaal, the planet really would be paradise. Even without Vaal, this place has exploding rocks and plants that shoot poison darts.

EQUIPMENT ODDITIES

• At one point Spock discovers a lightweight rock. When kicked or even gently tossed, it explodes with great force. For some reason, Spock snaps it in half with his hands, and the rock stays perfectly calm. Shouldn't it detonate because of this disturbance as well?

• When first approaching Vaal, Spock uses his tricorder to analyze the structure. Then he mumbles something about a force field before it knocks him backward onto his posterior. Finally he announces that the force field extends thirty feet in all directions. If Spock's tricorder could tell him that the field extended a specific number of feet in every direction, why did he run into it? (Spock definitely is not having a good day. He's already taken a chestful of poison darts. He was just repelled by a force field, and in a little while he's going to get hit by lightning!)

• During the attempt to break the ship free of Vaal's tractor beam, Scott flies backward into the captain's chair. The chair's pedestal actually lifts off the floor. Shouldn't a starship be a bit sturdier? Or did the designers purposely construct the pedestal to absorb the shock of hitting the chair?

CONTINUITY AND PRODUCTION PROBLEMS

• The final shot of the *Enterprise* warping off into space uses the "clipped nacelle" graphic. Watch the tips of the engines very carefully and you'll see the *Enterprise* move completely onto the screen before the entire nacelles show.

TRIVIA ANSWERS

1. Spot. (I'm sorry. Just a little joke. It was so easy, I couldn't ignore it.)
2. He helped the young James Kirk get into the Academy.

CLOSING STILLS

• *Enterprise* orbiting what looks like North America, "Miri"
• Kirk and android, "What Are Little Girls Made Of?"
• Kirk, Spock, and McCoy at the *Koon-ut-kal-if-fee* ceremonial grounds, "Amok Time"
• Phaser cannon, "The Cage"
• *Enterprise* and *Botany Bay*, "Space Seed"
• Kirk, Spock, and the Guardian of Forever, "The City on the Edge of Forever"
• Balok puppet, "The Corbomite Maneuver"

THE DOOMSDAY MACHINE

Star Date: 4202.9

Following a trail of smashed planets, the *Enterprise* comes upon the heavily damaged USS *Constellation*. Beaming over with a landing party, Kirk can only find the ship's captain, Commodore Matthew Decker. Decker reports that a giant vessel with the ability to slice up planets attacked them. With his ship disabled, Decker transported his crew down to a planet in the nearby star system. Unfortunately, the vessel then destroyed that planet as well. After sending Decker and McCoy back to the *Enterprise,* Kirk and Scott prepare the *Constellation* for towing. At this point the planet killer returns.

Decker now assumes command of the *Enterprise* and orders an attack on the vessel. It proves disastrous for the ship. Though still on the *Constellation,* Kirk orders Spock to take charge. Humiliated and grieving for the loss of his crew, Decker commandeers a shuttle. He flies it straight into the planet killer's maw and detonates the shuttle's engines. When Sulu registers a slight power drop during the incident, Kirk concocts a plan. Scott rigs the *Constellation*'s impulse engines to overload, and Kirk pilots the ship toward the planet killer. At the last moment, the crew beam him back to the *Enterprise*. Then the exploding engines destroy the planet killer from the inside out—providing some meaning to Decker's sacrifice.

Trivia Questions

1. What is the registry for the USS *Constellation?*

2. On the *Constellation*, who reported that the fourth planet in system L374 was breaking up?

SYNDICATION CUTS

• After Kirk orders an approach course to the *Constellation,* a flyby of the *Enterprise* and a reaction shot by Kirk and Spock.

• Kirk, McCoy, and Scott heading for Auxiliary Control.

• After a commercial break, a flyby of the *Enterprise,* a flyby of the planet killer, Spock giving Kirk a report on the object, and finally Kirk and the landing party's attempt to return to the ship just before the planet killer attacks. These edits do away with two problems. As Kirk and the landing party take their positions to beam back, they are missing a man. The original landing party consisted of Kirk, McCoy, Scott, and two lesser lights. McCoy has already beamed back with Decker, but when the rest of the landing party prepares to return to the ship, only Kirk, Scott, and Washburn get into position. The other guy is still down in Engineering! Then as the *Enterprise* prepares to bring the landing party home, Spock gives an order to drop the defensive screens. At this point the planet killer attacks. While not a certainty, it appears that the *Enterprise*'s shields drop *before* the planet killer fires. Wouldn't this result in a tremendous amount of damage? The *Enterprise* does lose a few systems, but shouldn't the blast take out a section of the hull?

• After Kirk begins work on the *Constellation* viewscreen, an establishing shot of the *Enterprise*, a pan of the bridge, and McCoy's report that there were no casualties in the attack.

• When Spock rebuffs Decker for trying to assume command, a pair of reaction shots from the two officers.

• Decker looking over the crew before giving the order to turn and attack.

• Several reaction shots following Sulu's acceptance of this order.

• After Scott pulls off the little panel in the *Constellation*'s engine room, the door to the left of the panel opens, and Scott removes the large device used to connect M5 to the engines in "The Ultimate Computer." The next scene shows Kirk working on the viewscreen.

• Escaping from his security

escort, Decker climbs down to the hangar bay and enters. An establishing shot of the *Constellation* follows, and Scott gives Kirk a progress update. In this update Scott says that he has hooked in ship's communications. There are two problems with this statement. Why is Scott wasting time fiddling with the communications system when the communicators are working fine? Also, why do Kirk and Scott continue to use communicators after Scott has hooked in ship's communications?

• A section of the sequence featuring Decker flying the shuttle into the planet killer and Kirk trying to dissuade him.

PLOT OVERSIGHTS

• Finding the *Constellation* deserted, Scott suggests that he, Kirk, and McCoy go to Auxiliary Control to play back the duplicate copy of the captain's logs. The next shot shows Kirk almost walking by a room, noticing Decker, stopping, and entering the room. The room looks suspiciously like Auxiliary Control, and Scott accesses the duplicate captain's logs a few moments after arriving. If this *is* Auxiliary Control, why did Kirk almost walk past it?

• The inability of McCoy to certify Decker as unfit for command seems a bit too convenient in this episode. Spock states that for McCoy to do so, the doctor must administer a battery of tests. "Court-Martial" indicates that McCoy is a specialist in space psychology. I'm no specialist, but Decker is obviously distraught, in shock, and behaving irrationally. Does it really make sense that Starfleet would require a complete examination during a crisis to relieve a commander from duty? Wouldn't the visual assessment of a trained medical professional—especially one with a background in psychology—be enough?

• Decker doesn't make a great showing in the episode. It sounds like he realized that the doomsday machine was chopping up the planets in the system, yet he beamed his people down to the next one in line for destruction. Also, prior to the first attack on the *Enterprise,* Decker doesn't bother to give Spock any information concerning the planet killer's weapon range. This leaves the Vulcan unprepared for the machine's onslaught.

• It is truly amazing that the designers of the planet killer went to all the trouble of constructing a "neutronium" hull and never accounted for the possibility that someone might try to fly a bomb down the mouth of their invention. The planet killer does have a powerful cutting tool. Doesn't it seem likely that it would use this tool to dissect any possible threat before gulping it down?

EQUIPMENT ODDITIES

• The production people saved themselves some money when McCoy and Decker return to the ship. The pair walk out of the room before beaming out. Why don't they just assume the same position as Kirk and the others do later? Answer: If they leave the room, the special effects department doesn't have to do a dematerialization sequence.

• Relieved of command by Spock, Decker hops a shuttle. As the bay doors slowly grind open, Sulu's panel light ups and he informs Spock that the bay doors are opening. Of course, Spock says to shut them, and Sulu says he can't because it's too late. There is no mention that Decker overrode the door control or jammed any systems. Evidently he strolled into the shuttle, hit the remote control, and the doors started opening. Wouldn't the door sensors fire off a message as soon as the process began? The doors sure don't look like they open very fast. Why isn't there time to stop them?

CONTINUITY AND PRODUCTION PROBLEMS

• Evidently the creators encountered a problem with the footage of the shuttle and the planet killer. The perspectives are way off. Earlier in the show, a side-by-side shot featuring the *Enterprise* and the planet killer gave the relative sizes of the two entities. When the shuttle appears in the same shot, it is much larger than it should be. It looks as big as the star drive section of the *Enterprise!* (Of course, if the creators had made it the correct size, I'm not sure we could've seen it.)

• Scott loses his Scottish accent when telling Kirk about the detonation trigger he has wired for the *Constellation*. Listen for the phrase, "and thirty seconds later . . . poof!"

TRIVIA ANSWERS

1. NCC 1017.
2. Science Officer Masada.

CLOSING STILLS

• *Enterprise* orbiting what looks like North America, "Miri"
• Lithium cracking station on Delta Vega, "Where No Man Has Gone Before"
• Talosian beast illusion, "The Cage"
• Kirk on trial, "The Squire of Gothos"
• *Enterprise* approaching energy barrier, "Where No Man Has Gone Before"
• Balok puppet, after attending his first *Star Trek* convention incognito and learning how much Shatner charges for an autograph, "The Corbomite Maneuver"

KIRK'S TOP TEN REASONS FOR VIOLATING THE PRIME DIRECTIVE

According to the Prime Directive, Kirk and company may not intervene in the normal social development of any planet. Also, if the inhabitants of the planet do not know of extraterrestrial life, Starfleet officers must not reveal their origins or operate any devices that may give the locals the impression that the officers come from the stars.

And now, for your reading pleasure, here are Kirk's top ten reasons for violating the Prime Directive:

10. The stupid machine that ran the planet didn't allow any touching and kissing. ("The Apple")

9. It was the beginning of a new duty cycle and I wanted to get it off to a great start.

8. The stupid computer that ran the planet didn't know how to throw a decent party. ("The Return of the Archons")

7. Women on backward planets are really impressed when you materialize in front of them.

6. The inhabitants were using a bunch of stupid computers to fight their warlike pantywaists. ("A Taste of Armageddon")

5. The desk-hugging commodores at Starfleet Command needed something to do.

4. I always wanted to conquer a planet. ("A Piece of the Action")

3. McCoy's blood pressure had dropped to 170/100.

2. It makes Spock's eyebrow twitch.

And Kirk's number one reason for violating the Prime Directive:

1. I noticed my hairline receding that day.

CATSPAW

Star Date: 3018.2

During a mission to Pyris VII, Kirk, Spock, and McCoy find a Halloween setting filled with fog, witches, and an old castle. In the castle's main hall, they meet a wizard named Korob and his associate, Sylvia. The exchange turns up a few facts. Korob and Sylvia are not indigenous to the planet, and they are very interested in learning about the science of humans. Apparently they plan some kind of invasion. A simple demonstration convinces Kirk of their powers. For a few moments Sylvia holds a pendant shaped like the *Enterprise* over a candle. At the same time, the crew reports a large heat increase on the ship.

Later, while spending time alone with Sylvia, Kirk guesses that she can be overcome with sensations. He caresses her and soon learns that she and Korob depend on a "transmuter" for their abilities. Suddenly Sylvia becomes incensed as she realizes that Kirk is using her. Korob, frightened by her rage, tries to help Kirk and the others escape, but Sylvia attacks him as well. Helpless, Korob gives his wand to Kirk. Realizing that it is the transmuter, the captain smashes it. In that instant, everything returns to normal, including the pair. They return to their original state. Unable to survive without the device, the small, feathered beings dissolve into nothing.

Trivia Questions

1. What is the name of the officer who dies at the beginning of the episode?

2. What are the two items Korob's race needs from humanity?

GREAT LINES

"*Very bad poetry, Captain.*"—Spock responding to a request from Kirk to comment on an apparition of three witches reciting a curse.

GREAT MOMENTS

The officer who is dead on arrival in the transporter room executes a beautiful fall off the transporter pad.

There also is a fun little nuance that Shatner throws into his performance during Kirk and Spock's second incarceration in the dungeon. While speaking, Kirk looks over at the skeleton hanging beside him and cocks his head sideways to mimic its position. Then the captain continues talking as if nothing happened.

SYNDICATION CUTS

• After losing contact with Jackson, Kirk gives orders to the transporter room and McCoy. Then Kirk leaves the bridge with Spock. The scene cuts to the transporter room, and Kirk arrives, followed by McCoy. Moments later, Jackson beams in. This footage contains an oddity, but its removal raises a question. In the uncut version, Spock leaves the bridge with Kirk but never shows up in the transporter room. However, in the syndicated version, McCoy shows up in the transporter room without being paged.

• Kirk tries to call the *Enterprise* just before heading into the castle.

• Kirk, Spock, and McCoy fan out from the entrance of the castle. A lengthy section follows concerning the efforts of DeSalle and the rest of the bridge crew to find and rescue the landing party. This section contains several moments of interaction between DeSalle and Chekov. In them, Chekov is not his playful self yet. In fact, he acts a bit like a twit. (This episode was the first show produced for the second season and therefore the first one for Chekov.) Also of note, the music for the establishing shot of the *Enterprise* can only be described as "Wagon Train to the Stars." A shortened version of this music appears in the syndicated version at two places.

• McCoy examines the gems at the dinner table and comments that they look real.

• A section of comments from Korob concerning the tests that Kirk and the others have passed.

• After a commercial break, several reaction shots as Sylvia dances the pendant of the *Enterprise* over the candle and Kirk suggests that DeSalle supplement the heat dissipation units.

• Chekov reports that the temperature has returned to normal, and Uhura's first attempt to reestablish contact with the landing party.

• A shot of McCoy staying behind so that Sylvia can question him, and a discussion about the force field between DeSalle and Chekov.

• Two lines of dialogue as Kirk wonders what is happening to McCoy, and Spock comments that they will find out shortly.

• For some reason, the creators moved a commercial break. In the uncut version, a commercial break occurs just after Korob brings Kirk and Spock out of prison and they are stopped by the large cat version of Sylvia. In the syndicated version, the commercial break is edited out and does not occur until Kirk hits McCoy for the first time. Little pieces of the episode disappear from both locations.

PLOT OVERSIGHTS

• Just after beaming down, Spock reports a life form reading in a certain direction at 137.16 meters. Moments later, he indicates another direction. For the distance, Spock offers, "just over 100 meters." Just over? What happened to the two decimal points of precision?

• After Korob fails to extract any information from Kirk, Spock, and McCoy through pleasant banter, Sylvia sends them back to the dungeon. Scott and Sulu, under her influence, act as their escorts. Scott holds the phaser, and Sulu carries the keys. Scott marches Kirk and Spock across the room to McCoy's location and *keeps on walking*. McCoy—having missed the first departure time—obediently falls in line *behind* Scott and starts following him out the door. At this point Sylvia calls the doctor back to begin his interrogation.

CHANGED PREMISES

• This DeSalle guy gets around. In "This Side of Paradise" he was a gold-shirted biologist. In this episode he's a red-shirted assistant chief engineer.

CONTINUITY AND PRODUCTION PROBLEMS

• Poor Chekov is having a really bad hair day. Granted, his hair is rarely fixed to perfection, but in this episode it literally does look like someone dropped a mop on his head.

• The witch apparitions that quote their bad poetry at the beginning of this episode seem to be wearing black turtlenecks. I'm assuming the creators meant them to look like bodyless heads, but there's a bit too much light to accomplish that effect.

• After Korob waves his wand— lighting the candles and setting the table with food—a close-up of the

wizard shows the candles unlit and the table's large centerpiece missing.

• After the incident with the *Enterprise* pendant, Korob relaxes and begins talking about their power. Sylvia soon snaps at him, and a close-up shows his reaction. The table and chairs that stood in front of him in the wide shot are suddenly behind him! (In fact, the creators pulled a piece of footage from later in the show to get this clip.)

• (I am not sure of this next nit, but it seems real enough that I thought I would mention it.) When Kirk arrives for questioning, Sylvia rises from her seat and begins to move forward. It looks like her body scarf gets caught in the chair. Once it grows taut, she stops and nonchalantly reaches back with her right hand to make it look like she is holding on to the arm of the chair. If you'll look closely, you'll see she isn't. (The only explanation I can find for this behavior is that she's stuck. Being a good actor, she covered the problem nicely.)

• Toward the end of the episode, Korob attempts to defend Kirk and Spock from Sylvia. In her large-cat incarnation, Sylvia bursts through the door to the dungeon, throwing it on top of Korob. As the door falls, Korob crumples forward. When he lands, he sticks out the side of the door. The shot changes, and Korob's body suddenly protrudes from the top of the door.

• I usually don't comment on the construction of aliens. After all, the show is more than twenty-seven years old. We have vastly better technology today. However, the true forms of Korob and Sylvia could have been done better. Clearly visible black threads operate the little puppets. (Aside from this, the feathered creatures are quite interesting.)

TRIVIA ANSWERS

1. Jackson.
2. Dreams and ambition.

CLOSING STILLS

• *Enterprise* orbiting what looks like North America, "Miri"

• Apollo's temple, Pollux IV, "Who Mourns for Adonais"

• Romulan warbird, "Balance of Terror"

• *Galileo* on Gamma Canaris N, "Metamorphosis"

• Engineering, "The Enemy Within" (This is the establishing shot just before the good Kirk and Spock walk into the scene.)

• Kirk and Spock wounding the Horta, "The Devil in the Dark"

• Balok puppet, "The Corbomite Maneuver"

I, MUDD

Star Date: 4513.3

Hijacked by an android named Norman, the *Enterprise* drops into orbit around an uncharted planet. In caves under the surface, Kirk meets his old foe Harry Mudd (see "Mudd's Women"). Mudd claims that he is the sovereign of this world. He explains that during a break from prison, authorities damaged his stolen craft. He drifted in space until arriving at this planet, where he found more than two hundred thousand androids looking for someone to serve. At his request, they built several series of young lovelies to entertain him. Yet even this has grown wearisome, and since the androids wish to study other humans, Mudd suggested they grab a starship.

The androids quickly beam the crew off the *Enterprise* and begin serving them. Many things about the place are quite appealing. Scott is very impressed with the engineering laboratory. McCoy can't believe the medical research equipment. When the androids announce that they intend to control the instabilities of all the humanoids in the galaxy, Kirk finally convinces everyone to act. They overwhelm their superior foe using completely illogical behavior. All are freed except Harry Mudd. As punishment, Kirk leaves him behind and asks the androids to construct five hundred exact duplicates of Mudd's ex-wife.

Trivia Questions

1. Who does Norman knock unconscious in Auxiliary Control?

2. Who crushes Kirk's communicator?

RUMINATIONS

This is a delightful episode, especially from a nitpicking viewpoint. The creators did an excellent job with the indentification tags for the Alice androids. I couldn't find a single instance where the creators made a mistake. All the close-ups match the wide shots. Kudos!

Also, I'm surprised Data hasn't visited this planet. He might be able to share technology with these androids.

SYNDICATION CUTS
• At the beginning of the show, McCoy's comments after telling Spock that Norman is unusual. This footage contains a biting rebuff by Spock after McCoy says that Norman hasn't shown up for a

153

physical. Spock suggests that Norman may fear McCoy's "beads and rattles." (If I didn't know better I might think that Spock is irritated with McCoy's description of Norman's oddness.)

• Spock's arrival on the bridge, and Sulu's attempt to cut in an emergency manual monitor after Norman visits auxiliary control.

• Norman adjusting the warp drive controls and then leaving Engineering.

• After Kirk says "Harry Mudd" the second time, Mudd advising the captain that to be absolutely correct he should call him Mudd the First.

• After a commercial break, Mudd ranting about his rulership on this planet before calling in his lovelies.

• Mudd waves to his right to call in the lovelies on his other side.

• The editors sandwiched in a new commercial slot just after Mudd introduces Stella the first time. Due to a transitional fade and music, several seconds disappear on either side of the commercial.

• Kirk and Uhura impressed with the Barbara series, after which Kirk comments that he likes their "styling." (I've said it before, I'll say it again. Starfleet needs to let their captains fraternize with the crew. This poor guy needs some companionship.)

• Scott in the Engineering lab.

• McCoy's report to Kirk on the androids' physiological and psychological states of being.

• After Kirk comments that the androids don't think the humans can do anything to stop them, Mudd grouses at the captain and Spock. Then McCoy grouses back.

PLOT OVERSIGHTS

• First of all, how did Norman get *assigned* to the *Enterprise?* Yes, there are ways by which he could assume someone's identity and reprogram the records to align with his statistics, but the show never offers one clue on how Norman actually accomplished this.

• Throughout the episode, whenever the androids want to sidestep a question, they say, "I am not programmed to respond in that area." For instance, when asked by Kirk who sent him to commandeer the ship, Norman responds with this statement. Yet Norman knows who sent him. Therefore, Norman's statement is a lie. He has the knowledge and the ability to relate that knowledge to Kirk. To be truthful, Norman would have to say, "I am programmed *not* to respond in that area."

• During the course of the show, the crew discovers that Norman is the head android and directs the activities of the others. If Norman is the director, what did all the other androids do while he was off hijacking the *Enterprise?*

EQUIPMENT ODDITIES

• The entrance to Auxiliary Control is missing a doorplate. The red "No Admittance" sign holds a prominent place beside the double door, but the actual identification of the room is nowhere to be seen.

• Kirk uses the top button on the right arm of his chair for most of his communications in this episode. In other episodes he uses the lowest button, as does everyone else on the ship.

• Evidently Norman made several good adjustments to the warp drive system. In "Arena," Spock comments that a sustained warp seven would be dangerous, but in this episode the *Enterprise* flies at warp seven for four days.

• Just after Norman explains the origin of the androids, two of the Alice series invite Kirk and company to peruse the planet's facilities. They speak their last sentence in unison, except for one word. One of the Alices says, "You are free to *visit* them," while the other one says, "You are free to *use* them."

• Throughout the show, whenever female androids are present, the creators have them "make a leg." (A quick explanation in case you aren't familiar with the term. In Colonial times, men of sophistication wore knee-high leggings to show off their calf muscles. Standing around at parties, men would elevate one of their heels to tighten the calf and give it a better shape. Reportedly, women would swoon upon seeing shapely calf muscles. The less-endowed gentlemen could even buy "falsies." This raising of the heel was called "making a leg.") For some reason, Alice 2 and Alice 118 forget to do this when Kirk calls them into the main room to watch the performance by McCoy, Scott, Uhura,

and Chekov. The entire time they stand straight-legged. Then, after they become "completely inner-directed," the camera angle changes and both are instantly making a leg. Evidently their "Are we looking good, or what?" sensors work even when the androids are unconscious.

• After receiving too much irrational input, Alice 3 and Alice 11 conk out. Interestingly enough, the lights on their ID badges do not stay on as did those of all the other androids who conked out.

CONTINUITY AND PRODUCTION PROBLEMS

• The outfit that Harry Mudd's ex-wife wears is very similar to the one Martha Leighton wears in "The Conscience of the King."

• The planet that the *Enterprise* orbits at the end of the episode sure looks a lot like Alpha 177.

• One final item: I'm sure you know that the Alice series of androids in this show was actually played by identical twins. In a moment of cuteness, the creators listed one of the young ladies in the credits as "Alice #1-250" and the other as "Alice #251-500." All well and good, except that one scene near the end of the show has Alice 3 and Alice 11 standing side by side. (I know. Picky, picky, picky, picky.)

TRIVIA ANSWERS
1. Ensign Jordan.
2. Alice 99.

CLOSING STILLS

• *Enterprise* orbiting what looks like North America, "Miri"

• Harry Mudd, "I, Mudd"

• Engineering, "The Enemy Within" (This is the establishing shot just before the good Kirk and Spock walk into the scene.)

• Talosian beast illusion, "The Cage"

• Kirk and Spock fighting, "Amok Time"

• Balok puppet watching "The Way to Eden," "The Corbomite Maneuver"

★

METAMORPHOSIS

Star Date: 3219.8-3220.3

O n the shuttle *Galileo,* Kirk, Spock, and McCoy transport Assistant Federation Commissioner Nancy Hedford back to the *Enterprise.* She suffers from a rare and fatal disease. Suddenly an energy cloud appears, grabs the shuttle, and brings it down on a planetoid. They are surprised to discover that Zefram Cochrane, the inventor of warp drive, lives here. More than 150 years ago, he set out in a craft, intent on dying in space. As he passed by this planet, the energy cloud—a being Cochrane calls the Companion—drew him down. Somehow it restored his youth and has provided for him these many years. Watching Cochrane and the Companion together, Kirk soon guesses that the energy cloud cares for him.

Cochrane then explains the reason for the capture of the shuttle. He had told the Companion that he was about to die of loneliness. So the Companion brought him friends. Kirk tries to reason with the Companion, arguing that it can

Trivia Questions

1. What planet is at war and needing Hedford's mediation?

2. Where is the Companion's planet located?

never truly love Cochrane without being human. Moments later, a fully recovered Hedford appears. The Companion has merged with her, giving up immortality for a chance to experience true love. When Hedford states that everyone is free to go, Cochrane stays behind. He wants to grow old with this one who sacrificed so much for him.

GREAT MOMENTS

T here's a lovely moment at the end of the episode after the Companion has joined with Hedford. Resting against a tree, Companion/ Hedford listens to Cochrane speak as she watches him through her upraised scarf. The sheer fabric of the scarf approximates the patterns that the Companion displayed as an energy cloud. For a moment, Companion/Hedford views Cochrane again as she perceived him for the past 150 years.

SYNDICATION CUTS
• The center section of Cochrane's approach to the shuttle.
• After Cochrane offers a hot bath, Hedford snaps that it was

perceptive of him to notice that she needed one. Kirk then grills Cochrane for more information.

• Shortly after arriving at Cochrane's house, McCoy's examination of Hedford, her grousing at him, McCoy informing Kirk that they have only hours to save her, and Kirk continuing to question Cochrane. This edit and the previous one significantly soften Hedford's overall tone in this episode. She still snaps a lot until the Companion joins with her, but the remaining incidents can be chalked up to frustration or fever.

• Kirk, McCoy, and Cochrane walk out of Cochrane's quarters, and Cochrane explains how he calls the Companion.

• After a commercial break, McCoy yells and pleads for the Companion to stop its attack on Kirk and Spock. The syndicated version rejoins the uncut version with Cochrane scrambling to his feet. Interestingly enough, the audio is blank on my syndicated version when Cochrane stands back on his feet. At first I thought this was simply a transmission or recording error, but the uncut version has McCoy continuing to shout until Cochrane stands, takes a breath, and closes his eyes. I'm wondering if the editors muted the audio to cover McCoy's voice, since they cut his footage.

• Ship's log, star date 3219.8. An establishing flyby of the *Enterprise*, Scott recapping events so far, and scanners following the shuttle trail and then losing it. This

section of film had three major nits in it! First, the flyby of the *Enterprise* uses the "bad starboard nacelle" footage I've referred to before. Second, when Scott uses the communications panel on the captain's chair, the indicator light shows that he is using it backward! At the end of the log entry, Scott presses the lowest button on the right arm of the chair. Look closely and you'll see the oval light next to the speaker turn *on*. Then Scott hits the button again to talk with the officers running the scanners. Again, when he hits the button to stop communicating, the indicator lights up. Third, while looking for the shuttle, Sulu comments that a certain area of space shows no antimatter residue. Do the engines of a shuttle actually spit antimatter into space? If they did, wouldn't the scant matter that exists in any section of the universe quickly combine with the antimatter in lots of tiny explosions?

• After a commercial break, Kirk and company walk back inside after attempting their first dialogue with the Companion before Cochrane joins them.

PLOT OVERSIGHTS

• In the tender moment just after the Companion and Hedford join, Cochrane looks at Kirk for permission to go for a walk. Kirk nods and says, "Go ahead, Gawgrun." Gawgrun? Who is Gawgrun? The man's name is Zefram Cochrane, and Kirk has called him "Cochrane" for the entire episode. It sounds like our beloved captain's mouth was temporarily stuck on the consonant "g."

• Cochrane wants to stay on the planet with Companion/Hedford but tells Kirk not to mention his existence. Kirk agrees to keep it secret. What about Hedford? She is an assistant Federation commissioner. Will McCoy fill out a bogus death certificate to keep inquiring minds away?

EQUIPMENT ODDITIES

• The top of the universal translator that Kirk uses to communicate with the Companion looks very much like the translator/recording/fire-starting device the Metrons gave Kirk in "Arena."

• After joining with Hedford, the Companion states that the shuttle will operate as before. As I recall, the initial problem with the shuttle was the energy dampening field, but after the Companion attacked Spock, it short-circuited all the electronics on the back side of the shuttle. Did the Companion instantly repair these as well?

CONTINUITY AND PRODUCTION PROBLEMS

• After Kirk speaks to the Companion about love, a wide shot shows Cochrane at some distance. Then a close-up shows Kirk. Next the scene cuts to Kirk, Spock, and McCoy. Very soon the camera pulls back to include Cochrane, who looks like he's been standing there for some time. The last we saw of him he was *way* over in the field. (Yes, there is time for him to run over to Kirk and company and assume a nonchalant standing position. It just looks funny.)

TRIVIA ANSWERS

1. Epsilon Canaris III.
2. In the Gamma Canaris region.

CLOSING STILLS

• *Enterprise* orbiting what looks like North America, "Miri"

• Korob and Sylvia in their natural state, "Catspaw"

• Kirk, McCoy, and Bones, "Catspaw"

• Kirk, Spock, and McCoy at the *Koon-ut-kal-if-fee* ceremonial grounds, "Amok Time"

• Sylvia, cat/woman, "Catspaw"

• Balok puppet, "The Corbomite Maneuver"

JOURNEY TO BABEL

Star Dates: 3842.3-3843.4

The *Enterprise* ferries one hundred Federation delegates—including Sarek, Spock's father—to a conference on the admission of Coridan, a planet with rich dilithium deposits. Disturbingly, sensors detect a small vessel following at extreme range. Then a delegate turns up dead, and suspicion falls on Sarek. The method of execution appears to be Vulcan. However, subsequent medical examination shows that Sarek is suffering from a coronary condition and probably was incapacitated when the attack occurred. Next, the assassin targets Kirk. With the captain severely wounded, Spock assumes command and throws the assassin in the brig.

When Sarek's condition worsens, McCoy decides to operate. Unfortunately, Spock refuses to relinquish command, given the current crisis. A short time later, Kirk strides onto the bridge and tells Spock to report to sick bay. The captain intends to return to his quarters as soon as he gets Spock off the bridge. Before Kirk can leave, the alien vessel attacks. It is faster and more maneuverable than the *Enterprise,* but Kirk finally defeats it by playing dead. McCoy succeeds as well and saves Sarek's life. Investigations later prove that the assassin and craft were Orion. Evidently they wished to start an interplanetary war so they could continue their illegal dilithium mining operations on Coridan.

Trivia Questions

1. How many ambassadors are on board the Enterprise?

2. What is Sarek's blood type?

RUMINATIONS

It may be just my imagination, but Spock seems suddenly harder and more Vulcan in this episode. If Leonard Nimoy did this intentionally, it was a very nice touch indeed. His father is on board. Of course he would alter his behavior, perhaps secretly looking for the approval that his father has withheld for so many years.

SYNDICATION CUTS

• Kirk, Spock, and McCoy walk down a hall, and the first part of the shuttle recovery sequence.

• The *Galileo* turns in the shuttle bay, and a few more moments of the guards primping before the hangar doors open. The edit removes the usage of shuttle bay footage from "The *Galileo* Seven."

• Most of Spock's initial report on the alien vessel, and Uhura's attempts to contact it.

• The alien vessel's first flyby. Spock's line about the vessel traveling at warp ten actually comes after the craft passes them.

• A shot of the Tellarite sitting at the table before Sarek enters the reception room.

• After a commercial break, Kirk asking how the Tellarite was killed.

• Reminding Kirk that worry is a human emotion, Spock sits and takes extra readings on the alien vessel. Turning to face his captain, he then rattles off the types of ships that it is not. At this point, Uhura calls for Kirk, telling him of the signals she is receiving. This edit creates an odd sequence for Spock. He sits and turns to study his instruments. Then the scene contains a reaction shot from Kirk and finally a wide shot showing Kirk on one side, Spock on the other, and Uhura in the middle, calling for the captain. In this last shot Spock is *facing* Kirk. There is time for him to whip around in his chair while the camera focuses on Kirk but no motivation for him to do so.

• After a commercial break, Chapel walks away from Sarek's bed before Kirk and Spock arrive in sick bay.

• Part of the discussion among McCoy, Spock, and Amanda concerning the experimental drug.

• Spock leaves sick bay, and the first part of the fight between Kirk and the assassin.

• After a commercial break, a log by Spock, star date 3843.4, recapping events so far, and McCoy's report on Kirk's condition. This edit does away with a nit. The assassin clearly stabs Kirk on his right side, but McCoy states that the captain has a puncture in his *left* lung.

• Just as Kirk awakens in sick bay, Chapel calls the doctor over.

• The start of Sarek's operation. This edit also takes care of a nit. When McCoy starts the transfusion from Spock, the clear tubes leading from the machine to Sarek fill with green blood, but the tubes running from Spock to the machine are empty!

• After a commercial break, a section of the battle with the alien vessel, including Kirk preparing to fire the photon torpedoes.

• Several reaction shots from Sarek's operation.

• Chekov's report that number 4 shield has buckled, Kirk's instruction to switch to auxiliary power, and Chekov complying before indicating that the shields are firming up.

PLOT OVERSIGHTS

• The fight between Kirk and the assassin bears scrutiny. When have we ever seen deck 5 devoid of personnel? (Aside from "The Mark of Gideon," of course.) Yet conveniently, in this episode, no one is around to help Kirk battle off his attacker. Next, Kirk does his little move where he jumps up and then falls on the ground. To begin with, I have never understood the strategic benefit of this move. Why would you want to fall on the ground in the middle of a fight? In addition, this move has Kirk landing with his posterior dangerously close to the assassin's knife. This is not a good thing. The attacker could simply cock the knife upward and make Kirk walk funny for the rest of his life. Then—while struggling to recover from this little move—our dear captain turns his back to his attacker! Of course, the guy stabs him, after which Kirk throws the attacker over his shoulder. As the captain struggles to his feet, the assassin takes a few moments to *adjust his outfit* so that Kirk can recover. Finally he decides that Kirk is close enough and reaches for the knife with his left hand. Kirk kicks the guy, and suddenly the knife is in the assassin's *right* hand.

• When Uhura discovers that the assassin is receiving a transmission in the brig, Kirk hits his communications button and says, "Security to the brig." Shouldn't security be stationed at the brig already?

EQUIPMENT ODDITIES

• At the beginning of the episode, Kirk needs to adjust his dress uniform. He has to squat in front of the mirror so he can see. Does this make any sense at all? It's *his* mirror. Why doesn't he adjust it so he can see his face without hunkering down?

• McCoy appears to have a Tantalus field device installed in the wall of sick bay! This device, made infamous in "Mirror, Mirror," can focus on a person and disintegrate him or her. What would the good doctor be doing with such a device? (Is it cheaper than malpractice insurance?)

• At one point, Amanda comes to Spock's quarters to plead for her husband. She wants Spock to relinquish control of the *Enterprise* and provide blood for Sarek's operation. Spock refuses, and Amanda storms out. Appropriately, Spock's door opens and then closes behind her. Then Spock walks up to the door and it stays closed. Puzzled by this behavior, Spock reaches out to touch the door, hoping to discover—from the Vulcan mind meld—why the door is behaving in this manner. (Just joking! Spock does reach up and touch the door, and it still stays closed. How does it know to do this?)

• For some reason, the machine in sick bay that lays across Sarek's chest generates smoke from time to time. It almost looks like someone has a cigarette lit behind it.

• After the power fails during Sarek's operation, McCoy orders Chapel to fetch the "old portable stimulator." Chapel heads around Sarek's bed, walks a few feet to a nearby cart, and picks it up. It amazes me that this "old" device was so easy to find.

• Just before Kirk fires on the attacking ship for the last time, Chekov puts it at a range of 75,000 kilometers. After firing, it takes more than five seconds for the phasers to reach their target. Light travels approximately 300,000 kilometers per second. Therefore, phasers must travel much slower than the speed of light. Yet in this episode, Kirk tries to hit a vessel going at warp eight with phasers. This is impossible. Even if you fired at point-blank range, the vessel could move out of the way before the phaser energy would reach it. You could only hope that the captain of the other craft was stupid enough to fly through the beams! This brings up another issue: If phasers travel at less than the speed of light, you definitely do not want to fire them while the ship is traveling at warp. If you do, you'll run into your own phaser energy as soon as the beam exits the warp field surrounding the ship and drops into normal space.

CONTINUITY AND PRODUCTION PROBLEMS

• I usually don't say much about alien makeup simply because this show was created so many years ago. However, the pig-face masks on the Tellarites really do need help.

• When Sarek enters the reception room to take a pill, a Tellarite sits against the wall with a drink in his left hand. Then a close-up shows the drink in his right hand. Of course, when the scene returns to Sarek, the drink has jumped back into the Tellarite's left hand.

• Just after Amanda asks Spock not to give her the odds on finding enough Vulcan blood for Sarek's operation, the episode transitions to a flyby of the *Enterprise*. If you look closely at the front of the saucer section you can see stars shining through.

TRIVIA ANSWERS

1. Thirty-two.
2. T negative.

CLOSING STILLS

• *Enterprise* orbiting what looks like North America, "Miri"

• Sarek and Amanda, "Journey to Babel"

• Roman television arena, "Bread and Circuses"

• Talosian beast illusion, "The Cage"

• Spock walking to shuttle, "The Immunity Syndrome"

• Mugato and Kirk, "A Private Little War"

• Balok puppet upon hearing from his agent that Paramount doesn't pay royalties to puppets, "The Corbomite Maneuver"

FRIDAY'S CHILD

Star Dates: 3497.2-3499.1

O n Capella IV, Kirk, Spock, and McCoy negotiate for Federation mining rights to a rare element. The local inhabitants are fierce warriors steeped in traditions. One misstep can mean instant death. To make matters worse, a Klingon named Kras is negotiating with the Capellans as well. Then a Capellan named Maab stages a coup and takes over the leadership. According to tradition, the old leader's wife must die. Unwilling to watch her slaughter, Kirk pulls Eleen out of the way at the last minute. This action angers the Capellans, and they place the officers and Eleen in a hut. Thankfully, the four manage to escape into the hills. Once there, McCoy delivers Eleen's baby.

Unable to accept that she should continue to live in violation of her traditions, Eleen soon turns herself over to Maab. She claims the child is dead and that she has killed the Earthmen. Wanting proof, Kras pulls out a weapon and demands that Maab verify her story. After assessing the situation, the new leader spares Eleen's life. He then sacrifices his own so his tribe can kill the dishonorable Klingon. By succession, the child becomes the new leader of the Capellans, with Eleen as his regent. She quickly concludes the negotiations, awarding the mining rights to the Federation.

Trivia Questions

1. From what two ships does the *Enterprise* receive distress calls?

2. What type of tablet does Kirk use to light up the cave?

SYNDICATION CUTS

• A call from the bridge during McCoy's briefing at the beginning of the episode. This edit creates a problem. Just prior to the call, the officers in the briefing room watch footage of the Capellans on the central viewer. When the call comes, the central viewer switches to Sulu. Afterward it switches back to the Capellans. In the syndicated version, Sulu never calls, but his picture shows for an instant on the viewer!

• Reaction shots of McCoy and Spock as Kirk chews out the doctor after the ensign dies.

• Scott's decision not to inform Kirk about the other ship, and Kirk walking over to apologize to McCoy.

• Reaction shots all around after one Capellan says his people will not negotiate with the Federation.

• After Kirk, Spock, McCoy, and Eleen escape, Kras paces beside the new Capellan leader.

• A section from the *Enterprise's* search for the freighter.

• Part of the Capellans' approach before Kirk and Spock cause the landslide. Moments later, several reaction shots.

• Coming back from the commercial break, dust rises from the landslide and Kras approaches the Capellan he kills.

• After Kirk goads McCoy into delivering Eleen's child, a fade transition to the captain crawling around the rocks.

• More Capellans walk up the hill before the scene changes to the *Enterprise* and Scott ponders the vessel's disappearance. This edit removes a production problem. At one point in this sequence, Scott stands beside the communications station and receives a report from Uhura. A close-up shows him considering the information. The background of the shot indicates that Scott stands well ahead of the captain's chair. In fact, the shot comes from footage several seconds later, after Scott has walked down to stand in front of the navigator's console.

• Eleen groans, and McCoy assures her.

• McCoy asks if Eleen wants his help the second time.

• After Eleen escapes, a fade transition to Kirk and Spock sitting up on the rocks.

• After a commercial break, Uhura hails the Klingon ship, and reaction shots all around.

• More Capellans walk.

PLOT OVERSIGHTS

• In the captain's first log, Kirk says that Capella IV has an abundance of a rare mineral vital to the life support systems of colonies. What is with this Federation, anyway? Why do they keep establishing colonies highly dependent on rare minerals? In "The Devil in the Dark" we discovered that many colonies need pergium to operate their reactors, and now we find out that they must have topaline for their life support systems.

• After the new leader takes over, he brings Eleen in for execution. Of course, Kirk hauls her out of the way. This makes Eleen furious, and she demands that Kirk die for touching her. The leader seems to agree that Kirk's actions warrant death. Then the scene changes to the *Enterprise*. When the action returns to the planet's surface, Kirk, Spock, McCoy, and Eleen are back in another tent. What happened to Kirk getting killed? The dialogue never mentions any stay of execution or even if Kirk is scheduled for execution.

CHANGED PREMISES

• Is the Organian Peace Treaty no longer in effect? (See "Errand of Mercy.") Why does McCoy say that the Klingons are their sworn enemies?

EQUIPMENT ODDITIES

• During the briefing at the beginning of the episode, McCoy describes a Capellan weapon that the warriors throw like a Frisbee. He shows them footage of a Capellan tossing this thing and cutting down a fair-size sapling. Close investigation reveals that the weapon completely misses the tree and bounces off a nearby bush! Somehow, the tree still manages to rip apart. (I suspect some trickery here. Perhaps the Capellans created the video to make themselves look more fierce than they really are. Good marketing can do that for you.)

• Deprived of their phasers, Kirk and Spock fashion primitive bows and arrows to fight the Capellans. I'm sorry, but I simply do not believe that these wobbly bows and crooked arrows could hit anything—let alone kill someone, as they do later in the show.

• The little viewer that pops out of Sulu's console when he calls battle stations doesn't rise very fast. Hopefully, enemy vessels will take this into account and attack *slowly.*

CONTINUITY AND PRODUCTION PROBLEMS

• During the battle for leadership, a Capellan fights with the current leader. The leader pulls back and stabs the man. When he does, the man's outfit completely changes. Most obviously, his white fake fur scarf is suddenly red.

• There's a really odd edit in the fight just after Kirk stops Eleen's execution. He hits a Capellan, and the man goes down. An instant later, the guy is shoving Kirk back with his foot.

• Eleen's baby seems to have rigor mortis. When McCoy hands the child to Spock, the Vulcan places one hand near the boy's lower back and the other near his feet. The bundle retains its shape. Anyone who has ever held a baby knows that if you don't support an infant's head, it will flop backward.

• Speaking of backward, the first time the *Enterprise* flies toward the viewer from right to left on the screen, the "NCC-1701" is mirrored (as if the creators edited the film backward).

• Supposedly Kirk shoots Kras in the leg with one of his crooked arrows, but when the camera switches to a wide shot, the arrow disappears.

TRIVIA ANSWERS
1. SS *Dierdre* and USS *Carolina*.
2. Magnesiteon-nitron.

CLOSING STILLS
• *Enterprise* orbiting what looks like North America, "Miri"

• Kirk, Korob, and Sylvia as the big cat, "Catspaw"

• The planet killer, "The Doomsday Machine"

• Kirk, Spock, and McCoy at the *Koon-ut-kal-if-fee* ceremonial grounds, "Amok Time"

• Gorn, "Arena"

• Spock and the Companion, "Metamorphosis"

• Balok puppet, having signed

up for acting classes, hoping that he can cash in on his popularity and make some money by

doing cameos, "The Corbomite Maneuver"

THE DEADLY YEARS

Star Dates: 3478.2-3479.4

A landing party beams down to the scientific station on Gamma Hydra IV. In one of the buildings, Chekov finds a dead man of extreme age. Caught off guard, Chekov bolts out the door, yelling for the captain. A quick inventory of the rest of the grounds proves that every scientist has died or will soon die of old age. Shortly after returning to the *Enterprise*, Kirk, Spock, McCoy, and Scott begin aging rapidly as well. Soon Spock determines that the aging is caused by an unusual type of radiation.

Unfortunately, none of the standard treatments work. Frustrated, Commodore George Stocker forces Spock to rule Kirk unfit for command. Then Stocker takes over and orders Sulu to set a course straight for Starbase 10, even if it does take the ship through the Neutral Zone. In no time, Romulans surround the ship and start pummeling it with their weapons. McCoy finally finds a cure, and a renewed Kirk quickly transmits a message to Starfleet.

He intends to blow up the ship. Of course, the Romulans fall back to escape the blast, and when they do, Kirk rockets to safety at warp eight.

RUMINATIONS

Of course, the plot idea of rapid aging was recycled into the Star Trek: The Next Generation *episode "Unnatural Selection."*

GREAT LINES

"*Maybe you'd like to relieve Dr. McCoy.*"— Kirk throwing a sarcastic remark at Spock after the Vulcan had held a competency hearing that resulted in Kirk's removal from the captaincy.

GREAT MOMENTS

Near the end of the competency hearing, Kirk continually refers to the planet below as Gamma Hydra II, when it is actually Gamma Hydra IV. The whole sequence is very well written and played superbly.

SYNDICATION CUTS

• The entire scene in the hallway between Kirk and former love inter-

---

Trivia Questions

1. The two remaining scientists on Gamma Hydra IV believe that the landing party has come to pay their respects to whom?

2. What is the name of the yeoman who brings Kirk the fuel consumption report?

---

est/visiting scientist Dr. Janet Wallace after Kirk orders another physical for Chekov. This sequence lasts almost two minutes, twenty seconds and contains its share of nits. For instance, why are they standing in a hall and discussing their personal relationship? If the captain is concerned with his reputation on the ship, wouldn't he usher her into a briefing room for this exchange? Also, a female yeoman disappears after approaching Wallace. She walks up and starts to go between the doctor and the wall. The scene cuts to a close-up of Wallace, and the yeoman never walks behind her. Finally, a male lieutenant comes striding down the hall and realizes at the last moment that he is about to run into the pair. The astute lieutenant executes a near ninety-degree turn and disappears from view.

• Stocker praises Kirk before asking Spock to convene a competency hearing.

• Kirk grouses at the beginning of the hearing, Stocker tries to take the responsibility for it, and Spock offers Kirk a chance to make an opening statement.

• Following a commercial break, Spock walks back to his chair after questioning McCoy.

• Lots of reaction shots just before Kirk makes a final comment and walks out of the hearing.

PLOT OVERSIGHTS

• Kirk orders Sulu to raise the orbit to 20,000 *miles* perigee, but

at the end of the show Kirk talks about the destruction in a diameter of 200,000 *kilometers*. Wouldn't it be confusing to switch continually between the imperial and the metric measuring systems?

• At the beginning of the hearing, Spock tells Kirk that he has a right to cross-examine the witnesses. Yet after questioning a blonde yeoman, Spock dismisses her, and she never reappears at the hearing.

• I realize that Stocker had to be in charge to make the bonehead decision to run the *Enterprise* into the Neutral Zone, but shouldn't Spock fight harder to see that Sulu assumes command? The navigator has command *and* combat experience ("Arena").

• And speaking of Stocker, if this guy is such a stickler for regulations—which the episode tends to assert—why would he violate the very important regulation "Stay out of the Neutral Zone"?

• After deciding that adrenaline must provide a cure, McCoy wants to admonish Spock and Wallace to get moving on a cure. He says, "Well, don't just stand there jawin', Spawnck." Spawnck?

• Do I need to say anything about the way the cure miraculously restores hair color and smooths everyone's skin?

EQUIPMENT ODDITIES

• During one scene, Kirk calls Spock from his quarters. He uses the viewscreen, and a picture of Spock on the bridge appears.

During the whole conversation, Kirk stands facing the screen with his shirt off. My question is this: What is Spock seeing the entire time? Kirk's belly button? Just where is the camera for these viewscreens?

• Kirk still hasn't gotten anyone to adjust the height on his mirror. He still has to hunch over to see himself.

CONTINUITY AND PRODUCTION PROBLEMS

• All the visuals for the battle with the Romulans come from other episodes. The footage of the Romulan ships comes from "Balance of Terror." The footage of photon torpedoes striking the Enterprise comes from "Errand of Mercy." Oddly enough, the Romulans fire their plasma weapon, but when the missiles reach the Enterprise, they have mutated into photon torpedoes! (The real problem here is that the plasma weapon in "Balance of Terror" was very powerful. The crew of the Enterprise desperately worried about even one hit from the device in that episode. Yet in "The Deadly Years," the Enterprise takes multiple hits and survives.)

• Evidently the Enterprise still hasn't solved its insect problem.

Near the end of the episode, Kirk, Spock, and McCoy recall the events on the planet's surface. Just after Kirk says "We were together all the time," a bug flies up the left side of the screen!

• The preview on my uncut video features "The Changeling." This isn't correct in either production order or air date order.

TRIVIA ANSWERS

1. Alvin.
2. Atkins.

CLOSING STILLS

• Enterprise orbiting what looks like North America, "Miri"

• Kirk and tribbles, "The Trouble with Tribbles"

• Jail set, "Bread and Circuses" (It is never seen completely empty in the episode.)

• Tellarite sitting in front of a red curtain. (This shot doesn't appear in any show.)

• Kirk and Spock wounding the Horta, "The Devil in the Dark"

• Lithium cracking station on Delta Vega, "Where No Man Has Gone Before" (I expect that the creators spliced it in backward to spice things up a bit.)

• Balok puppet practicing his smug look, "The Corbomite Maneuver"

OBSESSION

Star Dates: 3619.2-3620.7

When a gaseous creature kills three members of a landing party to Argus X by draining all the red blood cells from their bodies, Kirk becomes obsessed with hunting it down. He suspends the *Enterprise*'s scheduled transport of desperately needed drugs, and trains all the scanners on the planet below. As justification, the captain states that the creature poses a far greater threat to the Federation. He claims that the same creature attacked the crew of the USS *Farragut* eleven years ago. Record tapes show that something killed two hundred crew members, but the incident occurred on a planet thousands of light-years away. Kirk's suspicions prove true when the creature leaves Argus X and defies expectation by setting course at high warp for that planet. Kirk tries to kill it by using the ship's weapons but phasers and even photon torpedoes prove ineffective.

Then Spock comes to the worst conclusion: His observations show that the creature is preparing to spawn. Kirk orders Engineering to drain a small amount of antimatter from the ship's engines and place it in a magnetic container. Beaming down with Ensign Garrovick, Kirk waits for the creature to approach. At the last moment, they beam up and detonate the antimatter, thereby killing the creature.

Trivia Questions

1. With what ship is the *Enterprise* scheduled to rendezvous?

2. Where did Kirk first encounter the creature?

GREAT MOMENTS

Mark S. Painter, Sr., wrote me the following comments on this episode: "There is a wonderful scene in which McCoy and Spock confront Kirk concerning his bizarre, puzzling orders. In a dignified, respectful, but unapologetic manner, they quote regulations to him and note that he has given unusual orders. They politely request a fuller explanation. The implication, unspoken, but very much made, is that McCoy and Spock together have the power to relieve Kirk, and they are prepared to use it if he can't come up with a good explanation for his actions. It is all very military, very proper. I love that scene."

SYNDICATION CUTS

• Following a commercial, captain's log, star date 3619.6, recapping events so far and the initial questioning of Garrovick by Kirk. This edit covers a problem. When describing the size of the creature, Garrovick says, "ten to sixty cubic *meters*." A few moments later, he gives a distance of "twenty *yards*."

• Kirk asks if there are any more questions before he relieves Garrovick of duty.

• Garrovick enters his quarters before Kirk returns to the bridge.

• Just after McCoy arrives in his quarters, Kirk rises from his bed, checks with Chekov, talks with McCoy for a time, and then returns to his bed before the uncut and syndicated version sync back together.

• After a commercial break, the *Enterprise* chases the creature at warp eight, and Scott worries.

• Reaction shots all around before Kirk orders deceleration to warp six.

• A pan across Garrovick's quarters and the door buzzer before the door pops open and Chapel strides into the room. This creates a small problem in the syndicated version. It looks like Chapel just walks right into Garrovick's quarters, tossing aside his privacy because she brings him food.

• Chapel gives Garrovick a recap of current events.

PLOT OVERSIGHTS

• At one point this gaseous creature supposedly comes into the *Enterprise* through an impulse engine vent and attacks two crewmen before fleeing into the ventilation system. Wait a minute: The ship is out in the vacuum of space. There can be no direct path for any gas to travel between the interior of the ship and the exterior of the ship. If there was, all the air would rush *out!* Yet the dialogue makes it sound as if the only way the creature could get in was through that vent. Obviously, if the creature is inside the ship, it must be able to pass through the bulkhead, because anything else would mean the *Enterprise* couldn't contain its atmosphere.

• For a moment, Spock seems to forget the basic properties of a gas. As the creature invades Garrovick's quarters through a ventilation grille, the Vulcan puts his hands over the opening. Of course, the creature simply flows around them. (My daughter caught this at once.)

CHANGED PREMISES

• McCoy refers to Kirk as "Lieutenant" during his time on the USS *Farragut*. Kirk says that he served with Captain Garrovick (Ensign Garrovick's father) from the day he left Starfleet Academy. Yet in "Court-Martial," Kirk says that—as an ensign—he discovered a mistake made by Finney while serving on the USS *Republic*. If Kirk left the Academy and rose to the rank of lieutenant under Captain Garrovick, there are a limited number of ways to explain how he could be an ensign on the *Republic*. Did Garrovick switch from the *Republic* to the *Farragut* and take the young Ensign Kirk with him? Or did Kirk get busted back down to ensign after he left the *Farragut*? Or do midshipmen at the Academy somehow achieve a rank of ensign and spend their summers in space? (While this last explanation seems reasonable, Starfleet is built on the Navy model with respect to rank. It is my understanding that the rank of ensign isn't assigned until after you graduate from the Academy. Maybe Roddenberry decided to change this. Then again, maybe the creators just forgot what they said about Kirk in "Court-Martial"!)

EQUIPMENT ODDITIES

• The small tower that Scott admired in "I, Mudd," has made it aboard the *Enterprise* and resides in sick bay! On the android planet, the chief engineer walked around it and was amazed at its construction. Of course, that part of the episode was edited out for syndication. Does that mean that it never happened?

• Kirk can't decide which of the buttons on his chair opens a communications channel during this episode. He uses both the top and the bottom buttons on the right arm panel.

• Kirk also has a little trouble getting his communicator open as the creature approaches at the end of the episode. Granted, it is a high-stress situation, but it does look funny.

• This transporter is quite a device. Kirk starts the trip talking into his communicator but ends it with his arms lowered and his communicator put away.

• After beaming Kirk aboard, Spock opens a communications channel to the bridge so the captain can issue some orders. Oddly enough, the little light on the speaker mounted to the top of the transporter console stays off.

CONTINUITY AND PRODUCTION PROBLEMS

• Argus X sure looks like Alpha 177 ("The Enemy Within").

TRIVIA ANSWERS
1. USS *Yorktown*.
2. Tycho IV.

CLOSING STILLS

• *Enterprise* orbiting what looks like North America, "Miri"
• Apollo's temple, fired upon by the *Enterprise*, "Who Mourns for Adonais?"
• Tiger, "Shore Leave"
• *Nomad* scanning Uhura, "The Changeling"
• *Enterprise* orbiting Vulcan, "Amok Time"
• Balok puppet practicing his confident look, "The Corbomite Maneuver"

TRIATHLON TRIVIA ON INSULTS

MATCH THE INSULT TO THE PERSON WHO SAID IT TO THE EPISODE:

INSULT	PERSON	EPISODE
1. A traitor from a race of traitors	A. Korax about Kirk	a. "The Mark of Gideon"
2. Barbarian	B. Apollo about the crew	b. "Day of the Dove"
3. Bogus frat	C. Scott to Spock	c. "The Way to Eden"
4. Button-pushing brass head	D. Belle to Lokai	d. "This Side of Paradise"
5. Carcass full of memory banks	E. Anan 7 to Kirk	e. "Who Mourns for Adonais?"
6. Considerable interference	F Lokai about the crew	f. "Miri"
7. Denebian slime devil	G. McCoy about guard	g. "The Alternative Factor"
8. Elf with a hyperactive thyroid	H. McCoy to Spock	h. "Return to Tomorrow"
9. Fools	I. Van Gelder to Kirk	i. "The Trouble with Tribbles"
10. Fuzz-faced goons	J. Miri about Kirk	j. "I, Mudd"
11. Green-blooded halfbreed freak	K. Kirk to Spock	k. "Let That Be Your Last Battlefield"
12. Hard lip, Herbert	L. Adam about Kirk	l. "The Changeling"
13. Insane, filthy little plotter of ruin	M. Scott about Klingons	m. "A Taste of Armageddon"
14. Jelly in the belly	N. Tongo Rad to Kirk	n. "Dagger of the Mind"
15. Mechanical beastie	O. Korax about *Enterprise*	o. "Bread and Circuses"
16. Monocolor trash	P. Thalassa to McCoy	p. "Arena"
17. Mr. Lovie Dovie	Q. Mudd to Spock	q. "Where No Man Has Gone Before"
18. Muscleman	R. Scott to Mudd	r. "All Our Yesterdays"
19. Mutinous, disloyal halfbreed	S. Hodin about McCoy	s. *Star Trek III: The Search for Spock*
20. Overgrown jackrabbit	T. Scott about *Nomad*	t. "Whom Gods Destroy"
21. Pointed-ear hobgoblin	U. Kirk to Scott	
22. Pointy-eared thinking machine	V. Spock to McCoy	
23. Prancing, savage medicine man	W. Security guard to Sulu	
24. Sagging old rust bucket	X. Garth to Marta	

25. Sensualist
26. Simpering, devil-eared freak
27. Stiff-necked thistlehead
28. Stubborn, thickheaded Vulcan
29. Stupid cow
30. Swaggering, tin-plated dictator
31. Tiny
32. Unprincipled, evil-minded gulak
33. Useless pieces of bland flesh
34. Very excitable repairman
35. Vicious subverter of every decent thought
36. Walking freezer unit

Y. Mitchell about Dehner
Z. Chekov about Mudd
AA. Hodin about Scott

SCORING

(BASED ON THE NUMBER OF CORRECT ANSWERS)

0–5	Normal
6–10	Impressive
11 and up	You really love insults, don't you?

INSULT ANSWER KEY: 1. K d 2. E m 3. R j 4. I n 5. K d 6. S a 7. A i 8. K d 9. B e 10. M b 11. C b 12. N c 13. D k 14. L c 15. T l 16. F k 17. J f 18. G g 19. K d 20. K d 21. H o 22. Q j 23. P h 24. O i 25. V p 26. K d 27. U e 28. H r 29. X t 30. A i 31. W s 32. Z j 33. F k 34. AA a 35. D k 36. Y q

WOLF IN THE FOLD

Star Dates: 3614.9–3615.4

When Kirk and McCoy find Scott near the body of a murdered dancer on Argelius II, Chief City Administrator Hengist is satisfied with the chief engineer's guilt. Thankfully, Jarvis, an official on Argelius, wishes to probe further. During a ceremony, Sybo—his empathic wife—senses an evil thing filled with hatred for women. Darkness falls over the room, and she screams. When the light returns, Scott lets the dead woman slump to the floor.

The group beams up to the *Enterprise* to use its truth-verifying computer. It quickly shows that Scott did not kill Sybo. Using her last words and the library computer, Kirk and Spock piece together the truth. The murderer is actually an energy-based life entity that feeds on emotion, particularly fear. They trace its path from the murders of Jack the Ripper to a series of killings on Rigel IV only a year ago. It is called Redjac, and—knowing that Hengist came from Rigel IV—Kirk accuses the administrator. Hengist tries to

fight his way out, but Kirk knocks him to the floor. Suddenly Redjac flees to the ship's computer. While Spock regains control of the system, McCoy sedates the crew to keep them from fear. Redjac then becomes Hengist once again, but Kirk is prepared. McCoy sedates the mass murderer, and Spock uses the transporter to disperse his energy packets in space.

SYNDICATION CUTS

- More of the dancer wiggling near the show's beginning.
- Kirk and McCoy walking out of the pleasure pit.
- After a commercial break, Jarvis brings a stimulant for Scott, and the chief engineer awakens to the realization that the psychotricorder yeoman is dead as well.
- Jarvis wonders how any man could do such monstrous things after his wife dies.
- Following a commercial break, captain's log, star date 3615.4.
- Janus attests to his wife's abilities at the hearing on the *Enterprise*.
- After Redjac flees to the com-

Trivia Questions

1. What is the name of the cloud creature of Alpha Majoras I?

2. Who manufactured the murder weapon?

puter, Kirk and Spock ride the turbolift to the bridge. At the start of the journey, Redjac almost slams the door on Spock.

• Part of the scene on the bridge just after Kirk and Spock arrive to restore life support and prepare the crew to switch over to manual control.

• A section with Kirk on the bridge listening to Redjac's maniacal laughing and taunting.

• A transition fade from the bridge back to the briefing room.

PLOT OVERSIGHTS

• I'm not sure that Scott has a complete understanding of this "walk in the fog with a bonnie lass" thing. When recounting the experiences that led to the murder of the dancer, he tells Kirk that he was "up ahead, trying to lead the way." Isn't the whole point of this exercise to walk side by side and enjoy each other's company?

• After pronouncing Hengist dead, McCoy asks Scott to help him put the guy in a chair. Does this seem odd? The guy's dead! Chances are he will eventually flop out of the chair and onto the floor. Why not just leave him there?

EQUIPMENT ODDITIES

• The dancer at the beginning of the show never strikes her finger cymbals together. Are they just for show?

• During the hearing on the *Enterprise,* Kirk uses a truth-verifying computer. Before each person testifies, he or she places a small card in a slot on the front of the computer. The card sticks out of the top of the slot and is easily visible—in the wide shots, that is. In every close-up of the computer, the slot is empty.

• Before Sybo's empathic session, Kirk orders a scan of Scott's memory with a psychotricorder. This will supposedly record all his thoughts and actions for the past twenty-four hours. Of course, Redjac kills the woman who beams down to perform the scan. Then Kirk takes everyone up to the *Enterprise* and starts the hearing. At one point the captain states that after the hearing, the crew will do the scan. Wouldn't this be evidence? Isn't it normal practice to gather the evidence first and then hold the hearing? It can't take that long to do one of these things, because Kirk wanted to get it done while Sybo prepared for the ceremony. Also, why haven't we seen this device used in other episodes, such as "Court-Martial"?

CONTINUITY AND PRODUCTION PROBLEMS

• Evidently the musicians on Argelius II studied on Orion. The music they play is the same piece the instrumentalists played to accompany the dancing of everyone's favorite green Orion lust chicken . . . Vina! (See "The Cage." Oh, one other thing: I hereby apologize to IOWA for my insensitive remarks concerning one of their members. See the closing stills of the first season for more details.)

• At least we know what happened to Landru. You may recall that several millennia ago, he brought peace to Beta III and then left a sophisticated computer system in charge. Strange as it may seem, he eventually migrated to Argelius II and is living under the name of Jarvis. Surprisingly, Kirk doesn't seem to recognize him.

• At one point, Jarvis pours Kirk a drink. The captain receives the glass by grasping it from the bottom. The shot changes, and suddenly Kirk is holding it on the side.

• During Scott's testimony, a close-up of his right hand shows four perfectly formed fingers and a thumb. The creators continue their deception of the true nature of James Doohan's hand, obviously believing that if they show someone missing a finger, reality as we know it will screech to a halt.

TRIVIA ANSWERS
1. Mellitus.
2. The hill people of the Argus River region on Rigel IV.

CLOSING STILLS
• *Enterprise* orbiting what looks like North America, "Miri"
• Vaal, "The Apple"
• Kirk and *Nomad*, "The Changeling"
• Kirk, McCoy, and Bones, "Catspaw"
• Kirk, Spock, and McCoy at the *Koon-ut-kal-if-fee* ceremonial grounds, "Amok Time"
• Flower after firing its poison darts, "The Apple"
• Balok puppet practicing his angry look, "The Corbomite Maneuver"

THE TROUBLE WITH TRIBBLES

Star Dates: 4523.3-4525.6

After rushing to respond to a priority 1 distress call from Deep Space Station K-7, Kirk finds only a bureaucrat named Nilz Baris; his assistant, Arne Darvin; and tons of a hybrid grain called quadrotriticale. Baris informs Kirk that the grain is bound for Sherman's Planet and orders him to guard it carefully. Both the Federation and the Klingons lay claim to Sherman's Planet. Under the terms of the Organian Peace Treaty, the side that proves most efficient in developing this new world will gain possession of it. Angered by Baris's misuse of the priority 1 channel, Kirk begrudgingly posts only two guards around the grain bin and orders shore leave for off-duty personnel. When Uhura comes to the station to shop, she meets Cyrano Jones, a roving entrepreneur who gives her his latest find, a "tribble." Uhura takes the tribble back to the ship and soon finds that they breed very rapidly. In no time, the tribble population grows to disquieting proportions.

Trivia Questions

1. Where does the root grain for quadrotriticale originate?

2. According to Chekov, who invented scotch?

After discovering tribbles in the ship's food processors, Kirk races to the grain bins. As he guessed, the bins are filled with tribbles as well. While Baris rants, Spock notes that many of the tribbles are dead. McCoy later confirms that the grain is poisoned, and Kirk discovers that Darvin is a Klingon spy.

GREAT LINES

"*Before they went into warp I transported the whole kit and caboodle into their engine room, where they'll be no tribble at all.*"—Scott telling the captain how he disposed of the tribbles aboard the *Enterprise* by transporting them to a nearby Klingon ship.

GREAT MOMENTS

Many have nominated the avalanche of tribbles out of the storage bins as a great moment, and especially the rest of the scene, as Kirk is continuously pelted by descending tribbles. I personally like the little squeaks that the tribbles make as they land.

SYNDICATION CUTS

• A reaction shot of Spock after

finding K-7 peaceful.

• Kirk gripes to Spock in the bar about guarding grain before Uhura and Chekov enter.

• Jones offers the barkeep a vial of glow water.

• Jones compliments Uhura.

• Jones and the barkeep bargain over four credits a head for the tribbles.

• After sealing the deal, the barkeep asks when he can have the tribbles. In the syndicated version, this audio occurs under a close-up of a tribble eating the grain. Then the scene proceeds to Chekov noticing and commenting on this fact. Listen to the background music and you'll definitely hear the edit. In the uncut version, the barkeep asks when he can have the tribbles, Uhura asks the barkeep what he will be selling the tribbles for, the barkeep starts figuring his markup, and then Chekov notices the tribble eating the grain.

• Kirk walking out of sick bay, a fade transition to the captain encouraging the men in the transporter room to stay out of trouble as they visit the station, an establishing shot of K-7, and finally Scott and Chekov walking into the bar, followed a few moments later by Jones.

• The barkeep puts away his tribbles as the fight breaks out, and he hurries off to get security.

• After a commercial break, captain's log, star date 4525.6.

• The captain asks Ensign Freeman who started the fight.

• The close-up of McCoy's tribble

container before the shot pulls back and the discussion begins between Spock and the doctor in sick bay.

PLOT OVERSIGHTS

• To add to Kirk's troubles, a Klingon vessel shows up at K-7, demanding visitation rights. Kirk grants them, but only twelve at a time. The captain also beams twelve security guards onto the station to look after the visiting Klingons. Why, then, are there no security guards to be seen when the fight breaks out in the bar? Isn't this one of the main reasons the security guards are on the station, to guard the Klingons?

• After the fight, Kirk has a whole line of men he disciplines. Oddly enough, there were only a few men involved in the fight, and certainly no one with a blue shirt. Yet two of the men in the lineup have blue shirts. Was there another fight somewhere on the station at the same time?

• Cyrano Jones is definitely not a good entrepreneur. He doesn't know a bad product when he sees one. Every good businessperson knows that repeat sales are a healthy part of the game. There's no such thing as a repeat sale with a tribble. In fact, one tribble can instantly set up anyone as a supplier! That means Jones is going to all the expense of flying to a station to make only one sale. It's simply not cost-effective.

• When Kirk checks on the grain he stands directly under the opening to the bin and fiddles with the overhead door. This is not a good idea. What if the bin had still been filled with grain? Getting tons of grain dropped on your head will not improve your day in the least.

• After the fight, Kirk confines Scott to his quarters. A short while later, he's back on the bridge. Kirk probably realized that making Scott sit in his quarters and read technical manuals wasn't much of a punishment.

EQUIPMENT ODDITIES

• Evidently the Federation has visited so many alien worlds equipped with the trapezoid-shaped doors that they have decided to install them on their space stations! These doors first showed up in "What Are Little Girls Made Of?" They have made frequent appearances ever since.

CONTINUITY AND PRODUCTION PROBLEMS

• The creators continue to use the flyby of the *Enterprise* with the bad breakup on the starboard engine nacelle.

• Every shot of the *Enterprise* and K-7 shows the ship rotating around the station. Yet every shot of the inside of the station manager's office shows the *Enterprise* in a fixed position.

• Amazingly enough, that pesky little being Trelane—the one who irritated the crew of the *Enterprise* in "The Squire of Gothos"—has reincarnated himself as a Klingon! Trelane and the Klingon commander in this episode bear a striking resemblance.

• When Kirk comes to sick bay for headache pills, McCoy tells him about the results of his investigation of the tribbles. Turn up the volume on your TV when McCoy informs Kirk that the tribbles are geared for reproduction. You may hear a telephone ringing in the background.

TRIVIA ANSWERS
1. Canada.
2. A little old lady in Leningrad.

CLOSING STILLS
• *Enterprise* orbiting what looks like North America, "Miri"
• Gorn, "Arena"
• Starbase 11, "Court-Martial"
• Flower after firing its poison darts, "The Apple"
• Kirk, Korob, and Sylvia as the big cat, "Catspaw"
• *Galileo* departing shuttle bay, "The *Galileo* Seven"
• Balok puppet practicing his happy look, "The Corbomite Maneuver"

THE GAMESTERS OF TRISKELION

Star Dates: 3211.7-3259.2

When Kirk, Uhura, and Chekov vanish from the transporter pad, the crew institutes a full-scale search of the surrounding area. Finding nothing, Spock decides to follow a faint ion trail to its source. Meanwhile, the missing trio reappears in a large open area. A being named Galt explains that they are now "thralls." They will be trained to fight other thralls for the amusement of the Providers—pure mental beings composed only of brains. To enforce the wishes of the Providers, Galt fits each of the trio with a collar. At the first opportunity, they attempt an escape, but Galt's eyes light up and they drop to the floor in pain.

Shortly after the *Enterprise* arrives, the Providers conclude that Kirk and the others must be destroyed. The captain makes a desperate wager. He agrees to fight three of the thralls to the death. If he wins, he and the *Enterprise* will go free. If he loses, he will beam the crew down to the planet and they will spend the rest

Trivia Questions

1. Why does the *Enterprise* come to Gamma II?

2. What is the name of Chekov's drill thrall?

of their lives amusing the Providers. Of course, Kirk dies a horrible death and the show goes off the air (just joking!). As always, Kirk comes out victorious.

SYNDICATION CUTS

• After Galt announces that Kirk, Uhura, and Chekov will spend the rest of their lives on Triskelion, an establishing shot of the *Enterprise* and the entire sequence featuring Spock and the crew trying to determine what has happened to the officers.

• Uhura's first visit by Lars is shortened.

• After a commercial break, the captain's supplemental log.

• A discussion among Spock, McCoy, and Scott following Galt's assertion that any further disobedience will be punished by death.

• Following a commercial break, Kirk pleads with the Providers for leniency toward Shahna.

• Shahna gets to her feet and returns to the barracks with Kirk.

• After Kirk goads the Providers by saying they haven't the courage to show themselves, a Provider states that humanity has great curiosity. Kirk then reiterates that the Providers are afraid. This edit has Kirk speaking a sentence that makes no sense in the syndicated version. He says, "But these Providers haven't the courage to show themselves, but you are afraid."

• Shahna and the other thralls gather in the center of the fighting area before Shahna starts crying.

PLOT OVERSIGHTS

• After the Providers transport the trio to Triskelion, Kirk makes a log entry, star date 3211.8. How is he making this entry? Where is it being recorded? How does he know the star date? True, they have just left the *Enterprise* but Kirk has no way of knowing if they have just traveled through space or have traveled through time as well. Kirk even admits a few moments later that they may be in a parallel universe.

• The Providers continually praise the trio for their strength and spirit, but Chekov consistently turns in a very poor showing. In the initial confrontation, a large male named Kloog picks up Chekov and immediately subdues him. Then, when the trio attempt their first escape, Chekov hits a woman and runs. The woman shows no indication that Chekov did anything other than tap her.

• In one scene Kirk takes Uhura's punishment. After Kloog whips him for a while, Galt announces a rest period. That's an interesting concept: a rest interval during punish-ment.

• The first time Kirk starts to kiss Shahna, she has an interesting reaction. She tips her head to the side, leans forward, closes her eyes, and drops her jaw. All this from a female who has never kissed before! She certainly learns quickly.

• More intermixing of the imperial and metric measuring systems. Kirk tells Shahna that they must have covered two miles in their run, but the Providers tell Kirk that they exist a thousand "of your meters" beneath the surface.

• In the final battle, the Providers assign Kirk to the sections of the floor colored yellow and his attack-ers to sections colored blue. Anyone landing on an opponent's color supposedly will lose a weapon. Yet Kirk steps all over the blue areas and nothing happens!

CHANGED PREMISES

• At one point Spock asks McCoy for a suggestion. The doctor grumpily replies that this is the first time the Vulcan has ever asked him for anything, and it has to be on an occasion like this. I realize that McCoy is simply spouting off, but his statement isn't correct. Spock asks McCoy's opinion in "Obsession."

EQUIPMENT ODDITIES

• For some reason, the knives used on Triskelion look exactly like the ones used by the crew on the imperial *Enterprise* in "Mirror, Mirror."

CONTINUITY AND PRODUCTION PROBLEMS

• When Chekov's drill thrall visits his quarters for the first time, watch the rockface above and behind the pair. A shadow dances across it that looks suspiciously like a microphone mounted on a boom.

• When the Providers bring Kirk to their location, the painting that Kirk identifies as their power plant also appears in "The Devil in the Dark."

TRIVIA ANSWERS

1. To check on an automated communications and aspergation station.
2. Tamoon.

CLOSING STILLS

• *Enterprise* orbiting what looks like North America, "Miri"

• Lawgivers leaving Hall of Audience, "The Return of the Archons" (This scene is never shown in the episode.)

• Empire TV, "Bread and Circuses"

• Spock playing chess with Rojan, "By Any Other Name"

• *Enterprise* in energy barrier, "Where No Man Has Gone Before"

• Balok puppet waiting for his agent to call, "The Corbomite Maneuver"

A PIECE OF THE ACTION

Star Date: 4598.0

The *Enterprise* drops into orbit around Sigma Iotia II. The last contact with the planet came one hundred years ago, by the USS *Horizon.* At that time, no law existed stipulating noninterference. The crew is here to learn if the contact with the *Horizon* caused any cultural contamination. After contacting a man named Oxmyx, Kirk beams down with Spock and McCoy. They materialize in a violent, ruthless setting. In fact, the Iotians have based their society on a book left behind by the crew of the *Horizon, Chicago Mobs of the Twenties.* Moments later, Oxmyx's boys escort the trio to his office. Oxmyx demands that the Federation supply his henchmen with weapons so he can take over the world. When Kirk refuses, Oxmyx takes them as hostages.

The trio quickly escapes, but even the sociological computer on the ship can find no logical way to decontaminate the society. Improvising, Kirk uses the transporter to beam all the bosses into the same room and announces that the "Feds" are taking over. Knowing that Sigma Iotia II will benefit from a unifying leader, Kirk puts Oxmyx in charge and states that a Federation ship will return every year to collect their cut. Back on the ship, the captain discloses that the money will be used to guide the Iotians to a more productive society.

PLOT OVERSIGHTS

• At one point, another boss, named Krako, "puts the bag" on Kirk. His boys are not very smart. They imprison Kirk in a room with a letter opener and a heavy typewriter, either of which would make a handy weapon.

• Just before Spock and McCoy beam down for the second time, one of Oxmyx's men says, "They can't do nothing until they're through sparkling." How does he know this? He wasn't around when Spock and McCoy beamed down the first time. In case you're wondering, the *Horizon* probably didn't have transporters. While speaking with Oxmyx at the beginning of the

Trivia Questions

1. Kirk claims the game of fizzbin comes from what planet?

2. What component is the basis for virtually every piece of Starfleet equipment?

episode, Kirk has trouble explaining the transporter. Since the *Horizon* wasn't bound by the principles of noninterference, they probably would have told the inhabitants about transporters if the ship had them.

• Continuing with the second beam-down, it is amazing that an officer of Spock's intellect would not beam two security guards to a nearby location just in case Oxmyx tried to take them hostage again.

• Arriving at Krako's headquarters, Kirk ponders how to get past the guard. He says they can't use their phasers—presumably because it would violate the Prime Directive. Is Kirk really worried about the Prime Directive? He is in the process of strong-arming an entire world and forcing them to pay protection money to the Federation, and he's worried about someone seeing a phaser in action?

• After hearing that the Federation is taking over, Krako says that he thought they had laws against interfering. Where would he get this idea? The *Horizon* visited the planet before such laws went into effect, and Kirk has not said anything about noninterference to the gangsters.

EQUIPMENT ODDITIES

• Meeting Kirk and the landing party for the first time, Oxmyx enjoys a game of pool. At one point he uses the solid blue ball for the cue ball!

• Just after Oxmyx captures

Spock and McCoy the second time, the first officer manages to make a log entry without any recording equipment and without moving his lips.

• After rescuing Spock and McCoy from Oxmyx, Kirk decides to "bag" Krako as well. He and Spock jump in a car, and Kirk comments that the key is in the ignition. Does this seem right? In a lawless society, the keys are in the ignition?

• After grabbing Krako, Kirk and Spock head back to Oxmyx's office. They trudge back out into the street and hop into a car—a mode of transportation that Kirk describes as "faster than walking." That may be . . . but is it faster than beaming?

• Soon afterward, the scene changes to Oxmyx's office. McCoy holds a machine gun on the group assembled there. Wouldn't it be better to cover them with a phaser? If someone tried to jump him, would the doctor really "fill them full of holes"?

CONTINUITY AND PRODUCTION PROBLEMS

• Appearing on the planet's surface for the first time, Kirk, Spock, and McCoy stroll over to a bench. Kirk reaches out and touches the bench. Then the close-up shows Kirk walking up to the bench again.

• Just after Kirk, Spock, and McCoy beam down to the planet's surface, a woman in a peach-colored dress and red hat walks through the scene. The trio looks around for a few minutes, wanders down the street, and soon are stopped by Oxmyx's men. At this point, the woman in the red hat magically reappears in the scene.

• When asking one of the bosses if he has any objections at the joint meeting, Kirk points the gun directly at the man. Then a close-up shows Kirk's face, and the gun cocked up at a 45 degree angle. Then the shot changes again and the gun is pointing at the man once again.

• Both *The Star Trek Compendium* and *The Star Trek Encyclopedia* list the head gangster's last name as "Oxmyx." However, a poster in Krako's office spells the gangster's name "Okmyx." (Oh, the tribulations of being a nitpicker. Which is correct? That which is seen? Or that which is printed? If I believe what I see on TV—and, of course, I *really*

do—then Bela's last name is "Okmyx." But, if I use that name, hordes of Trekkers will descend on me, claiming that the authorities say the gangster's name is spelled "Oxmyx." As you can see, I chickened out.)

TRIVIA ANSWERS
1. Beta Antares IV.
2. The transtator.

CLOSING STILLS
• *Enterprise* orbiting what looks like North America, "Miri"
• Antimatter Lazarus's ship, "The Alternative Factor"
• Kirk, Spock, and McCoy as Nazis, "Patterns of Force"
• Hand holding phaser, "The Omega Glory"
• Fortress on Rigel VII (*sans* Pike), "The Cage"
• Balok puppet, "The Corbomite Maneuver"

THE IMMUNITY SYNDROME

Star Dates: 4307.1-4309.4

While investigating the disappearance of the USS *Intrepid* and all life from the Gamma 7A star system, the *Enterprise* encounters an area of darkness. Soon the crew begins experiencing deep fatigue, and power starts draining from the engines. Spock reports that the area emits some type of field that is incompatible with biological and mechanical processes. Realizing the threat to the galaxy, Kirk presses forward into the darkness. A short time later, a giant, single-cell organism approaches. Understanding the need for intimate knowledge about the creature, Spock pilots a shuttle into the cell to perform close-range testing.

Once inside, Spock locates the nucleus of the cell and makes another disturbing discovery. From the pattern of the chromosomes, it appears the cell is preparing to reproduce. When Spock's transmissions cease, Kirk takes the *Enterprise* into the cell. Arriving at the nucleus, the crew deposits a probe containing antimatter. Kirk then orders full astern. On the way out, they find Spock's shuttle and latch on to it with two tractor beams. Then the antimatter explodes, splitting the membrane and tossing both ship and shuttle to safety.

Trivia Questions

1. At the beginning of this episode, where was the *Enterprise* headed for rest and recreation?

2. What magnitude was the Gamma 7A system's sun?

RUMINATIONS

Obviously the crew of Picard's Enterprise *hasn't spent much time reading the logs of Kirk's* Enterprise. *In the* Star Trek: The Next Generation *episode "Where Silence Has Lease," Picard and company encounter an area of blackness as well. When Picard asks Data to check the records for any similar occurrence, the android can find nothing.*

GREAT MOMENTS

This episode contains some lovely graphics of the organism and the passage of the Enterprise *and the shuttle through it.*

SYNDICATION CUTS

• Just before the area of darkness appears, a sequence featuring an empty viewscreen, Chekov changing magnifications, and a conversation between Spock and Uhura. This conversation contains a production problem. Uhura asks what they are looking for. Spock says he would assume "that." Just before saying "that," the Vulcan taps his work area with his finger, and you can hear a distinct thunk. Spock acts as if he is pushing a button to put information on the main viewscreen, but the sound editor didn't dub in the button-pushing sound.

• Just after the area of darkness appears, several reaction shots and a small section of dialogue with Chekov making a guess at the area's composition. This edit is easy to find in the syndicated version. Listen to the background music and you'll hear an abrupt change.

• After the stars disappear, several reaction shots, and Kirk talking with Spock and McCoy before the captain speaks with Scott. The conversation between Kirk and McCoy contains a plot oversight. The doctor tells Kirk that things have gotten worse and his patients are backed up into the hall. His patients were *already* backed up into the hall. A previous scene showed Chapel giving shots near a sick bay exit, and the line pushed back into the corridor.

• Kirk asks McCoy for answers after the doctor comes to the bridge to administer stimulants.

• After a commercial break, Spock consoles McCoy before the Vulcan leaves in a shuttle.

• Just after the shuttle launch, the part of the scene showing Spock puttering around the shuttle, and Kirk's instructions to Uhura to route the shuttle's telemetry to the computers. This might be a plot oversight as well. Earlier in the show, the *Enterprise* launches a shuttle, and Kirk tells Chekov to route the probe's findings to the computer. Now the shuttle launches, and Kirk orders Uhura to do essentially the same thing. Why is Kirk passing around this job?

• When Kirk tells Scott that shields have unconditional priority, the uncut version shows the *Enterprise* extremely close to the organism before the episode returns to the bridge. The syndicated version deletes this footage, probably because the *Enterprise* shouldn't be this close to the organism yet!

• The editors must have needed to cut just a little more time from this episode, because they removed a pause in Kirk's dialogue. When McCoy suggests that Kirk lie down for a few minutes, the captain says, "I don't have a few minutes . . . maybe none of us do." The syndicated version is missing the pause.

PLOT OVERSIGHTS

• The intermixing of the imperial and metric measuring systems continues. Spock announces that the organism is 11,000 miles long, but later, Kirk says a probe could drift "thousands of kilometers" if they shot it into the organism.

• As Spock reaches up to open the doors to the shuttle bay so he can depart from the ship, McCoy grabs his hand. If you look closely at the atmosphere level indicator on the control panel, you will see that the shuttle bay isn't pressurized! Was Spock really going to open the personnel doors to the shuttle bay before it had a breathable atmosphere? In addition, didn't McCoy help equip the shuttle prior to this scene? If he did, why isn't the shuttle bay already pressurized?

• When Kirk suggests using anti-matter to destroy the organism, the crew seems genuinely impressed with the captain's brilliance. Didn't they recently use antimatter to destroy a creature in "Obsession"?

• After configuring the probe to carry the antimatter, Kirk has Chekov set the timer for a detonation in seven minutes. Then they lodge it next to the chromosomes and make a mad dash out of the organism. The episode gives no indication that the probe is drifting away from its target. Why, then, can't Kirk set the time for ten minutes or ten hours and give the ship a few moments to spare? (Answer: because it wouldn't be as exciting!)

CHANGED PREMISES

• There is an officer at the helmsman position for this episode who looks just like Lieutenant Kyle (featured in the episodes "The Doomsday Machine," "The Apple," and "Mirror, Mirror," among others). In addition, the credits list him as Lieutenant Kyle. Oddly enough, he wears a gold shirt—instead of his usual red—and Kirk consistently calls him "Kowel" (rhymes with "towel").

EQUIPMENT ODDITIES

• Somebody needs to sweep the floor in Engineering. At one point, the ship lurches forward and throws Scott from his chair. As he stands, you can see a large dustprint on his pants. (I would expect a little more cleanliness on the flagship of the Federation.)

• After McCoy refuses to wish him good luck, Spock boards the shuttle. It faces to the left. Then the shuttle rotates on its platform and finally departs. Therefore, when Spock boarded the shuttle it faced the front of the Enterprise. Then the shuttle turned around and finally flew out the back of the ship. Yet in "Journey to Babel," the shuttle carrying Ambassador Sarek lands, turns around, and the ambassador deplanes (deshuttles?). At this point the shuttle should be facing the back of the Enterprise, since the shuttle turned around. Yet the scene clearly shows that the shuttle faces left! (The only explanation that I can come up with is that Spock and McCoy used the doors on the other side of the shuttle bay. But wouldn't that mean that the creators would have to build two complete hallway sets to connect to the shuttle bay? Wink, wink.)

• Kirk still hasn't adjusted his mirror to the correct height. The scene in his quarters has the mirror chest high.

• Great confusion surrounds which button is the one for communications on the arm of the captain's chair. For most of this episode Kirk uses the top button, but at least once he uses one of the middle buttons.

TRIVIA ANSWERS
1. Starbase 6.
2. Fourth.

CLOSING STILLS
• *Enterprise* orbiting what looks like North America, "Miri"
• Penal colony, Tantalus V, "Dagger of the Mind"
• Spock inhabited by Henoch, "Return to Tomorrow"
• USS *Constellation* heading into the planet killer, "The Doomsday Machine"
• Android body doing a screen test, "Return to Tomorrow" (This shot never appeared in the episode.)
• Balok puppet after watching an entire week of QVC—during their fantasy and science fiction emphasis—and purchasing one of everything, "The Corbomite Maneuver"

A PRIVATE LITTLE WAR

Star Dates: 4211.4-4211.8

Revisiting a planet he surveyed thirteen years ago, Kirk finds that the once-peaceful villagers and the hill people are now at war. Even more surprising, the villagers have flintlocks, when they should have only bows and arrows. The beautiful planet holds other dangers, as well. Without warning, a large, furry, apelike creature called a mugato attacks, wounding Kirk with its poison-filled fangs. Since the *Enterprise* has left orbit, the captain tells McCoy that a local named Tyree knows of a cure for the bite. The doctor quickly locates the man. His wife, Nona, is a *Kahn-ut-tu*, one trained in herbal medicine. With her help, Kirk recovers.

That night, a reconnaissance mission to the nearest village confirms Kirk's worst fears. The Klingons are arming the villagers and trying to make it look like normal development. Kirk decides to arm the hill people with the same weapons to balance the planet. Both Tyree and McCoy object.

Tyree abhors killing, while McCoy believes Kirk would be violating the Prime Directive. When pressed for another solution, McCoy admits he has none, and—after the villagers kill Nona—Tyree finds he has a taste for killing after all. As soon as the *Enterprise* returns, Kirk orders a hundred flintlocks.

Trivia Questions

1. What was Kirk's rank when he visited this planet thirteen years ago?

2. What is the next improvement the Klingons plan for the villagers' flintlock rifles?

PLOT OVERSIGHTS

• At one point, Kirk says that if the Klingons are breaking the "treaty" by arming the villagers it could mean interstellar war. What treaty is Kirk talking about? Is he referring to the Organian Peace Treaty, mentioned only a few episodes ago in "The Trouble with Tribbles"? If the Klingons violate the treaty and start fighting with the Federation again, isn't there a good possibility that the Organians will intervene?

• The mugato bite must produce a condition similar to rigor mortis. As the hill people carry the wounded Kirk to a cave, his legs stick straight out, even though the two men transporting the captain have their hands under his thighs.

• Kirk's disregard for the Prime Directive goes back over a decade.

While doing the planetary survey thirteen years ago, he told Tyree about space travel, phasers, and the Federation.

• It's a fortunate thing for our captain that these villagers have no reflexes. During the night mission to the village, Kirk and McCoy are stopped as they try to exit a building. Two villagers with flintlocks apprehend them and begin to march them to an unknown destination. Without warning, Kirk elbows one in the stomach and McCoy wallops the other with a rifle barrel. There are several moments between these two actions, and the entire time, the second villager holds his rifle pointed directly at Kirk's chest. Thankfully, he never thinks to pull the trigger. (It is possible the gun wasn't loaded.)

EQUIPMENT ODDITIES

• After the hill people bring the wounded Kirk to a cave, McCoy uses his phaser to heat up some rocks. A close-up shows the phaser firing in short bursts. Oddly enough, McCoy's thumb stays perfectly still the entire time as it rests on the trigger.

• I've got to say one thing about these *Kahn-ut-tu* women: They have really nice shoes. Just after Nona heals Kirk, Tyree helps her to a bed. As she draws her feet under the blanket, she's wearing pumps. Later in the show, Nona runs across rocky terrain barefooted.

• During the first landing party mission to the planet, a villager

shoots Spock. For most of the show, he convalesces in sick bay. In one scene, a close-up of the medpanel shows that Spock has no pulse, even though the sound effects indicate that he does.

• After stealing Kirk's phaser, Nona meets up with a group of villagers. She threatens them with the weapon, but they attack anyway. A close-up shows her thumb moving from button to button on the phaser, but it never fires. Why doesn't it fire? If phasers are so hard to operate, why did Kirk cringe when Oxmyx and Krako played with them in "A Piece of the Action"?

CONTINUITY AND PRODUCTION PROBLEMS

• Here's another amazing fact from the galaxy of knowledge found in the fascinating study of exobiology. The mugato—that large, ferocious, terrifying beast with the dinosaur ridges down its back and lethal, venom-filled fangs—leaves *bunny* prints! In fact, the prints look identical to those left by the large white rabbit in "Shore Leave." It just goes to show you that you can't deduce an animal's viciousness from its tracks.

• As Kirk, McCoy, and Tyree make their escape from the village, the sound effects person forgot to dub in the "bullet ricocheting" sound used several times in the scene already. When the trio runs through the last arch, a puff of smoke blows silently outward.

• Just after the final fight with the

hill people, Kirk and McCoy stand pondering the new violence that has overtaken this peaceful world. Suddenly McCoy looks down, Kirk looks over, and the doctor pulls his communicator out of his bag. Was there supposed to be a beep dubbed in to create these reactions?

TRIVIA ANSWERS

1. Lieutenant.
2. A striker that will hold the priming powder more securely.

CLOSING STILLS

• *Enterprise* orbiting what looks like North America, "Miri"
• Rocky terrain
• Kirk and the Providers, "The Gamesters of Triskelion"
• Tellarite sitting in front of a wall (This shot doesn't appear in any show.)
• Kirk and Spock riding in a car, "A Piece of the Action"
• The *Enterprise* orbiting Deep Space Station K-7, "The Trouble with Tribbles"
• Balok puppet hearing the phone ring, "The Corbomite Maneuver"

BOYS IN THE HALL

AN EXAMINATION OF STAR TREK'S ATTITUDES TOWARD WOMEN

C reative efforts do not exist in a vacuum. Creators bring a life-set of beliefs and attitudes to everything they birth into existence. In addition, the current attitudes of the society often filter into these life-sets, especially in a medium as public and as far-reaching as television. With this in mind, I have compiled a list of statements and situations from the original television series that shed some light on the underlying attitudes toward women and their roles in the workplace. I have also selected a few statements and situations from the movies. The decade between the airing of "Turnabout Intruder" and the release of *Star Trek: The Motion Picture* saw many changes in our society's mainstream perceptions of women. The movies reflect this change. I find it interesting at times to stop and take stock of our recent history. Join me, then, for what you might find is a bumpy ride down memory lane.

1. *The role of the yeoman.* Most often in the original series, women are cast in the role of yeomen. Little more than glorified secretaries, they bring coffee, offer clipboards for senior officers to sign, and take dictation by using a tricorder. While it is true that these would be the normal occupations for yeomen, the gender of the yeomen engaging in these activities is disproportionately female.

2. *Leering as an accepted activity.* (This leering most often occurs in the halls, hence the title for this sidebar.) In "The Naked Time," Riley ogles a woman as he stumbles his way toward sick bay. In "Mudd's Women," a technician ducks his head around the corner to watch the three females pass. Kirk checks out a yeoman in "The Squire of Gothos." Christopher feasts his eyes on a yeoman just before he boards a turbolift with Kirk in "Tomorrow Is Yesterday." Sulu openly gapes at Ilia in *Star Trek: The Motion Picture.* Sulu and Chekov admire Vixis at the end of *Star Trek V: The Final Frontier.* (I guess this is an activity that remained constant through the 1970s and 1980s). By far the worst examples of leering occur in the first season of the television show. At the end of "The Enemy Within," Spock himself takes a long, hard look at Yeoman Rand, and in "Mudd's Women," the creators focus for several moments on the swinging posteriors of the three lovelies. The creators fill the screen with this apparition. In an appropriate tit for tat, Dr. Gillian Taylor appreciates the view as Kirk makes his way around her truck in *Star Trek IV: The Voyage Home.*

3. *The use of "girl" as an appropriate designation.* Vina is called an Orion slave girl, although she is clearly a woman. (She is also described as vicious, seductive, and actually appreciates being abused. I wonder . . . did a man or a woman invent this character?) During a discussion of his upcoming trial with Lieutenant Areel Shaw during "Court-Martial," Kirk attempts to talk her into representing him. When she replies that she has another case already, the captain responds that a girl with her abilities should be able to handle two cases at once. Referring to Dr. Miranda Jones—a trained telepath who will soon act as a liaison with the strategically important Medusans—McCoy cautions Kirk that she is not just another girl. In "The Lights of Zetar," Kirk, Spock, and McCoy all refer to Lieutenant Mira Romaine as a girl, as do the Zetarans. Bear in mind that Romaine heads a project to deliver new equipment to Memory Alpha, an important storehouse of information. On the flip side, Dr. Carol Marcus chides Captain Terrell of the *Reliant* by addressing him and his crew as "you boys" in *Star Trek II: The Wrath of Khan.*

4. *The subject of marriage.* Only minor clues exist as to the creators' beliefs on the ramifications when a female Starfleet officer marries. To my knowledge, no installment in the television series or movies ever shows a married couple serving aboard a starship. "Balance of Terror" does feature a wedding, but it is never completed. The husband-to-be makes a rather cryptic statement after Kirk calls battle stations, forcing the man and his fiancée to report to their duty stations. When she states that he won't get away from her this easily, the man replies that temporarily, he's still her commanding officer. This statement by itself is innocent enough. However, in "Who Mourns for Adonais?," Kirk muses about Lieutenant Palamas, saying that one day she will find the right man and off she'll go out of the service. I let you draw your own conclusions.

5. *Starfleet Command as a boys-only club.* "Turnabout Intruder" makes it clear that—at that time—there were no female starship captains. *Star Trek IV: The Voyage Home* breaks this barrier by showing us the first female captain, commanding the USS *Saratoga.*

6. *Vina.* According to "The Cage," Vina crash-landed on Talos IV. Having no pattern for her reconstruction, the Talosians rebuilt Vina as best they could. As shown at the end of the episode, Vina's true appearance is quite malformed—at least by the American populist standards of beauty. This physical disfigurement keeps her from rejoining human society. Her attractive appearance—even if it is merely an illusion—is more important to her than living in reality. What is most amazing in this matter is that Pike agrees with her reasoning.

7. *Uhura.* Some may look at the communications officer as little more than a telephone operator. Certainly her role in "The Corbomite Maneuver" gives this impression. However, over time the creators did allow Uhura's role to grow. In "Who Mourns for Adonais?" Spock assigns her the task of "rigging a subspace bypass circuit"—an operation she deems "delicate." In this episode Spock also comments that he can think of no one more qualified to do the work. On the other hand, *Nomad* in "The Changeling" identifies Uhura's mental processes as defective and chaotic. At this Spock replies—apparently as an explanation—that Uhura is a woman. *Nomad* then offers the final pronouncement that she is a mass of conflicting impulses.

8. *Dr. Miranda Jones.* Easily the most insulting treatment of any woman occurs in the episode "Is There in Truth No Beauty?" After deciding that Spock must mind-meld with Kollos, Kirk begins looking for a way to neutralize the suspected opposition Jones will have toward the plan. Instead of sitting down with her and discussing the matter intelligently, Kirk opts to impress her with his masculinity—certain that he can keep her distracted long enough for Spock to discuss the matter with Kollos. It is possible that Kirk takes this tack simply because he perceives her high level of jealousy with regard to Kollos and not because she is a woman. However, I have a hard time imagining that Kirk would send in a beautiful yeoman to distract Jones if she were a man.

9. *Other miscellaneous citings.* In "Shore Leave," Sulu puts his arm around Yeoman Barrows to help her as she walks through the forest. In "Who Mourns for Adonais?" Apollo comments that Lieutenant Palamas seems wise for a woman. "Wolf in the Fold" states that women are more easily terrified than men. Twice in "The Immunity Syndrome" Kirk comments that he is looking forward to a period of rest on some lovely planet. Both times he gazes lustfully at a yeoman. The Romulans—providers of equal command opportunities for men and women—dress their female commander in a miniskirt and go-go boots during "The *Enterprise* Incident." In "The Lights of Zetar," Scott comments to Lieutenant Mira Romaine that she is the sanest, smartest, and nicest woman ever to board the ship. (Does that mean Scott believes the rest of the women are only partly sane?)

RETURN TO TOMORROW

Star Dates: 4768.3-4770.3

Beaming down to a chamber beneath the surface of an uncharted planet, Kirk, Spock, McCoy, and Dr. Ann Mulhall find an entity named Sargon, who exists only as mental energy and is confined to a sphere. Half a million years ago, his race, once humanoid, grew until they considered themselves gods. A horrible war followed, destroying the surface. Ashamed, his race built this chamber and selected the best from both sides of the conflict. They transferred these chosen ones into the spheres to preserve their knowledge. Only three remain alive: Sargon; his wife, Thalassa; and Henoch, a former enemy. These three wish to transfer temporarily into Kirk, Mulhall, and Spock's bodies to build android bodies for themselves.

The potential for learning is too great to refuse, and the officers agree. Knowing Sargon will never allow him to keep Spock's body, Henoch plans for the leader's death. He alters the drug formula

Trivia Questions

1. What is Dr. Ann Mulhall's area of expertise?

2. How long ago did Sargon's race colonize nearby planets?

that the trio must use to stabilize their physical functions. Soon Sargon appears to die. At first Thalassa bargains to keep Mulhall's body as well but quickly realizes its temptations are too great. Sargon then speaks from the ship's computer, pleased that his wife has come to this realization. Together they overpower Henoch before departing.

RUMINATIONS

In one of those "stranger than fiction" occurrences, Thalassa views herself in the lid of a metal pan. (Actually she views the camera shooting the scene so that we can see her face and think she's looking at herself . . . but that's a side issue.) Startlingly enough, Shahna did the same thing just a few episode ago, in "The Gamesters of Triskelion." Even more astounding, both women use what looks like the same lid!

GREAT LINES

"But I don't suppose there'd be any harm in looking over diagrams of it."—Scott, talking himself into voting for the transfer after Kirk claims that Sargon could show them how to build warp drive engines the size of walnuts.

GREAT MOMENTS

Once again, Shatner and Nimoy add delightful touches to their performances. At the end of this episode, when Kirk finds out that Sargon temporarily placed Spock's consciousness into Nurse Chapel's mind, the captain turns and grins at his first officer while the Vulcan simply raises his eyebrow.

PLOT OVERSIGHTS

• Along with Kirk, Spock, McCoy, and Mulhall, two security guards step up on the transporter pad to beam down to the planet. As Sargon operates the controls, he leaves the guards behind. In discussing this turn of events, Spock and Scott refer to the "guards," but Kirk refers to them in the singular by asking if the "security guard" is still on the ship.

• The development of this plot rests on two necessary components. First, Henoch must overpower Sargon. The creators chose to use the metabolism drug as the mechanism for this first component. Unfortunately, this creates an unavoidable plot oversight. Why didn't Sargon just dictate the formula to McCoy? (I understand that their techniques for building android bodies require "hands-on" operation, but this is simply mixing some chemicals together. And McCoy *has* fiddled with the crew's

metabolism before. In "The Immunity Syndrome" he administered stimulants to keep the crew on its feet.)

The second component—Thalasa's temporary desire to stay in Mulhall's body—also has problems. The motivation for this change of heart comes from her abhorrence of the sterile-looking android body. Why can't they start out in a less-than-adequate body and keep upgrading it? Sargon apparently retained all his faculties even in the main computer of the *Enterprise.* And even if they can't, two episodes have shown us android bodies that are far superior—at least cosmetically—to the one manufactured by Sargon, Henoch, and Thalassa. I doubt that Thalassa would mind bodies like those displayed by Andrea or the Alices (see "What Are Little Girls Made Of?" and "I, Mudd"). If these three ancient beings are so smart, why can't they build an android body at least equal to the ones already displayed on *Star Trek?*

• While trying to convince Sargon to stay in Kirk's body, Thalassa kisses him and says, "Can robot lips do this?" Well . . . yes. They may not generate the same sensations, but they can touch.

• At one point Thalassa tries to make a deal with McCoy to stay in Mulhall's body. She says no one will know if the doctor keeps quiet. She better turn down the reverb on her voice if she expects to get away with this. Either that or refuse to speak unless she's standing in a room where everyone's voice echoes as hers does.

• At the end of the episode, Sargon and Thalassa borrow Kirk and Mulhall's bodies one last time for a parting kiss. Where do Kirk and Mulhall's consciousnesses go during this time? Always before, the officers' consciousnesses were transferred into the spheres or another person. At this point the spheres have been destroyed, and no one acts as if he or she has suddenly become possessed. Did Sargon stick them in the main computer?

CHANGED PREMISES

• When Spock declares that Sargon is "matter without form, pure energy," Kirk retorts, "impossible." The Companion in "Metamorphosis" was composed of energy. The vampire cloud in "Obsession" existed in the boundary between matter and energy, and Redjac in "Wolf in the Fold" could inhabit either a human body or the main computer. Why is Sargon's existence "impossible"? (Aside from the fact that pure energy doesn't have any matter in it, making Spock's statement nonsensical. Hmmm. Maybe that's why Kirk says "impossible." He's not referring to Sargon. He's questioning Spock's physics.)

EQUIPMENT ODDITIES

• In one scene, Scott brings Thalassa a curved object with a flip-top lid that looks very similar to Norman's stomach in "I, Mudd."

CONTINUITY AND PRODUCTION PROBLEMS

• As Kirk, Spock, McCoy, and Mulhall begin to beam down, the camera angle changes to show Scott at the transporter console. Watch the back of the hood in the center of the console. The shadow of someone's head appears and then quickly zips away. Evidently someone on the production crew got too close, realized his or her mistake, and made a hasty exit. Everyone else in the transporter room is supposed to be on the transporter pad.

TRIVIA ANSWERS

1. Astrobiology.
2. Six thousand centuries.

CLOSING STILLS

• *Enterprise* orbiting what looks like North America, "Miri"

• The *Enterprise* and the planet killer, "The Doomsday Machine"

• The old McCoy, "The Deadly Years"

• Tellarite sitting in front of a wall. (This shot doesn't appear in any show.)

• Mugato and Kirk, "A Private Little War"

• Kirk entering Proconsul Claudius Marcus's quarters, "Bread and Circuses"

• Balok puppet after his agent reports that Paramount has decided not to renew his contract for the third season, "The Corbomite Maneuver"

PATTERNS OF FORCE

Star Dates: 2534.0

The *Enterprise* approaches Ekos to check on Federation cultural observer John Gill. Gill arrived on the planet several years ago to monitor the progress of the primitive and warlike Ekosian people. Beaming down, Kirk and Spock find an exact re-creation of Nazi Germany, including its oppression of another cultural group. For years, people from Zeon—another planet in the star system—have aided the Ekosians in their development. Now the government has declared war on them and decreed that the Ekosian cities be cleansed of Zeons. The greatest shock comes when Kirk learns that Gill is the *Führer*.

Working with the Ekosian underground, Kirk and Spock infiltrate Nazi headquarters. They find Gill but quickly determine that he is heavily drugged and merely a figurehead. Originally Gill introduced the Nazi concepts into this society to make it more efficient. Then a ruthless Ekosian named Melakon took over and turned the movement toward viciousness. Just in time, Kirk rouses Gill enough to make a speech denouncing Melakon. This encourages the more peaceful Ekosian leaders to assume control and stop the killing.

Trivia Questions

1. What is the rank of the first Nazi uniform Spock dons?

2. Where do the Nazis send Kirk's and Spock's phasers?

RUMINATIONS

This episode had to be a continuity nightmare with all the uniform changes. The creators do an excellent job of keeping everything straight.

SYNDICATION CUTS

• A portion of the interrogation of Kirk and Spock after their capture by Nazis.

• A few moments just after Nazis confine Kirk and Spock to a jail cell.

• After the pair break out of the cell, the trip from the jail to the laboratory. During this sequence, Kirk bumps into a guard and picks his pocket for the keys to the lab. This causes a small glitch in the syndicated version. Later it shows the guard feeling his clothing and then returning to the lab. Since it does not contain the previous scene, the syndicated version provides no

201

clue what the guard has misplaced or why he would look for it in the lab.

• One line of dialogue just after Kirk and Spock meet the underground movement.

• Soon after gaining entrance to the Chancellery for Gill's speech, a section with Kirk taking more pictures of Daras before the group arrives at the historian's door. The edit does away with an obvious equipment oddity. Kirk uses a small, hand-held movie camera to film Daras. Anyone who's ever looked through a viewfinder will realize that Kirk is too close to her. The only thing on that stretch of film would be one large nose.

• After Gill's speech, the crowd actually says "Hail *Führer*" four times.

• Kirk and McCoy argue over giving Gill a second shot of stimulants.

• Following a commercial break, several seconds of McCoy approaching Gill's chair.

• After Kirk gives Gill a shot, the captain tries to talk with him. Listen to the music in the syndicated version and you'll hear it fade out just before the edit.

• Kirk slaps Gill and asserts that he must come out of it and tell the people what happened.

PLOT OVERSIGHTS

• There are several lines of dialogue in this episode that attempt to explain why a historian would reenact Germany under the Nazis. I don't buy any of them. Gill is sup-posed to be well versed in human history. He should know that "absolute power corrupts absolutely."

• To check on Gill, Kirk and the others walk out in the middle of the *Führer*'s speech. Wouldn't the other Nazis find this disrespectful?

EQUIPMENT ODDITIES

• One would think that sooner or later, Kirk and company would figure out that their communicators and phasers are going to get taken away during hostile missions. Yet they keep taking these sophisticated devices down to technologically primitive cultures. Worse yet, in this episode Kirk and Spock actually leave their phasers behind on Ekos!

• The camera that supposedly captures Gill's speech for broadcast to Ekos is mounted on the wrong wall. All the pictures come from a camera that should be mounted directly in front of Gill, but the lens on the camera sticks straight out from a sidewall. From that position it would take a lovely picture of the opposite wall. Does it use some sort of right-angle lens?

CONTINUITY AND PRODUCTION PROBLEMS

• The footage of the nuclear missile approaching the *Enterprise* comes from "Journey to Babel."

TRIVIA ANSWERS
1. Lieutenant.
2. Gestapo command headquarters.

CLOSING STILLS

- *Enterprise* orbiting what looks like North America, "Miri"
- Spock mesmerizing female, "The Omega Glory"
- *Enterprise* approaching giant amoeba, "The Immunity Syndrome"
- Kirk and his android doppelgänger, "What Are Little Girls Made Of?"

- Sylvia as the big cat, "Catspaw"
- Buildings, Eminiar VII, "A Taste of Armageddon"
- Balok puppet overcome with frustration, losing control, and erupting with an emotional outburst in a moment of weakness, "The Corbomite Maneuver"

BY ANY OTHER NAME

Star Dates: 4657.5-4658.9

After sending a false distress signal, a group of Kelvans take over the *Enterprise*. Though small in numbers, they possess powerful technologies. In addition to paralyzing crew members, they can store a humanoid body as a small block of chemicals. The leader of the Kelvans, Rojan, briefs Kirk on his plans. The Kelvans originate in the Andromeda Galaxy. They need a new home and sent out teams to look over the surrounding galaxies. Rojan intends to modify the *Enterprise* so it can make the trip back to Andromeda in only three hundred years. Once there, his descendants will inform the Kelvan government of the suitability of the Milky Way for conquest.

Quickly, the Kelvans carry out their plans and then reduce all but four officers to blocks. Although technologically disadvantaged, Kirk, Spock, McCoy, and Scott come up with a plan. In their natural state, the Kelvans are immense, multiarmed creatures with minds dedicated to efficiency. They assumed human form to utilize the *Enterprise* and are affected by the humanoid body's multiplicity of sensations. The four officers use whatever means they can to stimulate the Kelvans' senses. Eventually the officers convince the Kelvans that by the time the ship reaches Andromeda, they will be more human than Kelvan. In response, Rojan returns control of the ship to Kirk.

RUMINATIONS

When demonstrating the Kelvan ability to reduce a person to a block of chemicals, Rojan's people choose a man and a woman. Afterward, a Kelvan brings the two cubes to Rojan. He crushes one, in effect killing that person. Then Rojan tosses the other to the ground, and his people restore the man. This would be an easy place to make a mistake, but careful study of the cubes reveals that the creators did it correctly. Good job!

While stimulating a Kelvan with alcohol, Scott pulls out a new bottle and identifies it as "green." The creators of *Star Trek: The Next Generation pay homage to this*

Trivia Questions

1. Spock says that the bars across the cave on the surface of the planet are similar to what substance?

2. McCoy claims Spock suffered an attack of what disease ten years ago?

204

moment many years later in a scene between Scott and Data in the episode "Relics."

GREAT LINES

"I'm stimulating him."—Kirk to Spock and McCoy, explaining his fight with Rojan.

GREAT MOMENTS

*T*his episode contains several wonderful moments with Spock cast in the role of an anti-Cupid. His words barb Rojan's emotions and fuel his jealousy.

SYNDICATION CUTS

• Chekov's report that something is penetrating the ship from the planet, and Scott's reply to strengthen the shields just before the Kelvan appears in Engineering.

• Kelinda escorts the captured landing party to the cave.

• Spock's sensor descriptions of the energy barrier.

• Part of the aftermath of passing through the barrier.

• Two different sections of the progress in Scott's quarters as he "stimulates" the Kelvan.

• McCoy giving a Kelvan another shot.

• Part of the second discussion that Kirk and Kelinda have concerning kissing.

PLOT OVERSIGHTS

• Why does the female Kelvan named Kelinda have a European accent? These Kelvans have never been to Earth or even exposed to Europeans. Where would she get these speech mannerisms? For that matter, why do the rest of the Kelvans speak with American accents?

• To get Spock back to the ship, Kirk has the Vulcan place himself in a deep trance. Spock prepares for a moment and then falls over into the arms of Kirk and McCoy. Wouldn't it be more *logical* to lie down and then put yourself into a trance?

• After the *Enterprise* crosses the energy barrier, the Kelvans reduce all nonessential personnel to chemical blocks. Surprisingly, they leave Kirk intact. "The Ultimate Computer" suggested that the captain of a starship is needed for command decisions only. In "By Any Other Name" those activities rest with Rojan.

• It is also quite surprising that McCoy can "stimulate" one of the Kelvans by giving him hypos. Are the Kelvans so cocky about their abilities that they don't even suspect that the enemy doctor might put something detrimental in the shot?

• At one point, Kirk visits Kelinda to apologize for hitting her when he and the others attempted to escape from the cave. After the captain "apologizes," Rojan strides into the room. He uses a door on the sidewall of the cabin. I think this is a first for *Star Trek*. This episode demonstrates that people in space really do go to the bathroom! (I have no way to absolutely prove that the door leads to a bathroom from the television series, but the "official" blueprints of Kirk's *Enterprise* do mark it as such.)

• At the end of the show, Kirk suggests that Rojan make a deal with the Federation to offer the Kelvans planets in the Milky Way Galaxy for colonization. Has Kirk forgotten Rojan's attitude at the beginning of this episode? He indicated that the Kelvans were fixated on conquest. It is their way. Does the Federation really want to send an invitation to this type of race? Don't they have enough enemies to fight already?

CHANGED PREMISES

• At one point, Spock and Scott rig the ship to explode when it contacts the energy barrier. They correctly assess that the Kelvans must be stopped before notifying their superiors of the availability of the Milky Way Galaxy for conquest. Yet when they tell Kirk of the plan, the captain replies, "Are you mad?" He seems stunned that they would even suggest such a thing. Interestingly enough, several episodes later, in "Let That Be Your Last Battlefield," Kirk almost destroys the ship simply because Bele temporarily seizes control of of it.

CONTINUITY AND PRODUCTION PROBLEMS

• I don't think Shatner fully understood the effect that the "neural paralyzing field" was supposed to have. Rojan claims that it neutralizes nerve impulses to the voluntary muscles. Kirk's ability to move

his eyes back and forth is definitely under voluntary control—and therefore should be frozen—but the dear captain glances around continuously the first time the Kelvans entrap him with the field.

• Along the same line, Uhura manages to blink while under the influence.

• To stimulate a Kelvan, Scott takes the male back to his quarters and gets him drunk. In one scene, Scott tosses an empty bottle over his shoulder toward the door. The sound effects person dubbed in the sound of the bottle shattering. Later Scott collapses in front of the same door, and the bottle appears at his feet perfectly whole.

• The preview on the uncut version features "Obsession." This is neither the next episode in production order nor air date order.

TRIVIA ANSWERS

1. Diburnium.
2. Rigelian Kassaba fever.

CLOSING STILLS

• *Enterprise* orbiting what looks like North America, "Miri"

• Hand gripping *Enterprise*, "Who Mourns for Adonais?"

• Android removing spray latex, "Return to Tomorrow" (Of course, this scene never appears in the show.)

• Nazi headquarters, Ekos, "Patterns of Force"

• Kirk, Spock, McCoy, Scott, Uhura, and Chekov just before waving good-bye to Mudd, "I, Mudd"

• The *Enterprise* approaching Deep Space Station K-7, "The Trouble with Tribbles"

• Balok puppet, "The Corbomite Maneuver"

THE OMEGA GLORY

Star Date: unknown

Finding the USS *Exeter* in orbit around Omega IV and everyone on board dead, Kirk, Spock, and McCoy beam down to the surface. Once there, they meet up with the *Exeter's* captain, Ronald Tracey, who states that his crew died of a biological agent carried from the planet by a landing party. Fortunately, something on the surface inoculates against it. However, Tracey has apparently violated the Prime Directive. Believing that the inoculant also prolongs life, he used his phaser to assist the local villagers, the Kohms, in their struggles against their enemies, the Yangs. He sees a profit potential and demands that McCoy isolate the life-enhancing substance. The doctor's research shows only that the planet's inhabitants live longer because the strong survived a terrible biological war.

Meanwhile, the Yangs stage another attack and overwhelm the village. In stunned silence, Kirk watches the Yangs bring in a flag identical to that of the United States of America. On this planet, the Kohms, or "Communists," won the great battle and only now the Yangs, or "Yankees," are regaining control. Even more amazing, the Yangs' holy words include a document that exactly duplicates the U.S. Constitution. Before departing, Kirk urges them to implement their holy words, not only for themselves but for the Kohms as well.

Trivia Questions

1. How many shuttlecraft does the *Exeter* carry?

2. What was the name of the *Enterprise* officer who was killed by Tracey?

SYNDICATION CUTS

• Spock walks over to the science station of the *Exeter* to replay the logs.

• Three different sections of the fight between Kirk and Cloud William.

• A large section after Spock is injured by Tracey's phaser blast. In it, Tracey forces Kirk to order down more phasers, but Sulu abides by regulations and requests verification. Kirk then tells them to stand by.

• The buildup to the entrance of the flag.

• Coming back from the commercial, Cloud William sticking the knife in the floor before the fight between Kirk and Tracey.

PLOT OVERSIGHTS

• Kirk must have an incredibly hard head. While breaking out of a jail cell, a Yang named Cloud William wallops him with an *iron* bar! Not a light tap, mind you. The guy puts his whole body into it. Would a blow that forceful with an iron bar kill our good captain?

• This is one of those classic format science fiction stories exploring a "what if?" scenario—namely, what if the Communists had won a nuclear conflagration? The story would work in a "someone changed history through time travel" or "this is a parallel universe" setting. Unfortunately, it strains the "parallel Earth development" scenario a bit too far. Parallel development of slang ("Yangs" for "Yankees")? Parallel development of a flag identical to that of the United States of America? (Yes, it is a stirring moment when the guy with the flag marches into the room.) Parallel development of the Pledge of Allegiance? Parallel development of the U.S. Constitution—including the calligraphy?

• At the end of the show, Cloud William swears to Kirk that they will perform the words of the Constitution, and the captain seems very pleased with this response. There's only one problem with this: Cloud thought that the first three words of the document were "E Pleb Neesta." What in the world does "E Pleb Neesta" mean? At this rate, the Yang government will soon take on the qualities of fizzbin (the game Kirk invented in "A Piece of the Action"). "You can pass a law in Kongruss, except on Mondays when leaves are on the ground."

CHANGED PREMISES

• While agonizing over Tracey's interference with the evolution of life on Omega IV, Kirk says that a star captain's most solemn oath is that he will give his life, his entire crew, and even his ship to prevent a violation of the Prime Directive. Why are Tracey's actions fundamentally different from Kirk's actions in episodes such as "A Taste of Armageddon" and "The Apple"? Don't Kirk's actions constitute interference with the social development of life on those respective planets?

CONTINUITY AND PRODUCTION PROBLEMS

• Near the beginning of the show, a landing party beams over to the *Exeter.* Finding only empty uniforms and small piles of crystals, Kirk dispatches Spock to check out the rest of the ship. As McCoy examines a uniform draped over one of the large cylinders in the center of Engineering, Kirk pages the ship. The sequence that follows shows different sections of the *Exeter.* Astonishingly enough, a shot shows Engineering with all the lights suddenly on and completely empty. Shouldn't Kirk and McCoy be in this scene? Or is there another room that looks exactly like Engineering?

• The actor who plays Tracey turned in another excellent performance in the first-season episode "Dagger of the Mind."

• The editors spliced a piece of footage in backward at the end of the episode. Prior to the entrance of the flag, one scene shows Kirk's hair parted on the wrong side.

• After the entrance of the flag, Kirk stands, but the editors use the reaction shot of Kirk sitting down three more times before finally switching to close-ups that match the captain's current posture.

• At one point, Tracey attempts to discredit Spock by saying that the Vulcan is evil. He reminds Cloud William that the holy writings have a picture of the evil one's servant. At this, William opens a large book. Note the position of the bookmark. It isn't anywhere near the spot where William opens the book, yet it magically appears in the close-up. The same thing happens in reverse as William closes the book.

• As part of Spock's discreditation, Tracey also says that the Vulcan isn't human, that he has no heart. Just as William leans down to listen, the volume of the voices in the surrounding group of people swells. Oddly enough, many of them are speaking Chinese! The Yangs have just defeated the Kohms. Even if they had learned the Kohm language, I doubt that they would be speaking it during their victory celebration. (Evidently the sound effects person reused the voices from the beginning of the show when a group of Kohms were preparing to behead William.)

• As the landing party prepares to leave, there's a weird spot in the dialogue. Kirk says that they have shown the Yangs that freedom and liberty have to be more than just words. Then he says, "Gentlemen, the fighting is over." Between these two statements, Spock begins to say something, and McCoy looks like he's ready to jump into another discussion with the Vulcan. It appears that the creators cut a chunk of dialogue. It probably contained one of those trademark Spock/McCoy spats seen so frequently at the end of episodes. That would explain Kirk's second statement.

TRIVIA ANSWERS

1. Four.
2. Lieutenant Galloway.

CLOSING STILLS

• *Enterprise* orbiting what looks like North America, "Miri"
• Cape Kennedy, "Assignment: Earth"
• Gorn, "Arena"
• Apollo's temple, Pollux IV, "Who Mourns for Adonais?"
• Starbase 11, "Court-Martial"
• Balok puppet waiting for his agent to call, "The Corbomite Maneuver"

THE ULTIMATE COMPUTER

Star Dates: 4729.4-4731.3

With some reluctance, Kirk accepts orders to evacuate all but 20 members of his crew to the nearest starbase and replace them with an experimental new computer system called M5. Dr. Richard Daystrom—inventor of the M5 and father of all the computer designs currently used aboard the starship—claims that it can perform all the functions necessary for the operation of the vessel. Starfleet has chosen the *Enterprise* for the first "real world" test of the system. M5 will plot navigational courses, make recommendations for landing parties, and participate as an outmatched opponent in a simulated battle.

At first all seems to go well. Then M5 turns on an automated freighter and unexpectedly destroys it. Since M5 has taken control of the ship's functions, it is impossible to warn off the four ships closing for the simulated battle. M5 attacks them mercilessly as well. When Spock comments that M5 is not behaving logically, Kirk confronts Daystrom about his breakthrough. Daystrom claims that he has imprinted his own mental patterns onto the machine. Knowing that Daystrom abhors murder, Kirk drives the point home to M5 that it has murdered hundreds of people by its actions and reminds it of the penalty for murder. At this, M5 shuts itself off.

Trivia Questions

1. What is the name of the planet for which M5 makes landing party recommendations?

2. What is the name of the ensign who gets toasted by M5?

RUMINATIONS

At one point—when faced with M5's superior command of the Enterprise—Kirk goes to his quarters. McCoy follows him there with some refreshments. The scene is very reminiscent of one from the original pilot,"The Cage." In both, the chief medical officer provides an alcoholic beverage so the captain might soothe his emotions. In both, the captain contemplates other lines of work.

GREAT LINES

"You are great. I am great."—Daystrom conducting an affirmation session with M5. (These are definitely "great" lines. Sorry, sorry.)

SYNDICATION CUTS

• Daystrom reminds Kirk that M5 will plot the approach and orbit of a planet, Kirk forgets and asks Sulu to do it anyway, and Sulu tells Kirk that M5 has already done it.

• M5's explanation for the officers it selected to beam down. This edit removes the reason why M5 recommended Carstairs for geologist as opposed to Rawlens. M5 knew that Carstairs had visited the planet before while working with a mining company.

• Daystrom tells Kirk that M5 shut off decks 4 and 6 because they were unneeded.

• Several seconds from the "sneak attacks" by the USS *Lexington* and the USS *Excalibur.*

• After M5 destroys the freighter, Chekov comments that the *Enterprise* is returning to its original course and speed.

• Following a commercial, captain's log 4731.3.

• Just after the briefing room meeting, Spock and Scott work in the Jefferies tube.

• Several moments after a commercial, with Uhura trying to hail the "attacking" starships.

• Two sections from the second time Daystrom speaks with the computer.

• Kirk asks for battle status after Daystrom has a breakdown and security takes him to sick bay.

• Kirk begins his conversation with M5 by telling the computer that it will be under attack in a moment.

• Spock reports that the attack force is almost within phaser range.

PLOT OVERSIGHTS

• In *Star Trek: The Next Generation*, the creators make frequent mention of the Daystrom Institute of Technology. Was that institute named for the Richard Daystrom who appears in this episode? True, he is acknowledged as a genius but he also is responsible for the slaughter of more than four hundred Starfleet personnel. Wouldn't that be enough to get you kicked off Starfleet's list of the top ten most beloved scientists?

EQUIPMENT ODDITIES

• Why is Starfleet letting M5 operate a Constitution class starship? Wouldn't it be more reasonable to give it something like a freighter for its first "real world" test?

• The *Woden*—the old-style freighter that the M5 destroys—looks a lot like the SS *Botany Bay,* but they can't be the same type of ship. The *Botany Bay* was a DY-100 class ship meant for interplanetary travel and built in the 1990s (Could someone send me a postcard when these are ready to sail? I'd love to take a trip to Mars, and these are the '90s, after all.) Does the merchant marine actually have ships this old?

• The doors in sick bay show a marvelous sensitivity in this episode. After Kirk and Spock visit a heavily sedated Daystrom, McCoy joins them on the way to the bridge. For some reason the camera stays behind in sick bay, and the trio walks away from it and onto a turbolift. Thankfully, the doors in sick bay understand our need to watch our heroes depart and graciously stay open until Kirk, Spock, and McCoy walk across the hall and board the turbolift. Even more amazing, the doors know that Daystrom needs his rest and therefore open with absolute quiet.

TRIVIA ANSWERS
1. Alpha Carinae II.
2. Harper.

CLOSING STILLS
• *Enterprise* orbiting what looks like North America, "Miri"
• Sulu with foil, "The Naked Time"
• Giant amoeba on viewscreen, "The Immunity Syndrome"
• Penal colony, Tantalus V, "Dagger of the Mind"
• Scientific research center on Psi 2000, "The Naked Time"
• Balok puppet, "The Corbomite Maneuver"

BREAD AND CIRCUSES

Star Dates: 4040.7—4041.7

Tracing back the wreckage of the SS *Beagle*—a ship that disappeared six years ago—the *Enterprise* comes across a planet with remarkable similarity to Earth. Apparently on this world, the Roman Empire never fell. By monitoring television broadcasts from the surface, they discover that a few of the *Beagle*'s crew are still alive, and Kirk, Spock, and McCoy beam down to rescue them. The trio soon learn that the captain of the *Beagle*, R. M. Merrick, is now first citizen of the empire. Concerned that Merrick has obviously broken the Prime Directive, Kirk, Spock, and McCoy set out to find him. They land in jail, and a short time later Merrick arrives with Proconsul Claudius Marcus. Marcus explains that he refuses to jeopardize the stability of this world by contact with alien races. He wants Kirk to bring down the *Enterprise* crew a few at a time, after which the ship will be destroyed. When Kirk refuses, Marcus puts Spock and McCoy in the arena to die. This tactic forced Merrick into compliance but fails with Kirk.

Kirk's courage reminds Merrick how a ship's captain should behave. He locates a communicator and helps them return to the *Enterprise*. Unfortunately, these actions cost him his life.

Trivia Questions

1. Whom did Claudius Marcus kill the night before the *Enterprise* arrived?

2. What is the name of Proconsul Claudius Marcus's slave girl?

GREAT LINES

"I've heard it was similar."—Kirk commenting on the violence of Empire TV and comparing it to television programs on twentieth-century Earth.

GREAT MOMENTS

There is a wonderful sequence between Spock and McCoy in jail. At the time, the Romans haven't returned Kirk to the cell, and both are worried for the captain's safety. In the course of the dialogue, McCoy realizes why Spock isn't afraid to die. He's more afraid to live, worried that he might slip up and let his emotions boil through. Spock responds by pondering this observation for a moment. Then his countenance turns stoic, he faces McCoy and says, "Really, Doctor?"

SYNDICATION CUTS

• The back of the box for the uncut version of this episode entices potential viewers by stating, "Watch for one of the finest McCoy/Spock dialogues ever, usually cut in syndication!" This refers, no doubt, to the great moment mentioned above. Interestingly enough, the syndicated version of this episode is identical to the uncut version. For some reason, the editors skipped this show when preparing the tapes for syndication. The omission leaves television stations with only two options: Run fewer commercials, or "step on" portions of the show at their discretion. Since the discussion between Spock and McCoy isn't essential to the plot, I'm sure many television stations opt to drop a commercial over it. It is an easy location to grab some extra time. I find the situation ironic. Paramount hypes the fact that the uncut version has "one of the finest McCoy/Spock dialogues ever," yet it made no effort to preserve the dialogue by preparing a syndicated version of the episode with other elements cut so television stations could run as many commercials as they normally do during classic *Trek* episodes.

PLOT OVERSIGHTS

• McCoy is quite a fighter for a doctor. When the landing party makes its first escape attempt, McCoy strikes a guard on the chin with his fist and knocks the man down. One problem: The man is wearing a helmet with a chinguard. Wouldn't that hurt McCoy's knuckles . . . a lot?

• After deciding to kill Kirk, Marcus tells the captain that they have preempted fifteen minutes on the early show for his execution. Later Marcus tells the centurion that he wants him to kill Kirk with one clean blow. Will this really take fifteen minutes? Just how many commercials do they run per hour on Empire TV? Or do the fans like to watch the blood pour out? (This is, after all, a fairly gruesome world.)

CHANGED PREMISES

• This episode finally provides a complete definition of the fabled Prime Directive. "No identification of self or mission. No interference with the social development of said planet. No references to space or the fact that there are other worlds or civilizations." If Kirk really followed the Prime Directive he would never bring Spock along on missions. Every civilization they have ever visited has seen the Vulcan as an anachronism. Also, this definition confirms that Kirk has violated the Prime Directive several times (see Changed Premises for "The Omega Glory" for some examples) and has gone unpunished.

• To explain the startling similarities between this planet and Earth, Kirk states that it is another instance of Hodgkins' Law of Parallel Planet Development. If this is such a well-established law, why are Kirk and Spock surprised to find a Nazi civilization in "Patterns of Force"?

• Kirk states that Merrick lost the opportunity to command a starship because he failed a psycho simulator test. The captain says that all it takes is a split second of indecision. Didn't Kirk experience a split second of indecisiveness when he faced the vampire cloud eleven years ago—as recounted in the episode "Obsession"? Doesn't Spock also state in that episode that this type of indecision is a normal response for humans?

EQUIPMENT ODDITIES

• Great confusion surrounds the equipment the landing party carries. Why do they take phasers with them if the use of these weapons is so restricted? More to the point, why do they take Type II phasers when everyone on every planet they have ever visited consistently recognizes them as some type of gun? Type I phasers are easily hidden and have fooled less advanced civilizations in the past (see "Tomorrow Is Yesterday" and "A Piece of the Action"). Along the same line, shouldn't they have some type of homing signal installed in these things? Inevitably the enemy takes them away. Would it be logical to have some method for tracking them down and beaming them back to the ship? In this episode, for instance, they leave behind three

Type II phasers, three communicators, and a tricorder!

• Making sure the show lasts its allotted time, Kirk forgets to have McCoy inject them with the subcutaneous transponders used in "Patterns of Force." If he had remembered, Scott could have beamed the trio back to the ship anytime after Kirk called "condition green."

• Escaping from his execution, Kirk grabs a machine gun and runs to the cell holding Spock and McCoy. He blasts the door open with a barrage of bullets. Amazingly enough, when he opens the door there are no marks on it at all!

CONTINUITY AND PRODUCTION PROBLEMS

• As the guards usher Spock and McCoy into the arena, the bars part with a scraping sound. Then the scene cuts to Kirk and back to the pair. Now the bars are shut, but no sound accompanied their closure.

TRIVIA ANSWERS

1. Flight Officer William B. Harrison of the SS *Beagle*.
2. Drusilla.

CLOSING STILLS

• *Enterprise* orbiting what looks like North America, "Miri"
• Proconsul Claudius Marcus's quarters, "Bread and Circuses"
• Knight on horseback, "Shore Leave"
• McCoy beginning transfusion

from Spock to Sarek, "Journey to Babel"

• Kirk, Spock, and the Guardian of Forever, "The City on the Edge of Forever"

• Balok puppet hearing the phone ring, "The Corbomite Maneuver"

ASSIGNMENT: EARTH

Star Date: unknown

While doing historical research in orbit around Earth during the year 1968, the *Enterprise* is struck by a powerful transporter beam. Moments later, Gary Seven materializes on the transporter pad. He claims to be human, though he has lived for many years on a planet a thousand light-years distant. According to Seven, the inhabitants of the planet have trained a select group of humans to help Earth survive this difficult time. Kirk recognizes that another explanation may exist. Gary Seven may be a member of an alien invasion force. As Kirk and Spock discuss the situation, Seven escapes and beams down to an office in New York City.

Using the office's sophisticated facilities, Seven travels to Cape Kennedy. On this day, the United States will launch an orbiting platform containing a nuclear warhead. Quickly Seven makes his way to the actual missile and modifies it. Back in his office after liftoff, Seven alters the missile's course and arms the warhead. At this point Kirk and Spock arrive, brandishing phasers. Seven quickly explains that they must not stop him from detonating the warhead a hundred miles above the surface. This close call with disaster will frighten world leaders into rethinking the arms race. Kirk allows him to proceed, and Seven's mission is successful.

SYNDICATION CUTS

• Kirk tells McCoy to hurry with the physical analysis on Seven and then orders him to bring it to the briefing room.

• Kirk and Spock approach Seven's office building.

• Seven's reaction to the death of his two agents.

• Just after Seven's secretary, Roberta, calls the police, Kirk wrestles the phone away from her, Seven opens the safe, and Spock holds Roberta as Kirk fires his phaser at the door to Seven's office.

• After a commercial, Kirk sees the plans for the rocket base and walks out to speak with Roberta.

• Seven prepares to climb into the launch director's trunk.

Trivia Questions

1. What is the address of Seven's office?

2. Who is the launch director at McKinley Rocket Base?

218

• Three different pieces of Scott using the viewscreen to search for Seven.

• Seven hearing his cat, Isis, meow and commenting, "'Meow'? You are nervous aren't you, doll?" This edit takes away a small nit. Many other times during the show, the cat vocalizes sounds that could easily be classified as meows. If meows demonstrate the nervousness of the cat, it should have ulcers by the end of the episode.

PLOT OVERSIGHTS

• The big tension point at the end of the episode comes as Kirk tries to decide if he should let Seven operate the controls of his computer. Kirk isn't sure whether Seven will detonate the warhead or allow it to fall and begin World War III. If Kirk wants the warhead disposed of, why doesn't he just call the *Enterprise* and have them blow it out of the sky? Most likely, Scott could even fix it so it looks like the bomb actually exploded.

• At the end of the episode, Spock announces that everything happened just as it should have. To substantiate this claim, the Vulcan states that the library record tapes show the missile detonating at precisely the location that they just witnessed. What else would the record tapes show? The tapes come from the future. Let's say that the record tapes at the beginning of the episode show the warhead detonating at two hundred miles above the surface of the Earth. Those tapes would have

been recorded sometime after 1968—for the sake of argument, A.D. 2200. Now, let's say Kirk and Spock disrupt history, and the missile explodes at an elevation of 104 miles. It is now 1968. When 2200 rolls around, historians will record that the detonation occurred at 104 miles and put that fact on the record tapes. These tapes will be sent to the *Enterprise*. The *Enterprise* will travel back in time to 1968. Any change in history will instantaneously appear on the tapes, just as reality instantaneously changed when McCoy jumped into the Guardian of Forever in "The City on the Edge of Forever." (However, in that case, Kirk and the others on the surface weren't affected by the revision of history, because the Guardian evidently projects a local field to isolate itself and anyone close by from temporal disturbances. At least that's what the creators would like us to think.)

CHANGED PREMISES

• Kirk states that the *Enterprise* has traveled into the past to do historical research. Yet in the *Star Trek: The Next Generation* episode "A Matter of Time," Picard asks Rasmussen when historians will begin using time travel for their studies. Evidently Picard hasn't read the logs of previous *Enterprise* captains.

EQUIPMENT ODDITIES

• Up to this point, phasers have always fired a beam of light, even on stun. When Kirk fires at Seven in the transporter room, the phaser emits no beam.

• After Seven beams aboard, Kirk and Spock go to a briefing room to discuss the matter. At one point Scott talks to them from Engineering. His picture begins to fade as soon as he finishes relating his information, but Kirk doesn't reach over and "officially" turn off the viewscreen until a second or two later.

• Spock carries Seven's cat into the aforementioned briefing room. When Seven escapes the brig, the cat hurries to find him. When the cat leaves the briefing room, the doors open all the way, but when it enters the transporter room, the doors open only wide enough to let the feline slip through.

• Seven escapes from the Enterprise and uses the ship's transporter, but when he materializes in his office, it looks like he's using his own transporter.

• One of the displays on Seven's Beta 5 computer looks very similar to Dr. Richard Daystrom's M5 computer. Was Daystrom raised by aliens as well?

• At the end of the episode, Seven makes his final report on a typewriter that transcribes speech. Earlier in the show, Seven used the computer to record his intentions. Why then does he still work in an antiquated medium like paper? Why not just use the computer to record his final report?

CONTINUITY AND PRODUCTION PROBLEMS

• The opening shot of the Enterprise shows it near India and traveling east. The following shot of the viewscreen on the main bridge shows the Enterprise traveling west. Also, according to these graphics, the Enterprise was over Asia when the transporter beam hit them. If Seven is traveling to his office in New York, why is the beam hitting Asia?

• Watch the cat's tail when Seven beams off the Enterprise the first time. It flicks back and forth, then suddenly jumps and locks into position.

• There's a woman who's keeping close tabs on Kirk, Spock, and the entrance to Seven's office. She first appears in the background as Kirk and Spock head down a street looking for the correct building. She wears black boots, white hose, a striped gray fur miniskirt, and a striped gray fur coat. She next appears as Roberta rushes into the office building. Finally, this mystery woman walks past Kirk and Spock as they enter the building. (I first noticed her because her outfit looks similar to the one Lenore wore when she asked Kirk for a ride to their next performance in "The Conscience of the King." Apparently Lenore forgot to wear the skirt portion of the outfit.)

TRIVIA ANSWERS

1. 811 East 68th Street, Apartment 12B.
2. Cromwell.

CLOSING STILLS

• *Enterprise* orbiting what looks like North America, "Miri"

• Imperial Spock, "Mirror, Mirror"

• Vaal, "The Apple"

• Kirk and Spock wounding the Horta, "The Devil in the Dark"

• Lithium cracking station on Delta Vega, "Where No Man Has Gone Before" (I expect the creators spliced it in backward to spice things up a bit.)

• Balok puppet moments after learning from his agent that he will be recast as the stunt double for Beaker on *The Muppet Show,* "The Corbomite Maneuver"

1. Number of times Kirk snaps at a crew member: ten
2. Number of times Spock says "fascinating": forty-nine
3. Number of things that McCoy isn't (i.e., "I'm a doctor, not a . . . "): ten
4. Number of times Scott uses Scottish terminology: four
5. Number of times Sulu is "zoned": seven
6. Number of times Uhura says some form of "hailing frequencies open": eleven
7. Number of times Chekov falsely attributes something to Russia: six

REFERENCES

1. Twice at Uhura in "The Naked Time." At McCoy in "The Enemy Within." At Spock in "Miri." At McCoy in "The Corbomite Maneuver." At Spock in "The Conscience of the King." At Uhura in "Operation—Annihilate!" At Scott in "Who Mourns for Adonais?" At McCoy in "Friday's Child." As a group, at Uhura, Chekov, and Scott in "A Private Little War." (Interestingly enough, Uhura inherits a full 40 percent of the snapping.)

2. Concerning Balok's ship in "The Corbomite Maneuver." Concerning the state of the Organians in "Errand of Mercy." After almost getting hit by a car in "The City on the Edge of Forever." Upon hearing *Nomad* send a repeating symbol and seeing *Nomad* in "The Changeling." Also, after the mind meld with *Nomad* in "The Changeling." After seeing Sylvia's very large cat shadow and concerning Korob and Sylvia's true appearance in "Catspaw." After two of the Alices short out in "I, Mudd." Telling McCoy about getting a shock from the Companion and concerning Cochrane's parochial attitude toward love in "Metamorphosis." Concerning the imperial Kirk and the landing party in "Mirror, Mirror." On the matter of a project to test the length of time that atoms can retain their integrity in a transporter beam in "The Gamesters of Triskelion." Responding to the Provider's contest in "The Gamesters of Triskelion." Concerning Sigma Iotia's similarity to Earth in the 1920s and "The Book" in "A Piece of the Action." On hearing that Sargon will make it possible to beam through the rock in "Return to Tomorrow." That it will take only three hundred years to reach the Andromeda Galaxy in "By Any Other Name." Concerning the metal of the Kelvans in "By Any Other Name." That the missile had a nuclear warhead in "Patterns of Force." On realizing that John Gill is the *Führer* in "Patterns of Force." On finding that the *Defiant*'s helm was left on automatic in "The Omega Glory." Seeing Daystrom lose it in "The

Ultimate Computer." In response to slavery as an institution in "Bread and Circuses." Upon learning that he is a disembodied brain and finding out he is in a box during "Spock's Brain." Twice while expounding on the retograde civilization in "Spock's Brain." On discovering that Jones is blind in "Is There in Truth No Beauty?" Concerning the sensor readings, the shift to the Old West, and the dysfunctional tranquilizer in "Spectre of the Gun." On the reactions of the crew and the fact that the alien exists on negative emotion in "Day of the Dove." Concerning the Platonians' telekinetic power and the way it developed in "Plato's Stepchildren." After entering the room with two Kirks in "Whom Gods Destroy." After Bele's ship disintegrates and concerning the irrevocable hostilities between Bele and Lokai in "Let That Be Your Last Battlefield." Concerning Gideon's duplication of the *Enterprise* in "The Mark of Gideon." On the method used to sabotage the *Enterprise* in "That Which Survives." Concerning the match between Romaine's brain waves and the emanations of the Zetarans in "The Lights of Zetar." After Flint creates another M4 in "Requiem for Methuselah." On the appearance of Lincoln and the momentary mineral reading in "The Savage Curtain." Concerning the level of power generation from V'ger and the fact that Iliadroid says "Decker," not "Decker-unit," in *Star Trek: The Motion Picture*. Concerning Genesis in *Star Trek II: The Wrath of Khan*. Upon arrival at Sha Ka Ree in *Star Trek V: The Final Frontier*.

3. A moon shuttle conductor, "The Corbomite Maneuver." A bricklayer, "The Devil in the Dark." A psychiatrist, "The City on the Edge of Forever" (although he is a specialist in space psychology, according to "Court-Martial"). A mechanic, "The Doomsday Machine" and "The Empath." A scientist or a physicist, "Metamorphosis." An escalator, "Friday's Child." A magician, "The Deadly Years." A flesh peddler, "Return to Tomorrow." A coal miner, "The Empath."

4. Refers to "haggis" in "A Taste of Armageddon" and "The Savage Curtain." Calls Mudd a "bogus frat" in "I, Mudd." Refers to the engines as his "bairns" in "The Paradise Syndrome."

5. Asleep at the briefing room table in "The Corbomite Maneuver." Happy to be with Landru in "The Return of the Archons." Infected with spores in "This Side of Paradise." Under Sylvia's spell in "Catspaw." Pumped full of sedatives in "Wolf in the Fold." Under the children's influence in "And the Children Shall Lead." Stunned by Ilia in *Star Trek: The Motion Picture*.

6. Five times in "The Corbomite Maneuver." Once in "Tomorrow Is Yesterday." Once in "A Taste of Armageddon." Once in "The Trouble with

Tribbles." Once in "The *Enterprise* Incident." Twice in "Elaan of Troyius."

7. *Alice in Wonderland*, "Who Mourns for Adonais?" The Garden of Eden, "The Apple." The saying "Fool me once, shame on you. Fool me twice, shame on me," "Friday's Child." Claimed Sherman's Planet was mapped by Ivan Burkoff and a little old lady in Leningrad invented scotch, "The Trouble with Tribbles." Cinderella, *Star Trek VI: The Undiscovered Country*.

THIRD SEASON

SPOCK'S BRAIN

Star Dates: 5431.4—5432.3

A small craft with a sophisticated ion drive approaches the *Enterprise*. Without warning, a woman beams onto the ship, steals Spock's brain, and quickly departs. Kirk's pursuit leads the *Enterprise* to the sixth planet of the Sigma Draconis system. On the surface, Kirk and a landing party discover a retrograde civilization. At one time, the inhabitants maintained a very advanced society. With the advent of an ice age, the women moved underground while the men stayed above. In time, the males became primitive. The females still enjoy the benefits of their highly developed technology but understand it enough only to lure the males from the surface and control them as slaves.

The landing party soon discovers that Kara—the leader of the females—took Spock's brain to act as a master controller for their complex. Their machines contain a "Teacher," a device that floods the recipient with temporary knowledge. When Kara refuses to restore the brain to Spock's body,

Trivia Questions

1. How many M-class planets does the Sigma Draconis system contain?

2. What is the name of the first female Kirk meets on Sigma Draconis VI?

McCoy submits to the Teacher. At first the process of restoration seems simple, and the doctor proceeds rapidly. Then the knowledge fades. Frantic, McCoy concentrates on the Vulcan's speech centers. With additional help from Spock, the doctor completes the delicate operation.

GREAT LINES

"*Brain and brain, what is brain*?"—Kara, confused by the landing party's constant references to a word she doesn't recognize.

SYNDICATION CUTS

• Lots of reaction shots as the ion drive craft approaches. As usual, Sulu's viewer takes forever to lock into position. I guess the designers of the *Enterprise* didn't expect anyone to attack quickly.

• Before the captain's log, star date 5431.4, an establishing shot of the *Enterprise* and the crew chasing the ion trail left by Kara's vessel. In this edit, Sulu sets the ship to maximum warp, which he then refers to as warp six. In "Amok Time," Kirk pointed the ship at Vulcan and ordered the crew to engage at warp eight. According to the episode, they traveled at that speed for days!

• Most of Chekov's first report to Kirk after arriving on the planet's surface. This edit removes a plot oversight. Uhura detected energy emissions from orbit, and Scott will do so a bit later in the episode from the surface, but in his report Chekov states that there are no generations of energy.

• Four sections from the fight on the surface, and Kirk's questioning of the Morg afterward.

• A few lines of dialogue in which the first woman Kirk meets in the underground city introduces herself.

• A ship's log by Sulu. In this log, Sulu refers to the planet as Sigma Draconis VII. Everyone else has called it the sixth planet in the system.

• Scott comments that the females could never have set up a complex this technologically advanced.

• Spock, as the Controller, discourages Kirk from attempting to find him and restore his brain.

• Most of the footage showing Kara absorbing the ancient knowledge. Part of this sequence shows the display panel from the M5 computer. It sure does get around!

• After a commercial, Kara brandishes the phaser, threatening to kill Kirk, and states that the Controller must not leave.

• In the syndicated version, Kirk asks Kara—if she had the knowledge—could she restore Spock's brain? Kara replies with a forceful, "No!" In the uncut version, she responds, "I would not." Then Kirk tells her that she must restore what she has taken and Kara says, "No!"

PLOT OVERSIGHTS

• In the society on Sigma Draconis VI, men live on the surface and women live below. Supposedly it's been this way for thousands of years. Presumably the women mate with the men that they have taken as slaves and produce offspring. Do those offspring remain below with their mothers? If they do, how do the men on the surface procreate? When the children grow to a certain age, are the males banished to the icy region above?

• Why have the females deteriorated and lost the knowledge? Is it because they're *females?* They need a *man's* brain to tell them what to do?

• These Starfleet officers have amazing balance. They infiltrate the underground civilization on the planet, and Kara knocks them unconscious. Her little minions put pain belts on the men and sit them on stools. Mind you, they are still unconscious, and they are sitting on stools. Try going to sleep sitting on a stool. If you do get to sleep, you will wind up on the floor very quickly.

• After Kirk forces Kara to don the Teacher, she takes on a new persona—one of great calm and intelligence. Then she reaches under her skirt and pulls out a phaser. Scott notes that the phaser is set to kill, and Kara replies that the Teacher gave her the knowledge to operate the device. She does not seem surprised that the phaser is set to kill. In fact, she apparently wants the phaser on "kill." Note that Kara—from the time she pulls the weapon out of her skirt—never touches the setting. Also note that Kirk had the landing party set their phasers to stun. Therefore, when Kara confiscated the phasers, they were set on stun. Some time later, she set the phaser to kill and she did it before she received another dose of knowledge from the Teacher! If the Teacher is her only source for knowledge about the weapon, how did she know how to change the setting?

• Trying to convince Kirk to allow him to don the Teacher, McCoy says he might be able to retain some of the medical techniques and bring them to the "world." Which world? Wouldn't McCoy say that he might bring them to the "Federation" or the "galaxy"?

• Of course, when McCoy loses the knowledge of the Teacher, the simple solution would be for another member of the landing party to submit to the device. Instead, Kirk allows the doctor to bumble along with his natural abilities.

• Does Spock have a flip-top head? Twice in this show he has major cranial surgery and his hair looks perfect immediately afterward.

EQUIPMENT ODDITIES

• While trying to decide which M-class planet to visit in search of Spock's brain, Kirk looks at the back of the bridge on two different occasions and quotes how much time he has left. It's like he's looking at a clock, but I don't recall ever seeing a timepiece in that location.

• To make it easier to take Spock's body along during the search for the Vulcan's brain, McCoy and Scott rig a remote control device. With it, they march Spock's body around like a robot. (I had a fleeting thought that Nurse Chapel might want to get her hands on that remote for an afternoon, but that's not really the main issue here.) Whenever Spock's body moves, it makes a clicking sound. Why is it making a clicking sound? Does he need a little oil in those knee joints?

• The trapezoid-shaped doors serve once again. These doors first showed up in "What Are Little Girls Made Of?"

CONTINUITY AND PRODUCTION PROBLEMS

• The first time Kara knocks out the landing party in the underground city, Kirk falls to the ground with his left arm outstretched. In the close-up, his left arm is bent and his left hand rests on his stomach.

TRIVIA ANSWERS
1. Three.
2. Luma.

CLOSING STILLS

- Melkotian, "Spectre of the Gun"
- Kirk, Spock, McCoy, and Chekov preparing to beam over to the USS *Defiant*, "The Tholian Web"
- Kirk as Romulan, "The *Enterprise* Incident"
- Saloon, "Spectre of the Gun"
- Klingon ship used by Romulans, "The *Enterprise* Incident"
- Star field

THE ENTERPRISE INCIDENT

Star Date: 5027.3

pparently on his own, Kirk orders the *Enterprise* into Romulan space. Soon, three Romulan ships appear and demand Kirk's surrender. He refuses, knowing the Romulans desperately want the *Enterprise* intact. After a few minutes, the subcommander asks Kirk and Spock to beam over to the Romulan flagship to discuss the matter with his superior. During questioning by the Romulan commander, Spock reveals that Kirk acted alone, hungry for glory. Moments later, Kirk attacks his first officer for betraying him. Spock grabs the captain's face, and Kirk crumples to the floor. The first officer states he was not prepared and instinctively used the Vulcan death grip.

Back on the *Enterprise*, Kirk resuscitates. There is no Vulcan death grip. Spock merely used a nerve pinch to simulate death. The entire episode has been a ruse to give Kirk the opportunity to steal a Romulan cloaking device. The captain then beams back over—outfitted as a Romulan—and accomplishes the mission. As Scott rigs the device into the deflector shields, Chekov locates Spock with the sensors. After beaming Spock back to the *Enterprise*, Kirk blasts away at warp nine. The Romulan ships pursue, but Scott turns on the cloaking device and the *Enterprise* fades from view.

Trivia Questions

1. What is the name of the Romulan subcommander?

2. On what finger of her left hand does the Romulan commander wear a ring?

SYNDICATION CUTS

• After Kirk agrees to beam aboard the enemy ship, an establishing shot showing the *Enterprise* surrounded by three Romulan (i.e., Klingon) vessels. Then Kirk gives Scott some final instructions, and two Romulans beam onto the *Enterprise* as Kirk and Spock beam off. Interestingly enough, the Romulans pull their weapons as soon as they materialize.

• The Romulan commander expresses her disbelief that the *Enterprise* wandered into Romulan space because of an instrument malfunction.

• The Romulan commander decides to go to Kirk's cell, brings Spock with her, and orders him to have dinner with her. She then softens her tone and asks him to join her for dinner.

• Following a commercial break, an establishing shot of the *Enterprise*, and McCoy working over Kirk's "dead" body in sick bay.

• The Romulan commander hands Spock a blue drink and tells him that the Romulans have other recruiting inducements.

• The Romulan commander pours Spock an orange drink, explaining that the Romulan Empire offers him an alternative for service and entices him with the fact that Romulan women are not dedicated to the sterility of non-emotion.

• The Romulan commander and Spock walk back into her quarters after Kirk steals the cloaking device.

• Chekov informs Kirk that they are entering the Neutral Zone on the way back to Federation space.

PLOT OVERSIGHTS

• When the Romulan vessels surround the *Enterprise*, the Romulan subcommander announces with a smug tone, "You have been identified as the starship *Enterprise*." Big deal. So they can read. It says, "USS *Enterprise*" right on the saucer.

• When Scott comes down to sick bay, the newly resuscitated and "Romulanized" Kirk stands in the center of the room to greet him. The captain is supposed to be dead, yet he stands in full view of the hallway when the doors pop open. Wouldn't it be better to hide Kirk in a back room?

• The Romulan commander doesn't seem to know what a cloaking device looks like or where it's located. The Romulans keep the device in a special room on top of a large, centrally located pedestal. It is impossible to miss. Yet when the Romulan commander breaks into the room with Spock, she starts looking at the indicator panels along one wall. Bear in mind that she rushed to this room *specifically* because she feared for the cloaking device's safety. A few moments later, the Romulan subcommander finally informs her that the cloaking device is gone, and she turns around to see for herself.

CHANGED PREMISES

• When McCoy returns the "dead" Kirk to sick bay and claims the captain fell victim to the Vulcan death grip, Nurse Chapel quickly responds that there is no Vulcan death grip. Maybe so, but there is *tal-shaya,* a Vulcan method for snapping an opponent's neck. Does this qualify as a death grip?

EQUIPMENT ODDITIES

• At the beginning of the episode, three Klingon ships appear in Romulan space. When Scott expresses disbelief at this sight, Spock explains that intelligence reports have stated that the Romulans are buying their ship designs from the Klingons. (Now, isn't that convenient! It saved the creators from manufacturing a new Romulan ship.) Evidently the Romulans are also buying their hand phaser designs from the Klingons, because they look very similar to the ones seen in "Errand of Mercy."

• At the end of the episode, Spock escorts the Romulan commander to her quarters on the *Enterprise*. Kirk has promised to let her off at the nearest Starfleet facility. She and Spock board a turbolift on the bridge (deck 1) and travel to deck 2. The trip takes forever! They are traveling down only one deck. Why does it take this long?

CONTINUITY AND PRODUCTION PROBLEMS

• Amazingly enough, the Romulans dress their female commanders in miniskirts and go-go boots! Obviously, the Romulans aren't motivated to do this because of any sexist tendencies. After all, this woman commands an armada of Romulan vessels (which—as we find out in "Turnabout Intruder"—is more than we can say for *any* single vessel in Starfleet). So do the Romulan women *like* wearing miniskirt uniforms? And when the Romulan commander stands during her dinner with Spock and must tug at the bottom of her skirt to lower it past her posterior, is this action considered a "warrior" move?

TRIVIA ANSWERS

1. Tal.
2. Her index finger.

CLOSING STILLS

• Melkotian, "Spectre of the Gun"
• Medusan in a box, "Is There in Truth No Beauty?"
• Spock's brain as the Controller, "Spock's Brain"
• Asteroid, "Paradise Syndrome"
• *Galileo* in shuttle bay, "The *Galileo* Seven"
• Lawgivers leaving Hall of Audience, "The Return of the Archons" (This scene is never shown in the episode.)
• Cloaked Romulan warbird, "The *Enterprise* Incident"

THE PARADISE SYNDROME

Star Dates: 4842.6—4843.6

Kirk, Spock, and McCoy beam down to a planet endangered by an asteroid collision. The trio finds an Earthlike setting and people similar to Native Americans. As McCoy and Spock take a few extra readings, Kirk examines an unusual obelisk and then calls for beam-up. Suddenly the platform he stands on slides sideways. Kirk tumbles into the structure, and a bolt of energy knocks him unconscious. Spock and McCoy search for the captain but are forced to leave him behind. The *Enterprise* must rendezvous with the asteroid and push it off course.

Kirk awakes with his memory erased. When he stumbles out of the obelisk, the villagers proclaim him a god. Meanwhile, the *Enterprise* fails in its attempt to divert the asteroid, burning out many of its systems in the process. On impulse power, it retreats as Spock deciphers the writing on the obelisk. He learns that the "Preservers" built it as an asteroid deflector. Once in orbit, Spock and McCoy beam down to

find the villagers stoning Kirk because he can't operate the device. A Vulcan mind meld restores his memory, and with Spock's help, Kirk gains entrance. Moments later, the planet is saved, as the obelisk pushes the asteroid back into space.

SYNDICATION CUTS

• Spock's log entry, star date 4843.6, stating that they are proceeding at maximum warp, and Kirk's first moments in the natives' camp. This edit takes care of an equipment oddity (or changed premise, depending on your viewpoint). Two episodes ago, during "Spock's Brain," Kirk set course at maximum warp, and Sulu pronounced it warp six. In this episode, Spock says they are proceeding at maximum warp, and Scott calls it warp nine!

• Salish walks to the lake after Miramanee rejects him, and Kirk works on a lamp.

• McCoy storms out of Spock's quarters, and Miramanee speaks of her joining with the young maidens of the village.

• After a commercial break, part

Trivia Questions

1. What scents do Kirk and McCoy detect as they walk on the planet's surface at the beginning of the episode?

2. Spock equates the inhabitants of the planet to a mixture of what three Native American tribes?

234

of the fight between Salish and Kirk.

• Following the joining, an establishing shot of the *Enterprise* retreating in front of the asteroid, Spock in his quarters thinking, and McCoy entering to discuss the Vulcan's progress deciphering the glyphs on the obelisk.

• A section of Kirk and Miramanee's frolick in the woods.

• After a commercial break, an establishing shot of the *Enterprise* retreating in front of the asteroid, and McCoy entering Spock's quarters.

• Salish runs up to the obelisk with a group of people who begin to throw rocks at Kirk. In addition, Miramanee joins Kirk on the platform.

• Miramanee tells Spock that she saw Kirk coming out of the temple.

PLOT OVERSIGHTS

• At the beginning of the episode, McCoy wonders whether they should tell the inhabitants about the approaching asteroid. Spock replies that revealing themselves would only serve to frighten the inhabitants. There's another reason not to contact the natives and tell them about the asteroid. How about the *Prime Directive?*

• Not to be insensitive about the safety of the inhabitants of the planet, but since when did Starfleet take on the role of guardian angel for nonaligned worlds? From the looks of things, this planet runs through some sort of asteroid alley. McCoy expresses disbelief at the

beginning of the episode that the world isn't covered with crater holes. When the crew decided to save the planet from destruction, they were not aware of the asteroid deflector. Did they intend to send a starship by every so often to make sure other asteroids aren't endangering the world? Does Starfleet really have the resources to do this?

CHANGED PREMISES

• The creators need to decide whether this parallel Earth business should be considered an incredible occurrence or not. The first time they used it, in "Miri," everyone on the bridge crew expressed amazement. Then they were incredulous over the Nazi paraphernalia until they discovered John Gill's influence in "Patterns of Force." Then they were astounded at the replication of the struggle between the Yankees and the Communists in "The Omega Glory." So far, so good. But then Kirk shrugs off the similarity to Rome in "Bread and Circuses" by referring to Hodgkin's Law of Parallel Planet Development. Okay, so maybe parallel planets aren't that big a deal. With this episode, "The Paradise Syndrome," the crew is back to amazement!

EQUIPMENT ODDITIES

• In "The Alternative Factor" we see the dilithium crystals held in something like a flip-down bureau drawer. In this episode they are held in a small pop-up container on those big round things in the center of Engineering.

• Unable to deflect the asteroid, Spock orders full phasers to try to split it. When the power circuits burn out, the *Enterprise* spends the next two months retreating in front of the asteroid as it makes its way toward the planet. What happened to the photon torpedoes? Aren't they self-powered? Can't the crew fire them even if the warp drive and phasers are down?

• Speaking of the phasers, when they do fire, the beams travel outward from the ship, at an angle. Yet when hitting the asteroid, the beams converge at a single point. Just when do these beams start coming back together? If phasers shoot in a straight line, wouldn't the two beams keep getting farther and farther apart?

• And speaking of the warp drive being out, Scott claims they can't repair it just hanging in space. Does that mean they will have to dock at a starbase to fix it? How far away *is* the nearest starbase? It takes them almost two months just to get back to the planet.

• The transporter chief evidently told Nurse Chapel about the surface conditions on the planet before she beamed down. Materializing at the end of the episode in the strong, dust-filled wind, she keeps her eyes closed.

CONTINUITY AND PRODUCTION PROBLEMS

• Right in the middle of an agonized speech by Kirk about the dreams he has of a lodge that travels through the sky, a fly lands on his forehead. Consummate actor that he is, Shatner keeps right on performing through the scene.

TRIVIA ANSWERS

1. Honeysuckle and orange blossom.
2. Navaho, Mohegan, and Delaware.

CLOSING STILLS

• Melkotian, "Spectre of the Gun"
• Spock and McCoy standing by obelisk, "The Paradise Syndrome"
• Kirk and his android doppelgänger, "What Are Little Girls Made Of?"
• Imperial Spock, "Mirror, Mirror"
• Starbase 11, "Court-Martial"
• Talosian beast illusion, "The Cage"
• Star field

AND THE CHILDREN SHALL LEAD

Star Date: 5029.5

The *Enterprise* responds to a distress call from the scientific expedition on Triacus, only to find that all the adults have killed themselves. In addition, their children display no grief over the deaths. They have given themselves over to a Gorgan, a malevolent entity who lives on the planet. He used the children as a conduit to instill a deep anxiety and depression in the adults on Triacus. The Gorgan now uses the children to cause the crew to fly the ship toward Marcus XII, a colony of millions. When Kirk discover that the *Enterprise* no longer orbits Triacus, he confronts the children. They form a circle and summon their leader. The Gorgan reminds the children that they can control the crew through the enemy that lies within each adult. The children shake their fists and the crew imagines their greatest fears coming true.

Fleeing from the bridge, Kirk and Spock concoct a plan. They realize the children are the key. They use a recording of the children to sum-

mon the Gorgan again. Then they replay visual logs of both a happy picnic scene and the dead bodies of the children's parents. The contrast shocks the children back to reality. They begin to cry, and the Gorgan fades from view.

SYNDICATION CUTS

• After Kirk accepts McCoy's initial report on the children, one of them knocks over the United Federation of Planets flag and apologizes.

• A large sequence after Spock tells the captain that—at present—the planet is uninhabited. It contains Spock getting an odd reading on his tricorder from a nearby cave, he and the captain checking it out, and Kirk hurrying out of the cave due to feelings of anxiety. Kirk quickly dismisses these as sympathetic emotions caused by the mass suicide of the scientists. The pair then return to the ship to check out the tricorder tapes.

• Nurse Chapel helps Steve get his ice cream. This edit contains an interesting equipment oddity. At first Steve orders chocolate wobble and pistachio. Chapel looks

Trivia Questions

1. What are the last names of the children?

2. Kirk sets course for what destination at the end of the episode?

237

through the small number of cards in her hands and selects one. Then Steve adds peach to the list of flavors he desires. Chapel switches to another card, slips it in the slot of the processor, the door opens and Steve pulls out his ice cream. Note that Chapel did not press any selector buttons. The card was programmed for a combination of chocolate wobble, pistachio, and peach! It is simply unbelievable that this would be a common combination on board the *Enterprise*. Evidently Chapel has a card for any combination of flavors up to three different kinds. But that explanation causes its own problems. Let's say there are ten flavors of ice cream available. (If they've got peach and pistachio, there're probably more, but ten will work fine.) To order just one flavor, Chapel would need 10 cards. To handle any combination of up to two flavors, Chapel would need another 45 cards. Finally, to handle any combination of up to three flavors, Chapel will need another 120 cards—a grand total of 175 cards! (Hopefully my math isn't off, but even if it is, you get the idea.)

• A few more statements by Kirk to the children before the eldest starts saying, "Busy! Busy!"

• The reference to the cave when Kirk asks the eldest child what he saw on the planet. The editors had to delete this statement once they deleted the long sequence with Kirk and Spock in the cave. Since Kirk is never in the cave in the syndicated version, there's no reason to ask about it.

• After speaking with the eldest child, Kirk orders security to stand watch over them.

• Following a commercial break, an establishing shot of the *Enterprise*.

PLOT OVERSIGHTS

• The departure of the *Enterprise* from Triacus strands two security guards on the planet. No mention is ever made of going back for them.

• To bring up Uhura's greatest fear, the children cause her to gaze at an ancient version of herself in a mirror. Up to this point, the children must shake their fists before the illusion begins. With Uhura, the mirror appears on her workstation, the children shake their fists, and then she sees herself as old. How did the mirror get there before they shook their fists?

• As part of a process to bring the children back to reality, Kirk tells Spock to play the chant the children used to "summon up the Gorgan." How does Kirk know that the creature is called a Gorgan? The episode dialogue never refers to the being as such until Kirk uses the term.

EQUIPMENT ODDITIES

• After finding the dead scientists on the planet, Kirk uses the leader's tricorder to play back one of his log entries. Now, isn't that a convenient feature to have on a tricorder? A playback function. Sure would have been nice to have one of those on *Spock's* tricorder during "The City on the Edge of Forever"!

• Back on the ship, Kirk views the logs made by the leader of the expedition. During the playback, the leader holds his tricorder. If the tricorder is making the recording, how can it show up in the picture?

• And speaking of these log entries, the leader of the expedition gives the star dates as 5025.3, 5032.4, and 5038.3. Kirk gives the star date on his log at the beginning of the episode as 5029.5, and the leader died just after the *Enterprise* arrived. How could the leader make log entries after he died?

• After the children commandeer the ship, Kirk beams two security guards down to the planet to relieve those on duty. He is unaware that the *Enterprise* no longer orbits Triacus. The transporter chief beams them out into space. Does this seem right? Shouldn't there be some sort of sensor check to make sure the destination is actually there before beaming?

• Seeing the captain consumed by a fear of losing command, Spock hurries him off the bridge. The pair practically run into a turbolift. The ever-sensitive turbolift not only starts up without any instructions from Kirk or Spock, it also guesses their destination and takes them there!

CONTINUITY AND PRODUCTION PROBLEMS

• Evidently, the creators didn't have all the opticals done when they put together the trailer for this episode. The teaser shows the Gorgan with his face disintegrating, but he is solid. In the episode he is always transparent.

TRIVIA ANSWERS

1. Starnes, Janowski, Tsingtao, O'Connel, and Linden.
2. Starbase 4.

CLOSING STILLS

• Melkotian, "Spectre of the Gun"
• Kirk caught in memory beam, "The Paradise Syndrome"
• Kirk, Spock, and McCoy on the inner surface of the asteroid, "For the World Is Hollow and I Have Touched the Sky"
• Scott complaining about the present speed of warp 9, "The Paradise Syndrome"
• Sylvia as the big cat, "Catspaw"
• Spock approaching the *Galileo,* "The Immunity Syndrome"
• Gorn vessel at extreme sensor range, "Arena"

IS THERE IN TRUTH NO BEAUTY?

Star Date: 5630.7

The *Enterprise* ferries Medusan ambassador Kollos back to his home world. The Medusans are formless creatures so hideous that the mere sight of them drives humans mad. Even Vulcans are affected by their visage without the protection of a special visor. Two others accompany Kollos: Dr. Miranda Jones and starship designer Larry Marvick. Though human, Jones is blind and telepathic, a perfect candidate for a mind meld with Kollos. The Medusans are advanced navigators, and Starfleet hopes to access these abilities with the union.

Unfortunately, Marvick—jealous for Jones's affections—attempts to murder Kollos. Catching a glimpse of the Medusan, he goes insane. Immediately, Marvick runs to Engineering and puts the *Enterprise* into high warp. By the time the crew regains control, the ship has traveled beyond the galaxy, and there is no conventional means to navigate their return. Over Jones's objections, Spock mind-melds with Kollos. The two of them pilot the *Enterprise* to safety. Then, while breaking the mind meld, Spock forgets to wear his visor. The result is devastating. Kirk goads Jones into helping the Vulcan, claiming that she wants Spock to die because she is jealous of his union with Kollos. With great effort, Jones risks her life to bring Spock back to sanity.

PLOT OVERSIGHTS

• When Jones beams aboard with Kollos in his box, Spock actually greets Jones as if she is the ambassador. The Vulcan knows of the Medusans' reputation for hideousness. Does he actually believe Jones is the ambassador?

• At a dinner attended by the senior staff and Marvick, Jones senses that someone is plotting murder. The episode shows the image of Kollos's box impressing itself on Jones's mind. Later, Marvick visits Jones in her quarters. Suddenly she senses the intent again, and for the second time the episode shows us an image of Kollos's box. With a

---

Trivia Questions

1. What drink does Kirk offer Jones at their dinner?

2. On what does Scott bet Marvick that the designer cannot operate the controls of the *Enterprise*?

shocked expression, Jones confronts Marvick over his feelings and then says, "Who is it you want to kill, Larry? Is it me?" Well . . . maybe it's . . . *Kollos?* After all, she did see his image every time she sensed the desire to murder.

• After arriving at the conclusion that Spock should mind-meld with Kollos, Kirk takes Jones on a walk in the flower garden to distract her. In other words, instead of making her part of the process and convincing her of the necessity of allowing the mind meld, they resort to subterfuge. If I were Jones, I would find this highly insulting. True, she does have strong feelings about the matter, but isn't it inevitable that she will discover the plan? Was Kirk counting on wining and dining the woman for the next several hours? Does the esteemed captain really put that much faith in his charm? She does make a scene when she finds out, but she also eventually submits to the situation.

• At one point Jones says that she and Kollos had planned to mind-meld when they reached the Medusan "vessel." What Medusan vessel? At the beginning of the episode, Kirk says the *Enterprise* will take the Medusan ambassador back to his home world.

• Following his recovery, Spock stumbles into McCoy's office from the outside corridor. Why didn't he just walk through sick bay? Wouldn't it be more logical to take the direct route?

• At the beginning of the episode,

everyone vacates the transporter room, and Spock dons a special visor. Then the Vulcan beams Kollos and Jones aboard. At the end of the episode, Spock dons the visor again, but Kirk hangs around to watch them leave. Isn't this supposed to be dangerous, or was everyone being overly cautious the first time?

EQUIPMENT ODDITIES

• After Spock sees the Medusan, Kirk fires a phaser at the Vulcan to stun him. The captain clearly points the phaser at Spock's head, but the blast hits Spock in the stomach region. How can it do that?

• Moments later, the scene shows us Spock strapped to a bed in sick bay. Hopefully the attendants used heavy-duty straps, because the first officer broke through the regular ones in "Operation—Annihilate!"

CONTINUITY AND PRODUCTION PROBLEMS

• Apparently the fashion craze begun by Kelinda—that spunky European-accented alien from "By Any Other Name"—is catching on around the galaxy. Dr. Miranda Jones fixes her hair the same way.

• Of course, Diana Muldaur—who plays Jones in this episode—also starred as Dr. Ann Mulhall in the episode "Return to Tomorrow."

• At the very end of the dinner, Kirk drinks the final dregs from his glass. Then the action cuts to McCoy and back to Kirk. Now the captain holds an almost full glass of the blue liquid. Yet there is no sound of liquid pouring, and the other glasses within arm's reach also have liquid in them.

• After consulting with Kollos over the mind meld between him and Spock, Jones leaves the ambassador's quarters. In the very next close-up of Kirk, the captain's hair is parted on the wrong side.

TRIVIA ANSWERS

1. Antarean brandy.
2. A bottle of scotch.

CLOSING STILLS

• *Enterprise* in energy barrier, "Where No Man Has Gone Before"

• Fortress on Rigel VII, "The Cage"

• Floor game, Platonius, "Plato's Stepchildren"

• Balok puppet, "The Corbomite Maneuver"

• Romulan (Klingon) warship, "The *Enterprise* Incident"

• Star field

SPECTRE OF THE GUN

Star Date: 4385.3

Encountering a Melkotian buoy in space, Kirk ignores its warning to stay away and orders the *Enterprise* into orbit around their planet. He has instructions to establish contact with the Melkotians at all cost. On the surface, Kirk, Spock, and the rest of the landing party meet a Melkotian who reiterates that they were warned not to come. As punishment, the Melkotians stage an execution, taking the setting from Kirk's mind.

Immediately the scene changes to an Old West town. Kirk and the others retain their clothes but all their equipment is gone, replaced with holsters and six-shooters. They soon learn that the Melkotians have cast them in the role of the Clanton gang. The town is Tombstone, Arizona, and at five o'clock, the Earps and Doc Holliday will gun them down at the OK Corral. Unable to leave the town or reason with their opponents, the landing party constructs a tranquilizer grenade. When the device fails to perform during a test, Spock realizes that what they are experiencing isn't real. Using the Vulcan mind meld, he convinces the others. As the Earps and Holliday fire, the bullets simply pass through them. Kirk then declines the opportunity to kill Wyatt Earp. Impressed, the Melkotians invite the Starfleet officers for a visit.

Trivia Questions

1. On what day does the shoot-out at the OK Corral occur?

2. What is the name of the sheriff?

GREAT MOMENTS

When the Earps and Doc Holliday open fire at the end, Kirk and company stand with their backs to a wooden fence. The bullets chew away at the fence while the landing party remains unaffected. It's a very nice scene.

Also, the music at the landing party's first entrance to the saloon is my favorite of the entire television series.

SYNDICATION CUTS

• Chekov reports a range to the buoy of 45,000 kilometers.

• Kirk orders a course change, trying to elude the buoy.

• Kirk asks Uhura to try to raise the Melkotians a second time.

• The landing party looks around for a longer time just after arriving

243

in Tombstone.

• The landing party discusses the six-shooters.

• Spock assures the barkeep that they will watch "it" and everything very closely.

• Kirk asks the "young lady" a second time to release Chekov.

• Kirk tries to convince the barkeep that he is not Ike Clanton by stating that he hasn't been born yet.

• Two different sections during Kirk's talk with the Earps in Wyatt's office.

• After a commercial break, McCoy ministers to Kirk's lip, and the landing party discusses the properties of the bourbon. This edit takes away a possible inside joke by the creators. It sounds like McCoy reads the name of the bourbon as "Talos lightning." If he does, the creators slipped in a reference to the last encounter the *Enterprise* had with true telepaths. If you recall, in "The Menagerie, Part I" and "The Menagerie, Part II," the ship traveled to Talos IV to allow Captain Christopher Pike to spend the rest of his days with a race of telepaths.

• Kirk rejects Scott's suggestion that they can use the six-shooters against the Earps. This occurs shortly after the landing party discovers they cannot leave town.

• McCoy's exit from Doc Holliday's office and Sylvia's approach to the general store.

• Following a commercial break, the Earps egg Kirk on after Morgan Earp "kills" Chekov.

• McCoy tells Kirk that they all knew the risks in Starfleet, as the captain agonizes over Chekov's death.

PLOT OVERSIGHTS

• Shortly after arriving in the saloon, Morgan Earp confronts Kirk. Spock carefully explains to the captain that he should sit back down and not move a muscle— *especially* in his hands. The Vulcan states that doing so would initiate a most unfortunate series of events. What does Kirk do? He flexes his hands before sitting down!

CHANGED PREMISES

• In "Friday's Child," Kirk tells the Capellans that if they want to be left alone, the Federation will leave them alone. Why, then, has Starfleet given Kirk orders to contact the Melkotians?

EQUIPMENT ODDITIES

• Kirk has a little trouble with his communicator at the beginning of this episode. Just after beaming down to the planet, the captain pulls out the communicator, it flops shut, and then he has to flip it open again.

• At the end of this episode, the Melkotian buoy begins emitting radiation. In response, Kirk orders a standby on the "phaser guns." Phaser guns? (I suppose this is technically correct, but he's never called them this before.)

TRIVIA ANSWERS

1. October 26, 1881.
2. John Behan.

CLOSING STILLS

• Melkotian, "Spectre of the Gun"
• Saloon, "Spectre of the Gun"
• Lawgivers leaving Hall of Audience, "The Return of the Archons" (This scene is never shown in the episode.)
• Gorn, "Arena"
• Kirk, Spock, and the Guardian of Forever, "The City on the Edge of Forever"
• Viewscreen, just before the Orion raider comes into visual range, "Journey to Babel"

★ TREK SILLINESS

THE TOP TEN ODDITIES OF STAR TREK AND THE FIRST SIX STAR TREK MOVIES

1. *The "just like Earth" syndrome.* Many times in the original series, the crew would travel billions and billion of miles to some distant planet, only to find its culture was "just like Earth." I understand that this probably made the series possible because it allowed the creators to use existing props and buildings. There are times, however, when this ploy gets a tad silly. For instance, in "The Omega Glory," not only does the planet have Yankees and Communists, they also have an American flag, the Declaration of Independence, and the Constitution of the United States! As Kirk said in "Miri"—the first parallel Earth episode to be broadcast—"It seems impossible, but there it is."

2. *Able to cover vast distances in a single bound.* The dialogue in classic *Trek* and even in the movies makes the galaxy sound like a fairly small entity. "The Cage" has Pike telling the Talosians that he comes from a planet on the far side of the galaxy. Many times, characters speak as if the entire galaxy has been explored. A Starfleet commodore at the beginning of "The Alternative Factor" even states that some energy distortions were felt in every quadrant of the galaxy and *far beyond*, giving the impression that Starfleet has established communication with other galaxies.

3. *Seat belts, bottles, knickknacks, and other items.* The *Enterprise* is forever getting hammered with photon torpedoes and phaser blasts. Most of the time, this rocking violently throws crew members out of their chairs. Wouldn't it make more sense to give these people seat belts? On the other hand, the bottles always stay upright in sick bay, and everyone's quarters look great despite the multitude of breakables and loosely strewn items. How do these items stay in place?

4. *Production tomfoolery.* Granted, opticals such as matte paintings and ship shots are expensive to produce and should be reused whenever possible. However, the creators of classic *Trek* took film tricks to a new level. They routinely spliced pieces of film in backward to make Kirk look in the right direction. They often grabbed a close-up from later in an episode even though the background differed from the current scene. Sometimes they even slowed the film because the piece of footage occurred in the middle of a character's dialogue! In the third season they even began using a wide shot of the bridge with someone other than Chekov at navigation. Even though Chekov spends

a good deal of time at navigation in the final year of the series, he disappears every time the creators use the wide shot.

5. *The ends of the engine nacelles.* Evidently the original model of the *Enterprise* had vent covers on the ends of the engine nacelles. (The engine nacelles are the two cigar tubes that lie just behind the saucer section.) When *Star Trek* began filming for the first season, someone updated the model and put spheres on the backs of the engine nacelles. However, the creators never redid the ship footage created for the pilots. This footage includes the opening credits sequence. Therefore, the beginning of every episode shows vents on the back of the engine nacelles. Often the rest of the episode uses footage showing the spheres, and sometimes the creators freely mix the shots as the story unfolds.

6. *The "two-dimensional thinking" syndrome.* There is no "up" in space. Yet when one spacecraft meets another, both are usually facing each other at exactly the same level. This would occur only if space exploration occurred on a single plane—much like sailing a ship in the ocean. Also, all the battles in *Star Trek* occur in a very thin area. We never see ships slipping sideways as they drop and rotate around attacking vessels. The only evasive maneuvers used are hard turns to port or starboard—both of which put the ship in greater peril by increasing the size of the enemy's target. (Granted, I never expected to see a high degree of battle complexity in the television series. It was, after all, created decades ago. The movies, however, are a different story.)

7. *"The Way to Eden."* Yes, I know that this episode was created when hippies were "cool." Yes, I know that—at the time—the music featured in this episode was "groovy." Yes, science fiction is hard to write because you have to extrapolate far into the future and try to guess what things will be like then. However, this episode does some things that are just plain goofy. First, *Star Trek* has never been a musical. Yes, Uhura has sung once or twice, but a large section of "The Way to Eden" drones on with ad-libbed selections accompanied by twanging guitars. Second, in the case of music, it is somewhat simpler to project what elements will endure into the future. Bach has endured for over three centuries. He will easily endure for another three. The same holds true for any of the great classical composers. (By the way, *Star Trek: The Next Generation* does music precisely right. Maybe the creators learned their lesson with this episode!)

8. *The ever-changing ears on our favorite Vulcan.* What is it with Spock and his ears, anyway? Isn't he satisfied with how they look? Is that why he keeps having "ear" jobs between every movie? (Actually, there are times when it appears he has snuck off and had an ear job in the middle of the movie!)

9. *The ever-changing hardware on the* Enterprise. These Starfleet engineers must not have much to do. In almost every movie, the *Enterprise* looks completely different! On top of that, the phasers and communicators change. Can't Starfleet agree on a standard design for these things?

10. *The moving turbolift doors on the bridge.* This particular piece of changing hardware deserves its own category. Between *Star Trek IV: The Voyage Home* and *Star Trek V: The Final Frontier*, the turbolift doors move on the bridge. Then they move again between *Star Trek V: The Final Frontier* and *Star Trek VI: The Undiscovered Country*. Think about this for a minute. It would be like buying a twenty-two-story building on Earth and then telling the maintenance engineers that you are unhappy with the location of the elevators and want them moved five feet to the right!

DAY OF THE DOVE

Star Date: Armageddon

After responding to a distress call, Kirk and a landing party find that an entire colony has been destroyed. Moments later, a Klingon vessel approaches, but explosions suddenly disable it. Kang, the captain of the vessel, beams down with a group of Klingons. He claims that the *Enterprise* has fired on his ship and killed four hundred of his crew. In the distance, an energy being watches the confrontation. In fact, it attacked both the colony and the Klingon ship to stage a battle. The being then follows everyone back to the *Enterprise* and continues its preparations. It traps most of the crew in the lower decks, leaving equal numbers of Klingons and Starfleet officers above. It transmutates all weapons into swords and ensures that no one can die. The entity feeds on violent emotions, and it has created a setting where it can feast for thousands of years to come.

Once Kirk and Kang recognize the influence of the being aboard the ship, they call for a truce. They refuse to provide cruel entertainment for another life form. The cessation of hostilities weakens the being and—realizing that the captives will no longer cooperate—it departs.

Trivia Questions

1. On what planet is the colony supposedly destroyed?

2. Where did Chekov's fictional brother die?

GREAT LINES

"*For the present, only a fool fights in a burning house.*"— Kang, refusing to cooperate with the alien being any longer.

GREAT MOMENTS

At one point Chekov tries to rape Kang's wife, Mara. Kirk stops him and approaches her to enlist her help. He wants to speak with Kang and stop the fighting. When Kirk raises his hands in the conversation, Mara nervously looks at them. This is precisely the type of reaction she should have, given the circumstances—a lovely nuance that adds realism to the scene.

PLOT OVERSIGHTS

• When the alien seals most of the *Enterprise*'s crew in the lower decks, Kirk visits Kang and tells him about it. Does this seem sound strategically? Why would you tell your enemy that they are no longer vastly outnumbered? Additionally, during this discussion, Kirk and the security guards allow the Klingons to encircle them, almost completely blocking their way out of the room. Is the alien being causing the Starfleet officers to make these kinds of blunders?

• I've heard of a "glass jaw." As I understand it, the term refers to a person who gets knocked unconscious with even a light tap to the chin. Until this episode I had never heard of a "glass elbow." When the Klingons capture Engineering, two of the warriors chase Scott out into the hall. As the fighting threesome cross the threshold, a Starfleet security guard brings his weapon down on a Klingon's elbow. The Klingon promptly falls down, unconscious.

CHANGED PREMISES

• On the surface of the planet, Kang claims that Klingons have no devil. If that's true, it creates a changed premise in the *Star Trek: The Next Generation* episode "Devil's Due." In that episode, Ardra changes herself into the Terran and Klingon versions of the devil.

EQUIPMENT ODDITIES

• In "Arena," Sulu could sense when the Gorn ship engaged their transporters. Yet in this episode the Klingons beam down to the planet but no one informs Kirk that they are coming. Are the *Enterprise*'s sensors unable to detect Klingon transporters?

• This episode marks the first time that more than six people have beamed up to the ship simultaneously. Originally Kirk, McCoy, Chekov, and Johnson transport down to the planet. Then five Klingons arrive. Moments later, Scott brings everyone back to the *Enterprise*. In "The Apple," six officers beam down and then three more. This make sense, because there are only six transporter pads. On the other hand, it is possible that the transporter can scoop everyone off the surface but only reconstitute them six at a time.

• Desiring to speak with Kang, Kirk risks intraship beaming to transport to Engineering. From the bridge Spock sets the controls and tells Kirk that he will have eight seconds to get on the pad. Kirk flips the controls, goes to the pad, walks back to the transporter console, pauses, lays down his sword, and finally gets back on the pad. Depending on when you start the countdown, it takes twelve to fifteen seconds.

CONTINUITY AND PRODUCTION PROBLEMS

• At one point McCoy comes up to the bridge to chew out Kirk and Spock for their inaction. After the doctor storms off the bridge, the creators show us a reaction shot of Kirk. Look very closely at the upper-left-hand portion of the screen and you'll see what looks like wisps of cigarette smoke.

• After Kirk beams into Engineering with Mara, Kang engages the captain in a sword fight. Two Klingons hustle Mara out of danger. Then she pleads for Kang to listen to Kirk, and a close-up shows a communications panel over her left shoulder. However, the subsequent wide shot has her and her protectors standing in front of the large screen that sits between the room and the engines. There is no communications panel over her left shoulder.

TRIVIA ANSWERS

1. Beta 12A.
2. Archanis IV.

CLOSING STILLS

• Melkotian, "Spectre of the Gun"
• Kirk, Spock, McCoy, and Chekov preparing to beam over to the USS *Defiant,* "The Tholian Web"
• Kirk, Spock, and McCoy on the inner surface of the asteroid, "For the World Is Hollow and I Have Touched the Sky"
• Kirk and Spock in Athenian outfits, "Plato's Stepchildren"
• Spock's brain as the Controller, "Spock's Brain"
• Romulan (Klingon) warship, "The *Enterprise* Incident"
• Star field

FOR THE WORLD IS HOLLOW AND I HAVE TOUCHED THE SKY

Star Dates: 5476.3—5476.4

Discovering a large spacecraft designed to look like an asteroid, Spock calculates its projected course and informs Kirk that it will impact on a densely populated planet. Hoping to prevent the collision, Kirk, Spock, and McCoy beam over. They materialize on what looks like the surface of a world. Soon a woman appears who introduces herself as Natira, high priestess of *Yonada*. Their ancestors built this craft to replant their race from one star system to another.

When Natira takes a special interest in McCoy and asks to become his wife, the doctor agrees. Only recently he has learned that he suffers from an incurable disease, and he wants to make the most of the time he has left. Just after the ceremony, Natira shows her new husband a special book of knowledge. McCoy immediately recognizes it as the manual for the ship. With this book, Kirk and Spock restore the craft to its original heading and, in the process, find a storehouse of knowledge that includes a cure for McCoy. Bound by her duty to her people, Natira stays behind to help her people make the transition to their new home as the recovered McCoy departs with the *Enterprise*.

Trivia Questions

1. What is the name of the world that *Yonada* endangers?

2. With whom does Kirk consult at Starfleet command?

RUMINATIONS

The creators do a nice job in this episode of simulating the written Fabrini language and setting up the Oracle room. While it is true that all the triangles in the room are identical, flipping some of them upside down does give the impression of variation.

PLOT OVERSIGHTS

• At the beginning of this episode, McCoy tells Kirk that he has a terminal disease and makes two requests. Having a only year to live, McCoy asks that Kirk allow him to continue working and that the captain keep the information to himself. According to the captain's log, Kirk promptly asks for a replacement for McCoy. Then the captain almost refuses to allow him to go with the next landing party,

FOR THE WORLD IS HOLLOW AND I HAVE TOUCHED THE SKY

and a short time later tells Spock about the doctor's illness. Do these sound like the actions of a friend?

CHANGED PREMISES

• Beaming over to the inner surface of the asteroid, the landing party soon discovers several large cylinders. Suddenly the cylinders behind the landing party rise, and Yonadan guards jump out. The cylinders make a definite humming sound as they rise, yet Spock—with his supersensitive hearing (see "Operation—Annihilate!")—is taken by surprise along with the others. There's only one possible explanation for this: McCoy didn't get Spock's hearing hooked up correctly when he reinstalled the Vulcan's brain (see "Spock's Brain").

EQUIPMENT ODDITIES

• *Yonada* has a room where Natira speaks with the "Oracle," a computer that poses as the voice of the creators. After capturing the landing party, she leads them to the Oracle room. Once there, she holds out a phaser and a communicator and says of the landing party that they bear instruments that she and her people do not understand. Of course, the whole time one of the Yonadan guards holds a phaser trained on the landing party. For not understanding these devices, the Yonadans apparently know how to use them.

• Once again, a landing party from the *Enterprise* leaves weapons of sophisticated design

behind on a less developed world. No indication is ever given that Kirk recovered the three phasers confiscated by the Yonadans from the original landing party.

• It's an old problem, but the pulse light is way off on the close-ups as the medical panel thumps away at the end of the show.

CONTINUITY AND PRODUCTION PROBLEMS

• Before beaming over to *Yonada,* Kirk orders Sulu to match the speed of the apparent asteroid. Moments later, a graphic shows the *Enterprise* flying in front of *Yonada,* which is clearly gaining on the *Enterprise*.

• Coming back from a commercial break, Natira kneels beside McCoy's limp body. A weird shadow runs across the wall behind her.

TRIVIA ANSWERS
1. Daran IV.
2. Admiral Westervliet.

CLOSING STILLS

• Kirk and Spock shocked by Oracle, "For the World Is Hollow and I Have Touched the Sky"
• Imperial Spock, "Mirror, Mirror"
• Floor game, Platonius, "Plato's Stepchildren"
• Spock mesmerizing female, "The Omega Glory"
• Tiger, "Shore Leave"
• Earth outposts 2, 3, and 4 along the Neutral Zone, "Balance of Terror"

THE THOLIAN WEB

Star Date: 5693.2

When the *Enterprise* comes upon the USS *Defiant,* Kirk and a landing party find its crew dead, evidently by their own hands. Suddenly the *Defiant* begins to fade. The landing party makes a hasty retreat, but Kirk is trapped on board. Spock's subsequent research shows that this area of space is unstable, creating interfaces between parallel universes. At the next interface, he hopes to rescue his captain.

Meanwhile, a Tholian vessel approaches and demands an explanation for the intrusion into their space. In response, Spock predicts the next appearance of the *Defiant.* Unfortunately, the extra ship has disturbed the fabric of space. When the *Defiant* fails to appear, the Tholians attack. The battle cripples the *Enterprise* and disrupts the area even further. Soon another Tholian vessel appears, and the two begin encircling the *Enterprise* with tractor field filaments. At the same time, the unstable space begins to brew

an insanity in the crew, just as it did to the *Defiant's* crew. Then several officers report seeing Kirk. With these new data, Spock calculates the time of the captain's next appearance. At the last moment, Kirk rematerializes, the tractor beam engages, and a full-power pulse of the engines throws the *Enterprise* clear of the Tholian web.

PLOT OVERSIGHTS

• During the mission to the *Defiant,* McCoy passes his hand through a dead crew member and a table in sick bay. He reports these actions, and Kirk orders everyone to reassemble for transport. If the crew member is fading from reality as is the table, shouldn't the floors be fading from reality as well? (A similar problem occurs in the *Star Trek: The Next Generation* episode "The Next Phase.")

• With the captain presumed dead, Spock holds a wake for Kirk. At the end of it, Scott calls, "Attention!" Everyone stands. Some put their hands behind their backs, some in front, some at their side. Some slouch. Some stand up

Trivia Questions

1. What sections of the *Enterprise* sustain minor structural damage in the first Tholian attack?

2. What is the combination on Kirk's safe?

straight. I wonder what "at ease" looks like?

• Eventually McCoy discovers a substance to protect the crew from the effects of the unstable space. He mixes alcohol with a Klingon nerve gas called theragen. When administering the antidote to Spock and Scott, the Vulcan expresses surprise at the doctor's solution. Evidently Spock wasn't listening when McCoy told the Vulcan earlier in the episode that he was pursuing a cure based on theragen.

• With twenty minutes to go before the Tholians close their web and Kirk's last possible opportunity for rescue, Scott hoists a bottle full of the theragen-alcohol mix and strolls out the door. On the way, he tells McCoy that he will let the doctor know if it makes a good mixer with scotch. Supposedly it is a cute moment. Do the creators really expect us to believe that Scott is going off to get drunk at a time like this?

• Although not absolutely verifiable, it appears that Chekov is "in" on the playful banter at the end of the show concerning whether Spock and McCoy listened to Kirk's final instructions. He shouldn't be. He was in sick bay the entire time.

CHANGED PREMISES

• As part of the playful banter at the end of the episode, Spock and McCoy act as if they didn't listen to Kirk's final orders. Spock, in fact, purposely deceives the captain into thinking this. What happened to "Vulcans never lie"?

EQUIPMENT ODDITIES

• After the Tholians launch their first salvo, Uhura reports minor structural damage to the ship. In response, Spock increases power to the shields. Then the Tholians attack again. This time the weapon that caused only minor damage when the shields were set at a lower intensity suddenly shorts out some really important power thingamajigs. Does this seem right?

• Spock does repay the Tholians for their attack. He hits them with the phasers, a good, clean hit—a hit so good you can actually see stars shining through the back end of the Tholian ship.

• After Chekov wigs out, McCoy tells the security guards to take him to sick bay and put him in restraints. The next time we see Chekov he has the upper calf and biceps straps, but he also has a strap across his waist. It wraps around each wrist. This will not work. If Chekov twists his hands, the strap will pop right off. Tightening the strap will only make it easier to remove, because the action will force his wrists in the direction they need to move to break free.

• While we're on the subject of straps, I'm not sure why they even bothered with the one they put on Uhura. It is obviously just for looks.

• In "Journey to Babel" I mentioned that Kirk has to squat down to see himself in his mirror. In this episode it appears that the mirror in Spock's quarters is even lower, with respect to his person.

• Just as the Tholians close their web, Kirk appears and Spock says, "Ready to transport on my order." Then the Vulcan brings the ship to full power and the discharge throws the *Enterprise* clear of the tractor field. Moments later, Spock claims that the transporter beams had locked on to the captain and pulled him with them. Note that Spock never said, "Energize." In other words, the transporter chief locked a beam on the captain with only Spock's instruction to get ready to transport. (I suppose this isn't really impossible, but I always had the impression that locking a beam on someone came during the actual transportation process.)

• After Kirk beams aboard, McCoy gives him a hypo right through the spacesuit. Isn't the suit designed to be impervious to air and liquid? A porous spacesuit is as effective as the old screen door on a submarine.

CONTINUITY AND PRODUCTION PROBLEMS

• A short time after returning from the *Defiant,* Chekov goes bonkers. At one point his mouth forms a medium-size "O" and he lets out a hearty scream. It is possible, but it really looks funny.

• Several scenes later, McCoy's orderly loses it as well and attacks the doctor with a metal rod. For effect, the creators show

us the madman's viewpoint with a wide-angle lens. It distorts the image, giving the scene the appropriate feel. However, the perspective is shot from the orderly's right shoulder. Has this guy's head suddenly moved to the right? Is that why he's gone mad? (I'd certainly be mad if someone moved my head sideways.)

• And speaking of the fight scene in sick bay, the orderly forces McCoy crosswise onto the table. Then a distorted close-up shows the doctor lengthwise on the table.

• One last thing before I move on. During the fight, the bottles on the table fly everywhere. They don't look very heavy, and they certainly aren't bolted down. Yet when the Tholians attack and the impact of their weapon tosses McCoy and Chapel around in sick bay, the bottles stay perfectly still. (Is that amazing, or what?)

• During the transport of the captain at the end of the show, the creators used Scott's hands for the close-up on the transporter controls. The gold braid shows a rank of lieutenant commander, but the guy working the controls is only a lieutenant.

TRIVIA ANSWERS

1. A4 and C13.
2. Numbering the buttons from left to right: 5, 4, 3.

CLOSING STILLS

• Starbase 11, "Court-Martial"

• Melkotian, "Spectre of the Gun"

• Aged Uhura standing with hands raised, "And the Children Shall Lead" (This shot is cropped for use in the mirror showing Uhura's greatest fear.)

• Aged McCoy, "The Deadly Years"

• Star field

PLATO'S STEPCHILDREN

Star Dates: 5784.2-5784.3

An urgent distress call brings the *Enterprise* to Platonius. Beaming down, Kirk, Spock, and McCoy find the Platonian leader, Parmen, suffering from a massive infection in his leg. When McCoy attempts to give Parmen a shot, the hypospray leaps up, floats through the air, and injects the leader on its own. Telekinesis—the ability to move objects by thought alone—is common among the Platonians. Parmen recovers quickly, but when the landing party attempts to leave, the leader insists that McCoy stay behind. Of course, the doctor refuses. At this, Parmen uses his powers to force Kirk and Spock to play the fools in a series of humiliating performances.

Back in their quarters, the trio discover that the substance kironide is the source of the Platonians' power. With large doses of kironide injected directly into their bloodstreams, Kirk and Spock develop telekinesis as well and dominate the Platonians. As the landing party departs, Kirk delivers a stern warning to the Platonians to treat kindly any starships that happen by. After all, Kirk and the others have the knowledge to re-create the power any time they choose.

Trivia Questions

1. On what planet did the Platonians originate?

2. How long after their arrival on their current world did the Platonians develop their powers?

RUMINATIONS

In this episode, Michael Dunn turns in a wonderful performance as Alexander, the Platonians' court jester and the only one among them without the "power."

GREAT LINES

"I guess we weren't sufficiently entertaining."—Kirk upon seeing that the Platonians have forced Uhura and Chapel to beam down. (I once saw a commercial produced by a television station to announce that *Star Trek: The Next Generation* would be seen five days a week along with *Star Trek*. In a delightful little twist, the commercial ended with Kirk saying this line!)

GREAT MOMENTS

After the first humiliating session, Spock admits that the Platonians have aroused an intense hatred within him. While recommending that Kirk and McCoy release their emotions, the Vulcan states that he must control his. Spock stands during these statements and walks to a small table. As he speaks, he places his hand on a vase and proceeds to crush it, giving us yet another hint of the great power that the Vulcan keeps tightly reined.

SYNDICATION CUTS

• Spock and Philana discuss telekinesis and sleep.

• As Kirk tries to protect Alexander from Parmen's delirious mental attacks, Alexander yells for the landing party to let Parmen die. This edit removes a plot oversight. Later in the show, Alexander grows angry, smashes a pot, and grabs a shard. Using their mental abilities, the Platonians have become physically weakened. Even a scratch results in terrible infection and potential death. Alexander intends to cut them all. When Kirk talks him out of it, Alexander replies that it's the first time anyone thought of his life before his or her own. Actually, in the uncut version, it's the second, because Kirk takes several blows meant for Alexander during this edit.

• A "boop" just before the scene returns to Kirk after Scott reports that the turbulence has abated on board the ship. (Seriously, the editors cut only the "boop." They save themselves maybe a half second!)

• The last half of Kirk's second conversation with Scott and the first half of Alexander's song

before Kirk walks in to talk with Parmen.

• Kirk observes the pleasantries before demanding the release of his ship from Parmen. In the syndicated version, it appears that Kirk barges into Parmen's quarters and begins with rudeness. In fact, our good captain makes a polite attempt to reason with Parmen before things turn nasty.

• Kirk slaps himself several more times under Parmen's control.

• Following a commercial break, Kirk attempts to contact the *Enterprise*; the trio discuss the situation and then are drawn to Parmen's quarters.

• A section of Parmen's torture of Kirk.

• After Kirk makes like a horse, the scene zooms up to McCoy and breaks for a commercial. In these final moments, the syndicated version has slightly different music than the uncut version.

• Following a commercial break, a close-up of Spock pulling back to include McCoy standing over the Vulcan. The doctor then checks on Kirk, and they discuss Spock's difficulty coping with Parmen forcing emotion from him.

• After a commercial break, Uhura and Chapel wander into the entertainment hall.

• The second verse of Spock's song.

PLOT OVERSIGHTS

• In his second log, Kirk claims that the Platonians moved to Earth when their planet "novaed." Then, when the Greek civilization died, they moved to their current planet. First, planets do not go nova, stars go nova (picky, picky, picky). Second, the Platonians seem to have an amazing knowledge of Earth, given their departure several millennia ago. Parmen has Spock perform what looks like a Mexican hat dance around Kirk's head. And later in the show, Parmen refers to the *pièce de résistance*. Bear in mind that Parmen's power are tele-kinetic, not telepathic. He cannot read the minds of the crew members of the *Enterprise*, nor is there any indication that he can access their library files.

• Strangely enough, Kirk and company instantly forget they have the ability to create telekinesis after this episode. Think of the differ-ence telekinesis would make in a show like "The Empath." Kirk could easily turn the tables on the Vians. Conveniently forgetting new capa-bilities is standard fare for the crew of the *Enterprise*, however. They forget the amazing healing powers of the spores on Omicron Ceti III after "This Side of Paradise." They forget that the Romulan cloaking device worked at the end of "The *Enterprise* Incident." And they for-get that Scalosian water can accel-erate a humanoid after "Wink of an Eye." (Of course, if they remem-bered, most episodes would end very quickly.)

• To supply the Platonians with entertainment, Kirk dons a toga. (Actually, it's a miniskirt. Let's just see how *he* likes wearing one! But

I digress . . .) Presumably, our dear captain didn't jump into this outfit by himself. A Platonian "helped" him. (I'll let you decide if it was Parmen or his beloved wife, Philana.) Yet at the end of the show, Kirk reaches in back of the toga and pulls out a communicator. It was very thoughtful of the Platonian to allow Kirk to carry it along. I'm sure he or she realized that Starfleet officers just feel naked without them.

EQUIPMENT ODDITIES

• This little medical kit that McCoy carries is truly amazing. It doesn't look very big, but he manages to manufacture all sorts of chemical substances with it. At the begin-ning of the episode, Kirk says that Platonius has rich deposits of kironide—a substance the captain identifies as *rare*. When McCoy discovers that kironide has given the Platonians their powers, Kirk asks the doctor to inject him and Spock with the substance. McCoy rummages around in his kit for a few seconds and concocts the liq-uid. Just where did he get distilled kironide? Granted, it is supposedly in all the food and water on the planet, but when did McCoy have time to extract it? Or does he somehow magically carry around every chemical substance known to the Federation in that little med-ical kit?

• At the end of the episode, Parmen turns to sadism, attempt-ing to convince McCoy to stay behind. A table rolls out with a red-hot poker, a whip, a knife, and other implements of torture. Oddly enough, the knife is Rigelian in design! In fact—from the designs on the handle and given my vast knowledge on the subject—I'd say it was manufactured by the hill people of the Argus River Region on Rigel IV! (Are you impressed? I supposed I should confess. It's the knife that was used in the episode "Wolf in the Fold.")

CONTINUITY AND PRODUCTION PROBLEMS

• When Kirk, Spock, and McCoy materialize on Platonius, the wall behind them is identical to the wall behind the trio when they materialize at Starbase 11 in "The Menagerie, Part I."

• The actress who plays Philana, Barbara Babcock, also starred as Mea 3 in "A Taste of Armageddon."

• For the most part, the telekinetic effects (i.e., stuff flying through the air) are done well in this episode. When McCoy's hypo flies over to give Parmen a shot, however, you can see the strings.

TRIVIA ANSWERS

1. Sahndara.
2. Six months, fourteen days.

CLOSING STILLS

• Lawgivers leaving Hall of Audience, "The Return of the Archons" (This scene is never shown in the episode.)

• Nazi headquarters, Ekos, "Patterns of Force"

• Spock playing chess with Rojan, "By Any Other Name"

• Buildings, Deneva, "Operation—Annihilate!"

• *Galileo* taking off, "The *Galileo* Seven"

• The view just before Trelane creates Gothos, "The Squire of Gothos"

WINK OF AN EYE

Star Dates: 5710.5–5710.9

After luring the *Enterprise* to their planet with a phony distress call, five Scalosians slip on board. They live a hyperaccelerated existence and can move in the wink of an eye. Centuries ago, a terrible war devastated the planet, causing the original acceleration and leaving all males sterile. To propagate their race, the Scalosians lure ships to their planet. The remaining Scalosian women then choose men from the ships as their mates, after accelerating them with a drink of Scalosian water. Of course, the chosen men age much quicker in the accelerated time frame and—in a relatively short amount of time—they "burn up." Given the size of the *Enterprise* crew and the speed at which the Scalosian women go through men, the Scalosian scientists install a suspended animation device on the ship. The machine will freeze the crew until they are needed.

The queen of the Scalosians, Deela, chooses Kirk as her first mate. Kirk quickly learns all the relevant facts and passes them on to Spock, using a computer recording. After constructing an antidote to the Scalosian water, Spock accelerates himself. Together he and Kirk overpower the Scalosians and return them to the surface. Kirk then returns to normal time while Spock effects repairs on the ship.

RUMINATIONS

The creators used a nice technique to differentiate normal and accelerated existence in this episode. They shot all the scenes featuring Scalosians or accelerated Starfleet officers with the camera tipped at an angle. It gives those moments a more surreal look.

GREAT MOMENTS

After an ensign disappears on the surface, the landing party returns to the ship, and Kirk orders medical exams for everyone. As Kirk lies down on the sick bay table, McCoy says everyone checks out normal. Around this time, Deela takes the opportunity to kiss Kirk and tousle his hair. The creators actually went to the extra effort of attaching some type of mechanism to the captain's locks so they appear to jump up by themselves. (At this point in the episode, Kirk is living a normal existence while Deela is accelerated, so we cannot actually see her kiss him.) Kudos!

PLOT OVERSIGHTS

• The episode opens with Scott making a log entry. Kirk and company are on the surface, trying to locate the source of a distress call. Just how often do Starfleet officers make these log entries? Has the landing party really been gone long enough for Scott to record one, or did Kirk simply forget to do it before beaming down?

• Of course, the really big question with this episode is: How fast are these Scalosians? What is the ratio between hyperaccelerated and normal existence? There are a few hints. First, the crew can't see them. That means a Scalosian cannot be in one spot for more than one sixtieth of a second. Otherwise their image would "ghost" due to persistence of vision. Second, Deela *dodges* a phaser blast! Obviously—even though phasers use some type of electromagnetic energy—the discharge from a phaser must not travel at the speed of light. If it did, Deela would have to exceed the speed of light to get out of the way. According to our current understanding of physics, that's not possible. Third, Scott's entrance into the transporter room gives us a

final clue. From the time the chief engineer appears in the transporter room doorway until Kirk decelerates to normal time, there are about seven minutes of running dialogue in the accelerated existence. In that time, Scott barely moves a step—maybe one half-second in normal time. Using this ratio, the Scalosians would live 840 minutes for every minute of normal time (7 minutes times 60 seconds times 2, because Scott only moved half a second's worth). This estimate is probably low, because Deela did dodge a phaser blast, but it is sufficient for our needs.

Here's the nit. If it takes the Scalosians eight of their hours to install their deep-freeze device, how much time does the crew have to: (1) figure out that they've been invaded, (2) find the agent responsible for accelerating Kirk, (3) devise an antidote, and (4) dispatch Spock into hyperaccelerated existence to assist Kirk in thwarting the Scalosians' plans? Even with the low estimate of the ratio between normal and hyperaccelerated existence, our fearless crew would have only 34 seconds to accomplish these feats! (Just for the sake of argument, let's say the ratio is much lower, in the range of 120 to 1. The crew would still have only 4 minutes to stop the Scalosians. Hardly enough time for Spock and McCoy to argue over how to proceed!)

• After Deela accelerates Kirk, one shot shows Spock still moving. How can Spock be moving? Is it that incredible Vulcan physique again?

EQUIPMENT ODDITIES

• Deela claims that she gained access to the ship by beaming aboard with Kirk. Are the transporters really calibrated to lock on to a hyperaccelerated being? And even if they can, wouldn't Deela be frozen in place during the transport? And if she is frozen in place, wouldn't someone—such as the transporter chief—see her?

• Yet again, the pulse light is way off with the audible thumping on the close-ups of the medpanel in sick bay.

• Near the beginning of the episode, Kirk and Spock go to the life support area and examine the Scalosian equipment. The wall behind them holds a vertical stack of objects that look amazingly similar to the knowledge library that Spock discovered on Yonada in the episode (everyone take a deep breath so you have enough to get through this title) "For the World Is Hollow and I Have Touched the Sky." In that episode, Spock identified them as the accumulated knowledge of the Fabrini. (I would hate to think that Starfleet absconded with this very important information.)

• Turbolifts and doors provide an interesting challenge for accelerated existence. Do the Scalosians actually use the turbolifts? Wouldn't that form of transport be insufferably slow? And what about the automatic doors? The creators

conveniently sidestep this issue for the majority of the episode by showing the doors open. Most of the time there's no one near the doors, however. So why are they open? (Because it would take forever for them to open for those living in a hyperaccelerated existence, and it's only a one-hour program!)

• When Spock reviews the logs made by the landing party on the surface of the planet, the computer plays them out of sequence. On the surface, McCoy commented about the lack of life, and then Kirk mentioned a buzzing insect sound. During playback on the ship, the comments are reversed.

CONTINUITY AND PRODUCTION PROBLEMS

• The cityscape featured in this episode originally appeared in "A Taste of Armageddon."

• At the end of the episode, Kirk uses a Scalosian weapon to destroy the deep-freeze device. If you watch the explosion carefully, you can see some type of wick below it.

TRIVIA ANSWERS

1. Environmental Engineering.
2. Rael.

CLOSING STILLS

• Scientific research center on Psi 2000, "The Naked Time"

• Kirk on trial, "The Squire of Gothos"

• Talosian beast illusion, "The Cage"

- Pergium production station, Janus VI, "The Devil in the Dark"
- Engineering, "The Enemy Within" (This shot never appears in the episode.)
- Star field

THE EMPATH

Star Date: 5121.5

The star of the Minaran system will soon go nova, and the *Enterprise* arrives to pick up a scientific team. Kirk, Spock and McCoy find the research station abandoned but are quickly transported to an underground cavern. There they meet a beautiful mute empath whom McCoy names Gem. They also find the Federation scientists. Both are dead. Moments later, two Vians appear. They speak of necessary experiments and torture Kirk. Afterward, Gem uses her empathic abilities to heal the captain.

Soon the Vians return, claiming more testing is necessary. As Gem observes, McCoy tranquilizes the others and submits himself. By the time Kirk and Spock awake, the doctor is moments from death. The Vians explain that they can transport the inhabitants of only one Minaran planet to safety before the star explodes. Gem's people show the most promise, but the Vians must know that she can embrace the highest qualities

Trivia Questions

1. What animals appear as inanimate rock crystals until they attack?

2. What planet serves as home for a race of mutes?

of life, including self-sacrifice. McCoy's injuries are so severe that she might die if she tries to save him. Gem does try, but McCoy shoves her aside. At this, Kirk pleads with the Vians, claiming that her actions are enough, that no one needs to die to conclude the experiment. The Vians agree, heal McCoy, and disappear with Gem.

RUMINATIONS

The credits identify one of the Vians as Lal. This name revisits the Star Trek *universe in the* Star Trek: The Next Generation *episode, "The Offspring." In that episode, Data names his daughter Lal.*

I love this episode. It brings out the nobility and self-sacrifice of Kirk, Spock, and McCoy as each vies for an opportunity to protect the others.

GREAT LINES

"Everything that is truest and best of all species and beings has been revealed by you."—Thann complimenting Kirk, Spock, and McCoy on their performance during the experiment.

PLOT OVERSIGHTS

• OSHA, the Occupational Safety and Health Administration, must be out of business in the twenty-third century. To gain access to the research station, Kirk, Spock, and McCoy must walk down a narrow, steep, and winding staircase with no handrail.

• For some unknown reason, when the Vians torture Kirk; they take his shirt off and then dress him before sending him back to his friends. Were they concerned that he would stink up his shirt during the process and Gem might be offended by his body odor?

• Spock seems to have lost his motivation in this episode. Early on, he neck-pinches a Vian. At this, Kirk grabs the hand-held device the Vian uses to work his magic. Then the landing party and Gem escape to the surface. Once there, the Vians return Spock and McCoy to a holding area and torture Kirk as Gem watches. Afterward, Spock asks Kirk for permission to examine the Vian device. Why hasn't he done this already?

EQUIPMENT ODDITIES

• I am constantly amazed at the sophisticated manner in which visual logs are recorded. When Spock plays back the scientists' log, the camera pans and zooms to follow the action.

• After examining the Vian hand-held controller, Spock claims that it is operated by the specific brain patterns of an individual. He then tunes it to operate on his patterns. Yet near the end of the show, Kirk gives the device back to one of the Vians, and the guy uses it to heal McCoy. Wouldn't it still be tuned to Spock's brain patterns, or was our good Vulcan friend simply confused?

CONTINUITY AND PRODUCTION PROBLEMS

• During Kirk's torture, a wide shot from the back shows his arms outstretched, while the close-ups from the front show his arms cocked at the elbows.

• Evidently the preview for this episode was created before all the opticals were completed. In one scene, Gem heals Kirk's wrists. The episode shows the wounds dissolving away. On the other hand, the preview has edits between the various stages of healing.

TRIVIA ANSWERS

1. The sand bats of Manark IV.
2. Gamma Vertis IV.

CLOSING STILLS

• The *Enterprise* in the energy barrier, "Where No Man Has Gone Before"

• Kirk and Spock in Athenian outfits, "Plato's Stepchildren"

• Apollo's temple, Pollux IV, "Who Mourns for Adonais?"

• "Asteroid", *Yonada,* "For the World Is Hollow and I Have Touched the Sky"

• Roman Colosseum backdrop,

"Bread and Circuses"
 • System L374 after a visit from the planet killer, "The Doomsday Machine"

TRIATHLON TRIVIA ON OTHER CHARACTERS

MATCH THE CHARACTER TO THE DESCRIPTION TO THE EPISODE OR MOVIE:

	CHARACTER		DESCRIPTION		EPISODE OR MOVIE
1.	Alexander	A.	High-minded cloud dweller	a.	"Errand of Mercy"
2.	Andrea	B.	Redjac in disguise	b.	"The Empath"
3.	Appel, Ed	C.	The oldest boy	c.	"What Are Little Girls Made Of?"
4.	Ayelborne	D.	Sargon's nemesis	d.	"Catspaw"
5.	Companion	E.	She introduced Spock to emotion	e.	"Amok Time"
6.	Cromwell	F.	Rigged the engines to explode	f.	"Assignment: Earth"
7.	Daily, Jon	G.	Wrote Shakespearean poetry	g.	"The Gamesters of Triskelion"
8.	Daystrom, Dr.Richard	H.	Launch director	h.	"The Squire of Gothos"
9.	Deela	I.	Kirok's nemesis	i	*Star Trek III: The Search for Spock*
10.	Droxine	J.	Kirk's brother's wife	j.	"Dagger of the Mind"
11.	Drusilla	K.	The perfect wife for an immortal	k.	"The Trouble with Tribbles"
12.	Eleen	L.	Seductive cat woman	l.	"A Private Little War"
13.	Forever, Guardian of	M.	European-accented Kelvan	m.	"The Conscience of the King"
14.	Gem	N.	First android to kiss Kirk	n.	"The City on the Edge of Forever"
15.	Gorgan	O.	Bichromatic being	o.	"Mudd's Women"
16.	Hedford, Nancy	P.	Put the bag on Kirk	p.	"Metamorphosis"
17.	Hengist	Q.	Fought his alternate self	q.	"I, Mudd"
18.	Henoch	R.	Ruled a society of zombies	r.	"The Omega Glory"
19.	Jahn	S.	Did what no other woman had	s.	"The Devil in the Dark"
20.	Jones, Cyrano	T.	Her touch was deadly	t.	*Star Trek II: The Wrath of Khan*
21.	Jones, Dr. Miranda	U.	Energy being in disguise	u.	"The Mark of Gideon"
22.	Kalomi, Leila	V.	The Eymorg at the elevator	v.	"A Taste of Armageddon"
23.	Kapec, Rayna	W.	Regent of the new potentate	w.	"The Cloudminders"
24.	Keeler, Edith	X.	One of Mudd's women	x.	"For the World Is Hollow and I Have Touched the Sky"

#	Name		Clue		Episode
25.	Kelinda	Y.	Queen of the hyperaccelerated	y.	"Whom Gods Destroy"
26.	Kirk, Aurelan	Z.	High priestess of Yonada	z.	"That Which Survives"
27.	Krako, Jojo	AA.	Court buffoon	aa.	"The Ultimate Computer"
28.	Kryton	BB.	Female witch doctor	bb.	"Turnabout Intruder"
29.	Landru	CC.	Head android on Mudd I	cc.	"Requiem for Methuselah"
30.	Lazarus	DD.	Wanted revenge on Kirk	dd.	"By Any Other Name"
31.	Lester, Dr. Janice	EE.	Shot Horta before Kirk came	ee.	"This Side of Paradise"
32.	Lokai	FF.	Deceiver of children	ff.	"Return to Tomorrow"
33.	Losira	GG.	Led a program of depopulation	gg.	"Bread and Circuses"
34.	Luma	HH.	Captain of the *Astral Queen*	hh.	"Wolf in the Fold"
35.	Marta	II.	Skon's son	ii.	"Miri"
36.	McHuron, Eve	JJ.	Gateway to all times	jj.	"Wink of an Eye"
37.	Mea 3	KK.	Zephram Cochrane's lover	kk.	"Friday's Child"
38.	Natira	LL.	Trader of tribbles	ll.	"And the Children Shall Lead"
39.	Nona	MM.	Assistant Federation commissioner	mm.	"Plato's Stepchildren"
40.	Norman	NN.	Chekov's drill thrall	nn.	"A Piece of the Action"
41.	Odana	OO.	Had a duel with Kirk	oo.	"Operation—Annihilate!"
42.	Salish	PP.	Wanted to be disintegrated	pp.	"Elaan of Troyius"
43.	Sarek	QQ.	Nona's mate	qq.	"The Alternative Factor"
44.	Singh, Khan Noonien	RR.	Made insane by Adams	rr.	"Spock's Brain"
45.	Sylvia	SS.	Leader of the Yangs	ss.	"The Return of the Archons"
46.	T'Pau	TT.	Visionary in 1930s	tt.	"Let That Be Your Last Battlefield"
47.	Tamoon	UU.	Beautiful, blind telepath	uu.	"All Our Yesterdays"
48.	Trelane	VV.	Inventor of the M5	vv.	"Is There in Truth No Beauty?"
49.	Tyree	WW.	Mute empath	ww.	"The Paradise Syndrome"
50.	Van Gelder, Dr. Simon	XX.	Spock's 5,000 year-old love		
51.	William, Cloud	YY.	Official at Spock's wedding		
52.	Zarabeth	ZZ.	Slave babe to Marcus		

SCORING
(BASED ON NUMBER OF CORRECT ANSWERS)

0–8	Normal.
9–15	Don't worry. Your vast knowledge of *Star Trek*—while a bit on the excessive side—is no cause for concern.
15 and up	It may be time to seek professional help.

CHARACTERS ANSWER KEY: 1. AA mm 2. N c 3. EE s 4. U a 5. KK p 6. H f 7. HH m 8. VV aa 9. Y jj 10. A w 11. ZZ gg 12. W kk 13. JJ n 14. WW b 15. FF ll 16. MM p 17. B hh 18. D ff 19. C ii 20. LL k 21. UU vv 22. E ee 23. K cc 24. TT n 25. M dd 26. J oo 27. P nn 28. F pp 29. R ss 30. Q qq 31. S bb 32. O tt 33. T z 34. V rr 35. G y 36. X o 37. PP v 38. Z x 39. BB l 40. CC q 41. GG u 42. I ww 43. II i 44. DD t 45. L d 46. YY e 47. NN g 48. OO h 49. QQ l 50. RR j 51. SS r 52. XX uu

ELAAN OF TROYIUS

Star Date: 4372.5

The *Enterprise* travels to the Tellun star system. Civilizations on two of its planets, Elas and Troyius, have reached the stage where it is possible for them to destroy each other. To foster peace, both governments have agreed to a joining between the king of Troyius and the Dohlman of Elas. Having already picked up Troyius ambassador Petri, the *Enterprise* drops into orbit around Elas. The crew beams the Dohlman and her entourage aboard and Petri begins the process of acclimating his future queen—a female named Elaan—to the customs of Troyius. The people of Elas are fierce warriors, lacking in the social graces. During one session, Elaan stabs Petri, effectively removing him from the role of mentor.

Kirk picks up the challenge and begins to make progress when one of Elaan's guards sabotages the matter/antimatter chamber, burning up the dilithium crystals. A Klingon vessel appears, demanding that Kirk surrender. In the middle of the one-sided battle, Elaan appears on the bridge wearing a necklace made of common stones from her planet. The stones are dilithium crystals. Obviously, the Klingons knew of the rich deposits on Elas and wanted to abort the peace process. Using the crystals, Kirk beats back the Klingons and safely delivers Elaan to Troyius.

Trivia Questions

1. Who provided the wedding dress for Elaan?

2. Whom did Kryton kill while sabotaging the *Enterprise?*

RUMINATIONS

This episode shares a few themes with the Star Trek: The Next Generation episode "The Perfect Mate." In both, a woman given as a mate provides a vehicle for peace. In both, the woman has an enhanced power of sexual attraction. In both, the captain is smitten by the woman and must give her up for the cause of duty.

GREAT MOMENTS

France Nuyen, the actress who plays Elaan, does an excellent job with her portrayal, providing the episode with many great moments as she wars and loves with Kirk.

SYNDICATION CUTS

• The last half of Kirk's conversation with Petri in the hall outside the transporter room. In it, Petri reminds Kirk that the mission is important to the Federation as well.

• Spock states that the Klingon vessel is pacing the *Enterprise* just before security summons Kirk to Elaan's quarters.

• Petri recuperating from Elaan's knife wound and stating that he wants nothing to do with Kirk. He claims that Kirk's advice put him in sick bay and he intends to stay there.

• After Kirk tells Elaan that she will learn what she has been ordered to learn, several reaction shots, Elaan's demand that Kirk return her to Elas, and Kirk's refusal.

• Following Kirk's exit of Elaan's quarters, establishing shots of the *Enterprise* and the Klingon vessel along with Kirk's attempt to ask the Klingons their intentions.

• Kirk asks Uhura if she can pinpoint the source of the transmission, and Spock triangulates on it.

• After claiming they have no chance without dilithium crystals, Scott asks Kirk if they can contact Starfleet. Kirk refuses, claiming that it would tip off the Klingons that they succeeded in crippling the ship. These lines cause a plot oversight. Wouldn't it be standard procedure to contact Starfleet if an attack seems imminent from a Klingon vessel? Can't Starfleet

transmit in code and obscure the actual content of the message? Also deleted in this edit, Petri attempts to convince Elaan to wear a necklace containing "the most prized of royal jewels." Surprisingly enough, this same necklace shows up on Elaan's neck several moments later, and she tells Kirk that the necklace comes from her planet and the stones are common. (More on this nit later. Even though it is edited out at this point, the royal necklace is introduced earlier in the episode, making the nit ripe for picking!)

• A message from the Klingon vessel giving Kirk one last chance to surrender.

• Scott complains that the irregular energy flow from the crystals could blow them up, Kirk bargains for time by asking the Klingons to ensure the safety of Elaan, and the Klingons refuse.

PLOT OVERSIGHTS

• For a savage, Elaan of Elas is a clothes hound. She changes revealing outfits no less than four times in this show!

• At the end of the episode, Elaan dons a blue smock with gathers at the side. (Poor girl, the outfit barely fits her. Neither side closes, and both gaps are easily two inches.) She also puts on a necklace that contains several large crystals. Interestingly enough, the dress looks like the one Petri offered at the beginning of the episode as a wedding garment, and the necklace looks just like the one Petri offers in a box as "the most prized of royal jewels." Obviously the creators wanted to give the impression that Elaan had finally accepted her responsibilities and acquiesced to the marriage. However, when Spock discovers that the jewels in the necklace are dilithium crystals, Elaan acts as if the necklace comes from Elas and the stones are practically worthless. So did the necklace come from Troyius or Elas? Or were there supposed to be two necklaces and the creators fudged a bit? Also, if the necklace comes from Troyius, how will the rulers feel about the crew of the *Enterprise* appropriating some of their gemstones? Will they really believe Kirk when he says it was essential for the survival of the ship? Remember, these people don't have warp drive and obviously don't understand what dilithium crystals can do. If an alien culture transported a female Mars potentate to marry a British king on Earth, how would the queen mother feel if the aliens said, "Oh, by the way, we had to take some of your crown jewels to make our engines work"?

• At one point, Kirk barges in on Elaan as she eats. According to my wife, Elaan dines on green chicken. Obviously the cooks on the *Enterprise* found out that Elasians will eat anything. They took the opportunity to clean out the refrigerator. The meat had definitely been in there too long.

• Sulu has gotten into a bad habit. He looks back at the captain's chair even when Kirk isn't in it! In one scene, Sulu looks back, and at the same time, Kirk walks off the turbolift. There's nobody in the captain's chair, and Sulu cannot see Kirk from this viewpoint.

EQUIPMENT ODDITIES

• After seeing the pursuing vessel on the viewscreen, Kirk emphatically states that it is the Klingons. How does Kirk know this? Don't the Romulans fly ships of Klingon design?

• When Security calls Kirk to Elaan's quarters to rescue Petri, a close-up shows a workstation intercom and a hand reaching up to answer the hail. Two problems: The light is already on before the hand presses the button, and Kirk isn't standing at a workstation, he's standing beside his captain's chair.

• When Kryton skulks into Engineering, watch the guy on the upper level of the engine room. He checks some settings, walks a little farther, checks a few more things, and then tries to walk through a door. The door must have been daydreaming because the guy has to stop and wait for it to open.

• Kirk shows up in Engineering shortly after the security guards apprehend Kryton. Scott hands the captain the communicator Kryton used, and Kirk flips it open.

It promptly flips back shut, and Kirk pronounces it "Klingon." (I can't help but wonder if the captain is thinking, "Stupid communicator, obviously Klingon in design, won't even stay open when you flip it.")

• It's grungy nitpicking time! As the Klingon vessel makes its first flyby, Sulu counts off the distance: "100,000 kilometers, 90,000 kilometers, 80,000 kilometers." He pauses about two seconds between each number. The speed of light is about 300,000 kilometers a second, and Spock says moments earlier that the Klingon ship is approaching at warp six. Warp six is many, many times the speed of light. Sulu's countdown puts the Klingon vessel at approximately 5,000 kilometers a second, well *below* the speed of light.

CONTINUITY AND PRODUCTION PROBLEMS

• When the Elasians beam in at the beginning of the episode, those clever creators used Scott's hands on the transporter controls. Yet the chief engineer stands across the room.

• The prop guys got a little door plaque happy in this episode. Crew quarters have two entrances, one for each room. In Uhura's quarters the door near the big cylinder thing where Uhura keeps her unmentionables is covered by a large cloth with an African design. Yet when Kirk walks down the corridor outside Uhura's quarters, a blue plaque hangs beside this unused door. Blue plaques by doors indicate an official ship's operations room, such as Environmental Engineering. They have never indicated crew quarters. (Of course, maybe the plaque says, "This door purposely blocked off by tenant. *Do Not Use.*")

• At the very end of Elaan's tour of Engineering, the scene shows a close-up of Scott. However, the background shows a security guard. The guard is missing from all the wide shots. Evidently the creators grabbed a piece of film from later in the episode and spliced it in here for a reaction shot. (The exact camera angle and actor setup occur just before Scott talks to Kirk about finding Kryton in Engineering.)

• There are some kind of weird pulsating blue screens on the main viewer just after Kirk calls for battle stations.

• Right after Kirk fires photon torpedoes at the Klingon ship, a wide shot shows the bridge. On the main viewscreen the torpedoes detonate. There's only one problem. Chekov is missing! Before this point, Chekov mans the navigator's position. After this point, Chekov mans the navigator position. What happened to Chekov during this moment in the episode?

TRIVIA ANSWERS
1. The bridegroom's mother.
2. Watson.

CLOSING STILLS

• Melkotian, "Spectre of the Gun"

• Kirk as Romulan, "The *Enterprise* Incident"

• Romulan (Klingon) warship, "The *Enterprise* Incident"

• Nazi headquarters, Ekos, "Patterns of Force"

• Kirk, Spock, McCoy, and Chekov preparing to beam over to the USS *Defiant,* "The Tholian Web"

• Balok puppet, "The Corbomite Maneuver"

• Star field

WHOM GODS DESTROY

Kirk and Spock beam down to the maximum security asylum on Elba II and meet with Governor Donald Cory. Curious about the facility's newest inmate, Kirk asks to see Garth of Izar. An accident radically altered the former starship fleet captain's personality. After the inhabitants of Antos IV helped him to recover, he ordered their destruction. Unfortunately, a shock awaits Kirk at Garth's cell. Inside, he sees the real Cory. The other Cory now changes into Garth. As part of his healing, the people of Antos IV taught him to repair his cellular damage. Garth expanded on that knowledge and can assume any shape he chooses.

After locking up Kirk and Spock, Garth changes his appearance to that of the captain. He goes to the main control room and orders Scott to beam him aboard. Thankfully, the real Kirk left orders that no one could be beamed aboard without a special password. Garth tortures Kirk and even tries to trick him into revealing the password, but neither

tactic works. Later, Spock escapes and enters the control room, only to find two Kirks staring back at him. In short order Spock identifies the real Kirk, and the proper authorities soon resume control of the asylum.

Trivia Questions

1. What victory of Garth's did Kirk study at the Academy?

2. What two other emperor types does Garth evoke as examples of those who had gone before and failed?

RUMINATIONS

*T*o their credit, the creators did something about the awful pig masks they used in "Journey to Babel" to simulate a race called Tellarites. The makeup used on the insane Tellarite in this episode is a tremendous improvement.

GREAT LINES

"As you wish."— Spock acquiescing to Garth's request that he be addressed with the honorific "Lord."

GREAT MOMENTS

*T*he actress who plays Marta, Garth's consort, has some fun moments as she claims to have written poetry originally penned by Shakespeare.

PLOT OVERSIGHTS

• It has not been a good year for Starfleet. In "The Tholian Web,"

Spock emphatically states that—until the discovery of the mutinous crew of the USS *Defiant*—there has never been a mutiny aboard a starship. Yet this episode states that Garth's crew mutinied when he ordered them to destroy the inhabitants on Antos IV. So either Garth's mutiny happened some time ago and Spock simply forgot, or Starfleet has had *two* mutinies in very recent history. (In fairness to Spock, I suppose we could say that McCoy just didn't get that memory hooked back up when the good doctor reconnected the Vulcan's brain.)

• When Garth changes from the appearance of Cory back to himself, his clothes alter as well. The real Cory states that Garth's ability to assume different appearances comes from cellular manipulation. If that's true and the clothes change, then the clothes must be part of Garth's body. This actually makes sense because of the ring on Garth's right index finger. After Garth as Kirk discovers that the real captain has created a special password to gain access to the ship, he gets very angry. He pounds the floor and reverts to his normal appearance. In the process, the top of his ring goes bouncing across the floor. Yet, in a later scene, it is suddenly back together. If the ring is part of his body, Garth could simply pick it up, hold it against his skin, and command the cells to reconnect. Garth's abilities are even more amazing than this, however: When

he changes from Cory to Garth, a *working* phaser appears on his waist. Did he hide this phaser in his stomach, or can he actually create functioning machinery from body parts?

• Spock's behavior at the end of this episode is nothing short of ridiculous. There're a multitude of ways to determine which is the real Kirk, and Spock avails himself of none of them. The simplest way would be to stun them both—a suggestion that Kirk finally throws in the face of the Vulcan at the end of the fight, since Spock seems unable to conceive it. Only slightly more complex is asking information that only he and Kirk would know. For instance, "What was the first weapon used in the *Koon-ut-kal-if-fee*?" (It was the *lirpa*, for those of you who do not remember.) Of course, Spock exercises an option fraught with unpredictabilities. He lets Garth push him into a wall and then watches as the two captains duke it out. (I suppose we can allow this oversight, given that Spock's brain was reconnected by McCoy at the beginning of this season. Yes . . . it's the excuse that keeps on giving!)

• At the very end of the episode, Kirk talks with Spock about his method of flushing out Garth and comments, "Mr. Spock, letting yourself be hit on the head is not exactly a method King Solomon would have approved." Garth didn't hit Spock on the head. He shoved the Vulcan into a wall as Kirk watched. (I know. I know. I've read about this episode in *Star Trek Lives*. I know that the fight scene was rewritten because Nimoy adamantly refused to have Garth knock him out with one blow to the head. Quite correctly, Nimoy held fast to the premise that Spock had never been knocked unconscious before in a fight, and he felt it would violate his character. This is the wonderful thing about being a nitpicker. I don't have to deal in reality!)

TRIVIA ANSWERS

1. The victory at Axanar.

2. Li Kwong and Crotis

CLOSING STILLS

• Tiger, "Shore Leave"
• Lawgivers leaving Hall of Audience, "The Return of the Archons" (This scene is never shown in the episode.)
• Aged McCoy, "The Deadly Years"
• Romulan (Klingon) warship, "The *Enterprise* Incident"
• Balok puppet, "The Corbomite Maneuver"
• Bele's ship, "Let That Be Your Last Battlefield"

LET THAT BE YOUR LAST BATTLEFIELD

Star Dates: 5730.2-5730.7

The *Enterprise* intercepts a stolen shuttle and arrests its unusual pilot. His name is Lokai, and he is bichromatic—white on the right side of his body and black on the left. A few minutes later, another bichromatic being beams himself aboard the *Enterprise* just as his vessel explodes. He is Bele, chief officer of the Commission on Political Traitors from the planet Cheron, and he has come for Lokai—a person he characterizes as a murderer. Of course, Lokai has his own version to relate. He states that Bele's people have kept his race downtrodden, that they educated his people only enough to qualify them as slaves. In response, Bele speaks of the natural order and claims that Lokai has killed thousands. Bele requests that Starfleet turn Lokai over to him immediately and provide transportation back to Cheron. When Starfleet refuses to extradite Lokai, Bele uses the power of his will to force the ship toward Cheron. Unfortunately, much has transpired during the fifty thousand years Bele has chased Lokai through the galaxy. Everyone on Cheron is dead, murdered by the race hatred that permeated their world. The pair blame each other for the devastation and beam down to the surface to continue their battle.

> **Trivia Questions**
>
> 1. Where are Bele's guest quarters?
>
> 2. What are the letters and numbers in Scott's destruct sequence number 3?

SYNDICATION CUTS

• After Sulu puts Bele's ship on the viewscreen, Kirk asks for magnification, Chekov reports that there is still no visual contact, and reaction shots all around.

• Kirk gets out of his chair, and another shot of the star field on the viewscreen.

• Reaction shots all around upon the approach of Bele's ship, and the background voices droning on about emergency conditions.

• Following a commercial break, reaction shots before Bele announces his name.

• More reaction shots, as well as Kirk, Spock, and Bele departing from the bridge in a turbolift.

• Before a commercial break,

Kirk's comments that the dispute between Lokai and Bele is settled, "at least for the present."

• McCoy walks over to check on Lokai as Kirk leaves sick bay.

• The last half of Scott switching the ship's controls over to auxiliary, calling Kirk, and Kirk checking to see if the ship is back under control.

• When Bele announces that the ship is now under his control, reaction shots all around.

• Kirk asks the computer if it is ready to copy a destruct sequence, and then orders the computer to prepare to verify the destruct sequence.

• After a commercial break, the destruct countdown from twenty-five to twenty-one seconds.

• An establishing shot of the *Enterprise* approaching Ariannus.

• Two different pieces of the "*Enterprise* as crop duster" sequence. Listen to the background music in the syndicated version and you'll have no difficulty pinpointing the edits.

PLOT OVERSIGHTS

• Hearing that Lokai comes from Cheron, Kirk comments that the planet is in an uncharted region in the southern portion of the galaxy. If it's in an uncharted portion of the galaxy, how does Kirk know where it is? Spock later identifies Cheron's exact position by saying that the ship is heading directly for it. How do they know this stuff?

• Sensing the imminent impact of Bele's ship, Kirk jumps to his feet

and orders the crew to sound the warning for collision. (Let me say that again.) Kirk *jumps to his feet* and orders the crew to sound the warning for collision. Does this make sense? If your vessel is about to get slammed, wouldn't it be wiser to be seated? (Of course, the best body position would be seated with your seat belt fastened, but the *Enterprise* designers didn't believe in seat belts.)

• At one point, Spock tells Kirk that Cheron is on a course between 403 mark 7 and 403 mark 9. Is this another way to say Cheron is on a course 403 mark 8?

• For some reason, Kirk makes a log entry, star date 5730.7, and then *follows* it with another log entry, star date 5730.6.

• Kirk says Cheron lies in the southern part of the galaxy. Does that put the planet somewhere under the center of the galaxy? If it does, the *Enterprise* is much faster than it's successors. In the *Star Trek: The Next Generation* episode "The Nth Degree," Barclay arranges to plunge the *Enterprise* 30,000 light-years to the center of the galaxy. According to figures given in the *Star Trek: The Next Generation* episode "Q Who," it would take Picard's *Enterprise* at least eight years at maximum warp to return home from this distance.

• Finding their planet destroyed, Lokai and Bele commence a chase. On the bridge, Spock monitors their progress. Spock indicates that the pair is on deck 3. Then he says that Bele is passing rec room

3, approaching the crewmen's lounge, and Lokai is running past the crewmen's lounge. Next, Spock relates that the action has moved to deck 5 and says, "passing rec room 3." Is there more than one rec room 3? Or did Bele and Lokai run back to deck 3?

• Along the same line, Spock closely follows the progress of the chase, yet fails to mention that Lokai has entered the transporter room. Uhura has to tell Kirk that the transporter has engaged.

CHANGED PREMISES

• In "By Any Other Name," a group of invaders seizes control of the *Enterprise*. They intend to take it to the Andromeda Galaxy to inform their superiors that the Milky Way is ripe for conquest. Spock and Scott rig the ship to explode, but Kirk chickens out because everyone would die. Yet in "Let That Be Your Last Battlefield," Bele just wants to borrow the *Enterprise* to return Lokai to Cheron, and Kirk tries to blow it up using the auto destruct system.

EQUIPMENT ODDITIES

• Surprise! Bele's ship is . . . *invisible!* Well, that certainly saved a little on the budget for this episode. The creators have used many tactics to stay within the difficult restraints of time and money in producing *Star Trek*. However this one's a bit cheesy.

• At one point, Lokai tries to rally crew members to his cause by speaking with them in a lounge.

Spock walks by, stops, and listens through a crack in the door. Since when do the doors of the *Enterprise* stay open just a little bit?

• In this episode, the *Enterprise* travels to Ariannus and makes like a crop duster. It flies over the planet, spraying an antibacterial agent. Yet the entire time it appears that the *Enterprise* is well above the planet's atmosphere. Will this work? Would the particles float off into space, or would there be enough gravity to pull them downward eventually?

CONTINUITY AND PRODUCTION PROBLEMS

• The footage of the shuttle on the viewscreen comes from the episode "Metamorphosis."

• The footage of the shuttle landing in the shuttle hangar comes from "The *Galileo* Seven."

• For some reason, the director of this episode decided to do the *Batman* thing on the red alert light. You remember the effect. Zoom back and forth really fast. (Yes, kiddos, there was a television show before the *Batman* movies came along, and in many ways it was a lot more fun!) Was this done as a tribute to the actor who plays Bele? After all, he was the Riddler on that show.

• The wide shot of Cheron shows it in gray tones, but in the close-up, it's red.

• During the final chase through the ship, watch the first close-up of Lokai carefully. As he turns the corner, you'll see a rope in his left hand. (Some have speculated that this rope is attached to the camera dolly to help the actor know how fast to run.)

TRIVIA ANSWERS

1. Deck 6.
2. 1B2B3.

CLOSING STILLS

• Starbase 11, "Court-Martial"
• McCoy and Scott playing imagi-
nary instruments while Chekov and Uhura dance, "I, Mudd"
• Spock mesmerizing female, "The Omega Glory"
• Floor game, Platonius, "Plato's Stepchildren"
• Aged Uhura standing with hands raised, "And the Children Shall Lead" (This shot is cropped for use in the mirror showing Uhura's greatest fear.)
• Star field

THE MARK OF GIDEON

Star Dates: 5423.4-5423.8

The *Enterprise* travels to Gideon, a non-Federation planet that has suddenly requested Kirk's presence. Unknown to the captain, the Gideons have constructed an exact duplicate of the *Enterprise* on the surface. Just as Kirk beams down, they render him unconscious and transfer a vial of his blood into a woman named Odana. After letting Kirk wander through their crewless *Enterprise* for a few minutes, they send Odana in to meet him. She feigns ignorance of any knowledge about her planet of origin. The oddness and tension of the situation soon draws Kirk to Odana, just as the Gideons hoped. (Of course, it doesn't hurt that she's dressed in one of Theiss's costumes!) Then Odana falls ill, and the leader of Gideon's council appears from nowhere to rush to her side. His name is Hodin, and he is Odana's father.

Hodin knew that Kirk carried a rare disease in his blood. The planet of Gideon is vastly overcrowded because the people live very long

Trivia Questions

1. What is the name of the Gideon council member who beams up to the *Enterprise*?

2. What disease does Kirk carry in his blood?

lives. Hodin plans to use transfusions from Kirk to cut a swath of death through the populace. He predicts that Odana's death will rally the young people to come forward to sacrifice their lives to return Gideon to the paradise it once was. Thankfully, Spock beams down and rescues Kirk from this macabre existence.

PLOT OVERSIGHTS

• Just after coming aboard the fake *Enterprise,* Kirk says that he has searched every area of the ship. When Spock beams in, he states that the copy is an exact duplicate of the real *Enterprise.* First, how would Gideon, a nonaligned world, get exact specifications of a Starfleet vessel? Second, if space is at such a premium on Gideon, why go to all this trouble—and space—to build this rather large starcraft, which will be used for only a relatively short amount of time? (Presumably the Gideons didn't intend for Kirk to live there the rest of his life. Maybe they planned to use it as an amusement park.)

• At one point Kirk and Odana are

getting along famously, when the captain opens a view port to gaze at the stars. At first the captain sees a group of Gideons staring back at him. He rushes to Odana's side, evidently wanting to comfort her from this unexpected sight. Yet when Kirk grabs her, he leaves her facing the viewscreen. It makes it look like he's the one who's shocked and he's looking to Odana for comfort.

• All the group shots of Gideons show them dressed in bland unisex clothing and head-hugging hoods. Where did they get Odana's outfit—Frederick's of Orion? And why does she seem so comfortable in it even when she strolls around the real *Enterprise*? Is this standard attire for the council leader's daughter?

• As Odana grows sick, Hodin asks her, "What's it like to feel pain?" Come on . . . doesn't anyone stub his or her toe on this planet?

• The Gideons must have an amazing agricultural base. Normally, runaway populations are curbed by lack of resources. For some reason, this rule doesn't apply on Gideon. Odana claims that the entire planet is one mass of people. If that's true, how do they grow their food, and where do they get their water?

• The Gideons had planned for Kirk to fall so hopelessly in love with Odana that he would gladly stay and provide deadly transfusions to change the course of their world. They certainly miscalculated on this point! They had no idea just how fast our dear captain can fall in and out of love.

EQUIPMENT ODDITIES

• At the beginning of the episode Kirk beams on to the fake *Enterprise*. Thinking that he is still on the real *Enterprise* and upset that Spock left the room before completing the transport, Kirk marches off the pad and snaps on the intercom. He pages Spock and, receiving no answer, snaps it off and then on and then off before leaving. At the end of the episode, Spock does something very similar, except the intercom makes "boops" when the Vulcan flips the switch. What changed? Why is this fake intercom suddenly making sounds?

• The broadcast camera in the Gideon council chambers really is amazing. When it first transmits to the *Enterprise*, it takes its picture from behind a grille, giving the illusion of a people in great bondage—this in spite of the fact that the council chambers' viewscreen hangs in *front* of the grille. Then, as council leader Hodin concludes one of his conversations with Spock, the camera automagically switches to show a close-up of the off button before cutting back to Hodin and fading.

• Just after arriving on the fake *Enterprise*, Spock manages to make a log entry simply by thinking. (Is the psychotricorder used to record these log entries? If so, does it automatically screen out all personal thoughts?)

CONTINUITY AND PRODUCTION PROBLEMS

• As Kirk beams on to the fake *Enterprise*, he stands on one of the two front transporter pads. The scene then cuts to a reverse angle and shows the empty transporter room. Strangely enough, both of the front pads are empty.

• As Kirk pages the empty ship, the creators show us pictures of the main areas. For some reason, sick bay is on red alert.

• The opaque portions of Odana's outfit are similar to the opaque portions of the outfit worn by Lieutenant Marlena "Oiling my traps, darling" Moreau in "Mirror, Mirror."

TRIVIA ANSWERS

1. Krodak.
2. Vegan choriomeningitis.

CLOSING STILLS

• Starbase 11, "Court-Martial"

• "Asteroid" *Yonada*, "For the World Is Hollow and I Have Touched the Sky"

• The *Enterprise* in the energy barrier, "Where No Man Has Gone Before"

• Buildings, Eminiar VII, "A Taste of Armageddon"

• Hand with phaser, "The Omega Glory"

• Sargon and Thalassa leaving the *Enterprise*, "Return to Tomorrow"

THAT WHICH SURVIVES

Star Date: unknown

After discovering an unusual planet, Kirk beams down with McCoy, Sulu, and senior geologist Lieutenant D'Amato. Simultaneously, a woman appears and kills the transporter chief. Moments later, a tremor rocks the planet, and the *Enterprise* disappears. Without the ship, the landing party faces starvation and dehydration. A more immediate danger exists, however. A short time later, the woman—named Losira—reappears and kills D'Amato. When she comes for Sulu, Kirk determines that she is programmed to kill only one person at a time and must touch that person to accomplish her task. From then on, they protect the one she has "come for."

Meanwhile, Spock calculates that some energy force has thrown the *Enterprise* more than 990 light-years away from the planet. He sets a return course. On the surface, Kirk, McCoy, and Sulu come upon an underground entrance and soon arrive at a control room. The planet was constructed as an outpost for the long dead Kalandan

civilization. It is still functioning in defensive mode and suddenly creates three different versions of Losira, one for each of the landing party. Thankfully, Spock arrives in time to destroy the Kalandan main computer and save their lives.

GREAT MOMENTS

The creators used a nice transporter effect for Losira. She appears to flatten, squash into a black vertical line, and then the end points of the lines come together and disappear.

SYNDICATION CUTS

• Spock pages Lieutenant Rahda after Kirk leaves the bridge.

• The landing party discusses the "earthquake" that occurred just after they arrived.

• Initial damage reports on the *Enterprise*, and Spock ordering an autopsy on the transporter chief.

• Sulu walks off to do the geological survey. Also, Kirk and McCoy discuss D'Amato's death and grave.

• After Kirk says they have only questions and no answers, a reaction shot of McCoy and Sulu. Then

Trivia Questions

1. Who does the autopsy on the transporter chief?

2. What is Engineer, Grade 4, John Watkins' middle initial?

287

an establishing shot of the *Enterprise*, and Scott wandering around in Engineering.

• Following a commercial break, McCoy and Sulu discuss the navigator's injuries.

• The landing party walks into the cave, an establishing shot of the *Enterprise*, and Spock requests a computer readout.

PLOT OVERSIGHTS

• After conducting a "detailed" analysis of the planet, the landing party reports back to Kirk. They have a meeting, and the captain decides that finding water is one of the highest priorities. He sends D'Amato out to look for an underground source. Wouldn't a detailed analysis of the planet include this information?

• Kirk does an amazing job on the headstone of D'Amato's grave. It is nicely square and has "LT. D'AMATO" written on it. A few moments earlier, the episode demonstrated that the rock on the planet was almost impossible to cut with a phaser. How, then, did Kirk create this object to begin with? Also, with what did he write D'Amato's name on the stone? Have we ever seen Starfleet officers carrying pens? (Not to indulge in the macabre, but I suppose they could have fashioned a brush and used D'Amato's blood. That seems a bit gruesome.)

• After his first encounter with Losira, Sulu is amazed that someone so beautiful could be so evil. Didn't we just have an episode on this topic? Wasn't this one of the main themes of "Is There in Truth No Beauty"? Is Sulu not paying attention? Or did he not watch the reruns of the visual logs on the viewscreen's late night entertainment channel?

• After sending the *Enterprise* on its distant trip, the defensive computer on the planet programs a copy of Losira to sabotage the engines. Careening madly through space, Spock estimates that the ship and crew have only "14.87 minutes" left and relays this information to Scott. Moments later, he tells Scott they have "12 minutes and 27 seconds" left. Wouldn't it be better to standardize a format for telling time so that the crew doesn't have to convert mentally to the format they prefer?

• To fix the problem with the engines, Scott must fiddle with the magnetic containment field that holds the antimatter. After the process begins, Spock tells Uhura to monitor the magnetic force. He orders her not to take her eyes off the indicator. Of course, the entire time he's giving her these instructions, she's looking at him and not at the instruments!

• This episode has to be a first. To my recollection, this is the first time Kirk has actively refused the affections of a beautiful alien woman. She keeps saying, "I must touch you. I am for you," and our beloved captain keeps telling her, "No, no. That's okay." (I suppose the prospect of dying would have the same effect as a cold shower.)

• As Scott begins his repairs, Spock tells him he has 8 minutes and 41 seconds left. The action then shifts to the planet and finally back to the *Enterprise*. Soon after returning, Spock tells Scott he has 57 seconds left, and the scene shows Scott holding the same doohickey that he held before we went to see what was happening on the planet. What has this guy been doing for almost 8 minutes?

• After all the dramatic countdown and tension of the imminent destruction of the *Enterprise*, the deadline comes and goes and nothing happens. If Spock is so precise in his calculations, why was Scott able to work for several seconds *after* the Vulcan said the ship would explode?

CHANGED PREMISES

• At one point, Uhura asks Spock what the chances are that Kirk and the others are still alive. The Vulcan rebuffs her, stating that they are not involved in gambling, that they are merely pursuing the only logical course of action. Suddenly Spock doesn't want to calculate odds? Isn't this the same guy whose mother had to shut him up because he wanted to give her the odds on his father's survival in "Journey to Babel"?

EQUIPMENT ODDITIES

• Several times during the show, Spock fiddles with a hand-held control mechanism. Oddly enough, it is the same device McCoy used in "Spock's Brain" to control the movements of the Vulcan when his mind was missing. To me, this episode offers the most convincing proof that McCoy didn't get Spock's brain wired back in correctly. The poor Vulcan has to carry around the control mechanism to access the portions of his brain that our good doctor left unhooked!

• When Losira "comes" for Kirk, McCoy tries to take a reading on her. He says she shows no life signs. There is not even a mechanical signature. Yet earlier in the episode, when Losira attacks D'Amato, McCoy registered "a life form reading of tremendous intensity," and a biological one at that.

CONTINUITY AND PRODUCTION PROBLEMS

• After D'Amato dies, Kirk attempts to dig a grave for him using a phaser. The first shot has little effect, and the captain tries a second time. Touched by the phaser's beam, the surface explodes and starts a little fire. The only objects in the immediate area of the blast are rocks and dirt. If I recall correctly, neither of these usually burn.

TRIVIA ANSWERS

1. Dr. Sanchez.
2. B.

CLOSING STILLS

• Saloon, "Spectre of the Gun"
• Melkotian, "Spectre of the Gun"
• Garden scene, "Where No Man Has Gone Before"

• Spock's brain as the Controller, "Spock's Brain"
• Kirk zapped in memory beam,

"The Paradise Syndrome"
• Star field

THE LIGHTS OF ZETAR

Star Dates: 5725.3-5725.6

Lieutenant Mira Romaine joins the *Enterprise* on a mission to Memory Alpha, a Federation repository of knowledge. En route, the ship encounters an energy cloud, and Romaine collapses. The cloud then moves on to Memory Alpha, killing most of the researchers and wiping out its computer system. When the cloud moves off into space, Romaine and a landing party beam down to assess the damage but she soon warns them to return to the ship. She senses the cloud returning to the planet.

As the cloud approaches, Kirk orders a phaser attack. Unfortunately, Romaine doubles over in pain when the energy hits the cloud. Clearly it has established some connection with her. Spock's subsequent observations show that the cloud is in fact a collection of life entities. At this, Kirk suggests that Romaine give herself over to the entities. When she does, they explain that they are from Zetar. When their planet died, they willed themselves to continue living as an energy cloud and have searched the galaxy for a host in which to live out their lives. While Romaine still retains some control, the crew places her in a special chamber and increases the pressure until the beings die. Once freed, she returns to Memory Alpha to begin reconstruction of the facility.

Trivia Questions

1. Where was Mira Romaine born?

2. What are the names of Mira Romaine's parents?

RUMINATIONS

This episode gives us a rough idea when medical science finally came up with a cure to the common cold. At one point, Scott tells Romaine that McCoy can't cure her space sickness any more than he could cure a cold. Yet, in the first season of Star Trek: The Next Generation, *the crew says they no longer suffer from colds.*

PLOT OVERSIGHTS

• When discussing the visions that Romaine has had concerning the energy cloud, Scott claims that she foresaw the first attack on the ship. As far as I can tell, no other line of dialogue supports this statement.

• This episode contains a blatant

"we did it because we thought it would look cool" error. After placing Romaine inside the pressure chamber, Kirk orders the gravity to zero. This allows the creators to simulate the look of Romaine in a gravity-free environment, although the treatment is totally unnecessary and probably unwise. As soon as the crew cuts off the gravity, McCoy comments that the Zetars are growing stronger. Spock then chimes in, saying that the weightless state has become their natural condition. If you recall, the point of this exercise is to rid Romaine of the Zetars. It's not to make them more comfortable. If the Zetars like a gravity-free environment, why is Kirk supplying it? Answer: Because the creators thought it would look cool to strap this woman to a board and have her bob up and down.

EQUIPMENT ODDITIES

• Much of the equipment at Memory Alpha comes from previous shows, but one particular item is worth mentioning. One desk sports a Romulan control box just like the one seen on the Romulan commander's desk in "The *Enterprise* Incident."

• To kill the beings that inhabit Romaine, Kirk places her in a pressure chamber. Spock then increases the pressure until the beings die. Wait a minute: These beings invaded the ship. That means they passed through metal, since the *Enterprise* doesn't have open vents to the outside. What's stopping these beings from simply floating out of the pressure chamber?

CONTINUITY AND PRODUCTION PROBLEMS

• Supposedly the tapes I purchased from Paramount are uncut. However, there is a minor section on the syndicated tape recorded here in Springfield that doesn't occur on my uncut version! Just after the energy cloud appears for the first time, Kirk asks for magnification eight on the viewscreen, and the next shot shows an enlarged view of the cloud. These moments are missing from the "uncut" version.

• Lying in sick bay, Mira Romaine sees a vision of the dead people at Memory Alpha. Moments later, Kirk walks into the exact scene she sees. One dead man is slouched down in a chair with his back to the desk. In one shot, a viewscreen sits near his right shoulder. When the shot changes, the viewscreen now sits near his left shoulder.

• As the *Enterprise* races away from Memory Alpha, the energy cloud pursues. The viewscreen shows an aft view. The stars race away, but the cloud stays in the center of the screen. Kirk orders Sulu to turn to starboard. A graphic of the ship shows it turning to the right. This is correct. Moments later, the viewscreen shows the cloud moving back into the center of the screen, traveling right to left. Presumably this shows that the cloud has made the turn to starboard also. I don't think this is correct. If the *Enterprise* turns to the right and the cloud copies this motion, it should move from left to right onto the screen, not right to left. The only way it could go from right to left on the viewscreen is if it made a circle around the ship or if it overshot the turn and then had to approach the *Enterprise* from the opposite direction. Moments later, the creators do the same sequence again, this time to port, and they make the same mistake. The cloud moves back onto the screen from left to right when it should move onto the screen from right to left. (Is this thoroughly confusing or what?)

• Just after a briefing with Spock, McCoy, Scott, and Romaine, Kirk heads for the bridge. As the briefing room doors open, a male offi-cer springs into a walk. Apparently the extra missed his cue.

TRIVIA ANSWERS

1. Martian colony, number 3.
2. Jacques and Lydia.

CLOSING STILLS

• Scott and Spock working in Jefferies tube while Kirk watches, "The Ultimate Computer"

• Balok puppet taking a moment to check his cue cards, "The Corbomite Maneuver"

• Kirk, McCoy and Bones, "Catspaw"

• Kirk and Spock wounding the Horta, "The Devil in the Dark"

• Sylvia as the big cat, "Catspaw"

• Cloaked Klingon Bird-of-Prey, *Star Trek III: The Search for Spock*

THE UNSYNDICATED

By way of review, the program content of the episodes as they played on network television ran fifty-one minutes, including the opening credits, the teaser for the next episode and the closing credits. At some point Paramount prepared the episodes for syndication. In this process, they removed the teaser and edited the program content to allow for more commercials. As you know, commercials are the lifeblood of a television station. The more commercials a television station can play in an hour, the more money the station makes. The program content of the syndicated episodes runs forty-six minutes and thirty seconds. This gives the station six internal slots of two minutes, two seconds each and a final slot of one minute, fifteen seconds for a grand total of twenty-six commercials if all of them are thirty seconds in length.

To track the syndication edits, I set up two VCRs and two TVs. Simultaneously, I would play the uncut version of an episode purchased from Paramount and the syndicated version of the same episode recorded here in Springfield. A bit of practice with two remote controls allowed me to sync the two tapes together and instantly spot any scene edited out of the syndicated version. One of the great surprises during the creation of this book came as I encountered my first "unsyndicated" episode. I kept both versions of the show synced from start to finish and never caught an edit. For some reason, the episode had never been cut for syndication. Twenty episodes fall into this category.

I would imagine these episodes cause problems for the television stations. It means a station must keep track of which episode they will play in any given week and sell only enough advertising to fill the available slots. If the episode has not been edited down, they simply have less slots to fill (and consequently make less money). Of course, the station may opt to play the same number of commercials every week. In this situation, the station must add the commercials to the existing slots, running them over a section of the episode. The station can also play an extra commercial during the closing credits. I call this "stepping on" the episode. If you see an episode return from a commercial in a weird spot or notice the closing credits are cut short, the television station has probably stepped on the episode. This is most likely to occur on the episodes listed below. (Provided, of course, that Paramount sends the same set of tapes to stations around the country. I suppose it is possible that some of the stations may have received a complete set of syndicated tapes. I'm just a guy who sits in his living room and watches *Star Trek.* Although I've checked this with a number of other people, my knowledge about this situation is limited.)

The episodes played over the airwaves here in Springfield that do not contain cuts for syndication are:

"The Man Trap"
"Where No Man Has Gone Before"
"What Are Little Girls Made Of?"
"The Conscience of the King"
"A Piece of the Action"
"A Private Little War"
"Return to Tomorrow"
"Bread and Circuses"
"Is There in Truth No Beauty?"
"Day of the Dove"
"For the World Is Hollow and I Have Touched the Sky"
"The Tholian Web"
"Wink of an Eye"
"The Empath"
"Whom Gods Destroy"
"The Mark of Gideon"
"The Lights of Zetar"
"The Way to Eden"
"The Savage Curtain"
"All Our Yesterdays"

REQUIEM FOR METHUSELAH

Star Dates: 5843.7-5843.8

When Rigelian fever breaks out on board the *Enterprise*, the crew finds a deposit of the only antidote, ryetalyn, on a seemingly lifeless planet in the Omega system. Yet after beaming down, Kirk, Spock, and McCoy meet a man named Flint and his powerful robot, M4. After instructing M4 to gather and process the ryetalyn, Flint invites them to his home. There he introduces Rayna Kapec, a woman he claims was placed in his care at an early age.

Under Flint's guidance, Kirk and Rayna spend time together and fall in love. When M4 completes the processing of the ryetalyn, Flint reveals that Rayna is, in fact, an android—a woman he built as his perfect mate. Born on Earth in 3834 B.C., Flint quickly discovered that he could not be killed. Through the centuries he has assumed different personalities, amassing knowledge and wealth. Eventually he moved here and began his greatest project, to construct a woman equal to himself. Until Kirk

appeared, he could not evoke her emotions. Now that Kirk has done so, Flint seethes with jealously. At the same time, Kirk feels used, refusing to give up the woman he loves. Eventually the strain of conflicting emotions destroys Rayna and both men grieve, ashamed by their behavior. With ryetalyn in hand, the landing party returns to the ship.

RUMINATIONS

As a nitpicker, I have to wonder why Data (of Star Trek: The Next Generation) hasn't bothered to look up Flint, or at least his laboratory if the man is dead. According to this episode, Flint created a sentient, emotion-capable android. Maybe Data could learn a thing or two.

SYNDICATION CUTS

• Kirk asks for a full computer search on Flint and his planet and then comments about enjoying the brandy McCoy has just poured. This edit takes care of two minor problems. First, Kirk calls the planet "Holberg 917G," but the captain has already said that the planet resides in the Omega system.

Trivia Questions

1. According to Flint, where and when did the bubonic plague begin?

2. Who originally purchased the planet on which Flint resides?

Wouldn't that make the planet name something like "Omega V"? Second, when Kirk offhandedly asks for a computer search of Flint, Scott responds as if he knows what Kirk is talking about. Remember that when the landing party beamed down, the crew thought the planet lifeless. No dialogue indicates that Scott has since learned differently. His response should be, "What in the devil are you talkin' about? There's nobody else on that planet. Ya can't search for someone that doesn't exist. It canna be done, Captain. If ya know what I mean." Also, this edit creates a problem in the syndicated version. Once this section is removed, no dialogue indicates that the ship even knows of Flint's presence. Yet later, Scott calls down and says the computer has no information on the man!

• After a commercial break, the newly introduced Rayna and Flint approach the landing party.

• McCoy wonders what else interests Rayna besides gravity phenomena, and Rayna responds that everything does.

• Following Flint's comments that his pressures are none of Kirk's concern, the captain launches into a soliloquy about the complexity of being human.

• Flint's reflection that to be human means to dance, laugh, and enjoy pleasures as Spock sits to play a piece by Brahms. This edit causes a bit of a funny moment in the syndicated version. After Flint invites Spock to play the piece, the music begins immediately, as if the Vulcan literally jumped onto the piano bench. (I guess you don't have to ask twice to get that Vulcan to play a piece by Brahms!)

• A large section of the dance between Kirk and Rayna, including McCoy in the lab determining that the ryetalyn is tainted. The real shame here is that the editors had to butcher a lovely waltz (the music, that is).

• Kirk entering Flint's lab.

• Rayna indicates that Flint has ordered her never to go into a specific room in the lab. The dialogue in this section allowed an excellent spot for a splice. In the uncut version, Rayna answers, "I do not know" to two of Kirk's questions. The editor simply dropped out the first "I do not know" and all dialogue until the second.

• Following a commercial break, M4 approaches Kirk and Rayna, followed by Kirk pushing her away before trying to hide behind the screen.

• After a commercial break, Flint and Rayna discuss why M4 attacked Kirk.

• A pair of reaction shots after Spock reminds Kirk that the ryetalyn should be their immediate concern.

PLOT OVERSIGHTS

• When Flint first suggests that M4 process the ryetalyn, McCoy pipes up that he would like to supervise. Flint readily agrees, and the doctor follows M4 to the lab. Once there, M4 flies behind into the far end of the room, and a door blocks McCoy's path. True, the partition is made of a substance like frosted glass, but the doctor can't tell what M4 is doing back there. Yet the easily agitated McCoy takes it all in stride and opts to wait for the robot to return. Does this seem right? Wouldn't McCoy march out and grouse at Flint because he can't see what's going on?

• Presumably a person rises to the position of captain of a starship because he puts the needs of his crew and vessel above his own. In this episode, however, Spock continually reminds Kirk that they need to concentrate on procuring the ryetalyn. His crew is dying from a horrible plague, and in the space of fewer than four hours he goes so rabid for a woman that he seemingly loses all concern for the 430 men and women aboard his ship? Is this believable, or does he just need to visit Rigley's Pleasure Planet for a couple of weeks?

• Panting over Rayna, Kirk tries to convince her to come with him. He says he will make her happy. Just how is he going to do that? By leaving her for months or years at a time at home with the robot kiddies while he gallivants around the galaxy? (Even if he arranged for Rayna to be inducted into Starfleet, we've never seen a married couple on a starship during this series. The closest we came was the wedding in "Balance of Terror," but the guy died before the ceremony—and some of the dialogue between him and his bride hinted that she would be resigning her commission afterward.)

• At the end of the episode, time is short. The landing party finds the ryetalyn and then McCoy hangs around to look at the full-size Barbie dolls that Flint has created for his amusement. Shouldn't the doctor beam back to the ship immediately with the medicine? Compounding this oversight, the creators have the landing party chat about Rayna's true nature. Then Flint shows up and Kirk refuses to leave and they get into a fistfight—throwing each other around while the precious, life-saving ryetalyn sits on a table very near their altercation! Even if we accept that Kirk is hopelessly smitten with this android, what's wrong with McCoy? Is the scene too juicy to interrupt with something as mundane as saving lives?

• At the end of the episode, Kirk longs to forget Rayna, and McCoy mumbles that it would be better if the captain could forget her. In response, Spock wanders over, puts his hand to Kirk's head, and says, "Forget." If Spock can actually make Kirk forget Rayna, isn't the Vulcan required to fill in the gap with something? Wouldn't Starfleet Command be upset that their flagship's captain is missing several hours of his life? Would this mental deficiency be cause for concern? And even if Spock puts something in its place, isn't there still a problem in their reports? Kirk would remember the events one way,

Spock and McCoy another.

EQUIPMENT ODDITIES

• Flint appears to have a Romulan computer on the desk in his lab.

• Twice in this episode, Kirk makes log entries without a tricorder or moving his lips. (Also in the log entries, he mentions Flint. Yet at the end of the episode, Kirk claims that he can keep Flint's existence a secret. Doesn't Starfleet Command get a copy of the captain's logs?)

• Some of the computer panels in Flint's lab made a recent appearance in the episode "Whom Gods Destroy." Do they get paid extra for this?

• The first time M4 meets the landing party, the robot deactivates their phasers. Then, during its later attack on Kirk, it deactivates his phaser. Coming to the rescue, Spock walks into the room and shoots M4 . . . with his *phaser!* Why didn't M4 deactivate Spock's phaser? The creators tried to smooth this over by having the Vulcan say that it was fortunate the robot didn't detect his presence and deactivate his phaser. Well, that certainly was convenient, wasn't it?

• At one point, to demonstrate his power, Flint grabs the *Enterprise* out of space, reduces it to the size of a large model, and deposits it on a desktop. Either the desktop is very sturdy, or Flint has some way of decreasing the ship's mass at the same time he shrunk its size. If

not, the ship would retain its weight and crush the table into tiny pieces.

• Seeing his ship resting on a tabletop, Kirk wanders over and looks into the bridge. The shot changes to show Kirk peering into the main viewscreen. This actually makes sense, even though Kirk stands beside the ship and not in front of it! In all likelihood, while the ship orbits the planet, the viewscreen would be set to port. On the other hand, Kirk acts as if he can actually see the crew. The viewscreen isn't a window, it's an electronic display, and it isn't on the side of the ship, it's in front. Is Kirk seeing the crew through the bubble in the ceiling of the bridge?

• After Rayna collapses, McCoy hurries over and feels her neck for a pulse. Let's see . . . he feels the *mechanical woman's* neck for a pulse.

TRIVIA ANSWERS

1. In Constantinople, during the summer of A.D. 1134.

2. Mr. Brack, a wealthy financier and recluse.

CLOSING STILLS

• Fortress on Rigel VII, "The Cage"

• Spock playing chess with Rojan, "By Any Other Name"

• Spock's brain as the Controller, "Spock's Brain"

• *Galileo* departing shuttle hangar, "The *Galileo* Seven"

• Scientific research center on Psi 2000, "The Naked Time"

• Star field

THE WAY TO EDEN

The *Enterprise* intercepts a stolen spacecraft and beams its inhabitants aboard. They are Dr. Sevrin, a noted scientist, and his band of followers. Sevrin and the others desire a simpler form of life. Their goal is Eden, a mythical planet of abundant beauty. Curious about their cause, Spock uses the ship's computers to find Eden after Sevrin agrees to tell his students not to interfere with ship's operations. Unfortunately, Sevrin actually tells his disciples to learn what they can about the ship. In short order, they proceed to Auxiliary Control and take over the *Enterprise*.

On arrival at Eden, Sevrin rigs an ultrasonic broadcast to knock out the crew. He and his people then depart in a shuttle for the surface. Thankfully, Kirk manages to shut off the sound waves before they kill everyone on board. Beaming down, Kirk and a landing party find that Eden is indeed beautiful, but it is also deadly. All the vegetation oozes acid, and the fruit is poison. Sevrin refuses to accept this, grabbing a piece of fruit and thrusting it into his mouth. His death convinces the rest of the troupe to return quietly to the ship.

RUMINATIONS

I really have only one thing to say about this episode . . . groovy.

PLOT OVERSIGHTS

• This episode keeps referring to "starbase." Kirk will take them there. Kirk wants a message sent there at the beginning of the episode and at the end. However, Kirk never says which starbase.

• Evidently all the Romulans are down for their afternoon naps, because none of their ships shows up to challenge the *Enterprise*—even though the *Enterprise* flies into Romulan space to get to Eden. Yet again, fortune smiles on the flagship of the Federation.

• After Sevrin and his followers leave the ship, Kirk shuts off the ultrasonic sound and calls the bridge. He asks if they have control of the ship, and the answer comes back, "No." Moments later he asks if they can break orbit if they need

Trivia Questions

1. Who subs for Uhura in this episode?

2. What are Dr. Sevrin's fields of study?

to, and the answer comes back, "I think so." Did I miss something here? Don't you need control of the ship to break orbit?

• Soon after following Dr. Sevrin and his students to Eden, a landing party discovers one of them dead underneath a tree. You can tell he was a musician. Even in death, the index finger on his right hand keeps strumming.

• The landing party discovers that the plants on the planet are filled with acid. The vegetation burns the skin with a simple touch. Yet once the landing party locates Sevrin and the others inside the shuttle, they drag them outside! Since Sevrin and the others wear few clothes, their feet are already burned from the acid. Why, then, is Kirk hauling them out of the shuttle? Wouldn't it be better to leave them inside with the protection it affords?

EQUIPMENT ODDITIES

• In many episodes, Kirk consistently uses the top button on the right arm of his chair to open communications. According to "Court-Martial," that's the button to signal "Yellow Alert." Yes, it is possible that the crew rewired the chair because Kirk wanted to use the top button for communications. However, all the other officers consistently use the lowest button on the chair. For another thing, the light on the intercom speaker comes on only when the lowest button is pushed. Take this episode, for example. After Kirk

returns from sick bay to the bridge, Scott calls him. The captain walks to his chair and presses the lowest button. Look closely at the back end of the armrest and you'll see the oval light beside the speaker come on (just as the light does on every other intercom speaker when its button is pressed). Kirk talks with Scott and then uses his fist to hit the top button on the armrest. This is the same method he uses in many other shows. After performing this movement, Kirk acts as if the conversation is complete. Look closely one more time and you'll see that the intercom light is *still* on. If both the top and bottom switches operated the intercom, shouldn't the light go out when Kirk hits the top button?

CONTINUITY AND PRODUCTION PROBLEMS

• The stolen spacecraft is a Tholian vessel flipped around with engine nacelles attached.

• On three occasions, the creators either purposefully or accidentally spliced close-ups of Kirk in backward: once when Kirk walks out of sick bay after learning that Sevrin has a disease, and twice when watching Sevrin do his thing in the poisoned tree. You can find these places by watching Kirk's hair and the insignia on his shirt.

• When the ultrasound hits the crew, they crumple. Amazingly enough, they fall exactly the same way they did in "Spock's Brain." Even more amazing, Chapel's hairdo has suddenly reverted to the one she wore during "Spock's Brain." Is this what women mean when they talk about a "drop-dead gorgeous" hairstyle?

• The establishing shot of a lake comes from "Shore Leave."

TRIVIA ANSWERS

1. Lieutenant Palmer.

2. Acoustics, communications and electronics.

CLOSING STILLS

• Apollo's temple, Pollux IV, "Who Mourns for Adonais"

• The *Enterprise* leaving Deep Space Station K-7, "The Trouble with Tribbles"

• Giant amoeba on viewscreen, "The Immunity Syndrome"

• Jail set, "Bread and Circuses" (It is never seen completely empty in the episode.)

• Medusan ambassador Kollos in an open box, "Is There in Truth No Beauty?"

• Viewscreen just before the *Fesarius* appears, "The Corbomite Maneuver"

THE CLOUDMINDERS

Star Dates: 5818.4-5819.3

In need of zenite to stop a plant plague on another planet, the *Enterprise* drops into orbit around Ardana. This planet sports a city in the clouds called Stratos, where its dwellers concentrate on the mental arts. Their leisure is made by possible by Troglytes, those who work below the surface, mining the zenite. Unfortunately, the Troglytes are currently in a state of rebellion, forestalling the delivery of any more zenite. Instead of bargaining for the zenite, Plasus—the head of the City Council—turns to torture but accomplishes little.

Frustrated by the impasse, Kirk tries to win the confidence of a Troglyte leader named Vanna. McCoy has discovered that unrefined zenite emits a gas that causes temporary mental retardation and emotional instability. The captain offers Vanna masks that will screen out the gas. Instead, Vanna attempts to take Kirk hostage, but he uses his phaser to seal them in a side room of the mines. Kirk then has Scott beam Plasus to the room

Trivia Questions

1. What is the name of the planet endangered by the plant plague?

2. Whom does Kirk suggest to aid in mediation between Stratos and the Troglytes?

as well. In just over an hour, the gas reduces both men to animals, and even Vanna is convinced. The Troglytes deliver the zenite and Kirk departs, leaving a large supply of masks and the hope that the peoples of Ardana will work together toward equality.

RUMINATIONS

Plasus's daughter, Droxine, wears a gorgeous dress in this episode. The cut is a bit too provocative for daily wear, but the material is fabulous.

SYNDICATION CUTS

• Part of the fight between Kirk and Spock, and the Troglytes. This edit removes a continuity and production problem. Initially the Troglytes lasso the pair with leather thongs. The edited section shows Spock fighting without the thong, easily tossing his Troglyte attackers aside. Then the action returns and the Vulcan suddenly has the thong back on, as if the creators originally spliced the film together in the wrong sequence.

• Plasus and Droxine discussing the officers' arrival and the desperate actions of the Troglytes. The removal of this sequence causes a small problem in the syndicated version. When Kirk and Spock wander to their rest area, Plasus and Droxine stand in the council chamber's art gallery. The scene cuts to guards bringing in a Troglyte and then shows father and daughter suddenly standing on a viewing platform some distance from their original position. There is time to move, but the pair would almost need to sprint to arrive in time (an activity I find unlikely, given Droxine's attire).

• A portion of Plasus's interrogation of the first captured Troglyte.

• Vanna's assertion that starships do not carry cargo, and Kirk's response as the two speak in the rest quarters in front of Spock and Droxine.

• Kirk discusses Vanna's torture with Plasus.

• Following a commercial break, a captain's log, star date 5819.0, recapping events thus far. The planet the *Enterprise* orbits during both this and Spock's log looks very similar to Alpha 177 in "The Enemy Within."

• Kirk assures Plasus that McCoy has performed the necessary tests to show that the zenite is the cause of the Troglyte retardation, and Plasus continues to deny this.

• A portion of Kirk's attempt to elicit Vanna's trust while in her cell on Stratos.

• After a commercial break, Spock's log, star date 5819.3—again recapping events.

• Kirk pages the *Enterprise* from the cave several times before Spock responds.

• Spock and Scott discuss the fact the Plasus and Droxine stand too close together for the *Enterprise* to ensure that they transport only Plasus.

PLOT OVERSIGHTS

• The future seems to have some really bad plagues. In "Let That Be Your Last Battlefield," the *Enterprise* had to make like a crop duster and save an entire planet from some sort of bacteriological infestation. Now, in this episode, the *Enterprise* must hurry to another planet or all its plant life will die. Although we have our problems here on Earth, I can't think of any natural pestilence or disease that has ever threatened to destroy *all* life on the planet.

• Spock claims that Stratos is a completely intellectual society, that all forms of violence have been eliminated. Later, Droxine confirms that the people of Stratos believe this about themselves when she echoes the sentiments. Yet Plasus shows no remorse at torturing Vanna to obtain information about the rebellious Troglytes. Isn't torture a form of violence? (Spock himself refers to it as such.)

• Spock tells Kirk that the name Troglyte comes from an ancient Earth term. Why would members of an alien planet use terminology from our world to name one of their races?

• After deciding to take matters

into his own hands, Kirk beams down to Vanna's cell, violating Plasus's orders. When a guard appears, Kirk pulls out his phaser and flattens himself against a wall. He waits for the man to enter. Many moments later, the guard turns and sees Kirk. The captain then stuns him. Why not stun the guy before he turns around? In that way he couldn't confirm that you were the one who broke Vanna out of jail. Then—instead of calling the *Enterprise* to beam them down to the planet's surface—Kirk and Vanna go strolling through Stratos to find a transporter.

• At the end of the episode, the lovely Droxine—a female raised in the completely genteel world of Stratos, a world flooded with art, music, and beauty—tells Spock that she will go to the mines. She no longer wishes to be confined to the clouds. Yeah, right! Obviously this woman is trying to make points with Spock. There is no way this woman will last very long in the tunnels of the underworld. She'll get down there—presumably dressed in something other that her Stratos outfit—take one look at the surroundings, daintily pick up a digging tool between her thumb and index finger, and say, "Eeewwww." She will then turn around and head back home.

CHANGED PREMISES

• Spock certainly has changed in the romance department. Maybe it's just because he has finally met a living "work of art." The normally reserved Vulcan offers several scantily hidden compliments to Droxine and even proceeds to tell her about the Vulcan mating rituals. So much for, "It is a thing no out-worlders may know," and "It is a deeply personal thing"—statements made by Spock during his discussion of *Pon farr* with Kirk ("Amok Time"). Then again, maybe his *brain* didn't get hooked up right at the end of "Spock's Brain."

EQUIPMENT ODDITIES

• In Kirk's rest area, the intercom faces away from the bed on the far corner of the end table. Evidently inhabitants of Stratos never speak to anyone on the intercom during their rest times.

• The mask that Kirk offers the Troglytes has only a single band to secure it to the face. The band travels up from the mask and over the head. Does this seem secure? (I know the creators were trying to construct something that looked futuristic, but while Kirk wears the thing, it looks as if it's ready to fall off at any moment.)

CONTINUITY AND PRODUCTION PROBLEMS

• For some reason, Kirk has taken up ventriloquism as a hobby. Just after the opening credits, the show returns to Kirk and Spock— still lassoed with the Troglyte thongs. Angrily, the captain says, "Who are you and what is the meaning of this attack?" And—just to show these primitives that he's more than just a starship commander—Kirk fires his questions without moving his lips!

• Under the influence of the gas, Kirk hits Plasus and sends him flailing back into a rock face. Watch the upper part of the wall as Plasus hits it. It pushes in and then springs back out. (This planet has some very odd rocks.)

TRIVIA ANSWERS

1. Merak II.

2. The Federation Bureau of Industrialization (in other words, the FBI).

CLOSING STILLS

• Pergium production station, Janus VI, "The Devil in the Dark"

• Spock approaching the *Galileo*, "The Immunity Syndrome"

• Thann and Lal watching Kirk, "The Empath"

• Kirk, McCoy, Scott, and Uhura materializing in the transporter, "Mirror, Mirror"

• Scott complaining about the present speed of warp nine, "The Paradise Syndrome"

• Star field

THE SAVAGE CURTAIN

Star Dates: 5906.4-5906.5

As the *Enterprise* surveys Excalbia, Abraham Lincoln appears on the main viewscreen. After coming on board, he invites Kirk and Spock to the planet. Moments after their arrival, Surak—the father of all that Vulcans hold dear—appears. Next, a rock transforms itself into a being and explains the purpose of the gathering. The inhabitants of the planet do not understand the concepts of good and evil. They have set the stage for a battle to the death to see which is stronger. Out of the thoughts of Kirk and Spock, they have created Lincoln and Surak as partners for good. From the same source they create four personifications of evil. To ensure Kirk's motivation, the rock being explains that if good loses, the *Enterprise* will be destroyed.

As a man of peace, Surak refuses to fight. He goes to meet with the other side, and they kill him. A few minutes later, Lincoln dies in a rescue attempt. Despite the odds, Kirk and Spock attack and defeat the enemy. The rock being observes that good and evil are the same, that they use the same tactics. In response, Kirk points out that his only motivation was to save the lives of his crew. Satisfied, the rock being lets them depart.

Trivia Questions

1. According to Scott, Lincoln is as loony as what animal?

2. To whom does Lincoln compare Kirk as a military strategist?

PLOT OVERSIGHTS

• After beaming aboard the ship, Lincoln seems genuinely surprised by technological advances such as the transporter and taped music, but when he leaves the room he walks right out into the hall, as if he knew the doors would open automatically. A man from Lincoln's time would stop, look for a doorknob, reach out, and jump back as the doors opened by themselves.

• In a stunning display of Earthcentric attitudes, Kirk actually has to ask Spock to identify Surak. Spock claims that he is the father of all that the Vulcans hold dear. In other words, he is the greatest of the greatest heroes of the first officer's race. No one expects Kirk to know the intricacies of Vulcan existence, but a recognition of Surak's name seems pretty basic.

• Speaking of Surak, this guy is really tough on showing emotion. It appears that Spock reacts rather stoically to his hero's arrival, but later he apologizes for the emotional outburst. Instead of saying, "What emotional outburst?" Surak simply agrees that the circumstances were unusual.

• Spock makes a pitiful showing in this episode. He must be self-conscious about fighting with Surak around. In the first fistfight with the four bad guys, Spock ends up dancing with the woman, seemingly unable to overpower her. In the final battle, Spock wrestles around with Genghis Khan until Kirk can kill Kahless and rush over to help him. What happened to that great Vulcan strength and fighting ability that we've seen in other shows?

• At one point Kirk marches up to the rock creature and tries to hit it. Ever tried to hit a rock? Especially a rock that has smoke rising from it? What is he thinking?

CHANGED PREMISES

• Wanting to establish a time frame for their first face-to-face meeting, Lincoln asks Kirk if they still measure time in minutes. Kirk smugly replies, "We can convert to it." They can *convert* to it? Since when did they stop using minutes to measure time? Every close-up of the chronometers shows the time in hours, minutes, and seconds. On top of that, every evil adversary has given them deadlines in hours and minutes.

• At one point on the bridge, Spock gives Lincoln a readout on the altitude of the *Enterprise*. Referring to miles, Spock says, "Using your old-style measurement . . . " Old-style measurement, Mr. Spock? Then why did you refer to the amoeba in "The Immunity Syndrome" as 11,000 *miles* long.

• This episode contains a Klingon warrior named Kahless. He is said to be the forerunner of all things Klingon. *The Star Trek: The Next Generation* episode "Rightful Heir" also speaks of Kahless, and a clone of the great warrior actually makes an appearance. Interestingly enough, Kahless doesn't have the ribbed forehead in "The Savage Curtain" but somehow acquires it in "Rightful Heir."

EQUIPMENT ODDITIES

• Not to beat a dead horse, but in this episode Kirk uses the top button on the right armrest to initiate communications, and the shot clearly shows that the light on his intercom speaker does not come on.

• Kirk and Spock try to beam down to the surface of the planet with the standard complement of equipment, but the inhabitants of the planet tamper with the transporter so that the phasers and Spock's tricorder remain behind. It takes several moments for Spock to discover this. A phaser I can understand—it sits on the hip, out of the way. But a tricorder? It normally hangs from Spock's shoulder. Doesn't it seems likely that

Spock would instantaneously notice that this piece of equipment was missing?

CONTINUITY AND PRODUCTION PROBLEMS

• Once again, the creators spliced in a piece of film backward. Shortly after the rock being introduces all the bad guys, a close-up shows our dear captain with his hair parted on the wrong side.

• Oh, embarrassment of all embarrassments for our beloved Captain Kirk! Here he is engaged in an epic struggle of good versus evil, uncertain of his surroundings and all but one of his fighting compatriots. What could possibly make this situation worse? Well . . . he could split open his pants! In the first wrestling match between the good guys and the bad guys, Kirk struggles with Colonel Green. At one point Kirk lands on his back and uses his legs to give Green a shove. As Kirk draws his knees to his chest, you can see a white line appear on his posterior. (Not that I'm an expert or anything but it appears that the Starfleet uniform has lost its integrity.)

• Before leaving to speak with the enemy, Surak gives Kirk and Spock the Vulcan hand sign. Watch closely just before he does so and you'll see the actor drop his hand slightly behind his outfit. It looks like he's trying to get his hand into position to make the sign. Even so, he doesn't quite get it right, because when Surak lifts his hand to Kirk, his thumb is pressed against his index finger.

• The close-up of Lincoln just as Surak screams actually comes from the president's speech several moments later, about being a woodsman. The creators simply slowed the film down.

• The rock creatures did a very realistic job when they created Lincoln. They even supplied him with a really big wallet. When Abe crawls on his hands and knees to reach Surak, there's a large protrusion in his back hip pocket that's either a wallet or a small whiskey flask.

TRIVIA ANSWERS

1. An Alturian dogbird.
2. General Grant.

CLOSING STILLS

• The *Enterprise* leaving Deep Space Station K-7, "The Trouble with Tribbles"

• Romulan warbird firing plasma weapon, "Balance of Terror"

• Flower with poison darts, Gamma Trianguli VI, "The Apple"

• Kirk, Korob, and Sylvia as the big cat, "Catspaw"

• Kirk and the tribbles, "The Trouble with Tribbles"

• The *Enterprise* after Scott engages the stolen cloaking device, "The *Enterprise* Incident"

ALL OUR YESTERDAYS

Star Dates: 5943.7-5943.9

Three hours before the planet Sarpeidon's sun goes nova, Kirk, Spock, and McCoy beam down to find out why all its inhabitants have suddenly disappeared. They find a library and a Mr. Atoz. Unknown to the landing party, the Sarpeidon government has created a time portal, allowing its citizens to avoid the impending doom by living out the rest of their lives in the past. Atoz assumes they are from Sarpeidon and urges them to make their choices before it's too late. Through the time portal, Kirk hears a woman scream, and he jumps through to help her. He appears in a time frame filled with horse-drawn carriages and swashbucklers but with the help of a fellow time traveler manages to return to the library.

Chasing after Kirk, Spock and McCoy arrive in the planet's last ice age, five thousand years in the past. There they meet a young woman named Zarabeth, imprisoned in the frozen wastes. Spock falls in love with her as he reverts to a Vulcan of this time frame, savage and driven by emotion. With McCoy's help, Spock realizes what's happening, and the pair return to the library. Just before the Sarpeidon sun explodes, the trio beam back to the ship.

Trivia Questions

1. What is the name of Sarpeidon's sun?

2. What is the name of the tyrant who banished Zarabeth to the ice age?

GREAT LINES

"*I heard the spirit talk to him. He answered and did call it 'Bones.'*"—The arresting officer attesting to the fact that Kirk is a witch. (At the time of his apprehension, Kirk was trying to find the portal back to the library by having Spock and McCoy speak to him. While this is a great line—putting Kirk's nickname for McCoy in an entirely different light—I would be remiss if I did not note that the arresting officer never hears Kirk call McCoy "Bones.")

PLOT OVERSIGHTS

• While telling Zarabeth of his origins, Spock claims he comes from a world millions of light-years away. The galaxy is only 100,000 light-years from tip to tip. For Spock's statement to be true, Vulcan would have to lie in another galaxy.

• Zarabeth wears an interesting outfit in this episode. Once she sheds her heavy fur full-length robe, she reveals a rather skimpy animal skin ensemble. The bodice is composed of a single piece of skin, fashionably dyed in the ever-popular brown, secured with thin animal strips that intertwine sensually across her well-defined back. Her shorts are an intricate affair with well-placed cuts to allow plenty of movement and considerable thigh exposure. The thin strips of leather intrigue me the most. Just how did she manufacture them? Or perhaps the larger question would be, why would she construct this type of outfit in the first place? According to Zarabeth, she expected to be alone for the rest of her life. Wouldn't she make her clothing to fit only her basic needs? Why the jungle woman look? Does she put on fashion shows for traveling packs of wolves? Or is she trying to impress the local apes with the rewards of evolving faster?

• Supposedly, a tyrant banished Zarabeth to this time period. Tyrants aren't known for their benevolence. If a tyrant rules Sarpeidon, why would he arrange for all of the inhabitants to find safety in the past? Surely he has made enemies. If he knows Sarpeidon's sun will soon explode, why not lock away his antagonists and let the nova vaporize them? Depending on your theory of time travel, there might even be a considerable danger in allowing your enemies to escape into your past. On the other hand, perhaps the good people of Sarpeidon overthrew the tyrant years ago. The episode gives no indication of how long Zarabeth has been in exile.

• Along the same lines, Zarabeth manages to keep her hair looking lovely, including a stylish flip curl at the end of her tresses. How does she accomplish this? Does she roll her hair up in hot rocks just before going to bed? (Hopefully, she remembers not to bolt upright in the morning.)

• While in the jail cell, many, many years in Sarpeidon's past, Kirk makes a log entry. He has no tricorder. He doesn't move his lips, and he gives a star date of 5943.9. How can this star date be correct? He's hundreds of years in the past!

• While contemplating his stay with Zarabeth, Spock comments that they could use the natural hot springs to construct a "greenhouse of sorts." Where is he going to get the seeds to grow plants? This is a barren, ice-covered wasteland. None of the scenes shows anything resembling a plant. (I know. They can probably get the seeds out of McCoy's handy-dandy medical kit. They seem to be able to get everything else from it.)

EQUIPMENT ODDITIES

• The inhabitants of Sarpeidon must buy their computers from the race that sent Gary Seven to Earth in "Assignment: Earth." Seven's Beta 5 computer looks identical to Mr. Atoz's atavachron.

CONTINUITY AND PRODUCTION PROBLEMS

• The actor who played Mr. Atoz in this episode also played Septimus in "Bread and Circuses."

• As I said in "The Lights of Zetar," the tapes I purchased from Paramount are supposed to be "uncut." However, the syndicated version recorded here in Springfield contains several lines of dialogue missing from my uncut version! Near the beginning of the episode Kirk asks Mr. Atoz about recent history. In the uncut version, Mr. Atoz points Kirk to the reference desk. In the syndicated version he replies, "Really? Oh, that's too bad. We have so little on recent history. There was no demand for it." Then Kirk responds, "It doesn't have to be extensive. Just the answers to a few questions." At this point, Mr. Atoz heads Kirk to the reference desk.

• The base of the disk viewer that is nearest the time portal is recycled from Sargon's pedestal in "Return to Tomorrow."

• During a jail visit by the prosecutor, Kirk mentions that he was reading in the library. This statement elicits an immediate response from the prosecutor, and Kirk realizes that the man is from the future as well. In this sequence, the creators used a close-up of Kirk that actually comes from footage a few moments later, when the captain stands up.

• When the prosecutor visits a second time, Kirk places his hands on the bars of the jail cell. At this point there is one bar between the bars that the captain grasps. Then the shot changes and suddenly there are two bars between the ones he holds.

• McCoy has been taking ventriloquist lessons from Kirk (see "The Cloudminders"). The first time the doctor walks into Zarabeth's outer chamber, he speaks while his lips are sealed.

TRIVIA ANSWERS

1. Beta Niobe.
2. Zor Khan.

CLOSING STILLS

• Close-up of the opening of the planet killer, The Doomsday Machine"

• Jail cells, Triskelion, "The Gamesters of Triskelion"

• Kirk, Spock, and McCoy as Nazis, "Patterns of Force"

• Engineering, "The Enemy Within" (This shot never appears in the episode.)

• Spock approaching the *Galileo,* "The Immunity Syndrome"

• Star field

TURNABOUT INTRUDER

Star Date: 5928.5

The *Enterprise* arrives at Camus II. Disaster has struck the research team led by Dr. Janice Lester, a woman who attended the Academy with Kirk. Beaming down, Kirk and a landing party find Lester bedridden. When Spock's tricorder detects other weakening life forms, he, McCoy, and Dr. Coleman, Lester's physician, hurry off to investigate. As Kirk looks around the room, Lester suddenly bolts upright and presses a button. A force field reaches out, pinning Kirk to the wall. Lester takes her place beside him, and the ancient device places each person's essence in the other's body. Lester has always dreamed of being a starship captain and hated Kirk for his accomplishments. The landing party then returns to report that all the other scientists are dead. Lester—in Kirk's body—orders the landing party, including Coleman and Kirk—in Lester's body—beamed back to the *Enterprise*.

Lester believes that with a little practice, no one will know she isn't the real Kirk. The senior staff immediately notice a difference, however. Soon all are convinced that the exchange occurred. Desperate, Lester convinces Coleman to murder Kirk. In that way she can never be forced to return to her own body. Thankfully, the transfer occurs naturally during the struggle, and Kirk is restored as captain.

Trivia Questions

1. Where is the *Enterprise* scheduled to rendezvous with the USS *Potemkin*?

2. What psychological test does McCoy give Kirk?

RUMINATIONS

For the sake of clarity, I will refer to a character first using the physical appearance and then the essence. Therefore, I will call Lester in Kirk's body, "Kirk/Lester," and Kirk in Lester's body "Lester/Kirk."

GREAT LINES

"*It may not be scientific, but if Mr. Spock thinks it happens, then it must be logical.*"—Scott, trying to convince McCoy that the exchange occurred, even if medical science gives no indication that it has.

GREAT MOMENTS

Both William Shatner and Sandra Smith give excellent

313

performances in this episode as they switch personalities. Shatner, playing Kirk/Lester, is absolutely believable, and Smith really comes through with a strong performance as the displaced Kirk in a woman's body. They provide this episode with many great moments.

SYNDICATION CUTS

• In the transporter room, Scott comments to Kirk/Lester how fortunate Lester/Kirk is still to be alive.

• Kirk/Lester savors the feel of the captain's chair before ordering the course change to Benecia.

• Following McCoy's insistence that Kirk/Lester report for a physical, Sulu calls from the bridge to inform the captain that Starfleet Command wants additional details on the reason for their delay in meeting the *Potemkin.*

• A slow pan from the medpanel to Lester/Kirk as she wakes from the sedative.

• After Lester/Kirk begins to cut herself free, an extensive chunk of dialogue between Spock and McCoy discussing the captain's current condition.

• The physical portion of Kirk/Lester's exam by McCoy.

• Following a commercial break, a captain's log by Kirk/Lester. The editors took care of a fairly large problem with this edit. Kirk/Lester records a captain's log detailing how he no longer fears discovery. Captain's logs are part of a public record. I

doubt Kirk/Lester would want others listening in on this log. Kirk/Lester should have used a personal log. Also, the editors fiddled with this footage a bit to smooth the transition from commercial to show. The uncut version comes back from the commercial break with a wide shot that includes Scott standing near Spock, seated in the witness chair. The captain's log occurs over this footage. When the log ends, the scene cuts to a close-up of Scott saying, "Surely you must have more than that to go on." For the syndicated version, the editors used the opening wide shot and replaced the captain's log with Scott's line of dialogue. Then the two versions sync back together, and the scene cuts to Spock's response to Scott's statement. (It's difficult to tell, but I'm not sure Scott is actually moving his lips in the wide shot. I guess that means Scott is also taking ventriloquism lessons from Kirk! See "All Our Yesterdays" and "The Cloudminders.")

• Security laughs at Kirk/Lester's mocking statement that he is Lester, and reaction shots from the communications officer, Sulu ,and Chekov before Lester/Kirk responds.

• Kirk/Lester asks Spock if he's ever heard of· a case such as described by Lester/Kirk, and Spock replies that he hasn't. (I'll talk about this later, but doesn't anyone remember the total entity transfer in "Return to Tomorrow"?)

• A few other reaction shots during the trial.

• After a commercial break, an establishing shot of the *Enterprise*, McCoy contemplating the vote on Spock's court-martial, and Scott approaching.

• On the bridge, the first part of Sulu and Chekov's discussion over whether they are going to allow the executions of Spock, McCoy, and Scott.

PLOT OVERSIGHTS

• How is Kirk/Lester supposed to open the safe in his quarters? There's no indication that the transference allowed Kirk/Lester to access any of the real Kirk's memories.

• After cutting herself free, Lester/Kirk runs to sick bay. In the presence of Spock and McCoy, Kirk/Lester hits the woman, knocking her out. Two security guards approach, pick her up, and carry her back to her bed. In the process, a guard slips his hand under Lester/Kirk's bare leg very high up on her thigh. One wonders what words of advice Kirk will have for that security guard once the captain is restored to his body?

• The psychological test McCoy gives Kirk/Lester supposedly reveals the basic emotional structure of a person. Yet, during Spock's court-martial, McCoy admits that the test showed that Kirk/Lester's emotional state is comparable to that of Kirk's when he took command of the *Enterprise*. Either Kirk was having a *really* bad day when he assumed command, or this test isn't worth much.

• At one point, Spock claims that complete entity transfer has never been accomplished with complete success anywhere in the galaxy. Don't the transfers in "Return to Tomorrow" qualify?

• As in the episode "Whom Gods Destroy," Lester/Kirk misses the obvious method for proving who she is. She tries to prove that she is Kirk by citing instances that are part of the public record. The Vulcan correctly points out that anyone could know them. Why doesn't Lester/Kirk mention *Pon farr*?

• Don't the security guards understand Starfleet regulations? Why don't they turn on Kirk/Lester when he orders the execution of his senior staff? According to Sulu and Chekov, the executions are illegal.

CHANGED PREMISES

• In the most stunning changed premise of the entire series, Lieutenant Galloway is *back!* Some of you may recall that Captain Ronald Tracey vaporized the intrepid lieutenant in "The Omega Glory." Yet somehow he manages to get resurrected and reincarnated for the final episode.

• When Kirk/Lester orders the execution of his senior officers, Sulu objects, and Chekov says General Order 4 is the only Starfleet order that carries a death penalty. According to "The Menagerie, Part I," General Order

7 is the only Starfleet order that carries a death penalty.

EQUIPMENT ODDITIES

• Does McCoy really do anything with that little medical doodad he waves around, or is it just for looks? When the landing party beams down to Camus II, McCoy opens his medical kit and extracts the little cylinder. The scene cuts to Lester, and the sound of the medical wand plays in the background. Yet McCoy seems unable to determine that there is nothing wrong with Lester. As soon as the rest of the landing party leaves Kirk behind, she pins him to a wall and leaps out of bed, full of energy. Shouldn't McCoy be able to tell she is faking?

• The straps that the medical personnel use in sick bay must have some magical quality to them. Lester/Kirk takes precious time to cut herself free, when it looks as if she can simply slip out from under the one strap across her waist.

CONTINUITY AND PRODUCTION PROBLEMS

• Evidently, Nurse Chapel grew tired of being a blonde. Suddenly, in this, the final episode of the original *Star Trek* television series, she's a brunette!

• Arriving on the bridge, Kirk/Lester takes a moment to savor the big chair and then stands to give new orders. As he does, the scene cuts to a wide shot from near Spock's workstation. The footage that precedes this shot shows Chekov at the navigator's position. The footage that follows this shot shows Chekov at the navigator's position. But this shot has somebody else in that chair. Who is this guy, anyway?

• This episode contains one of the best-known production problems—immortalized in the book *Star Trek Lives* by Jacqueline Lichtenberg, Sondra Marshak, and Joan Winston. After calling for a vote on Spock's court-martial proceedings, Kirk/Lester heads away from Spock toward the wall of the room. No, he's not going to sulk in the corner until the vote. He's supposed to be leaving the room. The story goes that the director told Shatner to walk that way and Shatner tried to explain that there wasn't a door there but the director wouldn't listen.

• The uncut version I purchased from Paramount contains a preview for "That Which Survives" at the end of this episode. Someone is trying to play with our minds. This is the last episode of the original television series.

TRIVIA ANSWERS
1. The Beta Aurigae system.
2. The Robbiani dermal-optic.

CLOSING STILLS
• *Enterprise* approaching energy barrier, "Where No Man Has Gone

Before"
• Engineering, "The Omega Glory"
• Kirk and *Nomad*, "The Changeling"
• McCoy beginning transfusion

from Spock to Sarek, "Journey to Babel"
• *Enterprise* over what looks like North America, "Miri"
• Star field

DAMAGE TOTE BOARD

1. Number of times Kirk's shirt is torn: seven
2. Number of people who slap Spock: five
3. Number of times McCoy pronounces someone or something dead: nineteen
4. Number of times Scott is knocked backward while trying to help a woman: three
5. Number of times Uhura is thrown from her chair: nine
6. Number of episodes or movies in which Chekov screams: six
7. Number of times Spock "kills" Kirk: two
8. Number of senior staff members who die and come back to life: five
9. Number of women hit by male Starfleet officers: four
10. Number of episodes in which the *Enterprise*'s artificial gravity degrades to "point eight": seven

REFERENCES

1. Torn during the fight with Gary Mitchell in "Where No Man Has Gone Before." Ripped by McCoy at the end of "The Naked Time." Torn by himself during "Miri." Ripped during the fight with Finnegan in "Shore Leave." Torn during the fight with Finney in "Court-Martial." Sliced open during the fight with Spock in "Amok Time." Ripped during the whipping in "The Gamesters of Triskelion."

2. Kirk slaps him several times in "The Naked Time." His mother slaps him in "Journey to Babel." Nurse Chapel slaps him in "A Private Little War." Dr. M'Binga slaps him also in "A Private Little War." The Romulan commander slaps him in "The *Enterprise* Incident."

3. Green in "The Man Trap." The horned doggie in "The Enemy Within." The creature in "Miri." Adams in "Dagger of the Mind." Kirk in "Amok Time." Scott in "The Changeling." Jackson in "Catspaw." Scott in "I, Mudd." Galway in "The Deadly Years." Dancer in "Wolf in the Fold." Tracey in "Wolf in the Fold." Hengist in "Wolf in the Fold." Nona in "A Private Little War." Kirk in "Return to Tomorrow." Starnes in "And the Children Shall Lead." Marvick in "Is There in Truth No Beauty?" Chekov in "Spectre of the Gun." Old man in "For the World Is Hollow and I Have Touched the Sky." Female scientist at Memory Alpha in "The Lights of Zetar."

4. Apollo slings him backward as he tries to stop the Greek god from taking Palamas in "Who Mourns for Adonais?" *Nomad* knocks him over the rail-

ing as he attempts to help Uhura in "The Changeling." The Zetars shove him as he helps Romaine into the pressure chamber in "The Lights of Zetar."

5. Once in "The Corbomite Maneuver." Once in "Balance of Terror." Twice in "Tomorrow Is Yesterday." Once (sort of) in "The Changeling." Three times in "The Immunity Syndrome." Once in "That Which Survives."

6. On seeing Alvin interned in "The Deadly Years." When overcome with space madness in "The Tholian Web." After touching a flower in "The Way to Eden." Upon burning his hand in *Star Trek: The Motion Picture.* During the ear slug sequence in *Star Trek II: The Wrath of Khan.* Falling off the *Enterprise* in *Star Trek IV: The Voyage Home.*

7. During the *Koon-ut-kal-if-fee* in "Amok Time." By using the "Vulcan death grip" aboard the Romulan vessel in "The *Enterprise* Incident."

8. McCoy in "Shore Leave." Scott in "The Changeling." Kirk in "Return to Tomorrow." Chekov in "Spectre of the Gun." Spock in *Star Trek II: The Wrath of Khan* and *Star Trek III: The Search For Spock.*

9. McCoy slaps Eleen in "Friday's Child." Chekov slugs Tamoon in "The Gamesters of Triskelion." Kirk knocks Shahna unconscious in "The Gamesters of Triskelion." Kirk coldcocks Kelinda in "By Any Other Name."

10. For the second pilot, "Where No Man Has Gone Before," the creators put together some background voices to play on the bridge after the ship waddles out of the energy barrier. One of the voices clearly says, "Gravity is down to point eight." Of course, every time the creators need-ed some "noise" to fill the bridge after an impact, they grabbed this tape. So . . . gravity degrades a lot on the *Enterprise*! There may be more places where this tape is used, but you can hear it clearly in these: "Where No Man Has Gone Before, " "The Corbomite Maneuver," "The Squire of Gothos," "Arena," "Tomorrow Is Yesterday," "A Taste of Armageddon," and "The Changeling."

THE
FIRST
PILOT

THE CAGE

Star Date: unknown

The *Enterprise*, under the command of Christopher Pike, travels to Talos IV in response to a false distress signal. The Talosians quickly capture Pike, and the captain soon learns that his keepers can make him relive any experience of his life. Oddly enough, a previously unknown woman named Vina seems to appear in these imaginings. Vina actually lives on Talos IV. She survived a crash-landing there eighteen years ago. After doctoring her injuries, the Talosians became interested in humans and decided to lure a male of the species to the planet. Many years ago, war drove the Talosians underground. The surface is finally recovering, and the Talosians desire to repopulate the planet with another race. The Talosians will carefully control these inhabitants, caring for them and living vicariously through their dreams.

Eventually Pike escapes to the surface, even as the Talosians realize that humans have a strong hatred of captivity. This quality makes humans unsuitable for their needs, and they allow the *Enterprise* to leave. Vina chooses to stay behind. The Talosians didn't know what humans looked like when they reassembled her. Vina's actual appearance is quite malformed, and the Talosians have offered to let her live out her life in beauty.

Trivia Questions

1. What is the name of Pike's horse?

2. Where was Pike born?

RUMINATIONS

For those of you who do not know, this episode is actually the first pilot Gene Roddenberry creat-ed for Star Trek. *It was rejected by the network execu-tives, but in a rare move they asked him to create another. The net-work executives then accepted the second pilot, "Where No Man Has Gone Before," and the rest, as they say, is history.*

As the earliest incarnation of the Star Trek *universe, "The Cage" contains many elements and themes that are later revisited in the original television series. The episode begins with a radio wave racing toward the* Enterprise, *alert-ing the sensors to the imminent "collision." The bridge crew ner-*

vously suggests options while Pike calmly orders them forward. This type of sequence becomes vintage Kirk. Also, Pike complains about having a female yeoman, much as Kirk does in the early episodes (these two facts give the impression that women on starships is a recent phenomenon). On the planet's surface, Vina entices Pike away from the landing party with the lure of perfect health—an enticement that surfaces in "The Omega Glory." War sends the Talosians underground, just as it does to the "Old Ones" in "What Are Little Girls Made Of?" The Talosians exploit the inhabitants of their menagerie for entertainment, much like the Providers use the thralls for sport in "The Gamesters of Triskelion." Pike pleads with the head Talosian to punish him instead of Vina in the same way that Kirk pleads with the Providers to grant Shahna a reprieve in "The Gamesters of Triskelion." Pike offers himself for the safety of his ship, as Kirk does in "The Squire of Gothos." Number One, Pike's first officer, makes the same argument as McCoy in "The Apple," that it's wrong to keep humans as slaves.

In the sidebar "Boys in the Hall," I discuss Star Trek's attitudes toward women, but two items deserve special mention here. First, Roddenberry made the first officer of Pike's Enterprise a female. At the time, this action was as radical as creating a racially mixed crew. According to the

Great Bird of the Galaxy himself—in his comments on my prerecorded video—men and women had difficulty with his choice of first officer. Second, Roddenberry dressed the female members of the crew in shirts and pants, just like the men. To me, these two items indicate that Roddenberry foresaw a time when men and women would intermix freely in the workplace, with little or no regard to gender (even if Captain Pike still had a little trouble with the idea). Of course, Hollywood quickly squashed that idea, and even now the uniforms of men and woman within the Star Trek universe remain distinctly different.

And speaking of clothing, "The Cage" features coats for the landing parties, an idea that does not recur until Star Trek: The Motion Picture.

This is the premiere and therefore, in my mind, entitled to gentle treatment. It's also very difficult to nitpick a single episode of a particular setting. As always, I will make a valiant attempt. You would expect no less.

One last thing, this episode holds the distinction of submitting to the editor's knife not once but twice. The creators cut it down to fit into the episode, "The Menagerie" (Part I and Part II) and then the editors cut "The Menagerie" down again for syndication.

GREAT LINES

"The women!"—Spock informing the rest of the landing party that only the female members were transported to the surface.

PLOT OVERSIGHTS

• At one point, Pike turns and bumps into his female yeoman. He looks over the reports she brings and comments that he isn't used to having a woman on the bridge. Number One reacts to this statement, and Pike explains that she is "different." However, a few moments earlier, the scene showed Pike standing beside a woman seated at a console on the bridge. Is she different as well, or merely cross-dressing?

• After setting course for Talos, time warp factor seven, the creators overlay the bridge action with a star field and music. This gives the impression that the *Enterprise* is rocketing through space. Since the music is drowning out any possibility of conversation, the navigator gives Pike a hand signal to indicate that they have achieved time warp factor seven. (A hand signal? On the bridge of the *Enterprise*? Someone needs to turn down the music.)

• Why is Spock limping after beaming down to the planet? And why is Spock smiling and shouting and showing emotion?

• The landing party tells the *faux* crash survivors that they won't believe how fast they can return to Earth now that the "time" barrier has been broken. Presumably Roddenberry was referring to flying faster that the speed of light. So these crash victims supposedly

made it to Talos IV by traveling at less than the speed of light? Pike tells the Talosians that he is from a stellar group on the "other end" of the Galaxy. The galaxy is 100,000 light-years across. Depending on the exact position of Talos IV, it would take a sublight craft no less than 30,000 years to reach the planet from Earth. I don't think these survivors are supposed to be that old.

• Vina claims she is deformed because the Talosians had no guide when they rebuilt her. Why didn't the Talosians use their own form? They appear to be humanoid. On the other hand, why didn't they just read her mind and find out what she thought she looked like?

EQUIPMENT ODDITIES

• In this episode, Spock can wave his hand and change the setting of a viewscreen. Kirk's *Enterprise* lost this ability.

• Attempting to rescue Pike from the Talosians, the crew of the *Enterprise* bring down a laser cannon. As it fires, Number One gives instructions to the ship. Every time she calls for more power, she speaks into her communicator, but when she wants them to disengage, she lowers the communicator and shouts at the sky.

CONTINUITY AND PRODUCTION PROBLEMS

• When the first landing party beams down, the guy on the far right changes head and hand position.

• The actors' lip movements don't match the audio in two places. First, during Spock's briefing on the ship, when Number One comments that they just thought they saw survivors. Second, on the planet, when Vina is in the cage with Pike and she tells him that he can have anything he wants in the whole universe.

TRIVIA ANSWERS
1. Tango.
2. Mojave.

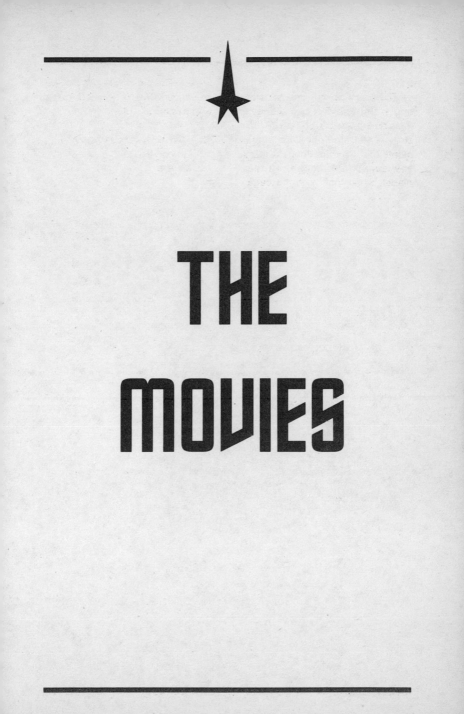

THE
MOVIES

STAR TREK: THE MOTION PICTURE

Star Dates: 7411.4-7414.1

An immense energy cloud travels toward Earth, destroying everything in its path. Knowing the *Enterprise* is the only ship in the area that can intercept the cloud before it reaches the Terran system, Admiral Kirk seizes the opportunity to sit in the "center chair" one more time. He convinces Starfleet to put him in charge of the ship and temporarily reduce its captain, Decker, to the rank of commander. Soon McCoy and Spock join the ship as well.

On arrival at the cloud, a tractor beam draws the *Enterprise* inside. Then a plasma probe dances through the bridge, disintegrating Lieutenant Ilia. Moments later, she reappears as a mechanized humanoid, a mouthpiece for V'ger—the entity inside the energy cloud. Through discussions with the mechanized Ilia and Spock's mind meld with a portion of V'ger, the crew learn more. V'ger is a living machine. It believes that it must return to Earth and merge with its creator. Upon arrival, V'ger transmits a simple binary message but receives no reply. Ilia states that Earth's biological infestation is interfering with the response of the Creator. In a few minutes, V'ger will destroy all carbon-based life on the planet.

In a desperate gamble, Kirk tells Ilia that he knows why the Creator is not responding but must be taken to V'ger before he will say. Ilia escorts them to a central structure. It is occupied by an old space probe from Earth. In fact, V'ger is *Voyager 6*, launched by NASA some three hundred years earlier. It fell into a black hole and reappeared on the far side of the galaxy. Once there, it drifted into the awareness of a planet of intelligent machines. The machines interpreted V'ger's programming literally: Collect all information possible and return it to the Creator. They outfitted *Voyager* with the capability to do just that. The crew searches the historical records and transmits the command to tell *Voyager 6* to release its data. Before receiving the final sequence, V'ger burns out its own

> **Trivia Questions**
>
> 1. What is the name, class, and registry of the vessel scheduled to rendezvous with the USS *Columbia*, NCC 621?
> 2. What is the name of the security guard present with Kirk, Spock, and McCoy when they find the mechanical Ilia taking a shower?

antenna leads. It wants to meet the Creator in person. Decker volunteers to key in the last few numbers. When he does, V'ger absorbs him and gains the knowledge of human emotions and intuition—the ability to move beyond mere logic. Moments later, V'ger disappears, leaving the *Enterprise* in orbit around Earth.

RUMINATIONS

*F*ans of Star Trek: The Next Generation *will notice the original implementation of some of that television show's elements in this movie. For one thing, the main musical theme for* NextGen *came from this movie. Also, note the hallways and the vertical matter/antimatter core, the little elevator in Engineering, and the beds in sick bay. At one point, a set of wall covers in the background matches those used in the transporter room on the* Enterprise 1701-D. *The orbiting space station Kirk beams aboard near the beginning of the film looks like one used in "The Measure of a Man." The only difference is that the creators turned it upside down. And finally, this movie features an alien female officer named Ilia, who comes from a sexually permissive culture. Years ago, this officer had a relationship with the executive officer, whose name is Will Decker. They meet for the first time since the breakup on the* Enterprise. *Does this sound familiar? It should. Just change the names to Deanna Troi and Will Riker.*

PLOT OVERSIGHTS

• Earth must not be very important to the Federation. Starfleet Command schedules a refit for the *Enterprise* and—knowing that it isn't ready for space flight—sends all its other starships off on missions. Does this make sense strategically? Why is the *Enterprise* the "only starship in interception range" of V'ger? If this is really true, Starfleet Command left themselves undefended.

• The *Enterprise* sure does get to Jupiter fast after leaving space dock. They are supposedly traveling at half the speed of light, yet in the movie it appears that they arrive at the huge gas giant in only seconds. The problem here is that even our solar system is *big*. It takes more than two hours for light to make the journey from Sol to Jupiter. (The creators probably just didn't bother to show us this part of the journey. After all, it would slow down this movie even more!)

• For some reason the pilot who ferries Spock to the *Enterprise* doesn't identify his passenger when he requests docking privileges. Even the ship's computer cooperates with this conspiracy of silence. As Chekov stands outside the docking bay doors, the coy computer will only identify the one boarding as "Starfleet inactive."

• McCoy hasn't decided to join the rest of the Federation on the metric system yet. While all the rest of the distance measurements in the movie are in kilometers, the doctor wonders if V'ger contains a crew of a thousand beings who stand 10 *miles* tall.

• In a dramatic moment well into the movie, Spock turns to Kirk and says, "I suspect there's an object at the heart of that cloud." Didn't Starfleet already figure this out? Didn't the little guy at Comm Station Epsilon 9 say something similar to this when he spoke with Kirk near the beginning of the movie?

• For some reason, V'ger decides to send its mechanized version of Ilia into a sonic shower. Of course, this allows the creators to show us water glistening on Ilia's presumably naked body, and it also provides the slightest possible excuse for the mechanized probe to spend the rest of the movie dressed in a *really* short robe. The origin of this robe deserves some scrutiny. When the door to the shower first opens and "Iliadroid" appears—seemingly oblivious to the fact that she isn't wearing any clothes—Kirk apparently remedies the situation by pressing a few buttons. The robe then magically appears. It's nice to see that Kirk hasn't lost his appreciation for the feminine form. Dressing Iliadroid in a full-length robe would have been a tragic misuse of resources. Yet not only does Kirk choose a miniskirted wrap for this freshly showered probe, he also fits her with high heels! This is a bit much. A simple tour of the ship rarely calls for a bathrobe and heels.

• At one point, Spock says that V'ger *obviously* operates from a central brain. How is this obvious? The current trend in computing is away from centralization toward lots of smaller computers hooked together over networks.

CHANGED PREMISES

• Well, the Klingons certainly have changed in the past several years! The movie opens with three Klingon vessels attacking V'ger. Instead of looking like humans with bushy eyebrows, these Klingons have a center ridge running up their forehead. Just how much time has elapsed between the last episode of the original television series and the beginning of this movie? According to the dialogue, this movie occurs approximately four and a half years later (assuming Kirk completed the last two years of the *Enterprise*'s five-year mission after the television show ended). Kirk claims he spent five years aboard the *Enterprise* and then two and a half more with Starfleet Command. I guess a lot can happen to alien races in four and a half years. On the other hand, a lot can happen to Starfleet officers. The crew of the *Enterprise* certainly look more than four and a half years older.

• The opening scene featuring Spock has the former first officer of the *Enterprise* meditating on the hot sands of Vulcan. Oddly enough, there's a really big moon and a large planet in the sky. During "The Man Trap," Spock told Uhura that Vulcan had no moon. In addition, the same scene in the movie has a wizened Vulcan female bidding Spock good-bye as she says, "Live long and prosper." Oddly enough, she doesn't give the Vulcan hand sign. Until this moment, the hand sign has always accompanied these words.

• Toward the end, Kirk tells Scott to prepare to carry out self-destruct. What happened to all the code stuff we saw in "Let That Be Your Last Battlefield" and will see again in *Star Trek III: The Search for Spock?*

EQUIPMENT ODDITIES

• During the television series it took only one transporter to get anywhere. If you had a transporter on a ship, you could beam to and from a planet. If you had a transporter on a planet, you could beam to and from a ship in orbit (Although we never actually saw Federation technology accomplish this, the Kelvans did it in "By Any Other Name.") Yet when Kirk needs to get to the *Enterprise*, he beams up to a nearby space station and Scott pilots him over in a shuttle pod. Scott claims the transporters on the *Enterprise* are temporarily out of order. This scene raises some questions. Aren't there transporters on Earth? If not, why not? And if there are, why not beam Kirk directly to the ship instead of the station? Along the same line, two officers die several minutes later, when the *Enterprise* tries to beam them aboard. The dialogue seems to indicate that two transporters are involved in the

process. Since when does it take two transporters to get someone from the surface of a planet to a ship?

• Shortly after coming aboard, Kirk calls together the crew on the recreation deck and shows them the transmission from the three Klingon vessels that initially intercepted V'ger. The recording shows V'ger easily destroying all three. In fact, the recording shows V'ger for several moments after the Klingon vessels are destroyed. If the Klingon vessels are transmitting these pictures, how can the recording contain a shot of V'ger after the vessels are obliterated? (I realize the dialogue in the movie mentions a sensory probe, but I got the impression that the probe was intercepting the Klingon transmissions, not recording pictures of the battle.)

• Along the same line, the *Enterprise* receives a transmission from Comm Station Epsilon 9 after it is destroyed.

• After beaming aboard, McCoy says, "Permission to come aboard," and the computer answers happily, "Permission granted, sir." Kirk stands in front of the doctor. Wouldn't this be the captain's job? (Several scenes later, Spock joins the crew and says the same thing. This time the uppity little computer lets Chekov respond, "Permission granted, sir.")

• In the first of his captain's logs, Kirk claims that they must risk engaging warp while still in the solar system to intercept V'ger at the earliest possible moment. Is this really risky? Didn't the old *Enterprise* warp out of a planet's orbit all the time? (If you require a specific example, Scott tells Kirk that they will be "warping out of orbit" one half-second after the captain gives the word in "The Naked Time.")

• The arms on Kirk's bridge chair fold down to secure the captain to his seat. If the planners thought far enough ahead to realize that the ship might get tossed around, why do the crew members along the sides of the bridge have to stand up to do their jobs? Wouldn't it be better to secure them in seats as well? Or are their jobs simply not that important?

• As V'ger's plasma probe sucks information out of Spock's computer station, a series of blueprints flashes across the screen. Unless I miss my guess, those are the plans to the original *Enterprise* drawn by Franz Joseph Designs. (Joe Ryan loaned me his copy for this project.)

• V'ger supposedly re-creates Ilia's body in precise detail, yet she sounds like a Transformer.

• For some reason, Kirk changes his space suit while he is *outside* the *Enterprise*. After Spock runs off for his mind meld with V'ger, the captain dons a spacesuit and follows him. The helmet of the suit has a tube that runs around the neck area. Following V'ger's expulsion of Spock, Kirk catches his friend, and suddenly the captain wears a suit similar to Spock's.

• When Kirk, Ilia, and the others emerge from the hatch on the front of the saucer, the navigation beacon has stopped blinking. Someone probably turned it off so the light wouldn't hurt the captain's eyes.

CONTINUITY AND PRODUCTION PROBLEMS

• Starfleet must have been going through a pastel phase when this movie occurs. Thankfully, by the time the next movie rolls around, the powers that be have rediscovered real colors.

• When Comm Station Epsilon 9 intercepts the transmission from the imperial Klingon cruiser *Amar,* the staff play it on a small monitor. The footage shown contains an edit. The Klingon captain speaks for several seconds, and then his face jumps to a lower position. Who's been editing this transmission?

• This movie has eternal stretches of visuals showing Klingon vessels; Starfleet vessels; V'ger; and, of course, the *Enterprise.* My theory is that the creators had *Star Wars* in mind when they shot the miniatures of the ships. Nowhere is this theory *more* supported than in the approach of Spock's shuttle to the *Enterprise.* I almost felt like singing the *Star Wars* theme when it passed overhead.

• As Kirk prepares to board the *Enterprise*, his travel pod passes between a floodlight and the ship. Correctly so, the floodlight illuminates the side of the pod.

However, the pod does not cast a shadow on the side of the *Enterprise*.

• As the *Enterprise* moves out of space dock, several of the floodlights click off instantly. They must have new bulb technology in the twenty-third century, because present-day floodlights would dim and then go out.

• You want real nitpicking? You came to the right place. Watch the flash as the *Enterprise* jumps into warp speed. The first time this occurs in the movie, the flash starts exactly where the ship disappears. This is correct. However, the second and third times the ship jumps to warp, the flashes begin off to the side.

• Chekov greets Spock as the former first officer of the *Enterprise* comes aboard. Spock then walks away from Chekov, and the next shot shows the Vulcan walking on to the bridge. Everyone expresses surprise at seeing him. Then Spock leaves for Engineering, and Kirk turns to give an order to Chekov. Chekov? When did he arrive on the bridge? Spock left the docking area before he did. He didn't ride up in the turbolift with Spock, and there's no sound of any doors opening during the bridge dialogue. Did Chekov arrive before Spock showed up on the bridge, and if he did, why didn't he tell the crew that Spock was on board? Or did he tell them and everyone is just faking their surprise?

• During the first meeting with Kirk and McCoy, Spock's ears seem to be different. Normally the tips of the ears point up, but in this scene, they point back at an angle.

• When Chekov returns to the bridge after burning his hand, there's an obvious edit on my videotape. The music jumps, but I have no idea what's missing.

• One of the worst production problems in both the television series and the movies occurs in this episode. After Spock leaves to mind-meld with V'ger, Kirk follows behind in a spacesuit. As Kirk leaves the *Enterprise*, you can see the scaffolding that supports the set!

• Just after Spock enters V'ger, the reflection on his helmet shows sunrise on a planet and rings passing over him. The shot also shows his jet pack firing. Then the scene changes to a reverse angle. The jet pack burns out, Spock approaches a set of rings, and sunrise begins on the planet. I think the creators had a real problem with this sequence. The way it's edited it looks backward, but if they put the reverse angle first, Spock's jet pack would burn out, and then the close-up would show it still firing.

• The first set of reflections on Spock's helmet are flipped correctly for a mirrored view. But when Spock approaches the images of the mechanized planet, the reflection in Spock's helmet shows it oriented the same way Spock sees it. Mirror images should be flipped. (And—if perchance I don't have this figured out correctly—at least one of these reflections is wrong, because they are done exactly opposite to each other!)

• At the end of the movie, Spock and McCoy chat with Kirk on the bridge. Spock wears a coat with an orange armband. McCoy wears one with a green armband. Then the shot changes. Suddenly Spock wears the coat with the green arm-band and McCoy wears the one with the orange armband. (Makes one wonder what these guys do in their spare time.)

TRIVIA ANSWERS

1. USS *Revere*, NCC 595, a scout ship.

2. Ensign Perez.

STAR TREK II: THE WRATH OF KHAN

Star Dates: 8130.3–8141.6

The USS *Reliant* drops into orbit around Ceti Alpha VI in search of a completely lifeless world for Project Genesis. Lead by scientist Carol Marcus and her son, David—the product of a past relationship with Kirk—the project has created a device that can terraform a lifeless planet in only minutes. The process has performed well so far, and the final stage of testing involves firing the device at a barren world. Finding one anomalous life energy reading, Captain Terrell and First Officer Pavel Chekov of the *Reliant* beam down to investigate. They are soon captured by Khan and his followers (see "Space Seed"). One year after Kirk left them on Ceti Alpha V, Ceti Alpha VI exploded and hurled Khan's planet into a wider orbit. Consumed with a desire for revenge, Khan puts sluglike creatures into the officers' ears. The creatures burrow through to their brains and make them susceptible to suggestion. With Terrell and

Trivia Questions

1. Who is the master of the *Kobayashi Maru?*

2. What is the prefix code for the *Reliant?*

Chekov's help, Khan commandeers the *Reliant* and learns of the Genesis Project.

Meanwhile, Admiral Kirk—on a training run with a group of cadets—receives a call from Marcus. The *Reliant* has signaled that Starfleet is seizing control of Genesis, and Marcus demands to know why. Kirk, realizing Starfleet gave no such order, takes command of the *Enterprise* and heads for Regula. The first encounter with the *Reliant* goes badly for the *Enterprise*. Kirk barely manages to beat back the attack and move his crippled ship on to Regula.

Soon Khan steals the Genesis device and moves in to destroy the *Enterprise*. With only one option, Kirk turns the ship into the Mutara Nebula. When Khan follows him, the ships are evenly matched. The nebula distorts sensors and renders shields useless. With his superior experience, Kirk disables the *Reliant*, but Khan refuses to give up. He sets the Genesis device to detonate, knowing the *Enterprise* is without warp and unable to outrun the resulting explosion. After Scott doesn't reply to Kirk's repeated pleas for warp drive, Spock goes to Engineering. He restores power just in time for the ship to blast to safety but receives a lethal dose of radiation in the process and dies. As the movie ends, Kirk and crew pay their respects and then fire a torpedo casing containing Spock's body at the planet newly formed by the detonation of the Genesis device.

RUMINATIONS

*T*his is a great movie! A bit gross in the ear slug department, but all in all an excellent excursion for the crew of the Enterprise. One really nice touch occurs in the scene between Kirk and McCoy at the admiral's residence on Earth. The conversation revolves around Kirk's birthday and growing old. All the while, a clock ticks in the background, providing an incessant reminder that time is moving forward. Another nice touch is the recurring theme of the Kobayashi Maru—the test given Saavik at the very beginning of the movie, the test that forces a Starfleet officer to face a no-win scenario. Friends tell me that the Kobayashi Maru has inspired more than one scene in the Star Trek novels.

By the way, there's a story going around Trekdom that this movie contains a major plot oversight concerning Khan and Chekov. In one scene, Khan tells Chekov that he remembers the Russian from his time on the Enterprise fifteen years ago. The story goes that Chekov joined the Enterprise in the second season and "Space Seed" occurred in the first season. Therefore, Khan could not have remembered Chekov. The problem with this story is that the Enterprise is a big ship. Nowhere does dialogue indicate that Chekov joined the ship in the second season. All we know is that he joined the bridge crew in the second season. He could have worked in the lower decks during the first season. There's only one piece of evidence to indicate that Chekov wasn't with the ship at the very beginning of the show. During "I, Mudd," Kirk has to explain Mudd's identity to Chekov. You will recall that Mudd first visited the crew of the Enterprise with three stunning lovelies in "Mudd's Women." If Chekov had been on the ship at the time of "Mudd's Women," he would have known Mudd's identity. As demonstrated over and over in that episode, men talk about beautiful women. Without a doubt, the entire ship buzzed with descriptions of them and their origin, an origin inexplicably tied to Mudd. There is plenty of time, however, for Chekov to join the ship after "Mudd's Women" and before "Space Seed."

One final caveat on the matter above: Do I think the creators had this explanation in mind when they had Chekov and Khan identify each other? No. But, as Ferengi Rule of Acquisition number 76 states, "Every once in a while, declare peace."

GREAT LINES

"*I have been, and always shall be, your friend.*"—Spock, spending his final moments with Kirk. (It was almost impossible to pick just one great line out of this movie. There were a bunch of them.)

GREAT MOMENTS

*T*he epic conflict between Kirk and Khan, the final touching moments between Kirk and Spock, along with the Vulcan's funeral, provide this movie with many stirring moments.

PLOT OVERSIGHTS

• During the simulation at the very beginning of the movie, Saavik, a Vulcan female, realizes that the *Kobayashi Maru* lies disabled in the Neutral Zone. At this, she lets out an expletive. Wouldn't this be considered illogical *and* emotional?

• The graphics depicting the Neutral Zone show a modified sphere. Why would the Neutral Zone look like a sphere? The only way this would work is if the Klingon Empire sat at the heart of the sphere, but the sphere doesn't look that big.

• As Terrell and Chekov look around in the cargo containers on Ceti Alpha V, a close-up shows a half-finished game of checkers. Let's think about this. These guys are genetically bred for intelligence, and they play checkers? Not to insult the accomplished and skilled players of checkers in the reading audience, but there simply aren't that many playable scenarios in the game, especially if you compare it to a game such as three-dimensional chess—a game Kirk and Spock routinely played on the classic *Enterprise*.

• Moments after entering the cargo containers, Chekov discovers a strap from the SS *Botany Bay*. He quickly realizes that Khan will soon arrive and hurries his captain outside. Wouldn't it be simpler just to call for an emergency beam-out from within the cargo container? Of course, if Chekov did this, it would be a very short movie!

• Khan's people seem very young. In "Space Seed," the superpersons were all about the same age. Yet, in this movie they look at least 20 years younger than their leader.

• Khan claims that Kirk abandoned him and his followers fifteen years ago on Ceti Alpha V. In the review of the previous movie, I calculated that *Star Trek: The Motion Picture* occurred approximately four and one-half years after the end of the original television series. So the question is: How much time has elapsed between the first movie and this one? In this movie Kirk watches a recording that he says Marcus made *one year* ago. The star date on the recording is 7130.4. So a star date of 7130.4 is approximately one year prior to the beginning star date of this movie, 8130.3. (Actually, this make sense, because several episodes in *Star Trek: The Next Generation* indicate that 1000 star date units equal one year.)

The first movie begins on star date 7411.4. If the star dates are to be believed, the first movie begins *after* Marcus made her recording, and Marcus made her recording one year ago. Therefore, the first movie began less than one year ago. Since the first movie occurred about four and one-half years after the end of the original television series, the second movie must occur about five and one-half years after the end of the original television series. Hold that thought for a moment. Kirk deposited Khan on Ceti Alpha V in the first season of the television show. Presumably each season of the television show equates to approximately one year. In other words, Kirk deposited Khan approximately two years *before* the end of the television series. Putting these two "facts" together, Kirk dropped off Khan and the others about seven and a half years ago, not fifteen—as is stated in this movie's dialogue. Somebody's numbers are wrong somewhere.

• Khan claims that one year after Kirk left them on the planet, Ceti Alpha VI exploded and hurled Ceti Alpha V into a wider orbit. What are the chances that Ceti Alpha V's new orbit would look just like Ceti Alpha VI's old orbit? Wouldn't Ceti Alpha V have some sort of eccentric orbit because of what it has endured? Wouldn't this orbit tip off the crew that something has happened? And even if Ceti Alpha V doesn't have an eccentric orbit, what happened to the charts for this system? Was the crew of the *Reliant* in such a hurry to find a lifeless planet that they didn't even bother to do a full sensor scan of the system and count those big blips on the screen? It's a planet, for crying out loud! How could they not realize that Ceti Alpha VI was missing? And why didn't Spock tell Kirk that the planet was unstable during "Space Seed"?

• At one point, Khan quotes a Klingon proverb. When did he learn this? The last time he had access to a library was aboard the original *Enterprise*. (By the way, "Revenge is a dish that is best served cold" is actually an old Sicillian proverb.)

• Supposedly, the sluglike creature Khan puts in Chekov's ear will burrow inward and find a home in his brain. Several scenes later, the creature decides to look for new lodgings and moves out. What does this say about Chekov? (Maybe the creature couldn't *find* a home in there? I know—that was unkind and I apologize.)

• To hide the Genesis device from Khan, Carol Marcus and her son flee to a deep cave created by stage two of the Genesis Project. Subsequent shots show the cave filled with luxurious foliage and steep precipices. They also show a very strong light source. Where is this light coming from? Did the Genesis device burrow out to the surface?

• Using the same gimmick employed in the first movie, the *Enterprise* is, once again, the "only ship in the quadrant" that can investigate the problems at Regula I.

• After Kirk finds Marcus, she sends everyone but him out into the cave so the two of them can have a heart-to-heart talk. After all, she never told him about their mutual son, David. While Kirk bares his soul, Chekov lies a few feet away, supposedly unconscious. I don't believe it for a minute. Look at Chekov's arm. He's holding his hand up to his ear. That arm could not stay in that position if Chekov were asleep. He's just faking it so he can eavesdrop.

• At one point during the battle in the nebula, Spock comments that Khan thinks two-dimensionally. Yet Kirk makes his own share of "two-dimensional thinking" mistakes in this movie. Meeting Khan head to head for the first time in the nebula, Kirk orders "hard a-starboard." This changes the target profile of the *Enterprise* from fairly narrow to very broad as the ship turns and exposes its entire side. On the other hand, if Kirk had ordered a course up or down while simultaneously rotating around Khan's ship, our good captain could have kept the smallest possible profile toward the *Reliant* and still moved the *Enterprise* out of its way. Also, when Kirk finally slips behind Khan's ship, why does Kirk fire as both ships reside in the same plane? Wouldn't it make more sense to rise above or drop below the *Reliant* and then tilt the front of the *Enterprise* up or down to give

Sulu a bigger target? Granted, it is difficult to see inside the nebula. However, the maneuver would be simple to accomplish once Khan's ship appears on the viewscreen. Don't they teach this stuff at the Academy?

• A truly touching moment occurs as Kirk says the final words over his friend's coffin. As an epitaph, Kirk claims that of all the souls he has met in his travels, Spock was the most human. This is not exactly a compliment as far as Spock is concerned. In *Star Trek VI: The Undiscovered Country*, Kirk says that everyone is human, and Spock replies that he considers that remark insulting.

CHANGED PREMISES

• Suddenly, the "Neutral Zone"— a term that has always referred to the boundary between Federation and Romulan space—now refers to the boundary between Federation and Klingon space. (This is probably because the creators didn't have any Romulan vessels to show flying toward the *Enterprise* in the *Kobayashi Maru* simulation. Of course, they could have used the same tactic they used in "The *Enterprise* Incident." A crew member could have said, "Oh, yeah, intelligence reports say that the Romulans are buying their ships from the Klingons again.") The creators even have Saavik refer to the Gamma Hydra system in her log during the simulation— the same system referred to in the episode "The Deadly Years." In that episode, Commodore Stocker takes the *Enterprise* on a joyride into the Neutral Zone and is promptly attacked by Romulans.

• After the simulated bridge blows up during the *Kobayashi Maru*, Kirk appears and advises Saavik to pray. He says Klingons don't take prisoners. I believe it's the Romulans who don't take prisoners, according to Chekov in "The Deadly Years." The Klingons took both Kirk and Spock prisoner in "Errand of Mercy."

• At the end of this episode, Saavik cries during Spock's funeral. Is she half human or something? Aren't Vulcans supposed to be emotionless?

• When is Kirk going to pay for his incompetence during this movie? At least two crew members die, possibly many more. In spite of this, everyone acts as if he's a hero at the end. No one had to die. If Kirk had followed regulations and raised his shields as the *Reliant* initially approached, the first battle would have gone much differently. Yet to my recollection, Kirk is never disciplined for his actions. Starfleet must be loosening up. In "Court-Martial," Starfleet almost drummed Kirk out of the corps because he supposedly caused a single man's death.

EQUIPMENT ODDITIES

• Interestingly enough, the creators have moved the science station from directly behind Kirk to the right on the other side of the turbolift door.

• Evidently the designers finally decided how to designate the decks on the redesigned *Enterprise*. Now both turbolift doors on the main bridge sport "A," and later in the movie Spock makes reference to a deck "C." Presumably the decks number from the top of the ship to the bottom, using letters.

• What is wrong with the sensors on the *Reliant?* Approximately seventy supermen and superwomen started out on Ceti Alpha V. Khan claims the slug creatures got twenty of them, so that leaves fifty humans running around on the surface of this planet near some huge metal cargo containers. Why did only *one* scanner pick up a *slight* reading?

• Beaming down to the surface of Ceti Alpha V, Terrell completes the transport with one leg raised against a sand dune. Did he stand this way as he left the ship, or did the transporter automatically adjust his leg because it sensed uneven ground at the destination?

• As the shuttle carrying Kirk arrives at the *Enterprise*, someone announces that the vessel will dock at the "port side torpedo bay." Sure enough, Kirk and the others walk into the ship in an area that is used later to launch photon torpedoes. This area resides in a rectangular box near the base of the connecting piece between the saucer and the Engineering section on the upgraded version of the *Enterprise*. (In fact, when the *Enterprise* flies up beside the science station near Regula I, a close-up of the ship shows a docking ring on what would be the starboard side torpedo bay. Presumably there's a docking ring on the opposite side of the torpedo bay, and that's where Kirk's shuttle supposedly hooked in.) Unfortunately, the creators opted to use the footage from the first movie for the shuttle approach and docking. That shuttle connected to the ship on the Engineering section, well below and behind the torpedo bay.

• The creators generate a cute moment when Spock has Saavik pilot the *Enterprise* out of space dock. This supposedly makes Kirk nervous. What's the big deal? Sulu's at the helm, and he's the one who's actually working the controls. He's not going to ram the ship into anything.

• At one point, Kirk boards a turbolift and reaches up to press a button to indicate his destination. Saavik rushes in, and Kirk turns to face her. First, don't the turbolifts respond to voice commands anymore? And second, Kirk never does hit the buttons, yet the turbolift very obediently travels to the appropriate destination. If the turbolift can read the officers' minds, why bother making a pretense of hitting buttons in the first place?

• Kirk's quarters seem to have lost that really nice viewscreen he had in the first movie.

• For the first and only time in the original television series and the movies, when Kirk asks for a damage report, Spock walks over to a wall diagram and points.

• After Khan's initial attack, Scott reports that the "main energizers" are out. Having never encountered this terminology before, I am forced to assume that the main energizers are similar to the matter/antimatter warp drive. Then again, maybe not. According to the previous movie, the phasers can't fire if the warp drive is out, yet Kirk fires the phasers while the main energizers are down.

• At the end of the initial engagement with Khan, Scott shows up on the bridge carrying a badly burned trainee. Isn't sick bay a better destination for an injured person? Or were the turbolifts not working correctly?

• Beaming across to the Regula I science station, Kirk orders McCoy and Saavik to set their phasers on stun. Kirk and Saavik's phasers show a solid light on top, but McCoy's shows a running sequence of lights. Does this seem right? Wouldn't the indicators be the same on all the phasers? Also, during the attempt to kill Kirk in the cave, Terrell's phaser flashes with the running sequence of lights, and we know that his phaser is set to kill at this point.

• How come the crew of the *Enterprise* have to carry around soapbox communicators when the crew of the *Reliant* gets really cool "Dick Tracy" wrist radios (especially since the crew of the *Enterprise* had the wrist radios in the previous movie)?

• Before giving Kirk a tour of the

Genesis cave, Marcus tells the captain that it took Starfleet ten months to tunnel out the storage area. Ten months? What happened to vaporizing phasers and transporters? Wouldn't these tools make short work of carving out the storage area?

• Preparing for the second battle with Khan, the crew manually lift up a bunch of grates so they can launch their photon torpedoes. Does this seem right? This advanced starship needs crew members to yank up the floor grates before it can go into battle? This is not a good design.

• Of course, no one bothers to try to beam the Genesis device off the *Reliant* and out into space with the widest possible dispersion, as they did to Redjac in "Wolf in the Fold."

• The tube that comes out of the floor in Engineering seems awfully wobbly. It teeters back and forth as Spock works with it.

CONTINUITY AND PRODUCTION PROBLEMS

• As Saavik participates in the *Kobayashi Maru*, the shots of her in the captain's chair include the starboard turbolift doors. A piece of paper hangs on the door, looking very much like the stencil that was used create the door's decoration. Then after Kirk arrives, a similar shot shows the paper suddenly gone and the decoration in its place.

• Of course, much of the early footage in this movie comes from the first movie. Those opticals are

expensive to produce. The creators might as well get some mileage out of them. These pieces are recycled: the footage of the three Klingon vessels, the shuttle pod's approach to the *Enterprise* in space dock, and the *Enterprise* leaving space dock. This conservation of resources does give rise to a few funny thoughts. First, are the transporters *still* broken? Kirk shuttled aboard the *Enterprise* during the previous movie because he couldn't beam aboard. What is the excuse this time? Second, when the shuttle passes the shuttle bay of the *Enterprise*, a person in a spacesuit floats downward upside down—exactly the way he or she did during the previous movie! Does this person know how to operate the controls on that suit? Third, when the *Enterprise* pulls out of space dock, someone—also in a spacesuit—waves good-bye. Again, just as someone did in the first movie. Does Starfleet have a designated "waver" to make all departing spaceships feel as if they will be missed?

• Okay, even I admit before I begin that this one belongs in the "picayune, overly obsessive, and needlessly stringent nitpicking" category. With that admission aside . . . when McCoy visits Kirk at his home on Earth, the pair walk past a ticking clock. It's hard to distinguish which hand is which, but one of the hands points just before two, and the other just after three. Two minutes and eleven seconds later, the clock chimes. Bear in mind that clocks like this sometimes chime on the quarter hour but often chime only on the hour and half hour. There's no configuration of time based on the hands of the clock that would account for it chiming when it does. (So tell me the truth: Is this one a bit over the edge?)

• The creators took the space station used near the beginning of the first movie and flipped it 180 degrees for use as the scientific research station near Regula I. This really isn't a problem. Starfleet designers would reuse successful designs, and there really is no "up" in space. I just thought I would note it.

• To demonstrate his great strength, Khan latches on to Chekov's spacesuit and hoists him into the air. Then he pulls the Russian back to the ground. Note: He *pulls* the Russian back to the ground. Is there some sort of odd antigravitational field effect in this cargo container? Shouldn't it be easier for Khan to return Chekov to terra firma?

• After the first battle with Khan, Kirk visits sick bay. Midshipman Preston reaches up and takes hold of Kirk's uniform, leaving a large bloodstain. When Kirk returns to the bridge, the stain has moved and changed shape.

• As the *Enterprise* enters the Mutara Nebula, everyone on the bridge lurches forward except Kirk.

• When his assistant dies with his eyes open, Khan pulls the man to his chest. Oddly enough, the man's eyes close during this action. Must be that incredible, genetically engineered physique.

• Hurrying to his friend's side, Kirk slides down a ladder in Engineering. At this point, his jacket is closed. Then he rushes toward Spock. McCoy and Scott instantly restrain him. Now Kirk's jacket is open. Then it varies in the amount it is open as the scene unfolds.

TRIVIA ANSWERS
1. Kojiro Vance.
2. 16309.

MAJOR THEMES IN STAR TREK

THERE ARE THEMES THAT CROP UP OVER AND OVER IN THE ORIGINAL TELEVISION SERIES AND THE MOVIES. I HAVE LISTED EACH ALONG WITH THE SHOWS I FEEL DEAL WITH THAT THEME.

1. *Humanoids can take actions that will threaten or lead to their own destruction.* In "What Are Little Girls Made Cf?" the inhabitants of Miri's planet create a series of viruses that kill all the adults. In "Return to Tomorrow," Sargon says that his race developed their mental powers to such an extent that the subsequent war destroyed their planet. "The Omega Glory" features the results of a terrible bacteriological war. In "Wink of an Eye," the Scalosians deal with the effects of global destruction. "Let That Be Your Last Battlefield" shows Bele and Lokai returning to a world eradicated by war. In "That Which Survives," McCoy speculates that the virus created by the construction of an outpost eventually annihilated the Kalandan race.

2. *The expulsion from Paradise (i.e., the Garden of Eden).* In "The Return of the Archons," Kirk destroys Landru, ending the Betans' life in "Paradise." In "This Side of Paradise," Kirk discovers colonists infected with spores that bring perfect health and serenity. The captain soon learns that violent emotions destroy the spores, and he uses this knowledge to evacuate the planet. In "The Apple," Kirk and his landing party find a small group of humanoids living an idyllic existence under the supervision of a machine named Vaal. Kirk destroys the machine and then congratulates the populace on their freedom before leaving. In "A Private Little War," Kirk refers to the flintlock rifles that he is supplying to the hill people as serpents in the Garden of Eden. In "The Way to Eden," a group of twenty-third-century hippies makes its way to a planet called Eden, only to find that the plant life is acid-filled and the fruit is poisonous. In *Star Trek VI: The Undiscovered Country*, Spock and Valeris discuss a painting in Spock's quarters depicting the expulsion from Paradise.

3. *Power and superior ability often breed corrupt behavior.* Charlie Evans in "Charlie X" uses his abilities in cruel ways. Kirk's friend Gary Mitchell becomes his enemy after Mitchell receives supernatural powers in "Where No Man Has Gone Before." The genetically engineered Khan in "Space Seed" feels justified in using his enhanced abilities to force his will on the weak. Thalassa in "Return to Tomorrow" admits that there is a great temptation to use her powers for her own whims. Zeons, at first simply primitive, turn to sadistic behavior once organized by John Gill in "Patterns of Force." Platonians in "Plato's

Stepchildren" lose all moral restraint after gaining the power of telekinesis. "Wink of an Eye" features hyperaccelerated Scalosians willing to use their speed to preserve their race no matter what the cost.

4. *Prejudice blinds.* In "Balance of Terror," Stiles believes that Spock is the enemy because the Vulcan looks like a Romulan. In "The Devil in the Dark," the miners view the Horta as evil, unable to discern that their actions have caused the deaths of thousands of her children. Prejudice temporarily blinds both Starfleet officers and Klingons in "The Day of the Dove" to the activities of an alien life form. In "Let That Be Your Last Battlefield," Bele and Lokai continue their blood feud even though it has destroyed their planet. In *Star Trek VI: The Undiscovered Country*, Kirk grapples with letting go of his hatred for all Klingons.

5. *Humans shouldn't be ruled by machines.* Kirk nukes Landru in "The Return of the Archons." Kirk zaps Vaal in "The Apple." Kirk talks M5 into committing suicide in "The Ultimate Computer." Kirk and Spock turn off the Oracle in "For the World Is Hollow and I Have Touched the Sky."

6. *The problems of immortality.* Long-lived children face starvation in "Miri." Cochrane is lonely and bored in "Metamorphosis." The chance to attain immortality drives Tracey to murder in "The Omega Glory." Flint has to build a wife to match his longevity in "Requiem for Methuselah."

7. *The needs of the one outweigh the needs of the many.* Spock risks his life, Kirk's career, and the *Enterprise* to return Pike to Talos IV in "The Menagerie, Part I." Kirk dedicates all the resources of the *Enterprise* to recover Spock's brain in "Spock's Brain." Spock puts the crew at risk to recover Kirk in "The Tholian Web." Kirk and company seriously violate Starfleet orders to recover Spock's body in *Star Trek III: The Search for Spock*.

8. *The needs of the many outweigh the needs of the one.* Kirk allows a woman he loves to die so that history will revert to its previous course in "The City on the Edge of Forever." Spock refuses to relinquish command and provide transfusions for his father in "Journey to Babel." Spock sacrifices himself to restore warp power to the *Enterprise* at the end of *Star Trek II: The Wrath of Khan*.

9. *Humans shouldn't be enslaved.* Number One threatens suicide as an option to enslavement in "The Cage." Kirk frees the inhabitants from their service to Vaal in "The Apple." Kirk fights for the freedom of the thralls in "The Gamesters of Triskelion."

10. *Man is no longer awed by beings with advanced capabilities.* Kirk is unimpressed by Apollo's bag of tricks in "Who Mourns for Adonais?" Kirk looks for scientific explanations for the magic of Korob and Sylvia in "Catspaw." Kirk questions "God" in *Star Trek V: The Final Frontier.*

STAR TREK III: THE SEARCH FOR SPOCK

Star Date: 8210.3

Returning from the battle with Khan, Kirk is confronted by Sarek—Spock's father—demanding to know why the admiral did not come to Vulcan. When a Vulcan anticipates death, he or she will place their *katra* in another person. In this way all that the person was, their knowledge and experience, can be preserved. There is even an ancient ritual that can restore a *katra* to the person's body. Kirk knew nothing of this, since Spock actually placed his *katra* in McCoy. Discovering this fact, Kirk makes plans to return to Genesis. Unfortunately, Starfleet has quarantined the entire area and has stated that the *Enterprise* will be decommissioned. With the help of the rest of the senior staff, Kirk steals back his ship and heads for the forbidden planet.

Meanwhile, a Klingon captain named Kruge learns of Genesis. He views it as an awesome weapon and vows to have its secret. His "bird of prey"—a small attack vessel carrying approximately twelve Klingons—sets course for the newly formed planet. On arrival, the Klingons destroy Starfleet science vessel *Grissom*, stranding Lieutenant Saavik and David Marcus on the surface with a unique individual. After beaming down, they found Spock's coffin empty and a young Vulcan boy. As the unstable planet ages in rapid spurts, so does the boy. Evidently the Genesis device revitalized the cells of Spock's dead body and they are growing into the Vulcan male.

By the time Kirk arrives, a landing party of Klingons has taken the trio prisoner. There is a brief battle between the *Enterprise* and the bird of prey, but Kirk's ship still isn't repaired from the altercation with Khan. Kruge soon demands Kirk's surrender and even kills David to let Kirk know he's serious. Unable to fight, Kirk invites the Klingons aboard and then sets the *Enterprise* to autodestruct. He and the senior staff quickly beam down to the planet. The resulting explosion eliminates most of Kruge's

Trivia Questions

1. Who is paged as Kirk walks away from his drink with the Starfleet commander of the space dock?

2. What is Sarek's lineage?

crew. Kirk then goads Kruge into coming to the surface by claiming that he knows the secret of Genesis. Arriving moments later, Kruge transports everyone except Kirk and Spock up to the bird of prey. A fight breaks out, and Kirk kills Kruge. Then he tricks the remaining Klingon into beaming Spock and himself up to the ship. The crew quickly overpower the Klingon and fly the bird of prey to Vulcan, where Spock's *katra* and body are reunited.

RUMINATIONS

*T*his movie contains many elements that reappear in Star Trek: The Next Generation. *As the* Enterprise *approaches space dock, Kirk asks Scott if he has always multiplied his repair time estimates by four. Scott responds that doing so maintains his reputation as a miracle worker. Scott confesses this tactic to La Forge in "Relics." Space dock in this movie serves for the first time as Starbase 74 in "11001001." The model for the USS* Grissom *also shows up several times in TNG. The episode "Night Terrors" comes to mind, wherein the model served as the USS* Brattain. *The bird of prey appears several times in TNG. I believe the first instance is in "A Matter of Honor." Finally, the model for the USS* Excelsior *shows up in "Encounter at Farpoint" as the USS* Hood.

One of the fun things the creators did in this movie occurs in the opening credits. Up to this point,

Leonard Nimoy's name always followed Shatner's. Of course, with Spock dead, the creators didn't want to list Nimoy in the opening credits, but instead of just dropping him out they put a longer-than-normal pause between Shatner and DeForest Kelley. I think they were just playing with our minds, knowing we would be watching to see if Nimoy was in the credits. By the way, you probably also noticed that the creators also went back to the original series and grabbed the ever-popular tribbles for the scene where McCoy tries to charter a ship in a bar.

GREAT LINES

"My logic is uncertain where my son is concerned."—Sarek to T'Lar after she states that it is not logical to request the ritual of *fal-tor-pan* since it is only legend. (This movie had a bunch of other great lines as well.)

GREAT MOMENTS

*S*hatner plays the moment of his son's death very well. The ever-strong Admiral Kirk stumbles backward and crumples to the floor after Saavik informs him that "David is dead." I really have to mention the self-destruct sequence with the Enterprise also. It is gorgeous.

PLOT OVERSIGHTS

• As the movie begins, Kirk comments that the ship feels empty, like a house with all the children gone. This is an interesting choice of simile for someone who's never been married.

• Amazingly, Kirk gets commended for his actions in *Star Trek II: The Wrath of Khan*. Does no one care that Kirk should have raised the *Enterprise*'s shields and that doing so would have kept Khan from gaining an early advantage?

• Starfleet Command certainly displays its Earthcentric attitudes in this movie. Kirk wants a ship to retrieve Spock's body and take it to Vulcan, and the only excuse the commander can come up with for refusing is, "Well, I never understood Vulcan mysticism." Vulcan is supposedly a founding member of the Federation. Spock comes from an extremely well-respected family. He served Starfleet for decades, and Starfleet can't let Kirk retrieve his body?

• How quickly did Saavik leave the *Enterprise* after the last movie? Why didn't she tell Kirk about this *katra* business? Because Spock died behind glass, did she simply assume that he couldn't accomplish the transfer?

• The creators evidently believe that momentum will be extinct in the twenty-third century. When the *Excelsior* loses forward thrust, it coasts to a stop!

• After conning Kruge's men into coming over to the *Enterprise* just before it blows up, Kirk and company beam down to the surface. Wouldn't it be better to beam over to the nearly empty bird of prey and commandeer the ship from Kruge?

• At the end of the movie, Sarek wonders at the great cost of bringing Spock back to Vulcan. Specifically he mentions the death of Kirk's son, David. David didn't die because Kirk wanted to bring Spock back to Vulcan. David probably would have died at the hands of Kruge no matter what happened.

CHANGED PREMISES

• When Kruge decides to blow up the freighter that brought him the information on Genesis, it looks as if his eyes tear. This is understandable, since blowing up the freighter will kill Valkris, his love. There's only one problem: In *Star Trek VI: The Undiscovered Country*, Spock will mention that Klingons don't have tear ducts.

• The Klingon captain claims he wants prisoners when his vessel first approaches the *Grissom,* but Kirk said that Klingons don't take prisoners in *Star Trek II: The Wrath of Khan.*

EQUIPMENT ODDITIES

• Who designed the *Grissom,* and just how are the crew supposed to get from the saucer section to the Engineering section? Or is that just fuel storage down there?

• Somehow, the starboard turbolift doors acquired a large burn mark between the end of the battle with Khan and the beginning of this movie. *Star Trek II: The Wrath of Khan* ends with the doors in fairly good shape, but *Star Trek III: The Search for Spock* opens with them badly burned. In addition, a panel to the right of the door simply disappears.

• Oddly enough, someone changed the interior of the turbolift between the two movies as well. There's a new control panel, and the displays showing the *Enterprise* look as if they've been moved. Does it seem reasonable—given the *Enterprise*'s severe damage—that someone would take the time to redecorate the turbolift?

• Suddenly everyone has new phasers! The phasers in *Star Trek II: The Wrath of Khan* had flat heads. The ones in *Star Trek III: The Search for Spock* terminate in little cones. Okay, so maybe they use a different type of phaser at the space dock, and Kirk took these along when he stole the ship. That doesn't explain why the football player—sorry, the security guard—who meets Kirk at Spock's quarters at the beginning of the movie is carrying a new phaser. Shouldn't he carry the kind shown in *Star Trek II: The Wrath of Khan?* The *Enterprise* has just barely arrived at space dock. There hasn't been enough time to restock the phaser supply.

• Searching for the repository of Spock's *katra,* Kirk consults the visual logs from the *Enterprise.* Note that these logs concern the death of Spock. They come from the *end* of the second movie. As the computer begins the first playback, it identifies the star date as 8128.78, an intriguing number given that the *beginning* star date

for the previous movie is 8130.3!

• Is it just me, or is the footage of Spock's last moments edited really well for a computer log?

• Heading the *Enterprise* out of space dock, Kirk calls for "one-quarter impulse." For the sake of argument, let's say that full impulse is one quarter the speed of light. That means that full impulse would be approximately 46,000 miles—or 74,000 kilometers—per *second.* One quarter of that speed would be about 11,000 miles—or 19,000 kilometers—per second. As the *Enterprise* makes for the exit of the space dock, Sulu claims the ship will reach the doors in one minute. In other words, space dock must have an interior diameter of at least 660,000 miles—or 1,060,000 kilometers. (Just take the speed at which they are traveling times 60 since there are 60 seconds in a minute.) The Earth has a diameter of approximately 7,000 miles. Therefore, the interior diameter of space dock is almost 100 times larger than Earth. Now, there's a feat of engineering for you!

• Along the same line, Kirk orders full impulse as soon as the *Enterprise* leaves space dock and it takes the ship 10 seconds to drop over the lip of the structure. If full impulse is one quarter the speed of light, that's a distance of more than 465,000 miles, or 744,000 kilometers. I have a hard time believing that the space dock is that big.

• Obviously McCoy doesn't know how to run the sensors. When the

Enterprise arrives at the Genesis planet, he doesn't even bother to let Kirk know that the debris of the *Grissom* is floating around in orbit.

• For some reason, the Klingons boarding the *Enterprise* need the assistance of the *Enterprise*'s transporters. Just before Kruge's men come over, Kirk calls and says he is engaging the transporters. Yet in the next movie, the Klingon Bird-of-Prey's transporters perform admirably by themselves, and in the previous movie the *Enterprise*'s transporters seem to have no difficulty functioning alone as well. Perhaps the Klingon ship is so damaged that the transporters needed help? In that case, why would Kruge even accept the help? Doesn't he know what Kirk and Scott did to the group of Klingons in "The Day of the Dove"? They beamed up the whole bunch and left them in the transporter buffer until lots of guys with phasers arrived in the transporter room.

• These Klingon ships can take an amazing amount of pounding. Kruge's ship received two photon torpedo hits—apparently while it was unshielded. Yet when Kirk commandeers it, Sulu reports they have full power. Just who repaired the damage? Most of Kruge's crew left for the *Enterprise* a few minutes after the battle.

CONTINUITY AND PRODUCTION PROBLEMS

• Wow! Saavik had a real makeover while the *Enterprise* put-

tered back home. Looks like she lost some weight and even had plastic surgery to change her face. I guess McCoy didn't have much to do. (Actually, the creators replaced Kirstie Alley with Robin Curtis for the role of Saavik in this movie. But I don't deal in reality.)

• After the *Enterprise* enters space dock, sensors detect an intrusion at Spock's quarters. When Kirk leaves the bridge to investigate, a close-up shows a layout of the *Enterprise* and a square to indicate the location of the intruder. I thought the graphic looked familiar, so I pulled out the blueprints of the *Enterprise* from the original *Star Trek* television series, and sure enough, there it was. The screen shows a section of sheet 8, deck 7 plan—starboard side at the bottom of the page near the impulse engines. The screen doesn't show the label for this area of the ship, according to the blueprints. It's the brig, the jail, the slammer, that final destination when you're heading up the river, and it's supposed to be Spock's quarters! (Granted, it is possible that Spock's quarters just happen to look exactly like the brig area of the original *Enterprise*. However, when Kirk gets there, they don't look much like the display on Chekov's monitor.)

• When Sarek visits Kirk's home on Earth, a pan across the glass shelving unit near the door reveals that the admiral has moved his mantel clock. This is the same clock immortalized by an over-picked nit in *Star Trek II: The Wrath of Khan.*

• I rarely comment on costuming (well . . . at least *men's* costuming). However, Chekov seems to be going through a "schoolboy" phase. Just after Kirk boards the *Enterprise* to prepare to steal back his ship, Chekov wears this fat white collar that makes him look like the little Dutch boy featured on the old housepaint cans.

• There's an interesting moment when the Genesis planet self-destructs. As the bird of prey warps away, a huge plume of lava rockets out into space. At the very end of the scene it begins *falling* downward. Wouldn't this debris be far enough out in space to keep on going?

• It sounds as if Scott loses his Scottish accent for a moment as he and Chekov look over the controls of the Klingon ship, trying to locate the antimatter inducer.

• Saavik must have given Spock several haircuts while on the surface of Genesis. According to the credits at the end, Spock aged more than twenty-five years during the movie, yet his hair remains approximately the same length. And what about shaving?

TRIVIA ANSWERS

1. Captain Styles.
2. He is the child of Skon, child of Solkar.

STAR TREK IV: THE VOYAGE HOME

Star Date: 8390

After three months of exile on Vulcan, Kirk and his crew decide to return to Earth to face charges for their actions during Spock's rescue. Spock—retrained by the Vulcans—accompanies them. Having facetiously renamed their stolen Klingon bird of prey the HMS *Bounty,* the crew set out for home.

Unknown to the *Bounty*'s crew, an immense cylinder approaches Earth, overloading the power systems of every object it meets. Once it arrives, the alien vessel begins transmitting a strange collage of sounds toward Earth's oceans. At the same time, the power emanations from the ship endanger all humanoid life on the planet. As the *Bounty* nears Earth, the crew listens in on a planetary distress call that warns off all ships and reveals the current danger. Kirk and Spock listen to the alien ship's broadcasts for a few moments and quickly identify them as the songs of humpback whales. Hunted to

Trivia Questions

1. What mineral does McCoy worry that the crew will spend the rest of their lives mining?

2. What is the registry of the USS *Enterprise* featured in the middle of this episode?

extinction in the twenty-first century, no whales remain to respond.

Desperate to save Earth, Kirk orders Spock to calculate the *Bounty*'s trajectory for time warp. Using the gravitation of the sun, the crew travel into the past, hoping to locate some whales. Although it takes a while to convince her of the truth, Kirk finds a willing ally in whale biologist Gillian Taylor. As it turns out, the place she works—the Cetacean Institute near San Francisco—has a pair of humpback whales. Unfortunately, Taylor's superiors release the whales earlier than planned, without telling her. With her help, the *Bounty* locates the whales on the open seas, and Scott beams them on board.

Using Spock's calculations once again, the *Bounty* slingshots around the sun and travels forward in time. They arrive seconds prior to their leaving, and the alien vessel immediately strips the *Bounty* of its power. After Sulu manages a crash-landing near San Francisco, Kirk blows the hatch to release the whales. A short time later, the male begins singing, and the alien ship moves off.

As the movie closes, the Federation drops all charges against Kirk and the crew save one, and that one applies to Kirk alone. For disobeying a superior's orders, the Federation demotes Kirk to captain and gives him the command of a starship, the newly commissioned USS *Enterprise*, NCC 1701-A.

RUMINATIONS

Isn't this movie fun? Just a romp through the grass and a nice change of pace from the very serious tone of the previous two. I can still remember the first time I saw Kirk and crew walking the streets of twentieth-century San Francisco. I burst out laughing, delighted by the juxtaposition of these accomplished, disciplined, futuristic heroes muddling around in our time frame.

GREAT LINES

"*Ah . . . the giants.*"—Literary critic Spock sarcastically passing judgment on the works of Jacqueline Susann and Harold Robbins.

GREAT MOMENTS

There's a very nice "wrap-up" moment at the end of this movie when Sarek tells Spock that his opposition to his son's choice of career may have been in error. It ties up a loose end the creators left open all the way back in the episode "Journey to Babel."

PLOT OVERSIGHTS

• Supposedly the monstrous probe comes to Earth looking for whales. Spock even goes so far as to say the probe has come to find out why "they" lost contact with the whales. So the whales transmitted to "them" until man hunted the large mammals to extinction? Just how did the whales accomplish this transmission? None of the humans on the planet ever noticed that whales could transmit across the vast reaches of outer space. Then again, maybe whale transmissions are nonintrusive and nondetectable. If that's so, why is the probe tearing everything up? Does it use a completely different technology?

• At one point, the top Starfleet officer tells the president of the Federation that they are launching everything they have against the probe. Yet several minutes later, the probe approaches space dock and there are ships that still haven't been launched. Also in this sequence, momentum suffers another setback. As the probe flies by, all the little craft inside lose power and stop. In space with no gravity, they should coast right into a wall.

• Just before leaving Vulcan, Saavik takes the time to tell Kirk how valiantly his son, David, died. She claims she hasn't had the chance until now. Kirk has been on this planet for three months. Even if she wasn't in the area, don't the phones work on Vulcan?

• As the probe wreaks havoc on

Earth, a Starfleet communications officer gives a readout on various cities around the globe. Specifically, he mentions Leningrad. If I remember correctly, Leningrad no longer exists. It's now called St. Petersburg. Unless this city reverts to Leningrad sometime before the twenty-third century, there will be no city by that name in Kirk's time. (Ah, the challenges of writing science fiction. Who could have predicted in 1986 the fall of the USSR?)

• Spock makes an amazing deduction at one point—one that is essential to move the plot forward. The crew of the *Bounty* listens to the distress call from Earth. In it, the Federation president indicates that the probe's transmissions are causing critical damage. He then lists four examples. He says the probe has almost totally ionized the atmosphere, caused all power sources to fail, left all orbiting ships powerless, and is proceeding to vaporize the oceans. He ends the message with an ominous warning about all life ceasing on Earth if they can't find a way to communicate with the probe. Moments later, Spock claims that the president said the probe was sending its message to the oceans. (I must have missed that part of the speech.) Of course, if Spock didn't direct Kirk's attention to the oceans, Kirk wouldn't ask Uhura to filter the transmissions, and Spock wouldn't determine that they were really whale songs. Hence, everyone on Earth would die.

• Why doesn't anyone put on a seat belt when riding in Gillian's truck?

• I've got to hand it to these whales. Spock says they are unhappy about how man has treated their race. The Vulcan obviously has told them that humanity will drive them to extinction in the near future. Yet in spite of this, they agree to return to the future and save us from extinction. (Kind of makes you wish you could grow flippers, doesn't it?)

• Needing high-energy photons to energize the *Bounty*'s dilithium crystals, Chekov and Uhura beam into a naval vessel, the USS *Enterprise*, and gather them from the ship's nuclear reactor. In the process Chekov is captured, injured, and winds up in the hospital. Kirk, McCoy, and Taylor stage a rescue, culminating in a "high speed" chase down the corridors of the hospital. Then Scott beams the four of them out of an elevator and deposits them outside the Bird-of-Prey. McCoy and Chekov hurry up the gangplank as Kirk says goodbye to Taylor. After he calls for transport, Taylor jumps him, wanting to go to the future. Kirk begrudgingly allows her to come. I reviewed this section of the movie because it is filled with contrivances. Yes, it is fun but "at what cost?" (To quote Sarek.) After McCoy repairs Chekov's injuries, the sensible thing at this point would be to call Scott and have him beam the four of them straight to the ship. (Yes, there are twentieth-century doctors and nurses watching from a locked room, but a well-placed sheet would take care of that problem.) Abandoning this option, Kirk leads a chase through the hospital until Scott transports them out of an elevator. Then, for some reason, Scott doesn't beam them into the ship, he dumps them in the park! This requires the weakened Chekov to struggle up the ramp with the help of Sulu. Kirk stays behind to bid Taylor farewell, and almost instantly, the ramp closes. Why is the ramp closing when Kirk isn't on board yet? Because the creators want to *beam* him on board so Taylor can jump him. (Definitely a cute moment, but hopelessly "staged.") Finally, after Taylor makes it on board, Kirk shrugs his shoulders and lets her stay. There is an exit door. He could boot her out. There is a transporter that could grab her and drop her almost anywhere on the planet. But Kirk would rather pluck her from her own time frame and haul her back to the future. Does he have an ulterior motive? (He does ask for her "telephone" number at the end of the movie.)

• I'm still not clear why traveling one way around the sun sends you backward in time and traveling the other way sends you forward.

• At the end of the movie, the Federation president enumerates the charges against Kirk and crew. He lists conspiracy, assault on Federation officers, theft of Federation property, sabotage of the *Excelsior,* willful destruction of the *Enterprise*, and disobeying direct orders from a Starfleet commander. By my count, that's six items. Yet at the beginning of the episode, the Federation president said Kirk had been charged with nine violations of Starfleet regulations. What happened to the other three?

CHANGED PREMISES

• Preparing to brave twentieth-century America, Kirk says that it is a foregone conclusion that none of the natives has ever seen an extraterrestrial. How can he say that? Doesn't he know that we watch *Star Trek*?

• All the worry expressed by the crew concerning the possibility of changing the future in "Tomorrow Is Yesterday" seems to have disappeared completely by the time this movie rolls around. Scott and McCoy have no problem giving a plant manager the formula for transparent aluminum, a substance that supposedly won't be invented for many years. McCoy heals a woman in the hospital. Even more amazing, Chekov leaves a Klingon phaser behind!

• Kirk sticks Taylor with the bill for dinner by claiming that they don't use money in the future. Was McCoy joking when he told Fish Face that he had money to hire his ship during *Star Trek III: The Search for Spock?*

EQUIPMENT ODDITIES

• At the very beginning of the movie, the Klingon ambassador shows the Federation council pictures of the destruction of the *Enterprise*. Just where did these visuals come from?

• One scene shows a set of computers testing Spock. The displays are composed of a transparent plastic. Several shots look through the displays and show us Spock on the other side, answering questions. Oddly enough, the writing on our side of the display runs left to right. If the displays are transparent and the questions are written correctly for Spock to read, shouldn't we see them backward? Also, why are all the questions in English? His mother, Amanda, tells him that he has been retrained in the *Vulcan* way.

• Over the three months of exile, Kirk's crew completely reworked the insides of the Klingon Bird-of-Prey. They moved all the control stations into positions more familiar to Starfleet officers. Interestingly enough, they even installed new non-Federation-issue doors. Yet with all these modifications, they didn't bother updating the actual displays to read in English instead of Klingon. (I'm surprised they didn't just install a new computer system. Surely Sarek would pop for it, given their sacrifice for his son.) One other thing: Sulu and Chekov were obviously ready for a change. Their positions are switched with regard to the television show.

• Is there some reason why the universal translator *doesn't* work on whale songs? It translated the emanations from the energy cloud

in "Metamorphosis" just fine.

• The *Bounty* kicks up a lot of wind when it lands and takes off near San Francisco, but it doesn't appear to kick up much dust when it takes off from Vulcan. Neither does it disturb the ocean as it hovers over the whales.

• It's really a lucky thing for our heroes that no one happened by Golden Gate Park while they used it as a parking spot for the *Bounty*. Probably no one ever visits this park, and even if people did, they wouldn't notice the two huge indentations in the ground or the huge invisible "something" in the middle of the park.

• Kirk originally meets Taylor at the Cetacean Institute, a whale museum. He and Spock arrive on the bus; line up for the next tour and, lo and behold, Taylor is the tour guide! Maybe I just haven't visited the right museums, but I can't remember ever having a person with a doctorate as a tour guide. The whales are leaving soon, making study time short. So why is Dr. Gillian Taylor giving tours?

• I'm not going to spend a great deal of time on this, but I have a Mac Plus—the computer that Scott uses to derive the formula for transparent aluminum. It's a cute scene but completely unbelievable. The machine simply doesn't have enough processing power to run the kind of calculations as fast as it looks like it's doing. Of course, all the graphics were created ahead of time and simply flashed on the screen.

• At one point, Spock constructs a machine to capture high-energy photons from a nuclear reactor. Chekov and Uhura take the device on a covert mission—trespassing on a naval vessel. Interestingly enough, the machine beeps! Do you really want a machine beeping if you are trying to proceed with all due stealth?

• Following the procurement of the whales, Kirk orders Sulu to set course for the sun. Sulu engages warp while still in Earth's atmosphere! In *Star Trek: The Motion Picture*, Kirk said they would have to *risk* engaging warp while still in the solar system. If it's risky to engage warp while in a relatively big area like the solar system, wouldn't it be a lot more risky to engage warp while in the atmosphere of the Earth? In addition, the *Star Trek: The Next Generation* episode "Redemption II" featured a Bird-of-Prey engaging warp near a star. The action caused a giant flare to erupt, as if a vacuum had been created. Shouldn't the same thing happen in Earth's atmosphere?

CONTINUITY AND PRODUCTION PROBLEMS

• Evidently, not only was Geordi La Forge's mother a Starfleet captain, so was his grandmother! The actor who plays the captain of the USS *Saratoga* also starred as La Forge's mother in "Interface."

• This really isn't a problem, more of an effect. The creators used dialogue from later in the show to underlay the first time travel sequence with the morphing heads.

• There's one of those classic continuity problems in the dinner scene between Kirk and Taylor. A globed candle sits between them, visible from both camera angles. It happily bobs up and down in height through the whole scene.

• After Scott finds a way to get a local company to produce a sheet of transparent aluminum, Sulu delivers it with a helicopter. As the pair lower it into position, a crate surrounds the sheet. A subsequent shot shows the crate descending into the cargo bay of the *Bounty*. Then suddenly the crate disappears and the sheet continues to drop. (This may not be an error. It's very blatant, and I can't believe the creators didn't do this on purpose. I just can't figure out how it's supposed to be correct.)

• It's difficult to see, but I am told by those who know that Kirk's phaser changes hands when he melts the door lock after herding the doctors and nurses into the smaller room in the hospital.

• The beginning of the movie shows us the letters "HMS BOUNTY" clearly written in red paint along the side of the Klingon ship. Yet in a very close flyby at the end of the movie, the words do not appear.

• At the very end of the movie, McCoy stands beside Kirk on the bridge of the new *Enterprise*. McCoy leans over and places his right hand on the railing. The camera angle changes, and suddenly McCoy rests his right elbow on the railing.

TRIVIA ANSWERS
1. Borite.
2. CVN-65.

TRIATHLON TRIVIA ON PLANETS

MATCH THE PLANET TO THE DESCRIPTION TO THE EPISODE OR MOVIE:

PLANET	DESCRIPTION	EPISODE OR MOVIE
1. Alpha 177	A. Fought their wars with computers	a. "Whom Gods Destroy"
2. Alpha Majoras I	B. Home to bichromatic races	b. "The Empath"
3. Antos IV	C. Rich in pergium	c. "And the Children Shall Lead"
4. Argelius II	D. Home to an aspergation station	d. "The Omega Glory"
5. Argus X	E. In dire need of zenite	e. "The Naked Time"
6. Beta Antares IV	F. Ruk's official place of residence	f. "Who Mourns for Adonais"
7. Beta III	G. Radiation turns researchers old	g. "Where No Man Has Gone Before"
8. Camus II	H. Trelane's planet	h. "The Savage Curtain"
9. Capella IV	I. The inhabitants stopped a war	i. "A Piece of the Action"
10. Cestus III	J. Home of the Mellitus	j. "Catspaw"
11. Ceti Alpha V	K. Plant spores bring happiness	k. "Amok Time"
12. Cheron	L. Telekinesis brings cruelty	l. "All Our Yesterdays"
13. Coridan	M. Home to a race of giants	m. "Errand of Mercy"
14. Delta Vega	N. Source of the alcoholic water	n. "Obsession"
15. Deneva	O. Emergency medical supplies go here	o. "Return of the Archons"
16. Eden	P. Destination of a fear-driven ship	p. "The Man Trap"
17. Elba II	Q. A place of witches and wizards	q. "The Cloudminders"
18. Eminiar VII	R. Home of the giant dryworm	r. "The Way to Eden"
19. Excalbia	S. Outpost destroyed by the Gorn	s. "Operation—Annihilate!"
20. Exo III	T. McCoy visited a cabaret here	t. "The Apple"
21. Gamma II	U. Home of the sex change device	u. "The Deadly Years"
22. Gamma Hydra IV	V. Miners look for wives	v. "Wolf in the Fold"
23. Gamma Trianguli VI	W. The surface drops to -120° at night	w. "What Are Little Girls Made Of?"
24. Gamma Vertis IV	X. Home of a lithium cracking station	x. "The Gamesters of Triskelion"
25. Gothos	Y. Home of fizzbin	y. "A Taste of Armageddon"
26. Hansen's Planet	Z. Its ice age houses a lonely woman	z. "Let That Be Your Last Battlefield"
27. Janus VI	AA. Scott is tried for murder	aa. "The Enemy Within"
28. M-113	BB. Home of Leonard James Akaar	bb. "Turnabout Intruder"
29. Makus III	CC. Gas vampire's second home	cc. "Journey to Babel"

30. Marcos XII	DD. Home to the salt creature	dd. "Space Seed"
31. Merak II	EE. Attacked by hordes of brain cells	ee. "The *Galileo* Seven"
32. Omega IV	FF. Home of Apollo	ff. "The Squire of Gothos"
33. Omicron Ceti III	GG. Final destination of the *Archon*	gg. "Friday's Child"
34. Organia	HH. Molten home of the rock creatures	hh. "The Devil in the Dark"
35. Platonius	II. Destination for quadrotriticale	ii. "This Side of Paradise"
36. Pollux IV	JJ. Sevrin's destination	jj. "Spock's Brain"
37. Psi 2000	KK. Home of the giant eel-birds	kk. "Shore Leave"
38. Pyris VII	LL. They feed Vaal here	ll. "The Cage"
39. Regulus V	MM. Home of Chicago-style mobsters	mm. "Arena"
40. Rigel II	NN. Vina crashed here	nn. "Dagger of the Mind"
41. Rigel XII	OO. Home to a race of mutes	oo. "Mudd's Women"
42. Sarpeidon	PP. Place of Garth's internment	pp. "Plato's Stepchildren"
43. Sherman's Planet	QQ. Home of the Yangs and the Kohms	qq. "The Trouble with Tribbles"
44. Sigma Draconis VI	RR. Males above, females below	rr. *Star Trek: The Motion Picture*
45. Sigma Iotia II	SS. Adam's penal colony	ss. "For the World Is Hollow And I Have Touched the Sky"
46. Talos IV	TT. Its hot sands purge emotion	
47. Tantalus V	UU. In reality, a spaceship not an asteroid	
48. Triacus	VV. Voted on for Federation admission	
49. Triskelion	WW. Home of super humans	
50. Vulcan	XX. Providers gamble on thralls	
51. *Yonada*	YY. Gorgan lived here	

SCORING
(BASED ON NUMBER OF CORRECT ANSWERS)

0-7	Normal
8-15	You trekkers scare me!
16 and up	You don't live in your parent's basement by any chance, do you?

PLANET ANSWER KEY: 1. W aa 2. J v 3. R f 4. AA v 5. CC n 6. Y i 7. GG o 8. U bb 9. BB gg 10. S mm 11. WW dd 12. B z 13. VV cc 14. X g 15. EE s 16. JJ r 17. PP a 18. A y 19. HH h 20. F w 21. D x 22. G u 23. LL t 24. OO b 25. H ff 26. M ee 27. C hh 28. DD p 29. O ee 30. P c 31. E q 32. QQ d 33. K ii 34. I m 35. L pp 36. FF f 37. N e 38. Q j 39. KK k 40. T kk 41. V oo 42. Z l 43. II qq 44. RR jj 45. MM i 46. NN ll 47. SS nn 48. YY c 49. XX x 50. TT rr 51. UU ss

STAR TREK V: THE FINAL FRONTIER

Star Date: 8454.1

A crisis interrupts the senior staff's shore leave. Terrorists have invaded the main city of Nimbus III, the planet of galactic peace. The Federation, the Klingons, and the Romulans each have ambassadors there to demonstrate the viability of the three governmental systems working together. Although the *Enterprise* 1701-A is not completely operational, Starfleet needs its most experienced captain to confront this crisis. Without a transporter, barely functioning doors, and a skeleton crew, Kirk sets course to rescue the ambassadors.

Meanwhile, the Klingon captain of a bird of prey grows weary of shooting at space garbage. Hearing that Kirk is heading for Nimbus III, Klaa sets course for the planet as well. He intends to engage the *Enterprise* and destroy Kirk, thereby becoming the greatest warrior in the galaxy.

Reaching Nimbus III, Kirk and crew fly down in a shuttle to rescue the hostages. Unfortunately, the ambassadors have joined forces

Trivia Questions

1. Who played the Starfleet commander in this movie?

2. What is the name of *Enterprise* shuttle number 3?

with the leader of the rebellion. He is Sybok, a Vulcan and half brother of Spock. He staged the attack on Nimbus III to draw a starship to this location. When Kirk and company arrive, they are quickly captured, and soon Sybok controls the *Enterprise*. Then he sets course for the center of the galaxy. Sybok has received a vision that God awaits them there.

Passing through a great energy barrier, the crew does indeed find a previously unknown world at that location. Sybok, Kirk, Spock, and McCoy take a shuttle down to investigate. At first the being they encounter seems to have the knowledge and attributes of God, but then it begins to speak of using the *Enterprise* to cross the great barrier. Kirk asks a simple question: "What does God need with a starship?" At this the being grows angry and knocks Kirk backward with an energy bolt. Sybok realizes that this cannot be God. He tells the others to flee while he engages the enemy. Kirk orders a photon torpedo attack on their location, and for a moment the being seems destroyed. However, upon returning to the shuttle, the trio find that the thrusters won't fire.

By this time Scott has repaired the transporter enough to beam Spock and McCoy aboard, but a photon torpedo from Klaa's ship knocks it out again. The Klingon captain has chased Kirk through the energy barrier. With the *Enterprise* disabled, Spock turns to the Klingon ambassador from Nimbus III, General Koord, for help. The Klingon general successfully orders Klaa to rescue Kirk from the planet just before "God" destroys him.

RUMINATIONS

In the Star Trek: The Next Generation *episode "Disaster," Picard and three children climb up a turbolift tube. Wanting to brighten the children's spirits, the captain asks them if they know any good songs. One of the children responds with the title "The Laughing Vulcan and His Dog." Every time I see the opening sequence of this movie, I wonder if that song refers to Sybok and his sidekick. (I know. That wasn't very nice.)*

And speaking of Next Generation *tie-ins, the shuttle craft in this movie eventually arrives on Picard's* Enterprise. *In addition, the actor who plays the Terran ambassador, David Warner, also stars as Gul Madred, Picard's torturer, in the episodes "Chain of Command, Part 1" and Chain of Command, Part 2." (Of course, he is also*

Gorkon in the next movie.)

GREAT LINES
"Actually, it's my first attempt."— Sulu, responding to Sybok's question about how many times the navigator has flown a shuttle into the shuttle hangar without using the tractor beam.

PLOT OVERSIGHTS
• At the beginning of this movie, a Starfleet commander claims they must send Kirk, because he's the only experienced commander available. So what justification are they using to send the *Enterprise*? In *Star Trek: The Motion Picture*, Kirk commandeered the *Enterprise* in a crisis situation. Why doesn't Starfleet put him in charge of the *Excelsior*? It's docked right beside the *Enterprise*, and last we heard, it was in pretty good shape. (True, Scott removed a few computer components, but couldn't they be put back?)

• Doesn't Sybok understand Starfleet technology? On the surface of Nimbus III, Spock uses a tricorder to locate the kidnapped ambassadors. Couldn't a normally functioning starship do the same from orbit? Couldn't a normally functioning transporter pluck the hostages from danger without sending anyone to the surface? (Yes, I remember that Picard's *Enterprise* faced a similar problem in "Legacy," but in that episode the hostages were far underground, invisible to the sensors.)

• I don't recall seeing any palm

trees on Nimbus III, yet Uhura appears with two fronds to do her fan dance. Does she carry them with her just in case the opportunity arises?

• Kirk makes a pitiful showing as an infantryman in this movie. He manages to get inside the city where the rebels hold the ambassadors, and then both he and his troops seem to forget that they possess superior firepower. The rebels defeat them with guns that shoot little rocks! Why doesn't Kirk just have his men put their phasers on stun, wide field, and shoot everybody (just as he did in "The Return of the Archons")? Doesn't it make more sense to sort through the bodies after you've established some control? Of course, the creators wanted to have Sybok steal the *Enterprise*, and defeating Kirk was the first step in doing that. But they didn't have to make Kirk look stupid. The collusion between Sybok and the ambassadors could have been used to allow Kirk to retake the city and still be defeated.

• As Kirk, Spock, McCoy, and Sybok fly down in a shuttle to investigate the planet, "God" takes control and lands the vessel for them. Oddly enough, the four humanoids must walk a fairly long distance to get to the meeting. It sure seems like "God" could have parked a little closer. It's not as if the lot was full or anything.

• After "God" fires his first lightning bolt, Kirk's shirt shows char marks in the front and the back. Does that mean the bolt went all

the way through him? And if it did, why isn't Kirk dead? (I can understand why Spock isn't dead. His heart is over on the left side of his chest.)

• One final question: Did someone build the barrier that kept the evil being enclosed? The being said it had been "imprisoned" there for millennia. Who imprisoned it?

CHANGED PREMISES

• After introducing herself to the Terran and Klingon ambassadors, Caithlin Dar—the new Romulan ambassador to Nimbus III—recounts the history of the planet by saying that twenty years ago, their three governments set up this planet as an example of what they could do if they worked together. To pick this nit, the time frame for this movie must be established. As discussed in *Star Trek II: The Wrath of Khan (STII)*, two possible time frames exist for the second *Trek* movie. According to Khan, Kirk abandoned the supermen's and superwomen's group on Ceti Alpha V fifteen years prior to their eventual escape. That figure puts *STII* slightly more than fifteen years after Kirk's first mission as captain of the *Enterprise*. However, other evidence suggests that *STII* occurs about eight years after the beginning of the television show. Given that *STII* occurs eight to fifteen years after the beginning of the television series, how much time elapses between *STII* and *Star Trek: The Final Frontier?* The events of *STII* lead directly into

Star Trek III: The Search for Spock. Kirk and company spend three months on Vulcan before heading for Earth in *Star Trek IV: The Voyage Home (STIV).* At the end of *STIV,* Kirk sits in the captain's chair of the new *Enterprise* 1701-A and says, "Let's see what she's got." Near the beginning of *Star Trek V: The Final Frontier, (STV)* Scott grumbles that the captain said, "Let's see what she's got, and we did." It gives the impression that after the run around the block, the impossible job of working out the kinks fell to Scott. When returning from shore leave, Kirk tells Scott that he gave him three weeks to fix the *Enterprise.* These factors lead me to believe that no more than one year elapses between *STII* and *STV.* If that's true, then Dar's statements have to be false, because the television series started fewer than—possibly much fewer than—twenty years ago. That means that the Terrans, the Klingons, and the Romulans agreed on the settlement of Nimbus III prior to the start of the television series. The first-season episode "Balance of Terror" strongly suggests that the last contact with the Romulans came a hundred years earlier, with the establishment of the Neutral Zone.

• All of a sudden, the level of profanity blossoms in this movie. Kirk must be slipping in his old age. Or did he find that he enjoyed swearing while he was on Earth during *Star Trek IV: The Voyage Home?*

• After the shuttle crash-lands in the shuttle bay, Kirk and Sybok duke it out, and Spock ends up with a rock gun. Sybok strides up to Spock, allowing the gun to press into the center of his chest. Kirk orders Spock to shoot, but the Vulcan refuses. Later, in the brig, Spock tells Kirk that if he had pulled the trigger he would have killed Sybok. How so? Vulcan hearts reside on the left wall of the chest cavity (see "Mudd's Women"). Because of this, Spock lived when he was shot in the center of the back with a flintlock rifle in the episode "A Private Little War."

EQUIPMENT ODDITIES

• Hot stock tip of the week: Buy Boreal! They make mountain climbing shoes. According to climbing enthusiast Robert Chisnall, Kirk's wearing a pair at the beginning of the movie. Evidently, they're still in business in the twenty-third century.

• At the beginning of the movie, a close-up clearly demonstrates that Spock's boots fire downward. Yet he saves Kirk by grabbing the captain's ankles while both of them are upside down. Wouldn't the boots accelerate instead of brake their descent?

• At the end of the previous movie, Kirk takes the new *Enterprise* out for a spin. McCoy stands beside him, and just over the doctor you can make out the top of the letter "A" on the port turbolift door. This makes sense. Starting with *Star Trek II: The*

Wrath of Khan, the decks were identified by letters, with the main bridge being deck A. Yet at the beginning of *Star Trek V: The Final Frontier,* the turbolift doors on the bridge no longer have "A" on them. Who changed this, and why was it changed? Didn't Scott have enough to do trying to get the new *Enterprise* ready for service?

• What's more, not only has the designation for the turbolifts changed, they have actually moved! Prior to this movie, there was one station between the turbolifts. Now there are two. Bear in mind that these turbolifts travel in tubes. You can't just move the doorway: you would have to tear out the entire tube, shove it over, and then rebuild every deck it intersects. Does this seem reasonable?

• As the *Enterprise* heads for Nimbus III, Kirk tries to make a log entry in a newfangled recording device. It's shaped like a book. Apparently the captain should open this book, say his log, and then shut it. The scene joins this process with the book open and a big rectangle on the book's control surface flashing, "System Failure." What is really odd is that this big rectangle is *etched* with the words "System Failure." Evidently the *only* function of the rectangle is to inform the user that a system failure has occurred. This is not a good sign. Just how often does this rectangle light up? The designers of the logbook allocated a considerable amount of space on the control surface for these words.

Does that mean that they expect this light to be needed quite often? (I've heard of putting products in the field before getting all the bugs worked out, but this is ridiculous.)

• This new *Enterprise* can flat-out burn up the space lanes. It apparently doesn't take very long for the ship to go from Earth to Nimbus III and less than half a day to go from Nimbus III to the center of the galaxy. (Sulu says 6.7 hours, but that's after they have been at warp for a short while.) For the sake of generosity let's say that it took the *Enterprise* a total of 30 hours to go from Earth to the center of the galaxy. Our planet is slung off at the end of the western spiral of the Milky Way, and the galaxy is 100,000 light-years in diameter. Just to make the math easier, let's say it's 30,000 light years from Earth to the galaxy's center. If that's true, the *Enterprise* can travel at a rate of 1,000 light-years per hour. That's 8,760,000 light-hours per hour (1,000 times 365 times 24), or 8,760,000 times the speed of light. In other words, the ship can fly almost 9,000,000 times the speed of light! This is really, *really* fast! In comparison, the *Enterprise* 1701-D just pokes along. According to dialogue in several *Star Trek: The Next Generation* episodes, it would take Picard's *Enterprise* over 8 years at maximum warp to make a journey to the center of the galaxy.

• According to the rocket ride up the turbolift tube, the *Enterprise* 1701-A has seventy-eight decks that number from the bottom of the ship to the top. This is quite intriguing, since decks have always numbered from top to bottom, and the larger NCC 1701-D *Enterprise* only has only *forty-two* decks. In addition, this turbolift tube has no doors and no side connections to horizontal turbolift tubes, *and* it is triangular in shape and much bigger than a turbolift! Is this the express freight turbolift?

• As Kirk, Spock, McCoy, and Sybok disembark from the shuttle on the surface of the planet, the crew of the *Enterprise* watch their progress. The picture on the viewscreen is shot from a ground perspective several feet away from the shuttle as the four walk toward a mountain range. Just where is this picture coming from? "God"-cam?

• These photon torpedoes must not be as powerful as we've been led to believe. "God's" meeting place takes a direct hit, and the stone pillars still exist. I would have thought that one torpedo would have vaporized the whole area. Of course, then our heroes would die as well.

• The transporter room on this *Enterprise* looks suspiciously like the ones on Picard's *Enterprise*. I guess transporter technology hasn't changed much in eighty years.

CONTINUITY AND PRODUCTION PROBLEMS

• Those clever creators pulled a fast one in the scene at the begin-

ning of the movie, where Spock catches Kirk just before he hits the ground. Instead of attaching a suspension wire to Shatner's foot and hanging him upside down, they attached the wire to his side and held him horizontally. Then they built the set to make it look like he is hung upside down, and tipped the camera on its side. Watch closely as the camera rotates and pulls back to show the full view of Kirk and you'll see the wire sticking out of his side.

• Spock causes a continuity problem while roasting his "marshmelon" over Kirk's campfire. At one point he pulls the stick containing the marshmelon back and holds it across his knee. The shot changes and instantly the marshmelon is back in the fire. This happens a few moments later.

• Is there a different protocol for marking shuttles? The emblem on the side of the *Galileo* has a "V" on its side, just like the Engineering section of the *Enterprise*. However, on the *Enterprise*, the "V" has its narrow side up, but on the shuttle the narrow side of the "V" is down.

• Approaching Nimbus III, Klaa gives orders to reduce speed to impulse. Evidently no one was listening, because the next shot shows the bird of prey traveling at warp.

• As the shuttle *Galileo* makes its suicide run on the *Enterprise*, a close-up shows the shuttle hangar doors closed, then the camera angle changes, and the doors are suddenly open.

• As Kirk, Spock, and McCoy rocket up the turbolift shaft, the deck numbers make no sense. They run in the following sequence: 35, 36, 52, 64, (60-something), 52, 77, 78, and 78 again.

TRIVIA ANSWERS

1. Harve Bennett (cowriter of *Star Trek II: The Wrath of Khan*, writer and producer of *Star Trek III: The Search for Spock*, cowriter and producer of *Star Trek IV: The Voyage Home,* and cowriter and producer of *Star Trek V: The Final Frontier.*)

2. Copernicus.

STAR TREK VI: THE UNDISCOVERED COUNTRY

Star Dates: 9521.6-9529.1

When the Klingon moon Praxis explodes, the loss dooms the Klingon home world. Seizing the initiative, Spock opens a dialogue for peace with Klingon chancellor Gorkon and even arranges a summit. The Vulcan then volunteers the *Enterprise* to escort Gorkon's ship safely through Federation territory to a peace conference.

Several hours after arriving at the rendezvous point, the *Enterprise* suddenly appears to fire two photon torpedoes at Gorkon's ship. The detonations knock out the artificial gravity aboard the Klingon vessel. Moments later, a pair of men in gravity boots beam on board. With calm efficiency, they murder their way to Gorkon and assassinate the chancellor. Understandably, Klingon general Chang is incensed and prepares to attack the *Enterprise*. Kirk immediately surrenders and beams over with McCoy to offer any possible assistance. Chang simply arrests the pair.

Trivia Questions

1. Spock claims the gravity boots will hang around the assassins' necks like a pair of what?

2. What deck houses Sulu's quarters on the *Excelsior*?

As the Klingon government tries Kirk and McCoy for murder, Spock investigates the incident. While it is true that the assassins came from the *Enterprise*, he deduces that the actual photon torpedoes came from a ship that could fire while cloaked. Meanwhile, the Klingons convict Kirk and McCoy, sentencing them to the penal asteroid of Rura Penthe. Those who conspired against Gorkon soon arrange a jailbreak. They plan to dispose of Kirk and McCoy in the wastelands outside the prison. Thankfully, Spock comes to retrieve the pair as soon as they escape from under Rura Penthe's magnetic shield.

Back on the ship, Kirk and Spock flush out the lead conspirator on the *Enterprise*, a Vulcan female named Lieutenant Valeris. Spock's mind meld with Valeris reveals a list of coconspirators, including Chang. Captain Sulu of the USS *Excelsior* provides the location of the rescheduled peace conference, and Kirk sets course. He knows the conspirators will disrupt the proceedings. The *Enterprise* soon arrives, and Chang begins pummeling it with his cloaked ship. The *Excelsior* joins the fray but can take only potshots from Chang as well. The extra time helps Spock create a photon torpedo that can home in on the exhaust gases of Chang's ship. When it detonates, Kirk and Sulu bring all their weapons to bear on that location and destroy Chang. Then—quickly beaming down to the conference— they disarm the conspirators and save the peace process.

RUMINATIONS

Although it's impossible to see on the screen, Maryann Smialkowski sent me pictures verifying that the bolts on Chang's eyepatch are engraved with little Klingon symbols. Now, that's attention to detail!

GREAT LINES

"*I've been dead before.*"—Spock to Scott after the chief engineer complains that they're "dead" due to the fact that they do not know the location of the peace conference and will not be able to stop the assassination certain to occur there. (This movie also has a bunch of other great lines to choose from.)

GREAT MOMENTS

The mind meld between Spock and Valeris is a lovely scene, revealing a previously unknown fact. In all the prior mind melds, Spock dealt gently with his subjects—not because he lacked the power to probe their minds forcibly, but because his respect restrained him. In this case, spurred on by the imminent destruction of the peace process, the Vulcan pushes forward, demanding that Valeris reveal what she knows.

PLOT OVERSIGHTS

• Shouldn't the energy wave from Praxis fan out in *all* directions (three-dimensionally)? And isn't it convenient that it just happens to hit the *Excelsior* in exactly the same plane as the ship? A few degrees different and it would have missed the vessel completely.

• In the initial Starfleet briefing, Spock claims the peace initiative will put an end to seventy years of "unremitting hostility." My dictionary says "unremitting" means "continuous, incessant, persevering." Didn't the Organian Peace Treaty—created during "Errand of Mercy" and mentioned during "The Trouble with Tribbles"—reduce the level of hostility between the Federation and the Klingon Empire?

• The initial briefing is "classified." The large group gathered for it makes no decisions on the status of the peace conference. Apparently the leaders of the Federation and Starfleet Command have already made all the relevant decisions. If the matter is classified, wouldn't it be more sensible to meet discretely with Kirk and his crew, thereby lessening the risk of an information leak?

• Spock tells Kirk that Valeris is the first Vulcan to graduate at the top of her class at the Academy. This came as a surprise to me. Aren't Vulcans suppose to be the intellectual giants of the Federation?

• Supposedly, the crisis with the Klingons comes because their home world will be unable to support life in fifty years. Is this one planet absolutely critical to the entire Klingon domain? Why don't they just move to another planet in their empire? Have they spent so much on the military that they can't afford the moving expenses? Is that part of the deal with the Federation? The Klingons agree to be good girls and boys if the Feds send enough money so they can rent some U-Warp freighters?

• For a Vulcan, Valeris really bootlicks Kirk when she visits his quarters. She tells him what an honor is it to serve with him. She tells him that she always wanted to fly a ship out of space dock at one-quarter impulse. Yeah, right. Is it logical to risk damage to a space vessel just because you want to get out of space dock a few moments quicker? Of course, maybe Valeris is simply trying to ingratiate herself with Kirk to make herself more valuable to the conspiracy.

• After the Klingons beam on board for dinner, Valeris catches two men making disparaging remarks about the visitor. When she reminds them that they have work to do, the pair responds, "Yes, ma'am." I thought Starfleet had done away with gender-specif-

ic titles. Women are continually referred to as "Mister." (Actually, I suppose it would be more proper to say that Starfleet has done away with *feminine* titles.)

• The laws of momentum and inertia suffer yet another blow in this movie. When the gravity shuts off on Gorkon's ship, everything starts leaping upward. To quote Newton, "A body at rest tends to stay at rest."

• After the Federation president meets with the Klingon ambassador over Kirk's disposition, Starfleet comes to discuss a possible rescue plan. The Romulan ambassador is present for *both* of these meetings. I can understand him being at the first, but why is he at the second? Are we really so buddy-buddy with the Romulans that we want them to know that Starfleet is proposing a rescue attempt?

• Why doesn't Chekov know that firing a phaser on kill will set off alarms on the *Enterprise?*

• At Kirk's trial, an officer on Gorkon's ship testifies that he was "weightless and unable to function." Evidently the Klingons don't train their officers to function in a weightless environment. Are their artificial gravity devices really this reliable in battle?

• Evidently the Klingons have forgotten that they were demanding Kirk's extradition at the beginning of *Star Trek IV: The Voyage Home*. They put the captain on trial only for the murder of Gorkon, ignoring the deaths of Kruge and his crew.

• During the trial, the Klingons play back a portion of Kirk's personal log. In it, Kirk talks about his feelings toward the Klingons and says, "I've never been able to forgive them for the death of my boy." Yet earlier in the movie, when Kirk made the recording, he actually said, "I could never forgive them for the death of my boy."

• As mentioned below, the Starfleet ships in this movie suddenly have bunks. Even more interesting, men and women bunk together. Oddly enough, the women seem to draw the top bunks. (I guess boys will be boys. "You go ahead and take the top bunk, Crewman Chantal. Rest assured that every night we'll watch carefully to make sure you reach it safely.")

• Explaining her motivations for joining the conspirators, Valeris repeats Kirk's comment about the Klingons, "Let them die." Yet Kirk makes this comment to Spock in the empty meeting room of the initial briefing. Was the room bugged? (Some have suggested that the background silhouette in the briefing room conversation may be Valeris, but I can't find a silhouette in the background during that scene. It probably got chopped off in the conversion to television. Unfortunately, I don't have the videotapes in "letterbox" format.)

• After revealing Valeris as a conspirator, Spock goes to his room to sulk. Kirk enters and is about to turn up the lights when Spock says he prefers it dark. Is that why he has a light shining in his face?

• On the subject of Spock's quarters, do they seem a lot larger than Kirk's?

• When the *Enterprise* arrives at Khitomer, it looks like it's the only ship in orbit. Shouldn't there be a few ships hanging around? This is a big conference, and security is an issue.

• To find the exhaust pipe of Chang's ship, Uhura suggests they use the equipment they are carrying to catalog gaseous anomalies. Was the *Enterprise* doing this as well as the *Excelsior*? At the beginning of the movie, Captain Sulu makes a log entry stating that they have just returned from a three-year mission cataloging gaseous anomalies.

CHANGED PREMISES

• Heading for the rendezvous with Gorkon's ship, Kirk orders Valeris to fly the *Enterprise* out of space dock at one-quarter impulse. To this, Valeris replies that regulations call for thrusters only. When did Starfleet make this rule? In *Star Trek III: The Search for Spock,* Captain Stiles—a "by the book" guy if I ever saw one—ordered the Excelsior to leave space dock at one-quarter impulse.

• After the rendezvous with Gorkon's ship, Kirk claims he's "never been this close" to a Klingon vessel before. He must have forgotten the events of the previous movie. At the end of it, Klingons and Starfleet officers enjoyed drinks together in a lounge on the *Enterprise* as it flew beside a Klingon bird of prey. (I realize there's a story going around Trekdom that Gene Roddenberry actually called *Star Trek V: The Final Frontier* apocryphal. I understand why some of the Powers That Be would like to think that it never happened. As far as I'm concerned . . . that's too bad. It was on the screen. It cost lots of money to make. Paramount is still *selling* it. It's canonical!)

• The Klingon death howl, as described in the *Star Trek: The Next Generation* episode "Heart of Glory," seems to be missing as Gorkon expires.

• In the *Star Trek: The Next Generation* episode "Redemption," Gowron states that women may not serve on the Klingon High Council. Obviously that rule didn't apply in this time frame, because Azetbur is definitely a woman, and she's the head of the High Council.

• After helping Kirk and McCoy escape from prison, a female reveals that she is a shape shifter. Kirk responds that he thought shape shifters were mythical. Wouldn't the salt creature in "Mantrap" qualify as a shape shifter? If not, how about Garth in "Whom Gods Destroy"?

• At the end of the movie, Colonel Worf determines that the gunman who was trying to kill the Federation president is merely dressed as a Klingon. His first clue is the red blood leaking from the guy. This movie makes a big point of establishing that Klingons have purple blood. Amazingly enough, Colonel Worf's grandson, Lieutenant Worf, has red blood! For one thing, we saw it in the *Star Trek: The Next Generation* episode "Redemption II."

EQUIPMENT ODDITIES

• At the beginning of the movie, Captain Sulu drinks from a china teacup. When the energy wave approaches, the cup dances off its platform and crashes to the floor. Why is Starfleet still using breakable containers? Shouldn't they have some sort of indestructible china by now? Or is Sulu simply a traditionalist?

• Evidently, none of the transporters on Earth, the *Enterprise*, or space dock is working. Once again, the crew take a shuttle back to their ship.

• With this movie, the creators finally return to their senses and make the main bridge deck 1.

• Speaking of the *Enterprise*, it seems to have passed through some sort of retrograde anomaly. As usual, it only somewhat resembles the *Enterprise* of the previous movie, *Star Trek V: The Final Frontier*. However, these changes can be chalked up to a refit that occurred when we weren't looking. On the other hand, the same ship that had touch screens the last time out now has push buttons and faders (that look like they came from a sound mixing board). In addition, there's a galley—a galley where individuals actually cook food. Yes, the original *Enterprise* had a galley, but in this movie there's also a food replicator in Kirk's quarters—a food replicator that looks just like the ones on *Star Trek: The Next Generation*. (And—in case you're wondering if it only *looks* like a food replicator—it has dishes in it.) Finally, the crew members sleep in bunks, three high. There are no bunk rooms in the plans for the original *Enterprise* (plans approved by Gene Roddenberry and displayed in *Star Trek: The Motion Picture*).

• And speaking of the refit, why in the world would the designers move the turbolifts *again?* (See the previous movie.) Are they trying to find things for the workers to do? This movie shows several stations between the turbolift doors.

• The assassins who beam over from the *Enterprise* to Gorkon's ship materialize in a yellow beam. That's the color for Klingons. Starfleet uses a blue beam. Did someone from Gorkon's ship beam them over, and if so, why do the assassins immediately kill the Klingon transporter chief?

• This *Enterprise* has phasers in the galley. Now, there's an incentive for the cooks to do a good job!

• When the *Enterprise* sneaks into Klingon space, there's a cute moment with the senior staff rifling through dictionaries to respond to a Klingon outpost's inquiries. Chekov claims they can't use the universal translator because the Klingons would recognize it. Are the Klingon sensors really so bad that they can't distinguish a freighter from a heavy battle cruiser? And why doesn't the crew use the universal translator to *receive* the broadcast from the outpost. In that way they could get instantaneous translation of the information the Klingons want. Also, why are they using books? Haven't these been fed into the computer's library banks? Even in our backward time we have little hand-held devices to translate between languages. Why is the technology of the *Enterprise* less advanced? (Answer: Because it was a cute scene, and the creators wanted to put in some comic relief.)

• At one point the crew discover that someone killed the assassins. Kirk concocts a plan and has the entire ship paged for the "court reporter." The captain wants the murderer to think that the assassins survived and are about to give statements. Surprisingly, Valeris actually falls for this. Up to this point, in the original television series and the movies, the computer has always functioned as the court reporter. Three examples of this occur: in "The Menagerie, Part I," "Court-Martial," and "Wolf in the Fold." (Of course, this may be another instance of that retrograde anomaly I spoke of earlier. Perhaps this *Enterprise does* use humanoid court reporters.)

• Even with all the amazing advancements in Picard's *Enterprise*, the warp core looks surprisingly similar to the one shown in this movie.

• The clock above the viewscreen

gets stuck when Kirk first hears Chang speak from his cloaked bird of prey.

• To fire the specially equipped photon torpedo, someone presses a button labeled "Mode Select." Does this seem right?

• Attempting to assassinate the Federation president, a gunman dressed as a Klingon cuts a small circle of glass from a frosted window-pane. Then he sticks the end of his rifle through the opening. Note that the rifle uses a scope. Note also the size of the hole. I do not believe that the gunman would be able to look through the scope and see through the hole. The scope sits too high above the rifle. The hole would have to be much bigger.

CONTINUITY AND PRODUCTION PROBLEMS

• As the energy waves approach and the *Excelsior* begins bouncing up and down, Sulu's science officer gives his captain a report. Then a shot shows the science officer at his station. Then a wide shot shows him making his way back to the science station.

• Sulu's helmsman reports the energy wave approaching from the port side of the *Excelsior*. When it hits, the graphics show the impact on the starboard side of the ship.

• The insignia on the turbolift doors for the bridge seem to indicate that the turbolift can go up from this location. Isn't the bridge the highest point on the ship? (I realize that the design may simply

be the standard symbol for the turbolift. However, the top floors of buildings on Earth have no "up" buttons on their elevators.)

• Why don't Valeris's shoulder strap and collar match? Everyone else on the ship has matching shoulder straps and collars. Is it because she's only temporary?

• For being an old guy, Scott really is fast. When the Klingons come to the *Enterprise* for dinner, one shot shows Scott in the transporter control booth, and the very next one shows him standing by his friends.

• The actor who played the Terran ambassador in the previous movie comes back as Gorkon for this one.

• Just before Valeris vaporizes the pot in the galley, a helper strolls into the scene carrying a tray of potatoes. She sees the weapon rise and quickly turns to walk the other way. Then the shot changes, Valeris prepares to fire, and the same woman turns around again.

• The Federation president's office sure does look like Ten-Forward, doesn't it? (The bar on Picard's *Enterprise*.)

• Sarek has a little trouble finding a good seat during the meetings in the Federation president's office. He starts out in the chair to the president's right. After the Klingon ambassador leaves and Starfleet arrives, he stands and wanders behind the president to take a seat to the leader's right. This movement is convenient for us because otherwise he would be out of the shot for the rest of the scene. (I have a hard time believing Sarek is this vain. I prefer to think that his eyes are growing weak with age and he just wants to get closer to West's chart.)

• When Valeris comes down the fireman's pole to speak with Spock, the panel behind her shakes when she lands. For a starship, it sure doesn't look very sturdy.

• After escaping from the prison, Kirk has a fight with a shape shifter. McCoy lies unconscious on the ground with his feet toward the altercation. Then Kirk and the shape shifter roll toward McCoy and plow over him—except now the pair

and the doctor are side by side.

• To increase the drama of Spock's mind meld with Valeris, the creators dubbed in a heartbeat that grows in volume as the scene increases in intensity. As a nitpicker, I am forced to ask, "Whose heartbeat is this?" It cannot belong to Spock or Valeris. They are Vulcan. Their hearts normally beat more than two hundred times a minute.

• Uhura's name is spelled wrong in the closing credits.

TRIVIA ANSWERS
1. Tiberian bats.
2. Deck 3.

THE INTRAGALACTIC TREK AWARDS

A COLLECTION OF UNUSUAL CATEGORIES FOR SERVICE ABOVE AND BEYOND THE CASTING CALL

The winner in each category will receive the ever-popular Bloopie—an anatomically incorrect statuette featuring the hair of Pavel Chekov, the ears of Mr. Spock, the eyes of James T. Kirk, the nose of Leonard McCoy, the lips and teeth of Uhura, the neck of Hikaru Sulu, the chest of Khan Noonien Singh, and the legs of Janice Lester.

1. In the category "Episode in Which the Most Starfleet Personnel Die in the First Sixty Seconds," the nominees are: A. "The Apple"; B. "Obsession"; C. "The Immunity Syndrome."

2. In the category "Least Dressed Alien Female," the nominees are: A. Shahna, "The Gamesters of Triskelion"; B. Tigerwoman, *Star Trek V: The Final Frontier;* C. Zarabeth, "All Our Yesterdays." (The shoulders-up shot of Iliadroid in the shower doesn't count because we aren't really sure of her attire before Kirk thoughtfully dresses her in the miniskirted robe.)

3. In the category "Worst Alien Effect," the nominees are: A. Korob and Sylvia, "Catspaw"; B. Gav, "Journey to Babel"; C. Excalbian, "The Savage Curtain." (Actually, this last one isn't too bad, but I needed a third for the category.)

4. In the category "Speech by Kirk with the Most Clichés Strung Together in a Row," the nominees are: A. "Risk Is Our Business," from "Return to Tomorrow"; B. "In Every Revolution, There Is One Man with a Vision," from "Mirror, Mirror"; C. "Maybe We Weren't Meant for Paradise," from "This Side of Paradise."

5. In the category "Fastest Leap from Behind a Transporter Control Console," the nominees are: A. Montgomery Scott in *Star Trek VI: The Undiscovered Country;* B. Lieutenant Kyle in "Mirror, Mirror"; C. John B. Watson in "That Which Survives."

6. In the category "Episode with the Longest Stretch of Forced Laughter at the End," the nominees are: A. "Shore Leave"; B. "The *Galileo* Seven"; C.

"The Tholian Web."

7. In the category "Yeoman with the Best Bunny Hop," the nominees are: A. Janice Rand, "Miri"; B. Tonia Barrows, "Shore Leave"; C. Mears, "The *Galileo* Seven."

8. In the category "Episode with the Highest Number of Near Fatal Encounters for Spock," the nominees are: A. "The Apple"; B. "A Private Little War"; C. "Operation—Annihilate!"

9. In the category "*Humanoid* Male with the Best Pickup Line" (if we let the Horta in on this one they would easily sweep the category), the nominees are: A. James T. Kirk in "By Any Other Name"; B. Khan Noonien Singh in "Space Seed"; C. Apollo in "Who Mourns for Adonais?"

10. In the category "Starfleet Officer Who Can Manufacture the Goofiest Looks," the nominees are: A. Hikaru Sulu in "Wolf in the Fold"; B. Pavel Chekov in "Mirror, Mirror"; C. Kevin Riley in "The Naked Time."

AND THE WINNERS ARE . . .
1. C. "The Immunity Syndrome," topping the death toll at more than four hundred Vulcans when the USS *Intrepid* expires.

2. B. Tigerwoman, *Star Trek V: The Final Frontier.* (Interestingly enough, the triple-breasted tigerwoman easily wins the award and appears in the only *Star Trek* movie written and directed by none other than William Shatner.)

3. B. Gav, "Journey to Babel," with his obviously fake pig mask.

4. C. "Maybe We Weren't Meant for Paradise," from "This Side of Paradise," winning with a stunning five clichés in a row. They are: "fight our way through," "claw our way up," "scratch for every inch of the way," "stroll to the music of the lute," and "march to the sound of the drums."

5. A. Montgomery Scott in *Star Trek VI: The Undiscovered Country*, with his instantaneous leap from behind the transporter console to stand with his friends just as the Klingons beam over for dinner.

6. B. "The *Galileo* Seven," after Spock continues to assert that his act of desperation was logical.

7. C. Mears, "The *Galileo* Seven," with her spring from her chair to a picture-perfect landing just as the *Galileo* lifts off from the planet.

8. A. "The Apple." In this one episode, Spock is hit with poisoned darts, knocked on his posterior by a force field, and struck by lightning.

9. B. Khan Noonien Singh in "Space Seed," with the ever-popular, "Please sit and entertain me."

10. A. Hikaru Sulu in "Wolf in the Fold," after receiving an armload of sedatives.

ATTENTION ALL NITPICKING TREKKERS!

JOIN THE NITPICKER'S GUILD TODAY.

Just send in a mistake that you've found in an incarnation of *Star Trek*—the original series, the movies, *Next Generation, Deep Space Nine* or *Voyager*— or even a mistake that you've found in any of the Nitpicker's Guides. Simply mailing that entry will make you an official member of the Nitpicker's Guild! (Please understand. I get a lot of mail and read every letter, but it is very difficult to send out personal responses.)

Send your mistake to:
Phil Farrand, Chief Nitpicker
The Nitpicker's Guild
P.O. Box 6248
Springfield, MO 65801-6248

Note: All submissions become the property of Phil Farrand and will not be returned. Submissions may or may not be acknowledged. By submitting material, you grant permission for use of your submission and name in any future publication by the author. Should a given mistake be published in one of the mediums of the Nitpicker's Guild, an effort will be made to credit the first person sending in that mistake. However, Phil Farrand makes no guarantee that such credit will be given.

INDEX

THE NITPICKER'S GUIDE FOR NEXT GENERATION TREKKERS

by Phil Farrand

We need to know:

When did Data graduate from the Star Fleet Academy?

How many times in the series has Picard been kidnapped?

But we also need to know:

How come everybody's got a cloaking device except the Federation?

Why is there a control panel in the turbo lift in only one episode?

If the transporter breaks down, why don't they just use
a shuttlecraft?

Yes, we're fans. But we're not unobservant. Some of us even have
Vulcan-like logic. So here's the ultimate analysis of *Star Trek: The
Next Generation* for those who are unafraid of pointing the finger
at oversights and who know it's great fun to find out not only the
facts, but also the mistakes (or cost-cutting cheating) in the show.
So get your video recorder ready and your mind set for hours of
enjoyment and mental stimulation with:

- Plot synopses for every episode of *Star Trek:
  The Next Generation*
- Trivia questions
- Plot oversights
- Continuity and production problems
- Changed premises
- Equipment oddities
- Great lines and great moments
- Fun facts
- And more!

THE MAKING OF STAR TREK

by Stephen E. Whitfield and Gene Roddenberry

Did you know:

- that Captain Kirk was originally Captain April?

- that Mr Spock was nearly dropped as a character?

- that Dr McCoy's medical instruments were salt shakers?

- why all buttons were banned?

- how the 'beam down' effect was achieved?

- what happens at Warp Factor Eight?

All this, and much, much more is revealed in this book that tells the complete behind-the-scenes story of the production of the science fiction series that became a phenomenon - *Star Trek*!

MR SCOTT'S GUIDE TO THE ENTERPRISE

by Shane Johnson

Aided by the logbooks of Chief Engineer Montgomery
Scott and recently declassified Starfleet material, Shane
Johnson has written the most accurate, in-depth look at the
U.S.S. *Enterprise* available.

For the first time anywhere, deck-by-deck in full,
fascinating detail, you will tour the inside of the U.S.S.
Enterprise, the United Federation of Planets' most
recognised intergalactic ambassador. Using dozens of
blueprints, sketches and photographs, you'll visit the
on-ship sites of Captain Kirk, Mister Spock and
Commander Scott's most famous adventures - and take a
never-before-revealed peek at the inner workings of
a starship.

From the engineering room to the captain's quarters, from
sickbay to auxiliary control, here is your complete guide to
the most famous starship of all - the U.S.S. *Enterprise*!

Newly revised and updated from Titan Books

THE STAR TREK COMPENDIUM

by Allan Asherman

The Star Trek Compendium is your official guidebook to the *Star Trek* universe. Relive the voyages of the *Starship Enterprise* with a complete show-by-show guide to the series (as well as the Emmy Award winning animated shows and the *Star Trek* movies), including plot summaries, fascinating behind-the-scenes production information and credits for each. Follow the creation of Gene Roddenberry's series step-by-step - and *Star Trek*'s road to the big screen. Illustrated with over 125 specially selected photographs - including at least one from each episode - and fully indexed, this is the indispensable reference work to one of the most memorable television shows of all time - *Star Trek*.

This newly revised edition includes new material from *Star Trek VI: The Undiscovered Country.*

ALL I REALLY NEED TO KNOW I LEARNED FROM WATCHING STAR TREK

by Dave Marinaccio

Every situation you will face in life has already been faced by the crew of the *Starship Enterprise* NCC 1701:

- how to respond to challenge
- how to treat your friends
- how to pick up girls
- how to get ahead on the job
- how to run a business
- how to bandage a wounded silicon-based life-form

Years ago, advertising executive Dave Marinaccio realised that the solutions to all of life's problems could be found in the episodes of *Star Trek*, the galaxy's greatest compendium of wisdom and experience.

Looking at life from this original perspective, he has put together his own inspiring collection of down-to-earth philosophy, based upon the example of Captain Kirk and his crew: an excellent handbook for anyone confronting the strange life-forms and alien civilisations that make up everyday life in the twentieth century.

BACK TO THE BATCAVE

by Adam West with Jeff Rovin

"Fans never simply want to shake my hand or get my autograph. They want to talk about what Batman meant to them...For better or worse, richer or poorer, I'm married to the cape"
- Adam West

One day in the sixties, he woke up a star. The *Batman* TV show had become an overnight smash, rocketing its little-known lead actor suddenly into the big time. He worked with a galaxy of top stars, including Burgess Meredith, Eartha Kitt, Liberace and Vincent Price. He was on the cover of *Life*, shared a publicity agent with Clint Eastwood, and sang with Bing Crosby. On one day seven thousand children poured into Central Park in New York to meet him; even the Pope was a fan.

But within two years Batmania had faded, the TV show was cancelled, and Adam West had to face an uncertain future, where being typecast as a comic book hero in tights would haunt him.

For the first time, Adam West tells the inside story of his helter skelter ride on the fairground of fame, and reveals, with a wry sense of humour, the impact on his life and career of his fateful decision in 1965 to don the cape and cowl of the world's most famous crime fighter.

THE AVENGERS DEADLINE

by Patrick Macnee

An original novel, featuring the characters John Steed and Emma Peel from the cult sixties TV series.

Someone is tampering with speeches reported in the continental editions of British newspapers: antagonising other nations and causing anti-British riots abroad. John Steed and Emma Peel are called in to go undercover at *The Courier* newspaper in Fleet Street. Their mission: to identify and track down the Brotherhood, a band of neo-fascist ruthless criminals who will stop at nothing - not even murder - to bring down the Government and scize power.

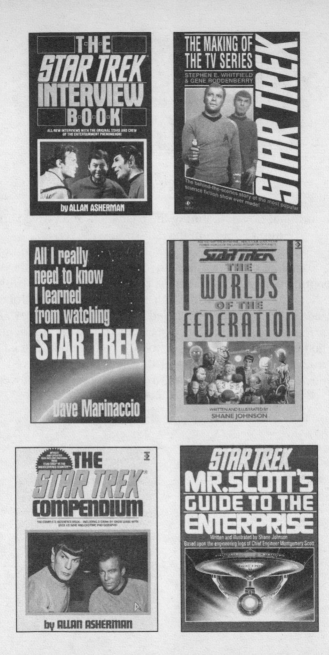

For a complete list of Titan's publications, please send a large stamped SAE to Titan Books Mail Order, 42-44 Dolben Street, London SE1 0UP. Please quote reference NPC on the envelopes.